"STRANGE LANDS AND DIFFERENT PEOPLES"

The Civilization of the American Indian Series

"STRANGE LANDS AND DIFFERENT PEOPLES"

Spaniards and Indians in Colonial Guatemala

W. George Lovell and Christopher H. Lutz

with

Wendy Kramer and William R. Swezey

UNIVERSITY OF OKLAHOMA PRESS : NORMAN

Also by W. George Lovell and Christopher H. Lutz

Demography and Empire: A Guide to the Population History of Spanish Central America, 1500–1821 (Boulder, Colo., 1995)
Demografía e imperio: Guía para la historia de la población de la América Central española (Guatemala City, 2000)
Historia sin máscara: Vida y obra de Severo Martínez Peláez (Guatemala City, 2009)
(eds.) *La Patria de Criollo: An Interpretation of Colonial Guatemala* (Durham, N.C., 2009)

Library of Congress Cataloging-in-Publication Data

Lovell, W. George (William George), 1951–
    Strange lands and different peoples : Spaniards and Indians in Colonial Guatemala / W. George Lovell and Christopher H. Lutz with Wendy Kramer and William R. Swezey.
— First edition.
        pages cm. — (The civilization of the American Indian series ; volume 271)
    Includes bibliographical references and index.
    ISBN 978-0-8061-4390-3 (hardcover : alk. paper)
    1. Indians of Central America—Guatemala—Government relations. 2. Indians of Central America—Guatemala—First contact with Europeans. 3. Indians of Central America—Guatemala—Colonization. 4. Guatemala—History—To 1821. 5. Guatemala—Colonization. 6. Guatemala—Foreign relations—Spain. 7. Spain—Foreign relations—Guatemala. 8. Spain—Colonies—America. I. Title.
    F1465.3.G6L69 2013
    327.7281046—dc23

2013011563

"Strange Lands and Different Peoples": Spaniards and Indians in Colonial Guatemala is Volume 271 in The Civilization of the American Indian Series.

The paper in this book meets the guidelines for permanence and durability of the Committee on Production Guidelines for Book Longevity of the Council on Library Resources, Inc. ∞

1 2 3 4 5 6 7 8 9 10

I equipped certain people to accompany Pedro de Alvarado to Guatemala. . . . I invested a considerable sum in horses, arms, artillery, and munitions, as well as giving money to members of the party to help them out. I believe that Our Lord God and Your Sacred Majesty will benefit greatly from all this because, according to my sources, I expect [Alvarado and his men] to discover many rich and strange lands and many different peoples. . . . Because they are engaged in God's service in His Majesty's name, they cannot fail to achieve a worthy and prosperous result.

Hernán Cortés to King Charles V, October 15, 1524

CONTENTS

List of Illustrations — ix

List of Tables — xi

Preface — xiii

List of Abbreviations — xix

PART I CONQUEST AND RESISTANCE

1. Advance and Retreat — 3

2. Alliance and Revolt — 32

3. Return and Surrender — 58

PART II SETTLEMENT AND COLONIZATION

4. The Emergence of Core and Periphery — 77

5. *Congregación* and the Creation of *Pueblos de Indios* — 96

PART III LABOR AND TRIBUTE

6. The Birth of the *Encomienda* — 123

7. Alvarado, Espinar, and the Booty of Huehuetenango — 129

8. Maldonado, Marroquín, and the Regulation of Excess — 149

PART IV DYNAMICS OF MAYA SURVIVAL

9. At First Contact — 173

10. The Cerrato Years — 184

11. Decline between Reforms — 196

12. The Valverde Years   212
13. Reaching the Nadir   224
14. The Slow Recovery   231
Conclusion   249

Appendix   255
Glossary   285
Bibliography   299
Index   327

ILLUSTRATIONS

MAPS

1. Core and periphery in colonial Guatemala   81
2. Proposed division of Indian landholding at Sacapulas   112
3. Demographic regions of Guatemala   180
4. *Pueblos de indios* in the Cerrato *tasaciones*   187

FIGURES

1. *Corregimiento* of Totonicapán and Huehuetenango   116
2. Parishes of Santiago Atitlán, San Pedro La Laguna, Sololá, and Panajachel   118
3. Mam fortress of Zaculeu   133

TABLES

1. *Departamentos* and *municipios* in Guatemala   255
2. Towns founded in the sixteenth century by
   regular and secular clergy   255
3. Tribute assessments of Alonso López de Cerrato, 1548–51   256
4. *Pueblos, parcialidades*, and *tributarios* in Totonicapán, 1683   257
5. *Chinamitales* and *parcialidades* in the pueblo of Sacapulas   258
6. Proposed allocation of land at Sacapulas, 1775–1800   258
7. Awards of *encomienda* in Guatemala, 1524–48   259
8. *Encomienda* succession in Chichicastenango, 1526–49   259
9. Population of Huehuetenango and subject towns,
   1530–31 and 1548–51   260
10. *Encomienda* obligations in Huehuetenango,
    1530–31 and 1549   261
11. Settlements burned, wholly or in part,
    in Huehuetenango, 1530   262
12. *Encomienda* obligations in Santiago Atitlán   263
13. *Encomienda* obligations in San Martín Sacatepéquez
    and Ostuncalco   264
14. *Encomienda* obligations in Jumaytepeque   265
15. *Encomienda* obligations in Tacuba   266
16. *Encomienda* obligations in Comalapa   267
17. *Encomienda* obligations in Momostenango   268
18. *Encomienda* obligations in Utatlán   269
19. Population of Guatemala at Spanish contact   270

20. Indian settlements and tributary population in the
    Cerrato *tasaciones*, 1548–51   271

21. *Pueblos de indios* in the Cerrato *tasaciones*, 1548–51   272

22. *Pueblos de indios* in the Cerrato *tasaciones* with no
    tributary data   273

23. Tributary populations of eight Guatemalan
    communities, 1548–82   274

24. *Tributario*-to-*reservado* ratios for six
    Guatemalan communities, 1562   274

25. Native populations of Central America, circa 1550   275

26. Native populations administered by secular clergy
    in the Bishopric of Guatemala, 1570   275

27. Native populations administered by the
    Dominican Order, 1570   276

28. Native populations administered by the
    Franciscan Order, 1570   276

29. Native populations administered by the
    Mercedarian Order, 1570   276

30. Comparison of tributary counts in towns that appear in
    both the Cerrato (1548–51) and Valverde
    (1578–82) *tasaciones*   277

31. Total payments made in the *Graduación de salarios*, 1684   278

32. Payments made in *Real servicio del tostón*, 1710   279

33. Payments made in *Real servicio del tostón*, 1719   279

34. Native parishioners and Ladino inhabitants of
    Guatemala, 1750   280

35. Tributary population counts, 1768–69   280

36. Population estimates for Spanish America, 1772   281

37. Indian tributary population in 1778   281

38. Comparative shifts in population, 1778–1812   282

39. Tributary population in 1802, 1806, and 1811   282

40. Native population of Guatemala, 1520–1811   283

PREFACE

Life as an academic is often a solitary concern, entailing long periods of private absorption. The job, to be sure, has its satisfactions and rewards but can be a tedious, sheltered affair. Collaborating with colleagues, not without its challenges, helps mitigate feelings of isolation and affords ample opportunity for the discussion, exchange, and refinement of ideas. It may actually be quite exciting, involving surprise finds and unexpected returns. The enterprise, at its best, operates on the principle of *gestalt*, and so (with any luck) the whole really does amount to more than the sum of its parts.

In our case we look back at a long and sustained collaboration. We first met in Guatemala in the late 1970s and early 1980s, got to know and appreciate one another, and started to work together—an archaeologist (Swezey), a geographer (Lovell), and two historians, Lutz and Kramer, the former already accredited as such, the latter just starting out. It was a unique moment for us, at times rather giddying. Kramer drove Lutz along back roads to decrepit churches huddled in the vicinity of Antigua, a city that in its heyday was the capital of all Central America, and helped him transcribe registers of births, marriages, and deaths for Maya communities named after ubiquitous Christian saints. Swezey, meanwhile, generated a host of ideas about colonial-era situations that Lovell did his best to develop, the two working happily away, traveling overland to Mexico to participate in a conference, accompanied in endless conversation by Guatemalan associates, among them anthropologists, architects, and art historians. The plans we made seemed to be fueled by an agreeable natural combustion.

Those same years, however, were tragic ones for Guatemala. The civil war that had been simmering for decades suddenly exploded, sending the country into mayhem. According to a United Nations truth commission conducted after a peace accord was signed in 1996, armed conflict and state repression took the lives of more than two hundred thousand people, the great majority indigenous Mayas. Events intervened that caused each of us to head off in a different direction—Kramer to Spain, where she honed her paleographic skills at the Archivo General de Indias in Seville before embarking on doctoral studies at the University of Warwick in England; Lovell to Canada, where he began teaching at Queen's University; and Lutz, after a scary experience resulting in unlawful detainment and false accusations, to the United States, where he established the publishing house of Plumsock Mesoamerican Studies and edited the scholarly journal *Mesoamérica*. Only Swezey stayed on in Guatemala, where he coped with the worsening political climate as best he could, steering the Centro de Investigaciones Regionales de Mesoamérica (CIRMA) through its first ten years of existence. Despite distance and separation, our commitment to working together endured all sorts of changes in personal and professional circumstances. This book, therefore, is the result of collective endeavors that began more than three decades ago. What do we hope to achieve with it?

Our aim is to engage the reader with a set of interrelated studies about fundamental aspects of the charged, adverse relationship between Spaniards and Indians in colonial Guatemala. Their antagonism was at its most visceral in the violent confrontations of the second quarter of the sixteenth century but surfaced, long thereafter, in mutual feelings of suspicion, resentment, and mistrust, still apparent among the country's inhabitants today. The chapters here are organized and grouped around (1) issues of conquest and resistance, (2) themes of settlement and colonization, (3) arrangements for the provision of labor and tribute, and (4) Maya survival in the wake of Spanish intrusion. Part I offers new information about the vicissitudes of conquest, contributing to a more nuanced appreciation of how prolonged and difficult it proved to be. In part II we concentrate on Spanish colonial objectives writ large and indigenous responses that tempered those objectives at the local or community level. The benefits and burdens of subjugation are our primary concerns in part III. Part IV sees us chart, for the three centuries between first contact in 1524 and Independence in 1821, the precipitous collapse and eventual recovery of the native population, whose demographic presence is still so striking.

While Guatemala was destined always to be of marginal importance to imperial Spain, especially when compared with the likes of Mexico and Peru, exploitation of its resources, physical and human, was not without reward. In shedding light on lands and peoples whose colonial experiences are not well known, we attempt to strike a balance between providing facts and presenting arguments. We lean heavily on the archival findings our research has unearthed, but at the same time, we subject empirical evidence to interpretive scrutiny, setting details, as much as we can, in context. Data, analysis, and synthesis thus go hand in hand, though they are never equally weighted in any given chapter. We also try to pay attention to the narrative potential of the sources we consult, which means that we ourselves recount, and do our best to make sense of, the stories that saturate the documents, articulated by Spaniards and Indians alike. This calls for us to be mindful of ulterior motives and hidden agendas, to be wary and on the alert, for the historical record is no more neutral than the all-too-human characters who penned it or who dictated it for others to write down. Recent theoretical literature insists on this realization, but it is often self-evident, indeed an inescapable modus operandi, when one examines documentation pertaining to colonial experiences in Guatemala. Predicaments arise in which it becomes difficult, if not impossible, to determine who is lying and who is telling the truth, to say nothing of infinite nuance in between. Should we take at face value, for instance, Pedro de Alvarado's account of how he subjugated the land, or are we better advised to listen to the views of native protagonists like the Kaqchikels, who assisted Alvarado at the outset of his mission, only to turn against him after he failed to keep his side of the bargain?

Weaving the studies together as chapters in a book has allowed us to rework some of them from their initial status as contributions to conference proceedings, edited collections, and scholarly journals.[1] These

---

1. Chapter 1 dates back to a collection edited by John M. Weeks (Lovell and Lutz 2001), chapter 4 to collections edited by Carol A. Smith (Lutz and Lovell 1990) and Julio Pinto Soria (Lutz and Lovell 1991), chapter 5 to a collection edited by David J. Robinson (Lovell and Swezey 1990), and chapter 7 to a collection edited by David Hurst Thomas (Kramer, Lovell, and Lutz 1991). A preliminary version of chapter 6 first appeared in the *Yearbook of the Conference of Latin Americanist Geographers* (Kramer, Lovell, and Lutz 1990). Chapter 8 builds on an article published in *Mesoamérica* (Kramer, Lovell, and Lutz 1986), chapter 9 on articles published in *Antropología e Historia de Guatemala* (Lovell and Swezey 1981), the *Canadian Journal of Anthropology* (Lovell and Swezey 1982), and the XVII Mesa Redonda of the Sociedad Mexicana de Antropología

items can be difficult to get hold of: books may have gone out of print, journals ceased publication. While portions of eight chapters appeared in such form previously, several in Spanish, but never in English, their configuration here often bears little resemblance to the original. They have not only been augmented and rewritten but also, we hope, improved upon. It would have been a barren exercise not to have reflected on our earlier efforts and incorporated new findings. Our thinking has evolved along with important advances in the field of Mesoamerican studies, prominent among them increased awareness of native agency and population history, two subjects on which our own research interests are complemented by the innovative labors and fresh insights of a new generation of scholars.[2] Eight chapters, most notably chapters 2 and 3 and chapters 11 through 14, as well as a substantive appendix, have been prepared especially for this book and reflect the synergy of Kramer, Lovell, and Lutz over the past decade, Swezey having died before further investigations had begun. Our book draws significantly on unpublished documents housed in the Archivo General de Centro América in Guatemala City and the Archivo General de Indias in Seville. We have been extraordinarily privileged to have spent considerable time working in these archives and perusing their remarkable holdings. We hope our findings will similarly delight our readers.

For better or worse, and with no slight to other players in the drama, our book has two main casts of characters: Spaniards and Indians, the former often individually identifiable by name, the latter usually not and thus generically called "indios." That designation is not ours but a matter of historical record, which we work with as best we can in this dizzying era of identity politics, particularly in Guatemala. For the most part, the "indios" in question are Mayas, who belonged (even if they never self-identified as such) to the more than twenty distinct affiliations found in Guatemala today. Our temporal focus is the early colonial

---

(Lovell and Swezey 1984), and chapter 10 on an article published in *The Americas* (Lovell, Lutz, and Swezey 1984). Kramer and Swezey thus contributed previously published work to three of these chapters, Lutz to six of them, and Lovell to all eight. Full particulars may be found in our bibliography. We thank the editors, journals, and publishing houses involved for their cooperation in allowing us to draw upon our earlier efforts.

2. The state of the art of Mesoamerican studies, as it developed in the course of the twentieth century, is discussed by contributors to the three volumes of *The Oxford Encyclopedia of Mesoamerican Cultures* edited by Davíd Carrasco (2002). For a critique of this massive undertaking, see Lovell (2004).

period, spanning the century between 1524 and 1624, although in the final chapter we track the slow recovery of the native population from its demographic nadir around the years 1624–28 through the seventeenth and eighteenth centuries into the nineteenth. Save for essential details necessary to our objectives in chapter 4, we do not deal with the presence of blacks and the emergence of *castas*, or mixed-blood populations, which two of us (Lutz 1993; 1994; Lovell and Lutz 1995; 2003) have examined in the past and hope to address again in a future work.

Our research has been facilitated by the financial support of several institutions, of which the Killam Program of the Canada Council, the Social Sciences and Humanities Research Council of Canada, Plumsock Mesoamerican Studies, Queen's University, and the John Carter Brown Library have all been especially generous. We have been ably assisted in preparing our manuscript by the secretarial patience of Sharon Mohammed, the digital savvy of Gabrielle Venturi and Guisela Asensio Lueg, the cartographic skills of Jennifer Grek Martin, and the copyediting prowess of Katrin Flechsig and Maureen McCallum Garvie. Jan Williams once again helped us compile an index. So, too, have we been well served by the archival foraging of Héctor Concohá and the contact we enjoy with scores of colleagues who have commented on our work, over the years, to positive effect. Jorge Luján Muñoz, a stern critic with whom we do not always see eye to eye, deserves special mention not only for his unfailing collegiality but also for his steadfast scholarly production, most recently in the form of the *Atlas histórico de Guatemala* (2011). Our original intent was to have more maps and illustrations, particularly of the conquest period, accompany our text, but we can now refer readers, without excusing ourselves unduly, to Don Jorge's fruitful labors in this regard. We thank Alessandra J. Tamulevich for asking us to have the University of Oklahoma Press consider our manuscript in the first place, and thereafter steering it to two readers whose critiques gave us much to ponder. We dedicate the book to the memory of our dear friend and colleague, William R. Swezey, whom we remember fondly.

ABBREVIATIONS

AGCA   Archivo General de Centro América

AGI   Archivo General de Indias

ASGH   *Anales de la Sociedad de Geografía e Historia de Guatemala*

BPR   Biblioteca del Palacio Real

CIRMA   Centro de Investigaciones Regionales de Mesoamérica

EEHA   Escuela de Estudios Hispano-Americanos

HSA   Hispanic Society of America

LSC   *Libro segundo de cabildo*

PARES   Portal de Archivos Españoles

RAH   Real Academia de la Historia

PART I

CONQUEST AND RESISTANCE

CHAPTER 1

ADVANCE AND RETREAT

The conquest of Guatemala was brutal, prolonged, and complex; fraught with intrigue and deception; confusing, perplexing, and daunting and not at all clear-cut. An epic clash of cultures and an arresting saga of personalities and controversies, it is also a challenging topic of inquiry, primarily because of problems inherent in the source materials, which include an array of indigenous as well as Spanish documents. Whether of native or Hispanic concoction, these materials tend to be restrictive in their coverage of certain periods, places, and peoples; paltry or negligent in others; and at times so distorted or plagued with self-interest as to be of questionable utility, no matter the allowances we are disposed to make. Yet a general view of the conquest persists: an armed confrontation whose stakes were evident and whose outcome (Spanish victory) was decisive. A critical reappraisal is long overdue, one that calls for us to reexamine events and circumstances in the light not only of new evidence but also of a keener awareness of indigenous roles in the drama.

Episodes in the initial phase of invasion swayed its very nature from what it might otherwise have been. We focus in this chapter on what unfolded between December 1523, when Pedro de Alvarado left Mexico to spearhead the assault, and August 1524, when his hitherto allies, the native Kaqchikels, abandoned their capital at Iximché to stage a rebellion against the Spanish presence. Their revolt lasted almost six years and possibly flared up again in the 1530s. An alliance between the invaders and the indigenous peoples they encountered, so crucial a maneuver in the conquest of Mexico, proved more problematic to forge and maintain in Guatemala. While our narrative is concerned, for the most part, with chronological reconstruction and of a mere, though pivotal, eight-month period, we try not only to furnish essential information but also to step back and reflect on motives and rationale, for these are not always apparent and cannot be taken for granted. Though native involvement, which we examine at greater length in chapter 2, needs to be better appreciated and given at least equal weight with Spanish accounts in telling the tale, it is difficult not to ascribe to Alvarado's actions a definitive, formative cast, for more than any other key player he influenced how conquest was destined to unfold, leaving a legacy of oppression that not even his death could erase.

OPENING MOVES

Hernán Cortés informs us that he made contact with Maya peoples in Guatemala shortly after his victory in 1521 at Tenochtitlán, the seat of the vast Aztec or Mexica empire. He had heard of "rich and strange lands and many different peoples," who perhaps numbered as many as two million, that lay south of Mexico in regions beyond Aztec control but to which Tenochtitlán had commercial ties and harbored territorial aspirations.[1] Sometime in 1522, Cortés arranged for two Spaniards to head there with "some natives from the city of Tenochtitlán, and others from the province of Soconusco." These Spaniards, via intermediaries, met with members of the two most powerful Maya nations in Guatemala, the K'iche's and the Kaqchikels. In the wake of this meeting, during which they learned of the defeat of the Aztecs, the Mayas reportedly sent emissaries back to Mexico to confer with Cortés. In the city of Tuxpán, Cortés informs us, he received "as many as one hundred natives from the cities called Ucatlan [Utatlán] and Guatemala [Iximché], some sixty leagues beyond Soconusco, who offered themselves in the name of their leaders as vassals and subjects of Your Imperial Majesty."[2] Such

1. Cortés ([1524–26] 1963, 162). His precise words, drafted on October 15, 1524, in his fourth letter to King Charles V, are "Pienso descubrir muchas y muy ricas y extrañas tierras y de muchas y de muy diferentes gentes." Our estimate of a contact population in Guatemala numbering some two million is developed and contextualized in chapter 9.

2. Cortés—see Mackie (1924, 12–13) and Recinos (1952, 54)—mentions these diplomatic missions, once again, in his fourth letter, stating "vinieron hasta cien personas de los naturales de aquellas ciudades . . . que se llaman Ucatlan y Guatemala . . . por mandado de los señores dellos, ofreciéndose por vasallos y súbditos de Vuestra Cesárea Majestad, [ciudades que] están desta provincia de Soconusco otras sesenta leguas." He makes it clear that contact with indigenous

rhetoric on the part of the Maya envoys may have been designed to slow the Spanish advance, or avoid being invaded altogether. In any event Cortés states that he hosted them cordially and sent them home with gifts for their lords.

Though his letters to King Charles V are detailed and expansive when viewed alongside Alvarado's missives—sketchy and slight by comparison—how much credence should we give Cortés's claim of having engaged in Mexico with ambassadors representing both K'iche' and Kaqchikel leadership? Jorge Luján Muñoz and Horacio Cabezas Carcache find it "difficult to accept the veracity of indigenous representation before Cortés, since we only have his word for it." They observe pertinently that "neither of the two major native sources, the *Popol Vuh* and the *Memorial de Sololá*, mentions such a visitation."[3] Daniel Contreras concurs, stating that he finds it even more implausible that "K'iche's and Kaqchikels would have gone together to parley with Cortés, since they were sworn enemies" of each other.[4] Francis Polo Sifontes is prepared to accept only part of what Cortés has to say, claiming, "we have good reason to believe that only Kaqchikels, not K'iche's, took part in the visitation."[5] Whether or not there was an exchange between Spaniards and Mayas at this juncture, Cortés ascertained that Indians from Guatemala were harassing his Mexican allies in Soconusco, who had already converted to Christianity and pledged allegiance to the Spanish Crown. The Kaqchikels, according to Polo

---

groups in Guatemala was a result of his having "enviado dos hombres españoles con algunas personas de los naturales de la ciudad de Tenuxtitán [Tenochtitlán] y con otros de la provincia de Soconusco." The city of Tuxpán ("Tuzapam" according to Mackie) was located between the province of Pánuco and Tenochtitlán, the latter the present-day Mexico City.

3. Luján Muñoz and Cabezas Carcache (1993, 50). The case they make, as do Contreras and Polo Sifontes (see notes 4 and 5, below), is founded on the assiduous work carried out by Adrián Recinos (1952). His analysis of the life and times of Alvarado is far more than a biography and remains an indispensable source for any examination of the conquest of Guatemala. Restall and Asselbergs (2007, 3) also note that "[n]o native sources mention the Tuxpán meeting, so we can only guess at the intentions or actual statements made by the Maya ambassadors." In our exposition, when drawing upon either the *Popol Vuh* or, more frequently and at greater length, the *Memorial de Sololá*, we cull from the Recinos editions (1950b; 1953) of "the two major native sources" because they are the best known, and most widely available, in English translation. In the case of the *Memorial de Sololá*, however, we refer throughout to translations rendered into Spanish by Recinos (1950a) and Otzoy (1999) and into English by Brinton (1885), Maxwell and Hill (2006), and Restall and Asselbergs (2007), especially when interpretations vary or, on occasion, are at odds. Though the scholars in question may disagree, we consider their efforts and those of Recinos to be far more complementary than contradictory.

4. Contreras (2004b, 51–52).

5. Polo Sifontes ([1977] 2005, 64).

Sifontes, "told the Spaniards that they were not the ones carrying out the aggression, and indeed offered their apologies," blaming the K'iche's.[6] Seizing the opportunity to exert his authority, Cortés ordered his loyal captain, Pedro de Alvarado, to go to Soconusco, determine who was responsible, and deal with them.

Alvarado is said to have received a second friendly overture on the part of the Kaqchikels, ruled by the lords Cahí Ymox and Belehé Qat from their stronghold at Iximché.[7] No rapprochement on the part of the K'iche's is recorded. According to Francisco López de Gómara, basing what he states on Pietro Martire d'Anghiera before him, the Kaqchikels sent "five thousand men" to Alvarado to convince him of their loyal intentions, along with gifts of clothing, cacao, and provisions, as well as gold and jewels valued at some twenty thousand pesos.[8] Adrián Recinos believes this show of solidarity, if it ever happened, to be exaggerated.[9]

6. Ibid., 47. Considering the extent of Guatemalan territory ruled by the K'iche's in late Post-classic times—see Carmack (1981) and Luján Muñoz (2011, 53–55, especially his map 26) for elaboration—what Polo Sifontes states makes logistical sense. Were the Kaqchikel indeed the culprits, they would first have had to traverse hostile K'iche' country before entering Soconusco to harass the Mexican allies of Cortés.

7. Recinos 1952 (55–56) and Recinos and Goetz (1953, 117). See Luján Muñoz (2011, 54–59, especially map 27) for an appreciation of Kaqchikel dominion. Regarding Iximché, Contreras (2004c, 35–44) makes a convincing argument that the *Memorial de Sololá* refers to the Kaqchikel capital or "tinamit," the stronghold city from where the court and its kings ruled over Kaqchikel country, as having been founded "en el paraje llamado Iximché"—in a place or region known as Iximché. He bases his information on the phrase "pa tinamit chi iximché" in the Kaqchikel text, which Recinos translates as "ciudad de Iximché" (city *of* Iximché) when it actually means "la ciudad en Iximché" (the city *in* Iximché). The name "Iximché" has thus been given to the city itself, but it properly refers more broadly to the area in which the city was established. Contreras points out that "our colonial chroniclers always called the capital of the Kaqchikel kingdom 'Guatemala, Tecpán Guatemala, Patinamit or Tinamit'—no one called it Iximché." The first to do so, in the nineteenth century, was "Archbishop Francisco de Paula García Peláez, who must have known about some translation of the *Memorial de Sololá* through his association with Juan Gavarrete and the Abbè Brasseur de Bourbourg." Gavarrete was a Guatemalan lawyer and history buff who, when working for García Peláez in 1844 or 1845, organizing documents in the archbishop's palace that had been deposited there from the former Franciscan monastery, first came across the Kaqchikel manuscript. Realizing its monumental worth, he showed the *Memorial de Sololá* to Charles Etienne Brasseur de Bourbourg, a French priest and scholar who made a translation of it but saw fit to take the original with him when he returned to France. After his death in 1874, the manuscript passed through the hands of another French scholar, Alphonse Louis Pinart (1852–1911). It was purchased in 1887 by Daniel G. Brinton (1837–99), who donated it (along with countless other treasures) to the library of the University Museum at the University of Pennsylvania in Philadelphia, where it remains today. For detailed discussion of the archaeology and ethnohistory of Iximché, see Nance, Whittington, and Borg (2003).

8. López de Gómara, and by inference Pietro Martire d'Anghiera, as cited in Recinos (1952, 55–56). The text of the former runs "les dió cinco mil hombres cargados de ropa, cacao, maíz, ají, aves y otras cosas de comer y veinte mil pesos de oro en vasos y joyas."

9. Recinos (1952, 56).

Robert Carmack, however, notes that both Anghiera and López de Gómara, who wrote during the second quarter of the sixteenth century, had access to a letter Alvarado wrote to Cortés from Soconusco, a letter Córtes acknowledges as having received but that is now lost.[10] Why would such a shrewd, self-serving operator as Alvarado register receipt of precious items valued at twenty thousand pesos, knowing full well that he would have to pay the Crown its *real quinto*, or royal fifth? Five thousand warriors, furthermore, were a significant complement to the Mexican forces already lined up on the side of the Spaniards, without whose participation the conquest would have taken an entirely different course.

Given what was happening at the time to the Kaqchikel population, experiencing precipitous decline as a result of horrific outbreaks of sickness to which native inhabitants had never before been exposed, the transfer of such manpower was sizable and significant. If it did occur, especially to that degree, it was a strategic gamble that would prove costly, as disease lingered rather than disappeared and military losses were incurred when the Kaqchikels first supported and then opposed the Spanish invasion.

What factors best explain these conciliatory gestures on the part of the Kaqchikels? Did they believe that they could fob off the Spaniards by delivering, voluntarily, a huge payment of tribute, one that would perhaps persuade the foreigners to leave them in peace? Did they hope to win over a powerful ally in their ongoing struggle against their enemies, the K'iche's and the Tz'utujils? Although the latter explanation seems more plausible, the Kaqchikels badly miscalculated if they thought Alvarado would head back to Tenochtitlán content with what they offered

10. Carmack (1973, 92–93). Alvarado also wrote to Cortés from Tehuantepec, but this letter, too, is missing. With an indignation that we emphatically share, Carmack (1973, 85) writes: "I am perplexed by the large number of important sixteenth-century documents from Guatemala that are known to be lost. Ethnographic treasures mentioned in later sources are missing: a report to the Crown on the condition of Guatemala prepared by [Pedro de] Alvarado, [Francisco] Marroquín's census, two descriptions of native religion prepared by [Domingo de] Vico and [Salvador] Cipriano, several *Relaciones Geográficas*, some of the Cakchiquel dictionaries, and a seventeenth-century chronicle (*Crónica Franciscana*) which referred to sixteenth-century documents. This is a complaint of all historians, but it seems an especially serious one in the Guatemalan case." See Kramer, Lovell, and Lutz (2011) for elaboration on what we consider to be the pillage of national patrimony. Though our survey of the holdings of the Hispanic Society of America in New York did not locate either of Alvarado's two lost letters, it did reveal the existence of a bounty of documents, the whereabouts of which scholars of Guatemala had little or no knowledge, including the second and third *Libros de cabildo* of Santiago de Guatemala, spanning the years 1530–41 and 1541–53 respectively.

him in Soconusco. The Kaqchikels played their hand successfully for a while, until the greed and venom of Alvarado made the role of cooperative ally intolerable. One conclusion is inescapable: Alvarado was impressed with the booty and must have become more interested in Guatemala as a result. On Cortés's orders, he did return to Tenochtitlán, by way of Pánuco on the Gulf coast, where his presence helped Cortés deal with the threat to his authority posed by Francisco de Garay, an ambitious rival who had arrived in Mexico from Jamaica. Once back in Tenochtitlán, Alvarado finalized preparations with Cortés for the armed campaign to commence.

The Conquest Begins

Alvarado left Mexico to embark on the conquest of Guatemala as 1523 drew to a close. Since his own account is frustratingly incomplete—he glosses over all sorts of matters, rather than document them at length— we turn to Cortés for details of the expedition's departure.

> I again fitted out Pedro de Alvarado and dispatched him from this city [Tenochtitlán] on the sixth day of December in the year 1523. He took with him 120 horsemen and, with spare mounts, a total of 160 horses, together with three hundred foot soldiers, 130 of whom are crossbowmen and harquebusiers. He has four pieces of artillery with good supplies of powder and ammunition. He is also accompanied by chieftains from this city, and from other cities in the vicinity, and with them some of their people. . . . The journey will be long.[11]

11. Cortés ([1519–26] 1963, 316–17). Bernal Díaz del Castillo—see Luján Muñoz and Cabezas Carcache (1993, 50)—records Alvarado's departure from Tenochtitlán as November 13, three weeks or so earlier than the date registered by Cortés. Recinos (1952, 61) states that Díaz del Castillo's date of departure "has been repeated by other historians, but the date given by Cortés himself, written at the time of the events taking place, is conclusive and should be considered definitive." Gall (1968, 74–76) records Cortés as having told Alvarado "always to take special care to prepare for me long and detailed accounts of what comes his way, so that I can pass them on to His Majesty." He observes that Cortés "had a keen eye for landscape and paid attention to detail" and developed his lengthy *Cartas de relación* from notes he took while engaged in action. A penchant for "historical and literary narration," alas, "was a quality that eluded the conqueror of Guatemala," resulting in his "not describing the inhabitants of the country he passed through" and "showing little interest in them and their creations." In Alvarado's "superficial" and "detached"

Cortés is vague about the size of the Mexican forces that accompanied Alvarado, but we know from other sources that they were substantial, hailing not just from Tenochtitlán but also from Cholula, Texcoco, Tlaxcala, and Xochimilco.[12] By late 1523, Alvarado was an experienced military commander not yet forty years of age. From Cortés he had learned how best to rally the troops at his disposal, inspiring them to superhuman efforts. In addition, according to Recinos, after observing "brave and astute Mexican warriors," Alvarado had adopted "the tactics and the cunning used in these parts of the New World."[13] Among the Spaniards who accompanied him were his three brothers, Gómez, Gonzalo, and Jorge de Alvarado; his cousins Diego and Hernando de Alvarado,

---

missives, Gall laments, "one does not find any thoughts inspired by the impact of the high culture and lush, magnificent landscapes he beheld for the first time." His focus instead "is on the atmosphere of the war he brought with him, in which thousands would die," and discussions of "superior tactics and the force of arms." Gall asserts that Alvarado's minimal compliance with what was expected of him, and his concentrating on military matters, "often covered up arbitrary acts committed by the Spaniards."

12. Writing in the first half of the seventeenth century, Fernando de Alva Ixtlilxóchitl (see Recinos 1952, 61) gives a figure for the Mexican forces that accompanied Alvarado of 20,000, one that is often cited, but all too uncritically. It is likely exaggerated, inflated by Ixtlilxóchitl to portray his fellow Mexicans in the most favorable light possible for the services they rendered during the conquest. Asselbergs (2004, 113) puts the figure at half that, "around 10,000." Matthew (2012, 78) presents useful, if non-quantitative, evidence from one Alonso López, "a native of Tlalmanalco near Chalco who later settled in Gracias a Dios, Honduras" after he served in the conquest of Guatemala. López states that the "great captain who had captured Mexico was sending Don Pedro de Alvarado to conquer the province of Guatemala." López adds that the "great captain" in question "brought together in Mexico all the chiefs and lords of the entire province . . . and ordered that Indians from each town be brought, and so a large number of Indians came," himself included. Matthew (2012, 90) furnishes more specific data courtesy of Pedro González Nájera, a "Spanish captain who acted as an interpreter during the original campaign," who recorded in 1564 that "approximately 7,000 allies from central and southern Mexico had participated in the invasions of the period." See chapter 3 for more on the role played by González Nájera in the conquest of Guatemala. Writing to the King on July 15, 1548, Fray Francisco de la Parra states: "Your Majesty knows that the Spaniards who conquered Mexico also were victorious here in the province of Guatemala, on account of having brought to assist them many Mexican Indian warriors, a great number of whom died in combat." De la Parra— see Archivo General de Indias (hereafter AGI), Guatemala 168, for further details—seeks reparations for the "wives and children who were left behind after the fighting was over, condemned to live here at a place called Almolonca [Almolonga] half a league distant from [Santiago] de Guatemala." The involvement of warriors from Tlaxcala is perhaps the best known, rendered with stunning depictions of battle scenes throughout Guatemala in Diego Muñoz Camargo's "Historia de Tlaxcala" (1582), a manuscript copy of which may be consulted in the Special Collections of Glasgow University Library (MS Hunter 242 U.3.15).

13. Recinos (1952, 62). He writes: "[D]e Cortés había aprendido el arte de mandar a los hombres y obtener el mayor provecho de su esfuerzo y valor; los valientes y astutos guerreros mexicanos le habían enseñado la táctica y artificio en uso en estas partes del Nuevo Mundo."

along with another cousin called Gonzalo de Alvarado y Chávez; and his trusted partner and future son-in-law, Pedro de Portocarrero.

The conquest began on February 13, 1524, when Alvarado crossed the Río Suchiate from Soconusco into Guatemalan territory, most likely with Kaqchikel guides to indicate the lay of the land and the path ahead to the K'iche' capital at Utatlán.[14] Without making specific reference to the *requerimiento*, or summons, that, under Spanish law, had to be read aloud to native peoples prior to battle, thus affording them an opportunity to surrender peacefully before hostilities began, Alvarado sent messengers to the K'iche's with directives to this effect, which went unheeded.

Alvarado and his troops passed through densely wooded terrain along the Pacific coastal plain, which would have been considerably more forested than at present. A three-day march took them close to Xetulul, the K'iche' name for the place later known as Zapotitlán. Three Indian spies captured near the Spanish encampment were sent ahead with instructions to dictate the terms of *requerimiento* to the rulers of Xetulul; again, no reply was forthcoming. Instead, the local population blocked trails in an attempt to impede the invaders. Nonetheless, Alvarado and his men proceeded toward Xetulul, crossing the Río Samalá with some difficulty and thereafter coming face-to-face with the enemy. They continued to advance, pursuing retreating K'iche' warriors for half a league beyond Xetulul. We have no record, as we have elsewhere, of houses being burned, crops destroyed, provisions seized, or people taken prisoner and branded as slaves of war. The invaders camped out in Xetulul's marketplace and spent two days pacifying the surrounding area. Abundant groves of "cacao, zapote, and other tropical fruits" created "a natural defense"

14. Mackie (1924, 53–90). Unless indicated otherwise, the quotations from Alvarado that follow come from Mackie's translation of his two extant letters to Cortés, the first written on April 11, the second on July 28, 1524. In his biography of Alvarado, Kelly (1932, 134–50) reproduces Mackie's "excellent translation" in its entirety, drawing upon it "for the sake of accuracy" time and again. Restall and Asselbergs (2007, 27–47) base their translation on an edition of the two letters first published in 1525, which they "checked against the text of [a] 1749 edition and against the text of [a] 1778 manuscript in the Real Academia de la Historia" in Madrid. While offering fresh glosses and insights, Restall and Asselbergs also remain faithful to Mackie's eloquent rendering. Kramer (1994, 30) provides a map of Alvarado's first *entrada*, as do Restall and Asselbergs (2007, 26). Luján Muñoz (2011, 74–84 and 164–72) reconstructs the initial invasion and subsequent expeditions of conquest with no fewer than eight maps and six illustrations, all nicely showcased in the *Atlas histórico de Guatemala*.

that favored the locals because it did not lend itself to the deployment of Spanish cavalry.[15]

On February 19, Alvarado's contingent left Xetulul and began its ascent into the highlands, where the principal K'iche' settlements were to be found and, at Utatlán, the court of the K'iche' kings. The upward trail, Alvarado comments, was "so rough that the horses could scarcely climb," thus making it necessary to stop for the night midway through their ascent.

THE BATTLE OF EL PINAR

The next morning, February 20, soon after breaking camp and continuing their trek up into the highlands, Alvarado and his forces came upon "a woman and a dog sacrificed, which my interpreter informed me was [issued as] a challenge." Alvarado did not have to wait long for the challenge to materialize, for soon afterwards his men became aware of a well-built palisade, though the fortification, located at a narrow point in the trail, was deserted. As he led his infantry at the front, his cavalry following in the rear, three to four thousand K'iche' warriors are reported to have attacked, forcing the Spaniards and their native auxiliaries to retreat. Then occurred, if not the turning point in the conquest of Guatemala, at least a crucial moment in how it unfolded.

Just as "thirty thousand men [came] toward us," Alvarado states, "I thanked God that there we found some plains." The Spaniards were able to move the scene of battle onto level space and so unleash their cavalry on the advancing K'iche' foot soldiers, whose numbers are surely exaggerated. From his combat experiences in Mexico, however, Alvarado was well aware of the impact that armed and armored men on horseback could have on people who had never before witnessed such a terrifying spectacle. K'iche' fear, together with cavalry expertise in keeping the battle out in the open, resulted in clash after clash, with the mounted invaders winning every fray. Alvarado describes one instance when, with his troops resting at a nearby spring, the K'iche's attacked yet again, but once more where cavalry could be put into action. K'iche' warriors were pushed a league back to the front range of some hills, where they turned

15. Recinos (1952, 65).

to face their attackers. "I [then] put myself in flight with some of the horsemen," Alvarado tells us, "to draw the Indians to the plains, and they followed us, until reaching the horses' tails. And after I rallied with the horsemen, I turned on them, and here a very severe pursuit and punishment was made."

While his account is articulated from the Spanish perspective and is admittedly one-sided and self-congratulatory, it does have the advantage of being written shortly after the events described. By contrast, virtually all the Maya texts on these same events were recorded much later, after members of the indigenous elite had been taught by Spanish friars to write in their languages using the Latin alphabet. The time lag, we suspect, inevitably resulted in inaccuracies and misrepresentations, as would appear to be the case of the celebrated, but some claim, mythical, K'iche' leader, Tecún Umán.

TECÚN UMÁN: MAN OR MYTH?

Grandson of the great King Quikab, whose counsel led to the Kaqchikels splitting from the K'iche' nation to form their own kingdom in the mid-fifteenth century, Tecún Umán passes without mention in Alvarado's firsthand account of the conquest. Neither is he named by Bernal Díaz del Castillo in his version of events, nor in that of the *Memorial de Sololá*.[16] Luján and Cabezas point out that the Spanish sources do not pick up on Tecún Umán (also known as Tecum) until the late seventeenth century. This hiatus causes them to question not only his participation in the conquest but also his very existence.[17] Four K'iche' texts, however, feature Tecum prominently, though none of them dates from the time of first encounter, or close to it: these are the *Título del Ahpop Quecham*, consulted and cited by the "criollo chronicler" Francisco Antonio de Fuentes y Guzmán, who wrote in the 1690s; the *Títulos de la Casa Izquín Nehaib*; the *Título del Ajpop Huitzitzil Tzunún*; and the *Título de los señores Coyoy*.[18] The last three documents even make reference to hand-to-hand

16. Díaz del Castillo ([1632] 1853) and Recinos and Goetz (1953).
17. Luján Muñoz and Cabezas Carcache (1993, 52–53).
18. See Fuentes y Guzmán ([1690–99] 1969–72) with respect to the *Título de Ahpop Quecham*; Recinos (1957, 71–94) for the *Títulos de la Casa Izquín Nehaib*; Gall (1963) for the *Título del Ajpop Huitzitzil Tzunún*; and Carmack and Tzaquitzal Zapeta (1993) for the *Título de los señores Coyoy*.

combat between Alvarado and the K'iche' leader at the Battle of El Pinar, which resulted in Tecum's death. Whom are we to believe?

Alvarado is not much help, but he does state that, in the course of the battle of El Pinar, "one of the four chiefs of the city of Utatlán was killed, who was the captain general of all this country." He reports that, after having set up camp in the abandoned K'iche' center of Xelajub', the present-day Quetzaltenango, toward noon on a Thursday, some twelve thousand warriors "from this city and surrounding towns" appeared and attacked near the area today known as Los Llanos de Urbina. Alvarado responded by sending out ninety cavalry and most of his infantry, first engaging the K'iche' forces and then pursuing them "for two leagues and a half until all of them were routed and nobody left in front of us." Along the banks of a stream that later came to be known, according to Fuentes y Guzmán, as "Xequiquel," or the "River of Blood,"[19] Alvarado claims that his troops "made the greatest destruction in the world," capturing all who sought to escape, "many of whom were captains and chiefs and people of importance." He fails to identify any K'iche' leaders by name in his letter to Cortés dated April 11, 1524. In a judicial inquiry, or *residencia*, conducted several years later, he does single out specific Spaniards and numerous place names, especially battle locations, though he is still unforthcoming about the names of native adversaries.

Luján and Cabezas observe that "no contemporary source nor one close to the conquest, whether indigenous or Spanish, informs us of the name of the Indian leader killed."[20] Furthermore, contrary to other sources that state that the leader killed at El Pinar was Tecún Umán, they contend that he was most likely one Ahau Galel from the Nijaib clan; the two support their case by citing the *Isagoge histórica apologética*, which records that, at the Battle of El Pinar, "it is only known that an Indian of royal blood died, named Galel Ahpop."[21] Luján and Cabezas also leave open the possibility, according to their reading of the *Popol Vuh*, that the leader in question may have been Ahtzic Vinac Ahau. They are critical of Carmack's reading of the sources, chastising him for treating the Tecún Umán issue "as if it dealt with a proven truth, but without analyzing the known historical doubts."[22] As the first to translate the

19. Luján Muñoz and Cabezas Carcache (1993, 51).
20. Ibid., 52.
21. Cited in Luján Muñoz and Cabezas Carcache (1993, 52).
22. Luján Muñoz and Cabezas Carcache (1993, 53).

Título de los señores Coyoy from K'iche' into English, Carmack is alleged
to have taken too literally that document's assertion that Tecún Umán,
"adorned with feathers and precious stones, was carried on the shoulders of K'iche' warriors for seven days before the battle [of El Pinar]
took place."[23] Luján and Cabezas are also skeptical of Carmack's suggestion that Tecum "supposedly lived" in Tzijbachaj in Totonicapán; they
query how this can be reconciled with his being from Utatlán—the
grandson, no less, of King Quikab.[24] With Tecún Umán today having
assumed symbolic significance for, among an array of disparate constituencies, the national armed forces and Guatemala's resurgent Maya
movement, it seems safe to assume that the controversy surrounding
him is far from over.[25]

On to Utatlán

Díaz del Castillo claimed that, as a result of so many K'iche' leaders
having been killed in the battles around Xelajub', "from that victory on,
those people very much feared Alvarado."[26] That fear, however, did not
stop surviving rulers from plotting to kill the man they called Tonatiuh
or Tunatiuh (meaning "the sun," an allusion to Alvarado's fair complexion) and destroy his invading army. The plot was veiled by an offer
of K'iche' surrender and obedience to the Crown. It entailed inviting
Alvarado to Utatlán—as he wrote to Cortés—"thinking that they would
lodge me there, and that when thus encamped, they would set fire to the

23. Ibid., 52.
24. Ibid., 53.
25. See Schirmer (1998, 114), Warren (1998, 154–56), and especially Van Akkeren (2007, 53–74)
for more on the Tecún Umán controversy. Schirmer views the K'iche' leader as a figure manipu-
lated ideologically by the Guatemalan military. Warren examines him from the perspective of
Maya cultural activism (see also Montejo 2005). Sáenz de Santa María (1969, vol. 1, liii) writes:
"The pre-Hispanic wars that Fuentes y Guzmán writes about could have occurred, the singular
dual between Alvarado and Tecún Umán, magic details aside, also. Is Fuentes y Guzmán's testimony sufficient for us to accept that these events really happened? I think not." Van Akkeren
(2007, 15 and 139) is of the opposite opinion, asserting that "there is now sufficient evidence to
accept the historical existence of this 'captain general' of the K'iche' army" and that "the national
legend, in truth, was a man of flesh and blood." A dossier on the subject, reviewing all evidence
then extant, was compiled and published by the Editorial del Ejército (1963). The Mesoamerican penchant for collapsing myth and history, of believing them to be one and the same, should
be borne in mind when dealing with the fact or fiction of Tecum's existence.
26. Díaz del Castillo ([1632] 1853, 220).

town some night and burn us all in it, without possibility of resistance." Upon arrival in Utatlán, which "more resembles a robbers' stronghold than a city," Alvarado sensed treachery and acted accordingly. Part of a wooden causeway, he found out later, had been undermined "so that that night they might finish cutting it" to ensure that neither the Spaniards nor their horses could leave the "robbers' stronghold" once they had been enticed there.[27] Fending off solicitations to stay overnight, eat, and rest in the fortress itself, Alvarado ordered his men to make camp on level ground outside, take control of the town gates, and prepare for action. Somehow they managed to turn the tables on the K'iche's, inviting their leaders to come to the Spanish encampment, and not vice-versa, whereupon Alvarado pounced, seizing prize captives. Yet, again he has very little to say about the incident, mentioning the loss of only one Spaniard but acknowledging the death of many of his Mexican allies.

Alvarado believed that only by "fire and sword" could he subjugate the K'iche's. To that end, he divulges, he exacted "confessions" from the captured rulers regarding their intentions, and had two of them burned at the stake. Utatlán was then razed to the ground. In the judicial hearing of 1529, it was alleged that when Alvarado demanded gold from the K'iche' lords, their failure to provide sufficient quantities to satisfy him was the reason he had them torched.[28] Recinos states that Alvarado received written confessions from the two rulers, Oxib-Queh and Beleheb-Tzii, before they died.[29] These testimonies, even though exacted under duress, would be useful to have, but like so many other documents, they are now unaccounted for. Indeed, there is no extant K'iche' version of events at Utatlán to confirm or counter the Spanish view. The *Popol Vuh* says only that the leaders of the plot were hanged, not burned.[30] The *Memorial de Sololá* backs up Alvarado's version of events, stating

27. According to Díaz del Castillo ([1632] 1853, 221), several observations made Alvarado suspicious, among them the absence of women and common people, a town surrounded by deep ravines, food that was bad and served late, and the fact that the lords sounded excessively animated in their verbal exchanges. Purportedly, Indians from Quetzaltenango had warned Alvarado that the Utlatecas wanted to kill him and his men if they stayed in town, and that many soldiers were waiting in the surrounding ravines to attack the Spaniards as soon as they saw the buildings burning. The origin of Díaz del Castillo's information is not known. See also the account by the Spanish soldier Francisco Flores in Alvarado's *residencia* (judicial review) carried out in Mexico in 1529, as cited in Recinos (1952, 76n42) and Ramírez (1847, 32).

28. Kramer (1994, 31–32), citing Ramírez (1930–33).

29. Recinos (1952, 75).

30. Recinos (1950b, 230) and Tedlock (1985, 224).

that the lords were tortured before they were burned alive. It gives the day 4 Qat—March 7, 1524, in our calendar—as the date of execution, noting that "the heart of Tunatiuh was without compassion."[31]

While camped outside the charred remains of Utatlán, Alvarado decided to test the good will of his allies, the Kaqchikels, by pitting them against their arch enemies, the K'iche's, in a classic strategy of divide and rule. He claims that "on the part of His Majesty," he ordered the Kaqchikels to send him four thousand men to attend to the annihilation of the K'iche's. Díaz del Castillo states that Alvarado demanded half that many, as do Recinos and Goetz in their reading of the *Memorial de Sololá*.[32] In any case, troops who "marched to the slaughter of the Quichés"[33] promptly arrived from Iximché.

What followed was a bloody campaign against K'iche' towns that had submitted to Spanish authority earlier but had afterwards participated in the Utatlán plot. This engagement lasted about eight days and consisted of forays all over K'iche' country, where settlements were laid waste and their vanquished occupants enslaved, branded, and later distributed among the victors. How many K'iche's died resisting capture is a matter of conjecture, but Francisco Hernández Arana, the author of the first entries of the *Memorial de Sololá*, describes the campaign as a "slaughter." Alvarado spent the rest of March and early April near Utatlán. During this time, on Tuesday of Holy Week, March 22, his Tlaxcalan consort, Doña Luisa Xicoténcatl, gave birth to their daughter, Leonor, named after Alvarado's mother, Leonor de Contreras.[34] Two questions arise from this union and event. First, could Doña Luisa's condition have

31. Recinos and Goetz (1953, 120). Recinos (1952, 75–76) adds that the kings met their end in a public execution "before a horrified citizenry," in keeping with "the penchant for vengeance and intimidation that was the trademark of Alvarado's character." Alvarado himself described his actions as designed "to strike terror into the land—atemorizar la tierra."

32. Díaz del Castillo ([1632] 1853, 221) and Recinos and Goetz (1953, 121). Carmack (1981, 146) suggests that the figure of four thousand soldiers is correct, the Kaqchikels having sent *two* separate deployments of two thousand soldiers each time. Kelly (1932, 154) notes that the *Annals of the Cakchiquels*—his bibliography includes the Brinton (1885) edition of the text, though he may also have consulted the original manuscript—states "four hundred," not four thousand. Otzoy (1999, 186), Maxwell and Hill (2006, 259), and Restall and Asselbergs (2007, 105) all furnish the lower figure of four hundred in their renderings. "Four hundred" in the Mesoamerican world meant symbolically "a great many," not necessarily a figure of mathematical precision.

33. Recinos and Goetz (1953, 121).

34. Mackie (1924, 27); Recinos (1952, 78); and Recinos (1958, 13). See Herrera (2007, 127–44) for elaboration of the importance of "intimate unions" between Spaniards and indigenous noblewomen in the early years of conquest.

prolonged Alvarado's stay in Utatlán, or were the additional three weeks spent there out of military necessity? And second, did his union with Doña Luisa and the birth of Leonor consolidate Alvarado's ties to the Tlaxcalans in ways he never could with the Kaqchikels?

KAQCHIKEL-SPANISH RELATIONS

Why did the Kaqchikels choose to cast their lot with the Spaniards? In the conquest of Mexico, the Tlaxcalans aligned themselves with the Spaniards against their powerful enemies, the Aztecs, and thereafter played a critical role in the successful Spanish campaign. The enduring Tlaxcalan-Spanish alliance had consequences far beyond central Mexico. By virtue of their prominence in Alvarado's army, Tlaxcalans afterwards were exempted from the onerous taxes and labor obligations imposed on Guatemalan Indians, albeit that this special status was one they had to lobby hard to maintain.[35] Usually with pejorative implications of being traitors to indigenous resistance, the Kaqchikels have been referred to as the "Tlaxcalans" of Guatemala.[36] The comparison is as unflattering as it is inaccurate.

Certainly the two polities shared similar concerns. Before the arrival of the Spaniards, both were in conflict with strong neighboring states. It would appear, however, that Tlaxcala was in a far weaker position in relation to Tenochtitlán than the Kaqchikels were with respect to the K'iche's, for the situation in Guatemala had become a contest between equals. The Kaqchikel decision to side with the Spaniards is not easy to resolve. How, for example, did the Kaqchikels assess the strength of their rivals—the K'iche's, the Tz'utujils, and the Pipils—against the might of the Spaniards? How could the Kaqchikels have known that the Spaniards would come and stay, when the more familiar Aztec strategy in *their* pursuit of empire was to rule indirectly from a distance, to be focused for the most part on the business of tribute and commerce after subjugation had been attained? While all possible motives may elude us, it is worth noting that, in the early stages of conquest, the Kaqchikel alliance proved

35. See Matthew (2012, 70–131) for detailed discussion not only of the Tlaxcalan case but also of the post-conquest experiences in Guatemala of other "Indian conquistadors" from Mexico.
36. See Polo Sifontes ([1977] 2005), Matthew (2007, 103), and Van Akkeren (2007, 43–44), among others.

to be a viable strategy for survival compared with what happened to
the K'iche's, who fought the invaders at every turn and paid dearly for
it. K'iche' losses are impossible to estimate. But did, for example, the
K'iche's of Utatlán suffer more for what Alvarado saw as their treacherous behavior than the K'iche's of other parts—Quetzaltenango, Totonicapán, and Momostenango, for instance? A case could be made that
Alvarado wanted events at Utatlán to serve as exemplary punishment,
because the use of the Kaqchikels in mop-up operations there may
well have resulted in a more violent campaign than was necessary. The
breakaway people from Iximché, the Kaqchikels, bore nothing but ani-
mosity for their former masters, the K'iche's.

Before departing from Utatlán, Alvarado wrote to Cortés:

On Monday, April 11th, I am leaving for Guatemala [Iximché], where
I mean to stop but a short time, because the town which is situated
on the water called Atitlan [Lake Atitlán] is at war, and has killed
four of my messengers, and I think with the aid of Our Lord [I shall]
soon subdue it to the service of His Majesty.

Two days later, Alvarado arrived in Iximché, where (in the words
of the *Memorial de Sololá*) "the kings Belehé Qat and Cahí Ymox went
at once to meet [him]," believing the conqueror "well disposed" because
"there had been no fight"; Francisco Hernández Arana, the eyewitness
author of this part of the account, notes explicitly that "Tunatiuh was
pleased when he arrived."[37] The Kaqchikel chronicler, however, also
records the following reaction: "In truth they inspired fear when they
arrived. Their faces were strange. The lords took them [to be] gods."[38]

---

37. Recinos and Goetz (1953, 121).
38. See Warren (1998, 154–56) for an illuminating debate about the meaning of these words.
Maxwell and Hill (2006, 260) render the passage thus: "In truth, it was frightening when they
arrived; their faces were not known. The lords perceived them as divine beings." Restall and
Asselbergs (2007, 106) opt for: "Truly it was frightening when they arrived; their faces were not
known. The lords wondered if they were godlike beings." We reiterate (see note 3, above) that, in
our opinion, the texts of Recinos—either alone (1950a) or in collaboration with Goetz (1953)—set
a standard with which later versions of the *Memorial de Sololá* more often coincide than diverge.
In this case, Otzoy (1999, 186), a native Kaqchikel speaker, words his translation into Spanish
much like Recinos (1950a, 126), who translates the passage in question as follows: "En verdad
dinfundían miedo cuando llegaron. Sus caras eran extrañas. Los Señores los tomaron por dioses."
One sentence, not three, is preferred by Otzoy: "En verdad fue cosa temible verlos entrar, sus rostros
eran extraños y los reyes los tomaron por dioses."

In contrast to his experiences at Utatlán, Alvarado felt sufficiently at ease to sleep in the Kaqchikel ceremonial center, in quarters ominously called Skull-Rack Palace. His night proved fitful, and he dreamed "that a frightening number of warriors came to him." Upon meeting the lords the next morning, he asked them: "Why do you make war upon me when I can make it upon you?" The lords replied that war with the Spaniards was not their intention, as "many men would die."[39] They made reference to the fact that Alvarado must have seen "remains there in the ravines." These words may refer either to corpses from some past battle with the K'iche's or, perhaps more likely, to those who perished in the deadly epidemics that had struck the Kaqchikels and are so movingly described by Hernández Arana.[40] Why Alvarado would broach the subject of the Kaqchikels making war on the Spaniards is unclear. Perhaps it had nothing to do with his nightmare and was simply his way of warning them that he was a ruthless partner and, if crossed, would be a lethal adversary.

The next subject raised by Alvarado was more appeasing and demonstrated some concern for Kaqchikel standing with respect to their neighbors: he asked the lords "what enemies they had." Without hesitation, knowing that the K'iche's had been disposed of, the rulers of Iximché replied: "Our enemies are two, oh Lord: the Zutuhils and [those of] Panatacat."[41] This response must have pleased Alvarado, in light of his earlier statement to Cortés that he would not stay long in Iximché because he had a score to settle with the belligerent Tz'utujils. The people of Panatacat, Pipils of the Pacific coast, whose stronghold was also known as Izcuintepeque, later Escuintla, would be dealt with after the Tz'utujils were brought to heel.

39. Maxwell and Hill (2006, 261) and Restall and Asselbergs (2007, 106) render Alvarado's nightmare in exactly the same words as each other, namely that "a frightening number of warriors came to him" during his sleep, prompting him to ask upon awakening: "Why will you make war on me? Is there something I am doing to you?" The Kaqchikel lords replied: "It is not that way; it is just that many warriors have died here." Recinos and Goetz (1953, 121) concentrate more on Alvarado's hostile mood upon awakening.

40. Recinos and Goetz (1953, 115–16). MacLeod ([1973] 2008) estimates that as much as one-third of the native population succumbed in these epidemics. It is very likely that many of the stricken went unburied, as evidenced by Hernández Arana's (Recinos and Goetz 1953, 116) vivid description: "Great was the stench of the dead . . . Half of the people fled to the fields. The dogs and the vultures devoured the bodies. The mortality was terrible." For further analysis of the relationship between epidemic disease and native depopulation, see Lovell ([1992] 2001), Lovell and Lutz (1995, 9–12), and Van Akkeren (2007, 41–42).

41. Recinos and Goetz (1953, 121–22).

Defeat of the Tz'utujils

Alvarado did not take long in subjugating the Tz'utujils. He left Iximché after several days, and by April 18, in the words of Hernández Arana, "the Zutuhils were destroyed by Tunatiuh."[42] Alvarado provides more detail, telling us that two messengers were sent to the Tz'utujils demanding their capitulation. In response, the Tz'utujils killed the messengers. So Alvarado set out with sixty cavalry, 150 foot soldiers, and the "chieftains and people of this land," traversing in short order the seven leagues between Iximché and the Tz'utujil capital, Tziquinahá, which lay on the southwest shore of Lake Atitlán at the foot of Volcán San Pedro.[43] Alvarado gives a vivid description of his assault on a fortified outcrop that jutted into the lake. He says that he and his men stormed the fortress after passing over a narrow causeway. The Tz'utujils defended their position bravely, but to no avail; many gave up the fight and threw themselves into the water, swimming to the safely of a nearby island. There they were able to regroup, "because my allies, who were bringing three hundred canoes across the lake, did not arrive soon enough" to finish them off. Alvarado camped that night in a cornfield and the next day approached the main Tz'utujil settlement. The Spaniards captured three locals and sent them as "messengers to the chiefs, advising them that they should come and render obedience to His Majesty." These messengers were spared and, shortly after, the Tz'utujil rulers appeared before Alvarado. He pardoned them for resisting his forces but warned them henceforth to be compliant and not make war on any of their neighbors, "as all were now vassals of His Majesty." Satisfied that his objectives had been achieved, Alvarado returned to Iximché.

Three days later, "all the chiefs, principal people and captains of the said lake" arrived in Iximché bearing gifts. They announced to Alvarado their hope that they were now on friendly terms; he recorded that the leaders "considered themselves fortunate to be vassals of His Majesty," at last "being relieved of hardships, wars, and differences that they had

42. Recinos and Goetz (1953, 122). See also the "Relación de los caciques y principales del pueblo de Atitlán" (1952).

43. Recinos (1953, 24) translates Tziquinahá as meaning "the house or stream of the birds" and states that "the ruins of the Zutuhil capital still exist in the place presently known as Chui-Tinamit." Van Akkeren (2007, 75) identifies the Tz'utujil capital as Chiya, meaning "at the water's edge," which "in Nahuatl is precisely Atitlán."

amongst themselves." Alvarado takes pains to note that he received the Tz'utujils warmly. He gave them some of his jewels and sent them back home "with much affection [as] they are the most pacific [people] that are in this land." While much of this may sound patronizing to modern ears, we must remember that the Tz'utujils would have known of the fate that had befallen their neighbors, the K'iche's, a fate they presumably wished to avoid. While the terms of submission were as yet unknown, the price of resistance was not.

The Road to Cuzcatlán

The *Memorial de Sololá* makes only brief mention regarding Alvarado's next target, the Pipils of Guatemala's Pacific coast and what is today western El Salvador. "Twenty-five days after his arrival in the city," it states, "Tunatiuh departed for Cuzcatán [Cuzcatlán], destroying Atacat [Panatacat] on the way. On the day 2 Queh [May 9] the Spaniards killed those of Atacat. All the warriors and their Mexicans went with Tunatiuh to the conquest."[44]

Alvarado has more to say about this phase of the conquest than about the defeat of the K'iche's. During his stay in Iximché, envoys from the coast arrived with offerings of peace, complaining to him that the people of Panatacat (Izcuintepeque) had obstructed them en route to their meeting. They claimed that the Izcuintecos had told them not to make peace with the Spaniards and that they might better allow the invaders to enter their territory, where, Alvarado wrote, "all would make war on me." In response to these disclosures, and under the pretext that the Pipils were the declared enemies of the lords of Iximché, he departed for the Pacific coast with 100 cavalry, 150 foot soldiers, and as many as five to six thousand Mexican and Kaqchikel warriors. Because the Mexican contingent had not yet been reinforced from their homeland, the majority of these auxiliaries had to have been Kaqchikels. Before arriving in Izcuintepeque, Alvarado's army traveled for three days through abandoned territory. As with the first skirmishes at Zapotitlán back in February, Alvarado declared that he was apprehensive when his troops had to travel through thick patches of forest. His solution was to deploy

44. Recinos and Goetz (1953, 122–23).

crossbowmen in the vanguard "because the horsemen could not fight there on account of the many marshes and wooded thickets." In the midst of heavy rain, his men reached Izcuintepeque without being detected, surprising the locals when they entered town. Despite their disarray, the Izcuintecos managed to wound some Spaniards and many of their native accomplices. The town, however, soon fell under Alvarado's control, after which he ordered it set on fire. Messages were sent to the lords of Izcuintepeque, reported to be hiding in the surrounding countryside, ordering them "to come and give obedience to Their Majesties." Alvarado warned that he would punish them severely if they did not come, threatening also to "lay waste their maize fields." His intimidation had the required result, and the lords arrived and agreed to be "vassals of His Majesty." The Spaniards stayed at Izcuintepeque eight days, during which time representatives from "many other towns and provinces" arrived in peace and surrendered.

Alvarado then left Izcuintepeque and, marching east toward present-day El Salvador, entered Xinca country. The first town he mentions is Atiepac, today Atiquipaque, where the Xinca-speaking inhabitants, lords and commoners, received him in person only to flee town soon thereafter, a common occurrence during the campaign and an act that Alvarado considered rebellious. Polo Sifontes, in agreement with Recinos, suggests that Xinca flight had more to do with a pragmatic desire to avoid having to feed hordes of hungry soldiers, "more than six thousand men."[45] Alvarado decided to push on and cover the next hundred leagues expeditiously, leaving the unfinished business of pacifying Atiquipaque for his return. The next day, at Tacuilula, he and his men experienced a similar reception of welcome, then flight, so they moved on to Taxisco, another Xinca town "which is very strong and has many people." There they spent the night. Alvarado left for Nancintla the following morning. But the wily conquistador's suspicions had been aroused. He positioned ten of his cavalry at the rear of his column and another ten in the midst of the carriers bearing their supplies. After two or three leagues, the Spaniards were attacked from behind. Alvarado informs us that many of his Mexican allies were killed and, despite precautions, supplies raided and lost, including strings for the crossbows and a quantity of iron.

---

45. Polo Sifontes ([1977] 2005, 70) and Recinos (1952, 87). Luján Muñoz (2011, 84) maps the location of Xinca and possible Xinca towns at the time of conquest.

Alvarado dispatched his brother Jorge with forty or fifty cavalry to try to recover the valued items. But even though Jorge succeeded in catching up with the raiders and routing them, he was unable to retrieve the lost goods. Stolen cloth had been torn to shreds. Back in Nancintla, local inhabitants were restless, abandoning the town for nearby hills. Alvarado sent Pedro de Portocarrero into the hills with foot soldiers to pursue the fleeing population and persuade them to come down, but the mission failed due to the impossibility of knowing where to search in such inhospitable terrain. The Spaniards stayed in Nancintla some eight days, after which time Indians came in peace from Pasaco, a Xinca town farther along on the road to Cuzcatlán. Alvarado welcomed this delegation, gave them presents, and beseeched them to surrender peacefully. He left for Pasaco toward the end of May, arriving to find the entrance to town blocked and arrows stuck in the ground, clearly a warning. Then, as at El Pinar, Alvarado noticed Indians quartering a dog, according to Recinos a ritual sacrifice that was "a sign of war."[46] Alvarado then heard raucous yelling and found himself confronted by "a great multitude of people," whom he and his allies attacked and pursued out of town.

After Pasaco, Alvarado left Xinca country and reentered Pipil territory, specifically the towns of Mopicalco, Acatepeque, and Acaxual, all in present-day El Salvador. The first two towns he found completely abandoned. At Acaxual (Acajutla) on the Pacific coast, fierce fighting broke out and the Spaniards' troubles began in earnest.

About half a league from Acajutla, Alvarado reports seeing plumed, well-armed warriors bearing their insignias and awaiting his arrival. His troops approached "within a [cross]bow-shot of them" and waited. Next he ordered an advance within "half a bow-shot," at which position he realized that the enemy were not moving, observing also that they were close to a wooded area where they could seek protection. He then resorted to the same tactic that had worked so well at Quetzaltenango, namely a feigned retreat to lure Pipil forces out into the open, once again "up to the horses' tails." After simulating withdrawal for a mere quarter of a league, his forces, "who were a hundred horsemen and a hundred and fifty foot, and about five or six thousand friendly Indians," turned and unleashed themselves, cavalry up front, on the

46. Recinos (1952, 88).

now more vulnerable Pipil warriors. "The destruction that we made amongst them," he wrote, "was so great that in a short time none were left alive." Alvarado claimed victory, but it came at considerable cost: several Spaniards were wounded and many auxiliaries killed. Alvarado himself sustained a wound from a Pipil arrow that pierced one of his legs and penetrated his horse's saddle. Complications related to the injury would cripple him for life, leaving him with one leg "four fingers" shorter than the other. So draining was the battle at Acajutla that Alvarado admits he was "forced to remain five days in this town to cure our wounds."[47]

From Acajutla, Alvarado limped on, northeast toward Tacuxcalco. Portocarrero captured two spies who revealed that, up ahead, Indians from Tacuxcalco and surrounding towns were gathered in force. Laid low by his injury at Acajutla, Alvarado passed command of the Spanish troops over to his three brothers, positioning himself on a hill overlooking the battlefield, from where he observed the ensuing confrontation. With the open charge of cavalry again decisive, the Spaniards and their allies crushed the Pipil forces and pursued them for more than a league into Tacuxcalco itself. There they carried out a "great massacre and punishment," after which they rested for two days. Alvarado reckoned that the Pipils now knew that the Spaniards were at their invincible best on open terrain, as the natives started to abandon their towns to the enemy and hide out of harm's way up in the hills. This happened at Miahuaclán, the present-day Azacualapa, where the inhabitants "left for the woods like the others." From Azacualapa, Alvarado headed for Atehuan, present-day Ateos, not too far from his planned destination, Cuzcatlán.

In Atehuan the conquistador received messengers from Cuzcatlán who told him that their rulers "wished to give obedience to Their Majesties." Alvarado claims he believed that they "would not lie like the others," so he agreed to meet them. He reports that he was indeed received in Cuzcatlán by "many Indians." Yet, when the Spaniards prepared their encampment, Alvarado records that not a man remained in town—all had fled. He sent messengers to remind the Cuzcatlán elite that they

47. Recinos (1952, 90) notes that in Alvarado's *residencia* in 1529, the conqueror testifies that he was gravely ill from this and other wounds, going so far as to state that he almost died as a result of the injuries he sustained at Cuzcatlán. Luján Muñoz and Cabezas Carcache (1993, 55) imply that he was exaggerating, stating that Alvarado himself "appears not to have given much importance to the incident," which is manifestly not the case. Luján Muñoz (2011, 61) maps the location of Pipil towns in El Salvador at the time of conquest.

had already pledged obedience. Their response was that they would not come out from their hiding places, would not obey, and if Alvarado wanted something from them, they were there "waiting with their arms." Alvarado made various threats, sent messengers who did not return, and ordered armed expeditions to find and fight the lords and their warriors in the mountains, resulting once again in casualties among the Spaniards and their native allies. Frustrated, if not incensed, Alvarado tried convincing the lords to return with a series of public proclamations, announced by criers, which came to naught. He then sentenced the rulers to death as traitors. He also declared that all Pipils who had been captured during the war, as well as those who might be apprehended subsequently, were to be enslaved and branded, so that their sale might cover the cost of "eleven horses that had been killed in conquering them," as well as any other future losses and expenses. He lamented that he had spent seventeen days in Cuzcatlán with absolutely nothing to show for it, save a better appreciation of what it would take to fulfill the goals of conquest. He puts it succinctly thus: "Here I learnt of very great countries inland, cities of stone and mortar, and learnt from the natives that this land has no end, and to conquer it, as it is large, and of very great cities, much time is required."

Having an arrow pierce his leg at Acajutla was bad enough, but the stalemate at Cuzcatlán was much worse, a low point in Alvarado's first seven months of conquest. "They suffered untold hardship, hunger, and calamity, our people [Mexican auxiliaries] and the Spaniards," the Texcoco author Fernando de Alva Ixtlilxóchitl says of the trek to Cuzcatlán. "They found little gold and treasure while engaged on this expedition, even though other provinces were won and subjugated."[48] Alvarado made his way back to Iximché empty-handed, in a mood of intense agitation, which the pain from his war wound would have done little to still.

Return to Iximché

The *Memorial de Sololá* records Alvarado's return to Iximché summarily, but then notes a more controversial topic, the handing over of a young native woman:

48. Cited in Recinos (1952, 94). Ixtlilxóchitl's precise words are "Padecieron hartos trabajos, hambres y calamidades los nuestros y los españoles. Poco oro y riquezas hallaron en este viaje, aunque se ganaron y sujetaron otras provincias."

On the day 10 Hunahpú [July 21, 1524] he returned from Cuzcatán;
it was two months [forty days] after he left for Cuzcatán when he
arrived at the city. Tunatiuh then asked for one of the daughters of
the king and the lords gave her to Tunatiuh.[49]

Alvarado makes no mention of this incident in his second missive to
Cortés, written one week later. It has become confused with another
charge—that the conquistador also took the Kaqchikel king's wife. In
1529, when Alvarado was put on trial in Mexico for misconduct and
abuse of power, one of the charges brought against him was that, on
returning to Iximché after the defeat of the Tz'utujils, he apprehended
the Kaqchikel king, Cahí Ymox, whom the Spaniards called Sinacán
or Sinacam, and his wife, Súchil. According to the court record, Cahí
Ymox beseeched Alvarado to let Súchil go, even offering a ransom of
gold, jewels, and slaves for her release. Alvarado is reputed to have
tricked Cahí Ymox by taking the ransom but not freeing his wife until
some time later. Alvarado justified his actions by claiming that Cahí
Ymox had been disloyal and that he wanted to teach him a lesson. Whatever the reason, Alvarado's behavior infuriated the Kaqchikel leadership,
precipitating a marked deterioration of relations that a few months later
sparked outright rebellion.

In his defense, Alvarado stated that his seizure of Súchil was to gain
information from her, specifically about the Pacific coast, which would
enable him "to see and know the secret of the land."[50] He claimed that
Kaqchikel lords told him not to bother exploring the region because it
contained many estuaries, rivers, mountains, and fierce animals. These
revelations were at odds with reports from a Spaniard named Falcón,
"who had been informed by an Indian woman called Súchil that the
land was good and rich." Alvarado alleged that he told the lords to bring
Súchil to him in order to find out the truth, but the lords refused to
cooperate. Believing it was to his advantage, as well as the Crown's, to
hear directly from Súchil, Alvarado apprehended an Indian called Toche,
in whose house Súchil was staying. With Súchil in his custody and

49. Recinos and Goetz (1953, 123). Otzoy (1999, 187) records the date as 11 Ajpu, not 10
Hunahpú, and has Alvarado asking for "una hija de los señores" not "una de las hijas del rey."
He registers the period that Alvarado was absent as "40 días," not "two months." In the Maya
calendar, twenty days constitute one month, eighteen months one year.
50. See Ramírez (1847, 99–100).

serving as his guide, Alvarado soon verified that "the land ahead was very good, rich and populated," even though his Cuzcatlán exploits had yielded nothing.

Recinos queries the veracity of the charge that Alvarado took Cahí Ymox's wife, noting that the *Memorial de Sololá* omits the episode altogether. He also questions Alvarado's claim that the Kaqchikel lords dissuaded him from venturing into the Pacific region, as it was in their interest to have Alvarado destroy their enemies in Izcuinte-peque, to which end they sent a strong contingent with the Spanish-Mexican expedition.[51]

Recinos contends that "the pathetic account" of the Súchil affair, which Alvarado did not deny, is riddled with contradictions, not at all easy to resolve. Alvarado acknowledges that he did indeed request to be given a woman, a *daughter* whose father was either the king himself (according to Recinos) or a Kaqchikel lord (according to Otzoy). In the lawsuit, however, he testified that it was common practice for native rulers to give Spaniards their wives, daughters, and sisters. Doña Luisa, after all, had been given to Cortés by her father, Xicoténcatl. Cortés, in turn, passed her on to Alvarado, telling Xicoténcatl that Alvarado was his "brother and captain" and that he would treat her well.[52] Perhaps the Kaqchikel rulers thought that the gift of a daughter of noble lineage would somehow be of benefit to them and their people. It is worth remembering that the *Memorial de Sololá* states that it was the lords, not the king, who "gave her to Tunatiuh." The significance of the wording remains unclear.

If Alvarado's request for a woman of high social standing was within the capacity of Kaqchikel rulers to meet, his next demand (and the very next entry in the *Memorial de Sololá*) triggered a chain of events that even the capricious conqueror might later have regretted. Manifestly upset at not finding sufficient riches on the road to Cuzcatlán, Alvarado issued to the Kaqchikel elite a demand for gold:

> Then Tunatiuh asked the kings for money. He wished them to give him piles of metal, their vessels and crowns. And as they did not

51. Recinos (1952, 97–99).
52. Ibid., 26–27. Pedro's brother Jorge was given Doña Luisa's sister, Lucía, to serve as his royal concubine; once again, see Herrera (2007, 131–37) for further discussion of the significance of these "intimate unions."

bring them to him immediately, Tunatiuh became angry with the kings and said to them: "Why have you not brought me the metal? If you do not bring with you all of the money of the tribes, I will burn you and I will hang you," he said to the lords.

Next Tunatiuh ordered them to pay twelve hundred pesos of gold. The kings tried to have the amount reduced and they began to weep, but Tunatiuh did not consent, and he said to them: "Get the metal and bring it within five days. Woe to you if you do not bring it! I know my heart!" Thus he said to the lords.[53]

On top of this demand, a few days later, Alvarado made a series of administrative decisions with far-reaching implications. On July 27, 1524, with total disregard for any sense of Kaqchikel sovereignty, he founded a Spanish capital at Iximché, awarding himself the right to receive tribute from its inhabitants. He allocated neighboring communities to members of his expedition so they, too, could receive tribute. Alvarado writes:

So it is that I come to this city on account of the heavy rains, where, for the better conquest and pacification of this land, so great and so thickly inhabited, I made and built in the name of His Majesty a Spanish city which is called the city of our lord Santiago. . . . And I elected two Alcaldes Ordinarios and four Regidores, as Your Grace will see by the election.[54]

In reality nothing close to resembling a Spanish city was built then or in subsequent months at Iximché.[55] When, three years later, Santiago came to be founded, it was located not at Iximché but on the slopes of Volcán Agua overlooking the Valley of Almolonga thirty-five kilometers to the southeast. Any dream that Alvarado had of making Iximché the Guatemalan equivalent of Tenochtitlán soon evaporated, one of many consequences of his wanton, rapacious behavior.

---

53. Recinos and Goetz (1953, 123–24).

54. Contreras (2004b, 45–50) and Kramer (1994, 47–62).

55. Commendably continuing the work of George Guillemin, whose untimely death cut short his plans for full-fledged, systematic excavation, Nance, Whittington, and Borg (2003, 332) conclude: "Because of the paucity of direct historical information about Iximché, it is a site that must be examined using primarily prehistoric archaeological techniques. . . . Thus it is not surprising that George Guillemin did not design his original excavations at Iximché as a project in historical archaeology."

RISING TO REBELLION

While the impact of Alvarado's symbolic moves to install Spanish forms of government may have been minimal, the demand for gold was not. The *Memorial de Sololá* records a dramatic sequence of events:

> They had already delivered half of the money to Tunatiuh when a man, an agent of the devil, appeared [*Hun achí qaxtok*] and said to the kings: "I am the lightning. I will kill the Spaniards; by the fire they shall perish. When I strike the drum, [everyone] depart from the city, let the lords go to the other side of the river. This I will do on the day 7 Ahmak [August 26, 1524]." Thus that demon spoke to the lords. And indeed the lords believed that they should obey the orders of that man. Half of the money had already been delivered when we escaped.[56]

The Kaqchikel account continues:

> On the day 7 Ahmak we accomplished our flight. Then we abandoned the city of Yximché because of the agent of the devil. Afterwards the kings departed. "Tunatiuh will surely die at once," they said. "Now there is no war in the heart of Tunatiuh, now he is satisfied with the metal that has been given him."[57]

56. Recinos and Goetz (1953, 124–25). Restall and Asselbergs (2007, 107) consider the Kaqchikel words "Hun achí qaxtok" to be "ambiguous," literally meaning "one man enemy." They note, however, that *qaxtok* may be translated as "demon" and that "in lowland towns it also refers to a warrior with a hand-mace." They base their interpretation on Maxwell and Hill (2006, 267–68), who translate the passage in question as follows: "In the middle of paying the precious metal to Tunatiw, a demon-man appeared: 'I am thunder; I will kill the Spanish people,' he said to the lords. 'They will be consumed in fire! Let me strike the town! Let the lords go across the river! Let it be on seven Ajmaq that I do this!' said the man, the k'axtok, to the lords. In truth, the lords believed him. The man's words were obeyed by them. In truth, the delivery of the precious metal was half completed when we dispersed." Otzoy (1999, 187) translates "Hun achí qaxtok" as "un hombre *poseído* de K'axtok' [el demonio]," a man "possessed by the devil," with which Mondloch (2002, 169) takes exception, stating "there is nothing in the Kaqchikel original to justify use of the word 'possessed'" and pointing out that the word "k'axtok" is better rendered as "deceiver, one who deceives." He suggests that a closer approximation would be "se presentó un hombre engañador," meaning "a man of deception presented himself." Mondloch's preference is close to how Vázquez ([1688] 1937, vol. 1, 40 and 74) deals with the term.

57. Recinos and Goetz (1953, 124–25). Closely following Maxwell and Hill (2006, 268–69), Restall and Asselbergs (2007, 108) render the extract thus: "On 7 Ajmaq the dispersal occurred. Then the town of Iximche' was abandoned; because of the demon-warrior the lords then left. Now, truly, Tonatiuh will die!' they said. There was no war in Tonatiuh's heart; he was happy because precious metal was being given." His handling of "K'axtok" apart—see note 56, above—Otzoy (1999, 187) words things similarly.

The "agent of the devil," however, in all likelihood a warrior-priest or soothsayer, failed to deliver on his promise: Alvarado did not die, nor was he "satisfied with the metal" delivered him. And there proved to be plenty of war still left in his heart, even if the toll of the Cuzcatlán expedition, along with the departure of many of his native allies back to Mexico, prevented him from waging it with the force he knew would be necessary to bring about a speedy end to the Kaqchikel insurrection. The *Memorial de Sololá* states:

> Tunatiuh knew what the kings had done. Ten days after we fled from the city, Tunatiuh began to make war upon us. On the day 4 Camey [September 5, 1524] they began to make us suffer. We scattered ourselves under the trees, under the vines, oh, my sons! All our tribes joined in the fight against Tunatiuh. The Spaniards began to leave at once, they went out of the city, leaving it deserted.[58]

Alive but stymied, Alvarado was in a mire of his own making. The forward momentum begun six months ago had ground to a halt. Indispensable allies had fled to the hills and were now bitter enemies ready to resist until death. Realizing the futility of collaborating any further with the Spaniards, and finding themselves under attack, the Kaqchikels rose up in arms. In need of reinforcements to deal with such a marked reversal of fortune, Alvarado considered his situation at Iximché so vulnerable that he ordered his men to retreat west to the safer confines of Olintepeque, a few kilometers to the north of Quetzaltenango. The conquest of Guatemala had suffered a major setback and was far from over.[59] It was not the first time Alvarado's behavior ended up creating a situation contrary to Spanish interests. What he accomplished by treating

58. Recinos and Goetz (1953, 124–25). Again aligning themselves with how Maxwell and Hill (2006, 269–70) tackle the text, Restall and Asselbergs (2007, 108) continue: "However, Tonatiuh missed the lords. So ten days after we dispersed from the town, the war was begun by Tonatiuh. On 4 Kamey began our being killed by the Castilians. Then our suffering began; we dispersed beneath the trees, beneath the vines, you, my sons! The whole kingdom was in a fight to the death with Tonatiuh. At the peak of it, the Castilians went elsewhere. They left the town; they abandoned it." Otzoy (1999, 187) varies only slightly, preferring (like Recinos and Goetz) to have "all the tribes" as opposed to "the whole kingdom" wage war "to the death," which by all accounts they did.

59. See Luján Muñoz (2011, 78–84 and 113–16, especially maps 37, 56, and 57) for informed discussion and cartographic rendering of native resistance throughout the colonial period.

his Kaqchikel hosts with such arrogance, contempt, and disdain was a prelude to even more intensified conflict, which their continued allegiance surely would have helped curtail. We turn next to sustained acts of resistance on the part of the Kaqchikels and other native groups.

CHAPTER 2

ALLIANCE AND REVOLT

An alliance that lasted barely six months ended in a revolt that lasted the better part of six years. The questions that arise are myriad, answers to them often elusive. Two matters emerge as particularly important. First, when can we consider Kaqchikel fealty to have begun? And second, why was it so short-lived?

Engaging both issues calls for us to contemplate further what motives best illuminate the Kaqchikels' decision to cast their lot with the Spaniards only to reverse it soon thereafter. Chronology is again crucial, but not easy to establish from the sources at hand. For comparative purposes, detailed discussion of the plight of the Kaqchikels will be interspersed with periodic mention of what happened to other native groups in Guatemala as conquest ran its variable, jagged course—an indigenous enterprise as much as, if not more than, a Spanish one.

ORIGINS AND RATIONALE OF THE KAQCHIKEL ALLIANCE

Kaqchikel awareness that foreigners of a different sort were about to reach Mesoamerica perhaps dates to 1510. That year, writes Adrián Recinos, "Emperor Moctezuma II sent an ambassador to the court of Yximché, probably to acquaint the kings with the anxiety he felt because of the presence of the Spaniards in the Antilles."[1] The *Memorial de Sololá* records the arrival of the Mexican delegation in Iximché, though it does not make any specific reference to Moctezuma's reasons for making contact: "[T]he

1. Recinos (1953, 18). How news of the Spanish presence on the Antilles would have reached Moctezuma is not addressed.

kings Hunyg and Lahuh Noh received the Yaquis of Culuacán. On the day 1 Toh [July 4, 1510] the Yaquis, messengers of the king Modeczumatzin [Moctezuma], king of Mexicu, arrived. We saw the Yaquis of Culuacán arrive. These Yaquis, who came many years ago, were very numerous."[2]

Hearing about the Spaniards though a third party was one thing, meeting them face-to-face quite another. If we believe Hernán Cortés, first contact would have occurred after the two Spaniards he dispatched to Guatemala from Tenochtitlán in 1522 arrived in Iximché, but the *Memorial de Sololá* does not mention the event. The Spaniards' unhindered transit through hostile K'iche' country was made under Mexican escort. Francisco López de Gómara, on the basis of information relayed by Pietro Martire d'Anghiera before him from a source no longer available for consultation, relates that during this encounter, the Kaqchikel leadership announced that it "wished to be the friends of such men and furnish them with 50,000 soldiers to conquer their neighbors and destroy their lands." The two Spaniards responded "that they would let Pedro de Alvarado know this."[3] If we accept the account, then that moment marks the beginning of Kaqchikel allegiance. If we do not— Recinos considers it "a fantasy, lifted from a book of stories about knighterrantry"[4]—we must consider the alliance as having been struck and acted upon later, in 1523, during one of Alvarado's two forays to Soconusco,

2. Recinos and Goetz (1953, 112–13). Restall and Asselbergs (2007, 1) observe that "Culhuacan is in the Valley of Mexico: these guests, whom we would call Aztecs, had come from their vast imperial capital of Tenochtitlán . . . [T]hese Aztec (or more properly Mexica) visitors comprised a diplomatic and trading embassy. They were clearly designed to impress upon the Maya the awesome power and reach of the Mexica emperor, perhaps as a prelude to an eventual incorporation into the empire—but the 1509 visitors were not an invasion force. Nor did one come in their wake." An "invasion force" in which Mexica warriors were well represented, we now know, did eventually penetrate Guatemala in 1524, but under markedly different political circumstances than prevailed a decade and a half earlier. Restall and Asselbergs (2007, 1), based on the chronology of Maxwell and Hill (2006, 237), give the year of the Kaqchikel-Mexica rendezvous as 1509, not 1510. Otzoy (1999, 217) concurs with Recinos and Goetz and correlates 1 Toj with July 4, 1510.

3. López de Gómara, cited in Recinos (1952, 55–56). His precise words are: "El señor dijo entonces que quería ser amigo de tales hombres y darles cincuenta mil soldados para que conquistaran unos sus vecinos que le destruían la tierra. A esto dijeron los dos españoles que lo harían saber a Pedro de Alvarado, capitán de Cortés para que viniese." Offering a fighting force of "fifty thousand soldiers" is surely a wild exaggeration. López de Gómara (see chapter 1, note 8) states two sentences later that "five thousand men," not "fifty thousand soldiers," were dispatched. How the two Spaniards knew, a year or more prior to the event, of Pedro de Alvarado being the person chosen by Cortés to head the Spanish offensive is not made clear.

4. Recinos (1952, 56). See also chapter 1, notes 8, 9, and 10.

the launching ground for his Guatemala campaign.[5] Alvarado is typi-
cally unforthcoming about whether or not Kaqchikels fought alongside
the Spaniards and their Mexican allies in the opening battles against
the K'iche's. His earliest mention of Kaqchikels engaging in combat
is not registered until after the fall of Utatlán, when Alvarado asked
Iximché to send him reinforcements. The *Memorial de Sololá* confirms
compliance, adding that Kaqchikel troops served the Spanish cause
in other ways besides waging war:

> Soon a messenger from Tunatiuh came before the [Kaqchikel] kings
> to ask them to send him soldiers: "Let the warriors of the Ahpo-
> zotzil and the Ahpoxahil come to kill the Quichés," the messenger
> said to the kings. The order of Tunatiuh was instantly obeyed.
>
>   Only the men of the city went; the other warriors did not go down
> to present themselves to the kings. The soldiers went three times only
> to collect the tribute from the Quichés. We [members of the nobility]
> also went to collect it for Tunatiuh.[6]

The above extract hints at what the Kaqchikels may have expected
from siding with the Spaniards, even if it does not entirely reveal their
rationale for doing so: strike an alliance, negotiate terms, act as co-con-
quistadors, and serve thereafter as collectors of tribute as opposed to
being obliged to pay massive amounts of it. "How local elites drew on
Mesoamerican traditions of alliance formation to deal with the Spanish
invasion," assert Michel Oudijk and Matthew Restall, is "the real story"

---

5. Mackie (1924, 13) notes that Cortés initially "dispatched Pedro de Alvarado with eighty-
odd horsemen and two hundred foot soldiers, amongst whom were many crossbowmen and musketeers; he took four field pieces and artillery, and a great supply of ammunition and powder."
Alvarado's first foray was interrupted because of Cortés having to deal with the ambitions of
one of his rivals, as Mackie (1924, 13) explains: "This expedition was about to start when news
was received of the arrival of Francisco de Garay at Pánuco, and Alvarado was sent to oppose
this incursion. It was not until the end of 1523 that he finally left Mexico." When he did so, Cortés
emphasizes, Alvarado left with men and munitions "in addition to what I had already provided
for the last expedition," all in all a considerable undertaking, especially when one bears in mind that a
substantial number of Mexican auxiliaries were also part of, indeed the bulk of, invader ranks.

6. Recinos and Goetz (1953, 120–21). Borg (2003, 25) informs us that the Ahpozotzil was
"the principal ruler of Iximché" and that the Ahpoxahil, "the second ranking Cakchiquel king,"
was the ruler of Tzololá [Sololá], which "was conquered by Iximché in 1517 during a period
when the Cakchiquel were engaged in continuous warfare with the Quichés." The tribute schedule
referred to, three deliveries in as many months, strikes us as implausible, even for such a ruthless
taskmaster as Alvarado.

of the conquest. These authors draw on Ross Hassig's depictions of "pre-conquest political organization and imperial strategy" to shed light on post-conquest scenarios whereby "members of such alliances were not centrally controlled," nor did they share "a common ethnic identity," but, rather, sought to function as "special-purpose institutions, arising from perceived needs and persisting as long as needs were satisfied."[7] Restall also observes that, in the Aztec empire as well as during the war that brought about its demise, "Mesoamerican city states were aware that forging an alliance with an imperial aggressor might help preserve their status."[8] His observation fits the Kaqchikel case well. Florine Asselbergs concurs. "When the Spaniards arrived," she notes, "they were immediately incorporated into this Mesoamerican system. Their arrival was regarded by many as an opportunity to establish a new alliance through which they could turn the existing socio-political relationships to their advantage." Furthermore, she asserts, "indigenous communities did not regard their [subjugation] to the Spanish Crown as a humiliation, but instead as an alliance of two equal forces [that], together, would be able to conquer other communities."[9] Again, her reasoning helps us better understand Kaqchikel maneuvers. We are fortunate in having the *Memorial de Sololá* and other indigenous sources to assist us in our analysis, as they portray (in the words of Oudijk and Restall) "a far more complex process of alliances and negotiations," proffering a view of colonial confrontation in Guatemala "as a continuation of precolonial processes of conquest and domination."[10]

In his ruminations on the actions of the Kaqchikels, Francis Polo Sifontes sets up "premises" and "hypotheses" that allow him to envision two "alternative" responses to the invasion.[11] He lays them out as follows:

Option 1: Voluntary submission to Spanish rule, which for indigenous peoples entailed (1) paying tribute with men, in order for them to participate in the conquest of other territories; (2) paying tribute in gold, as dictated in the

7. Oudijk and Restall (2007, 43–44).
8. Restall (2010, 192). See also Van Akkeren (2007, 43), who views "forging an alliance as simply a strategic maneuver to come out on the winning side."
9. Asselbergs (2004, 95–96).
10. Oudijk and Restall (2007, 57).
11. Polo Sifontes ([1977] 2005, 44–45).

terms of surrender; and (3) paying tribute in provisions so as to feed the invading army, an onerous obligation given the many such mouths to feed.

Option 2: Involuntary submission through force of arms, which thereafter entailed (1) the enslavement of members of the vanquished group, branded as slaves of war later sold at public auction to enrich the victors; (2) paying considerable tribute in gold; and (3) seizure of goods and provisions.

Polo Sifontes argues that the Kaqchikels' actions caused them to suffer the consequences of both options, in effect a "double punishment" for first having aligned themselves, only to revolt and be defeated. While other native polities in Guatemala chose Option 2 and fared accordingly, he contends that "on Kaqchikel shoulders the burden of conquest fell twice," adding that "this feisty people, inured to war, were probably exploited even more than any of their neighbors."[12]

If the precise origins of the Kaqchikel alliance cannot be established, nor all the nuances behind it, we are on firm ground as to when collaboration ended and resistance began: 7 Ahmak, August 26, 1524. That was the day, the *Memorial de Sololá* records, "we abandoned the city of Yximché" and "scattered ourselves under the trees" to "fight against Tuniatiuh."[13] What triggered such a dramatic volte-face on the part of the Kaqchikels, and what were the long-term implications for Spanish goals?

FROM ALLY TO ENEMY

Pedro de Alvarado, by all accounts, had an explosive temperament. Once provoked, he was quick to react, capable of committing or orchestrating acts of violence judged to be extreme even by the grim measures of his day. A man of arms rather than a strategic thinker, Alvarado exhibited a penchant to strike first and deal with consequences

12. Ibid., 13 and 45. He points out that "in whatever of the two situations, the conqueror also had the right to take from the defeated their lands and women."

13. Recinos and Goetz (1953, 124–25). Van Akkeren (2007, 77) correlates "7 Ajmaq" with August 28, 1524.

later, his sense of judgment often blinded by impulse. In his reconstruc-tion of Alvarado's life and times, Recinos furnishes abundant examples of how Alvarado's rash and vengeful behavior not only destroyed native welfare but also threatened Spanish interests. No better instance of his reckless ways, manifest before he undertook the conquest of Guate-mala, is the slaughter he unleashed at the Temple of Huitzilopochtli in Tenochtitlán on May 19, 1521.

Thousands of people had assembled with their lords to celebrate festivities honoring the Aztec god Tezcatlipoca at a location directly in front of where Spanish forces and their Tlaxcalan allies were garri-soned. Alvarado was acting commander at the time, Cortés having left with a sizable contingent of Spaniards to ward off the challenge to his authority by Pánfilo de Narváez, dispatched from Cuba by Governor Diego de Velázquez to hold Cortés to account for having embarked upon the conquest of Mexico without Velázquez's sanction. Believing that paying homage to one of their gods was cover for an intended assault, and no doubt feeling vulnerable in the face of such a mass, Alvarado targeted and pounced on a core group of leaders, unarmed but adorned with gold, feathers, and precious stones, just as they were about to perform the culminating ceremony. "The outcome of this attack," Recinos states with a poignant air, "was the death at the hands of the Spaniards of the flower of Mexican nobility, which turned the entire city against the invaders."[14] Returning the following month to a sullen, seething Tenochtitlán, and being apprised of what had taken place during his absence, an incensed Cortés, so Bernal Díaz del Castillo relates, declared the attack "a very wrong thing to do, the act of a madman."[15] He surely sensed, given the gravity of the incident, that a backlash was

14. Recinos (1952, 38). In his seminal study, the same author (1952, 189–211) offers insight-ful reflections about "Alvarado's character," drawing on the views of an array of commentators, from "unconditional apologists" Vázquez and Fuentes y Guzmán to "Black Legend" polemicist Bartolomé de Las Casas and the "serene and impartial judgment" of José Milla. The attack and its repercussions are vividly described by Padden (1967, 192–202). He views Alvarado as "a capable officer and a good leader of men" but a psychopath who "did not possess the genius of his commander." According to Padden's reading of the sources, "only those who feigned death survived," with Cortés considering the carnage wrought by Alvarado "ill done and an error of tragic proportion."

15. Díaz del Castillo, as quoted in Recinos (1952, 39). Francisco López de Gómara ([1552] 1964, 208), who served as secretary to Cortés, words his master's reaction far more circum-spectly. "Cortés, who must have felt badly about the affair," he writes, "dissembled his feelings so

inevitable. Stones hurled from Aztec slings, Cortés wrote later, soon "rained down from the heavens," trapping the Spaniards in their quarters, to which the Aztecs had laid siege, intent on starving out the invaders as well as bombarding them. Realizing that a retreat from Tenochtitlán to the safe haven of Tlaxcala was their only chance of survival, on the evening of June 30 (*La Noche Triste*), Cortés, his countrymen, and their native allies began a five-day battle to save themselves. They did so, but at a cost, according to Cortés, of 150 Spanish and two thousand "friendly Indian" lives—and six times that many Spaniards in the reckoning of Díaz del Castillo. "There were few left in the end," the latter recorded, "some 440 of us, with twenty horses, a dozen crossbowmen, and seven musketeers. We had no powder, and everyone was wounded, crippled or maimed."[16] Cortés regrouped and, with vital native assistance, set about the reconquest of Mexico, somehow seeing fit not only to overlook Alvarado's foolhardiness but to entrust him with the conquest of Guatemala two years later.

When he wrote to Cortés from Iximché on July 28, 1524, Alvarado signed off as follows: "I pray Your Grace to give [His Majesty] an account of who I am and of how I have served [him] in these parts . . . and how, in his service, I am lamed in one leg, and how little return I and these *hidalgos* [noblemen from Spain] in my company have received up to the present, and the little profit that we have made so far."[17] Mindful of the riches he had seen at Tenochtitlán and elsewhere in Mexico, and resentful that he had nothing remotely like them to show for his arduous trek from Guatemala to El Salvador and back again, Alvarado again fell prey to his own volatile nature. Soon after composing the above lines to Cortés, not content with what the K'iche's and Tz'utujils furnished as tribute, he turned on the Kaqchikels, whose leaders must have been as perplexed as they were angered to find themselves insulted, threatened, imposed upon, and expected to help make up for the "little return" and "little profit" that had until then fallen Alvarado's way. Instead of being treated respectfully as partners who had pledged allegiance, furnished fighters, provided food, shelter, and the comfort of women, served as

---

as not to irritate the perpetrators, for it happened at a time when he had need of them, either against the Indians, or to put down trouble among his own men."

16. Díaz del Castillo, as quoted in Recinos (1952, 43).

17. As rendered by Mackie (1924, 89–90).

guides, translators, and go-betweens, offered support and sustenance in every way imaginable, the Kaqchikels were ignominiously slighted, made to feel like dirt. By insisting that they deliver an inordinate amount of bullion or suffer the consequences for not doing so, through his rash, myopic behavior, Alvarado turned allies into enemies, an asset into an adversary, sparking a costly insurrection that was to drag on for years.

CONFLICTING VIEWS OF THE KAQCHIKEL REBELLION

Of the carnage at Tenochtitlán that led to *La Noche Triste* and the retreat to Tlaxcala, Díaz del Castillo states: "Some persons say that Pedro de Alvarado made war out of greed, [upon seeing] that the Indians who were dancing were covered in golden ornaments and jewels of great value. I do not believe that: I think that he struck to fill them with fear."[18] No either/or stakes were evident at Iximché. Instead, a toxic combination of both avarice *and* intimidation sent Kaqchikel country into mayhem.

The Kaqchikel rebellion is one of the murkiest episodes in Guatemalan history. From early on to the present, views of it have varied significantly, at times incompatibly so. Even the chroniclers Francisco Vázquez and Francisco Antonio de Fuentes y Guzmán, fellow criollos and close friends who shared information, have markedly different things to say about the uprising.[19] Two present-day commentators, Jorge Luján Muñoz and Horacio Cabezas Carcache, maintain that the Kaqchikels mounted "a heroic but fruitless war of resistance," as opposed to "a revolt or rebellion" per se, although they concede that in their fight against the Kaqchikels, "the Spaniards and their Indian auxiliaries suffered more losses and incurred greater damages than when fighting,

18. Díaz del Castillo, as quoted in Recinos (1952, 38). His precise words are: "[Dicen] algunas personas que el Pedro de Alvarado por codicia de haber mucho oro y joyas de gran valor con que bailaban los indios, les fué a dar guerra, yo no lo creo, ni nunca tal oí, ni es de creer que tal hiciese . . . sino que verdaderamente dió en ellos por meterles temor." The chronicler Antonio de Remesal—see García Añoveros (1987a, 257)—concurs, stating that Alvarado "wanted to be feared more than loved by all under his authority, Spaniards as well as Indians," adding that the trait led to "excesses" being perpetrated "with very little justice or reason."

19. See Polo Sifontes ([1977] 2005, 74–80) and Contreras (2004b, 50–64) for elaboration.

earlier in 1524, against the Quichés."[20] In a similar vein, and somewhat surprisingly so, the staunchly pro-indigenous Asselbergs opts to describe it as the "so-called 'Kaqchikel rebellion,'" despite acknowledging (as Luján and Cabezas also do) that because "the ones who were affected most were the Kaqchikel," they waged "six years of almost continuous warfare."[21]

Francisco Vázquez wrote his *Crónica de la provincia del santísimo nombre de Jesús de Guatemala* toward the end of the seventeenth century.[22] Around the same time, Luján Muñoz believes, the *Memorial de Sololá* was sent, for study and safekeeping, from Sololá by a friar who served there to the Franciscan convent in Santiago de Guatemala. There can be no doubt that Vázquez consulted the *Memorial de Sololá* while composing his chronicle, for he lifts several key passages from it. He says of Kaqchikel record-keepers in one excerpt:

> They write that before them appeared a *Caxtok*, which in their language means the Devil, the one who deceives, and he said to them: What are you waiting for with those few foreigners who remain in Almolonga? Tonatiuh [Pedro de Alvarado] has left already for Spain, and many foreigners (this is how they refer to Spaniards) have gone with him. What are you afraid of? I am the flash of lightning. I will make dust and ashes of them, I will wipe them out. If you prove to be cowardly, I will annihilate you too. Do you wish to live as the slaves of such cruel people? Do you wish to abandon the laws by which you have lived, the laws that your forefathers raised you to respect? Prepare yourselves, bring together those of our nation, who are many, and be done with such misfortune.[23]

Vázquez makes clear that he is extracting this information from an indigenous source to which he has access, one readily at hand. "So it is written in their accounts by the very Indians themselves," he records.

20. Luján Muñoz and Cabezas Carcache (1993, 59). See Luján Muñoz (2011, 78–80) for more on his views of the rebellion, including two maps (numbers 35 and 36) of Kaqchikel country at the time of the conquest.

21. Asselbergs (2004, 85–86).

22. Luján Muñoz (2004, 8). Swezey (1985, 161) also notes that Vázquez "had access to many ecclesiastical documents and primary sources housed in the rich archive at the Franciscan convent, as well as to the city archive where the *Libros de cabildo* and other civil records, now lost, were kept."

23. Vázquez ([1688] 1937, vol. 1, 74). See chapter 1, notes 56 and 57, regarding the word "Caxtok."

"Caxtok, devil and deceiver, whose false promises it was that caused these rebellions and inopportune disturbances."[24]

Judging from translations into Spanish made by Recinos and Otzoy of the same passage, Vázquez captures a sense of the Kaqchikel text reasonably well, flourishes and all.[25] The same cannot be said, however, of his reading of other parts of the *Memorial de Sololá*, nor of his handling of available contemporary sources. He dates the rebellion as having ignited in 1526, not 1524, over excesses inflicted on "the entire Kaqchikel nation, which is made up of more than sixty towns," not by Pedro de Alvarado but by one of his brothers, Gonzalo. The turmoil occurred, he alleges, after Pedro had left for Honduras to confer there with Cortés. "That gentleman," Vázquez writes of Gonzalo, "sought to take advantage of the occasion to enrich himself, and so imposed on the well-populated capital an abnormal levy of tribute: each day four hundred young women and an equal number of young men, under threat of being made slaves, would wash for gold on the slopes of a mountain called Chahbal and in a stretch of land called Punakil."[26] The *Memorial de Sololá*, on the other hand, tells us this demand was made by Pedro, not Gonzalo de Alvarado, and took place not in 1526 but in 1530.[27]

According to Vázquez, Gonzalo and his men were so hard pressed when the Kaqchikels rebelled that they were forced to retreat to Quetzaltenango and Olintepeque—"those who escaped with their lives, that is, as Spaniards and Mexicans were killed at will." There they are said to have licked their wounds, awaiting the arrival from Honduras of their

---

24. Vázquez ([1688] 1937, vol. 1, 40). Carmack (1973, 188) notes that "Vázquez claims to have had several Indian *títulos* in his possession, probably many of those used by his friend, Fuentes y Guzmán. Yet he makes almost no use of them." Two *títulos* that Vázquez may have consulted, Carmack reckons, are the *Título Huitzitzil Tzunun* and the *Título Nijaib*, but the chronicler makes no specific mention of the *Memorial de Sololá*.

25. See Recinos (1950a, 129) and Otzoy (1999, 187) for comparative evaluation, Maxwell and Hill (2006, 267–68), Van Akkeren (2007, 77), and Restall and Asselbergs (2007, 107), too.

26. Vázquez ([1688] 1937, vol. 1, 73–74). Like Fuentes y Guzmán, Vázquez was an ardent admirer of Pedro de Alvarado. By attributing to his brother, Gonzalo, deeds associated with Pedro, Vázquez may have acted so as not to tarnish the latter's reputation. In the Mesoamerican mindset, we must recall, invoking the number "four hundred" should not be taken literally but instead to mean "many." The "stretch of land called Punakil" most likely refers to today's San José Poaquil.

27. Recinos and Goetz (1953, 129). Maxwell and Hill (2006, 279) and Restall and Asselbergs (2007, 110) concur.

commander-in-chief. Pedro de Alvarado led what Vázquez depicts as a veritable *re*conquest of Kaqchikel country by targeting Nimaché, the "Great Forest," a mountainous redoubt to the east of Tecpán Guatemala, where the two leaders of the uprising were hiding out, "rebellious and obstinate" to the end. The Ahpozotzil and the Ahpoxahil, however, proved no match for Alvarado. Both Kaqchikel kings, Vázquez declares, upon being captured "were held prisoner, trophies of victory, until the year 1540, their lives spared by the merciful Don Pedro de Alvarado." He is adamant about Alvarado's "noble and Christian intentions," stating that even though they were "evil and obstinate," the leaders of the revolt were neither "hanged" nor "burned" but kept alive, "and it is believed that Alvarado would have taken them with him" on a voyage he planned to the Spice Islands.[28]

    If Vázquez shared his knowledge of the *Memorial de Sololá* with Fuentes y Guzmán, his kindred spirit appears not to have benefited much from it. In the *Recordación florida*, written during the decade after Vázquez penned his chronicle, Fuentes y Guzmán refers to numerous native texts and distills their contents, usually frustratingly from the standpoint of modern scholarship.[29] The *Memorial de Sololá*, however, seems not to have been among them. His version of the uprising, "the military action of which gave rise to, and may be considered the origin of, the *Fiesta del Volcán*,"[30] runs as follows.

28. Vázquez ([1688] 1937, vol. 1, 40 and 77). Customarily an astute reader of the sources, Recinos (1947, 261) appears to have put too much credence in Vázquez's version of events before thinking better of it. He states that "King Sequechul, also known as Tepepul, was imprisoned until 1540, when Alvarado took him aboard one of his ships, along with the Cakchiquel king Belehe-Cat, or Sinacán." Recinos compounds his error by correlating "Belehe-Cat" with "Sinacán," two lords he later acknowledges in a subsequent study as distinct individuals, the latter dying in 1532 while made to pan for gold (Recinos 1950a). Contreras (2004b, 63) also alludes to "the two captives" as having "departed with Alvarado and his armada, never to be heard of again." He is careful, however, to attribute this fallacious version of events "to the chroniclers, for whom Alvarado was good and generous." Contreras himself is well aware that the fate of "the heroic Kaqchikel kings" was quite different.

29. Carmack (1973, 184) would likely consider our assessment too harsh, for he writes "though Fuentes y Guzmán has been severely criticized for his exaggeration, disorganization, confusion and errors of fact, rambling, flowery style, and his obvious bias in favor of the conquistadores . . . it is my considered opinion that [he] was a better student of Indian culture than is usually recognized, and that his work is of inestimable importance."

30. Fuentes y Guzmán ([1690–99] 1882–83, 159–63). Contreras (2004a, 70–71) is of the opinion that Fuentes y Guzmán, "instead of calling it the Fiesta of the Volcano should have named it the Dance of the Conquest of Guatemala," which he claims it most decidedly is. "In a Dance of the Conquest of Guatemala," Contreras (2004a, 75–76) adds, "the character who, for historical reasons,

In 1526, the Kaqchikels (led by Cahí Ymox, whom the Spaniards referred to as Sinacán or Sinacam) and the K'iche's (led by a king called Sequechul) joined forces and rebelled, "their belligerent actions creating havoc in towns that remained loyal and obedient, often disrupting the entry of provisions into the [capital] city of Goathemala" from their base atop a mountain near Quetzaltenango. The uprising took place when Pedro de Alvarado was off in Spain. During his absence, Pedro de Portocarrero served as acting governor, and in response to native unrest, he assembled an army that advanced toward Quetzaltenango to crush the rebels. A strategic assault caused "disarray and confusion" among the rebels, who capitulated only after "valiant resistance." Recruited by Portocarrero from towns friendly to the Spaniards, a "goodly number of Indian bowmen" are said to have played a decisive role. Among those who surrendered were "Sinacam and Sequechul," who were taken captive and who remained in prison "for fifteen years, until Don Pedro de Alvarado left for the Molucas or Spice Islands."[31]

---

should represent Guatemala is the Apozotzil Kahi' Imox, also known as Sinacán, the most notable indigenous leader of his time." He points out that "the hero of the modern and better-known Dance of the Conquest, Tecún Umán, had but a moment of glory, falling in one of the first armed confrontations. Most certainly he never got to know [Pedro de] Alvarado, who found out about the death of the Lord of Utatlán after he had fallen on the field of battle, and not in man-to-man combat with him. Had that been the case, Alvarado would surely have informed Cortés. Legend and folklore have converted the Lord of the K'iche's, whom it is said was called Tecún Umán, into a heroic symbol of indigenous resistance." Contreras (2004a, 70) laments: "Almost no one today remembers the Apozotzil Kahi' Imox, the rebellious Sinacán, but during the colonial period his name was never forgotten, nor his act of rebellion, as each year on the occasion of royal festivities was celebrated what Fuentes y Guzmán called 'the admirable and splendid Fiesta del Volcán,' a spectacle that evoked the struggle and imprisonment of Sinacán and B'elehe' K'at, the leaders of the Kaqchikel revolt." Hill (1992, 1–9) opens his study of Kaqchikel-Spanish relations in the seventeenth century with a colorful description and incisive analysis of the "Fiesta del Volcán," a mock battle in which "we see the Colonial order in microcosm." He stresses that "like their role in the Fiesta del Volcán, [Kaqchikel] responses, their *adaptations* [Hill's emphasis] to the demands of the Colonial situation were largely worked out by the Cakchiquels themselves, usually without the Spaniards' knowledge or understanding." Matthew (2012, 180–200) also depicts the Fiesta del Volcán with a keen eye for detail and meaning, singling out the role in the drama of the "Mexicanos from Ciudad Vieja" as "Indian conquistadors in the Valley of Guatemala." The "symbolic surrender" of Sinacán, the climax of the Fiesta del Volcán, is noted by Asselbergs (2010, 201), too.

31. Fuentes y Guzmán ([1690–99] 1882–83, vol. 2, 155–59). Carmack (1973, 187) believes that Fuentes y Guzmán "was probably less successful at writing history than describing native culture and history," and all told "was a better ethnologist than historian." The chronicler's portrayal of the Kaqchikel rebellion certainly conforms to Carmack's views of him.

Francisco Ximénez, writing soon after Vázquez and Fuentes y Guzmán, took both chroniclers to task for their portrayal of the rebellion, having some especially severe criticism to level at the latter. A manuscript copy of his *Historia de la Provincia de San Vicente de Chiapa y Guatemala* (1715–20) indicates that he had the work of his two predecessors in mind when he was composing, for notes citing them appear in the margins of his folios as well as mention being made of them in the body of his text. "Not all native groups rose up," he states. "The K'iche's had no involvement, nor did they have a king called Sequechul. This person would have been some other powerful Kaqchikel ruler, or someone from elsewhere."[32] Ximénez, however, who had the *Popol Vuh* to draw upon as one of his sources, but not, it seems, the *Memorial de Sololá*, is himself not above reproach, for he, too, considers the revolt to have begun in 1526, regarding it "as little more than a ploy to gain some respite from tyranny," downplaying its significance as an armed confrontation of any consequence and chastising Vázquez and Fuentes y Guzmán for depicting it otherwise.[33]

The Kaqchikels themselves tell a different story.

KAQCHIKEL ARTICULATIONS

Daniel Contreras laments that "the account of the war against the Spaniards takes up hardly ten brief paragraphs in the *Memorial de Sololá*, without going into much detail. What it has to say, however, is of particular importance because information is accompanied by dates that anchor the rebellion properly in time." The Kaqchikel count is at odds with the chronology of the chroniclers, he states, but should be considered "the more reliable source," one that indicates that the rebellion "broke out in 1524 and was still going on in 1530." Contreras regrets

32. Ximénez, "Historia de la Provincia de San Vicente de Chiapa y Guatemala" (1715–20), Biblioteca Provincial de Córdoba, manuscript 128, fol. 133v. Aside from the manuscript in Córdoba—the venerable Dominican was born in nearby Éjica—printed editions of his work are available. The extract we have quoted appears, for instance, in Ximénez ([1715–20] 1929–31, vol. 1, 151), alongside some particularly stern words leveled at Fuentes y Guzmán, "who deceives a great deal by what he has to say."

33. Ximénez ([1715–20] 1929–31, vol. 1, 152–53). "I cannot fathom," he writes sharply, "the nerve of these two authors, coming up with such contradictions, each feeding off the other in flights of total fancy."

especially that "the authors of the *Memorial de Sololá* did not include entries about the resistance of other native peoples who, according to the chroniclers, also rose up in arms, following the Kaqchikel example," among them the Poqomams of Mixco, the Pipils of Cuzcatlán, a group of Tz'utujils in the Atitlán region, and Mam peoples in the Sierra de los Cuchumatanes.[34] We do well to work with the source as diligently as we can, listening to Kaqchikel voices as we place their testimony alongside the Spanish record, refusing to let the volume of the latter drown them out.

Arguably Guatemala's most accomplished modern scholar, whose translations of the *Memorial de Sololá*, first into Spanish and then into English, make his renderings the ones that have reached the widest readership, Adrián Recinos makes some trenchant remarks about the cause of the fighting:

> It is clear that the demands and threats of [Pedro de] Alvarado were what sparked the Cakchiquel rebellion. So great were one or the other that they obliged his former friends and allies to abandon their homes and scatter themselves in the mountains. Too late did the trusting lords comprehend that they had sacrificed the freedom of their people for a house of cards.[35]

He describes the clarion call most dramatically:

> The cry of insurrection resounded through the valleys and mountains. Cakchiquel warriors seized their arms and attacked the Spaniards at close quarters, showering them with arrows and lances, bellowing: "Here, take your gold, Tuniatuh!"[36]

Recinos points out that "Spaniards themselves denounced Alvarado for his extortions as well as his acts of violence against the natives, and thus originated the criminal proceedings instituted in Mexico . . . in 1529."[37] One of the charges leveled against him, the twenty-seventh

34. Contreras (2004b, 54); Luján Muñoz and Cabezas Carcache (1993, 57–58).
35. Recinos (1952, 105).
36. Ibid.
37. Recinos (1953, 19). One of the Spaniards who spoke out at the trial, declaring that Alvarado had been well received by the Indians, only to incur his wrath, was Francisco Flores. According to Recinos (1952, 105), Flores testified that the Kaqchikels rebelled "because Alvarado asked them to supply a considerable amount of gold, a demand they could not meet."

to be exact, ends with a monetary value being placed on the cost of his actions:

> Upon arrival in Guatemala, Pedro de Alvarado told the lords and inhabitants of the province that he wished to colonize it, and so they took him at his word. Then Alvarado ordered that within twenty days the lords give him one thousand gold leaves, each worth fifteen pesos. They began to collect the gold so as to comply with Alvarado's command, and indeed some eight to nine thousand *pesos de oro* were collected, but time ran out on them, because Alvarado would settle only for the finest of gold. The lords became fearful, knowing the cruelties he was capable of, this avaricious, hard-hearted man. Thus they made war on him, and for a long time, just as they did all over the country. The lords and inhabitants let it be known that, as long as Pedro de Alvarado remained in charge, there would be no peace with the Christians, even were they to die fighting. One consequence of all this is that Your Majesty and his fellow Spaniards have lost upward of 500,000 *pesos de oro*.[38]

For his part, Alvarado denied any wrongdoing, alleging that "the very night of the uprising, many lords and leaders dined at his table with him."[39] One wonders what he served them. To the specific accusations made above, Alvarado defended himself with a mix of denial and assertions of his own:

> I declare that I never abused the lords of the said province, who received many fine things from me. If they did give me some gold it was because I was entitled to receive it as part of my tribute payment. I did not compel anyone to deliver gold, and so that is not the reason why the Indians rose up in arms. This they do commonly, on a mere whim. Believing that I would give up on Guatemala and not colonize the land, they rebelled, resorting to crude warfare, digging pits with stakes placed at their bottom, covering the tops of them with branches, earth, and grass, into which many horses fell and many Christians were killed or wounded.[40]

38. *Residencia,* or court proceedings, against Pedro de Alvarado (1529), as cited in Polo Sifontes ([1977] 2005, 78). How much a *peso de oro*, back then, would be worth in our day is not easy to determine. France V. Scholes—see Sherman (1969, 200 and 206) for elaboration—estimated that, in 1957, one gold peso was the equivalent of between five and six dollars.

39. *Residencia* against Pedro de Alvarado (1529), as rendered by Recinos (1953, 20).

40. *Residencia* against Pedro de Alvarado (1529), in Polo Sifontes ([1977] 2005, 78–79. See Asselbergs (2004, 123) and Van Akkeren (2007, 106) for a vivid rendering of Kaqchikel traps as depicted in the *Lienzo de Quauhquechollan.*

On the last point, at least, the native scribes agree, recording their guerrilla strategies thus:

> Then the Cakchiquels began hostilities against the Spaniards. They dug holes and pits for the horses and scattered sharp stakes so that they should be killed. At the same time the people made war on them. Many Spaniards perished and the horses died in the traps. . . . The Quichés and the Zutuhils died also; in this manner all the people were destroyed by the Cakchiquels. Only thus did the Spaniards give them a breathing spell.[41]

Two disclosures here are worthy of comment. First, when the Spaniards went after the Kaqchikels, they incurred casualties not only among themselves and their Mexican allies but also among the K'iche's and the Tz'utujils. Having helped the Spaniards defeat both these peoples, the Kaqchikels (in the Mesoamerican scheme of things) were surely not surprised to find two of their former adversaries fighting alongside a former ally to defeat them. Recinos and his translator Delia Goetz, drawing upon Tz'utujil testimony in the "Relación del pueblo y cabecera de Atitlán," mention that "Don Pedro de Alvarado took out of the town a great many people, sometimes six hundred Indian soldiers, to make war on the Indian town and headquarters of Tecpán-Quauhtemallan and other rebellious provinces."[42] And second, Kaqchikel resistance appears to have been effective enough to have earned them, albeit momentarily, a "breathing spell" that allowed them to regroup and prepare for further "hostilities."

The fighting that broke out in September 1524 either resumed or was already underway again a year later, for the *Memorial de Solola* records that "the war with the Spaniards continued." By this time, Alvarado "had moved" the base of Spanish operations "to Xepau," a place that Contreras reckons lay some seventeen kilometers north of Iximché.[43]

---

41. Recinos and Goetz (1953, 125).

42. As rendered in Recinos and Goetz (1953, 125). They add: "In the same way the Spanish captain must have secured the aid of some of the Quiché people against their old enemies the Cakchiquels." Drawing on the contents of AGI, Guatemala 53, Restall and Asselbergs (2007, 114) also record that, "having arrived at our town of Santiago de Atitlán . . . Pedro de Alvarado and the other Spanish conquistadors" recruited Tz'utujil warriors "as allies in peace and companions to subject the rest with force of arms, up into the Provinces of Verapaz, Gracias a Dios, and San Miguel and León."

43. Recinos and Goetz (1953, 125) and Contreras (2004b, 55–56).

From an encampment at Xepau—which Recinos and Goetz, Maxwell and Hill, and Restall and Asselbergs all locate much farther west, correlating it with Olintepeque, four kilometers north of Quetzaltenango—the *Memorial de Sololá* acknowledges that "they made war on us and killed many brave men."[44] To Xepau in the spring of 1525 came much-needed reinforcements in the form of two hundred Spanish soldiers under the command of Pedro de Briones, sent by Cortés from Honduras with an undisclosed number of native auxiliaries.[45] While Pedro de Alvarado headed off "toward Lacandón and Puyumatlán" in an unsuccessful attempt to rendezvous with Cortés and traversed the Sierra de los Cuchumatanes only to find the rainforests of Chiapas almost impenetrable, Briones joined ranks with Gonzalo de Alvarado and Diego de Rojas in keeping up the offensive against the Kaqchikels.[46] Rojas claims that the Spaniards made some gains, to such an extent that, on Don Pedro's return to Xepau, a Kaqchikel delegation went to meet him with overtures of peace. If this did occur—the *Memorial de Sololá* offers no clues—nothing came of it.[47] Awaiting word from two parties he had dispatched in different directions to see if they could make contact with Cortés, Alvarado received news first in the form of a letter, in which Cortés again requested that Alvarado go to Honduras to assist him.[48]

On January 30, 1526, Alvarado appeared before the *cabildo* (municipal council) and told its members of his plans to comply with Cortés's instructions. The decision was not welcomed by members of the *cabildo*, who considered it unwise for him to leave for Honduras at such a vulnerable time. Alvarado retorted that "he did not need their advice, and that he knew full well what he was doing," adding for good measure that

44. Recinos and Goetz (1953, 125–26); Maxwell and Hill (2006, 272); and Restall and Asselbergs (2007, 108). Mackie (1924, 17) located Xepau "probably in the Tzutuhil country."

45. Recinos (1952, 112) and Recinos and Goetz (1953, 126).

46. Kramer (1994, 42) and Recinos (1952, 113). According to the latter, citing Díaz del Castillo, Briones was hanged four years later "for stirring things up and inciting mutiny." As did subsequent forays to conquer the Lacandón Mayas of lowland Chiapas, the one led by Alvarado had to give up and make its way back to Guatemala, demoralized and debilitated, on account of "raging rivers that run through the region and inhibit passage." Asselbergs (2004, 86) states that "during this journey [Pedro] left control in the hands of his brother Jorge," mistaking one brother for another, as it was Gonzalo to whom Pedro delegated command, alongside Rojas.

47. See Kramer (1994, 42), who bases her information on the contents of AGI, Patronato 54-5-2 ("Probanza de Diego de Rojas," 1528).

48. See Recinos (1952, 111–17) and Kramer (1994, 36–46) for a detailed discussion of this key period.

"Cortés had given him all that he had, and that with him he wished to die."[49] He named his brother, Gonzalo, to serve as acting governor during his absence and prepared his departure.

On February 7, a week after Alvarado's stormy encounter with the *cabildo*, some fifty to sixty of his soldiers mutinied, making it clear that they, too, wanted no part in a dangerous expedition to Honduras. Their dissent was manifest not at Xepau but at Iximché, where they were billeted. The would-be deserters set part of the capital on fire, a ruse to divert attention from their exodus, effected under cover of darkness. Allegedly making off with ecclesiastical ornaments that had graced the Spanish church, and accompanied by a disgruntled priest, they headed west to Soconusco, sacking towns along the way. Once in Mexico, they laid charges against Alvarado, so enraged that they hanged him and his henchmen in effigy.[50] The *Memorial de Sololá* diligently records the date, though it attributes the burning of the Kaqchikel capital to Alvarado, not the mutineers who managed to escape being commandeered to Honduras:

> Then Tunatiuh left Xepau and began hostilities against us because the people did not humble themselves before him. Six months had passed of the second year of our flight from the city, or [from the time] when we abandoned it and departed, when Tunatiuh came to it in passing and burned it. On the day 4 Camey [February 7, 1526] he burned the city; at the end of the sixth month of the second year of the war he accomplished it and departed again.[51]

Alvarado, of course, considered the mutineers the worst kind of traitors, who had abandoned not only him but the campaign of conquest in an hour of need. Before he "departed again" for Honduras, on February 20 Alvarado wrote to the highest authorities in Mexico City, giving them his version of events, anticipating correctly that the defectors would give them their version in due course.[52] Iximché was in a state of near-ruin.

49. See Recinos (1952, 115) and Kramer (1994, 44). The latter bases her information on the *Proceso de residencia contra Pedro de Alvarado, 1529* (Ramírez 1847).

50. Recinos (1952, 115–16). Among the deserters were two artillerymen of notable utility, whose defection Alvarado could scarcely afford.

51. Recinos and Goetz (1953, 126). Nance, Whittington, and Borg (2003, 189) report that when George Guillemin conducted his excavations at Iximché, he found "traces of fire almost everywhere" at Great Palace II.

52. Recinos (1952, 116).

By the time he left to meet up with Cortés, Alvarado had all but given up on the site, which had never served Spanish objectives as it had those of the Kaqchikels; it was a far cry from the viceregal capital then under construction on the ashes of Tenochtitlán.[53]

IN THE WAKE OF HONDURAS

As with his trek to, and travails in, Lacandón and Puyumatlán, Alvarado never did connect with his mentor in Honduras. At Choluteca he came across a party of Spaniards headed by Luis de Marín, which also included in its ranks Bernal Díaz del Castillo, chronicler-to-be. They informed Alvarado that Cortés had headed back to Mexico by sea, sailing from the port of Trujillo to deal with a series of issues detrimental to his interests. Cortés had intended, so he informed King Charles V on September 3, 1526, to return to Mexico from Honduras "by way of the South Sea," his plan being to cross over to the Pacific coast of Central America in order to take better stock, in person, of what he understood to be the deteriorating situation in Guatemala under Alvarado:

> Otatlán [Utatlán] and Guatemala [Iximché], where Pedro de Alvarado [has] always resided, having rebelled in consequence of various offenses done to them by the Spaniards, have never since become peaceable, but on the contrary have done, and are still doing, much harm to the Spaniards settled in their neighborhood, and to their Indian friends. Your Majesty must know that the country there is very broken, and the population very dense, and the people so warlike and brave and at the same time so trained in all kinds of warfare, offensive as well as defensive, that they have invented pits and other engines to kill the horses; and although the said Pedro de Alvarado has never ceased making war upon them with upwards of 200 horses and 500 foot, all Spaniards, besides 5,000, and at other times even 10,000 Indians, he has hitherto been unable to reduce them under Your Majesty's rule, but on the contrary, they become stronger every day through the people who join them.[54]

53. Kramer (1994, 44). "Given the circumstances," she writes of Santiago at Iximché, "it is amazing that the 'city' had survived that long." Cortés, meanwhile, had already invested four years of resources laying out and constructing Mexico City, in the effusive words of López de Gómara ([1552] 1964, 324), "the greatest city in the world" and certainly "the noblest of the Indies."
54. Cortés to King Charles V (September 3, 1526), as rendered by Mackie (1924, 19–20).

There is much here to ponder. First, Cortés acknowledges that rebellion has occurred as a result "of various offenses" perpetrated by his fellow Spaniards. Though abuse of the Kaqchikels (the natives of "Guatemala") sparked the insurgency, not the mistreatment of the K'iche's (the natives of "Otatlán"), who were now Spanish allies, indigenous resistance was growing "stronger every day" because of other disaffected groups "who join them." Second, Cortés recognizes that "Indian friends" participate on the Spanish side, "5,000, and at other times even 10,000" in number, sizable contingents without whose support the Spaniards could not have accomplished anything. And third, he alludes not only to "warlike and brave" Kaqchikel combatants but also to their tactical prowess, "offensive as well as defensive." The veteran conquistador, surely well aware of the extent to which "the said Pedro de Alvarado" was responsible for the sorry state of affairs, closes his "Fifth Letter to the Emperor" with a palpable air of regret. "I believe," Cortés writes, "that if I were to go among them, I could, by mild treatment or otherwise, bring them to a knowledge of what, God permitting, they owe to Your Majesty."[55]

It was Alvarado, however, who went back "among them," his own forces, native and non-native, bolstered by those of Marín. Bernal Díaz del Castillo, a member of the entourage, has left us with a memorable description, written years later, of how difficult things were en route to Guatemala, and of how the Spaniards were assailed upon arrival:

> On our march towards Guatemala . . . we entered the province of Cuscatlán, which was hostile, [though] we found plenty to eat, and from there we came to some pueblos near to Petapa. The Guatemaltecos had some hills entrenched on the road and some very deep gullies, where they awaited us, and we were there three days in capturing and passing them.[56]

One observation: the party not only found the natives of Cuzcatlán "hostile" but also reported no trace of occupation where, a year or so before, Alvarado's cousin, Diego, had ventured with Mexican and Mixtec allies to establish the city of San Salvador, to which Diego de Holguín had been dispatched as mayor.[57] The chronicler continues:

55. Cortés to King Charles V (September 3, 1526), as rendered by Mackie (1924, 20).
56. Díaz del Castillo, as rendered by Alfred P. Maudsley, in Mackie (1924, 120–21).
57. Recinos (1952, 107 and 117–18) and Asselbergs (2004, 86). See also Ximénez ([1715–20] 1929–31, vol. 1, 148–49), who transcribes an entry from the *Libro primero de cabildo*, dated May 6,

Then we came to Petapa, and the next day came upon . . . the valley
of the cross-eyed [Panchoy] where now [1541 on] this city of Guatemala is settled. At that time it was altogether hostile and we found
many barricades and pits and we fought with the natives to force
a passage.[58]

A second observation: far from being localized, the hostility encountered at Cuzcatlán is depicted as widespread, an obstacle hindering
Spanish movement at every turn. Díaz del Castillo concludes:

Then we went to the site of the old city of Guatemala, where the
caciques named Zinacan and Sacachul used to reside. Before entering the city there was a very deep gully where the squadrons of Guatemaltecos were awaiting to prevent our entry, and we made them
flee, unfortunately for them, and went on to sleep in the city, and the
lodgings and houses were good and the buildings very fine, in fact
befitting the *caciques* who ruled all the neighboring provinces. From
there we went out onto the plain and built *ranchos* and huts and stayed
in them for ten days, for Pedro de Alvarado sent twice to summon
the people of Guatemala and other pueblos in the neighborhood to
make peace, and we waited . . . to learn their reply. As none of them
would come, we went on by long days' marches without halting where
Pedro de Alvarado had left his army settled, for it was hostile country
and he had left his brother, Gonzalo de Alvarado, there as captain.
The village where we found them was called Olintepec.[59]

Again, there is much here to unwrap, but two comments will suf-
fice. First, Díaz del Castillo states categorically that it was the "old city
of Guatemala" they entered after a struggle, meaning Iximché, which
the Kaqchikels had apparently reoccupied while Alvarado was off in
Honduras and his brother, Gonzalo, was headquartered in Olintepeque.
Despite sleeping at least one night in the well-equipped facilities of the
Kaqchikel court, "for ten days" thereafter the "*ranchos* and huts" that

---

1525, "in which Don Pedro de Alvarado states that, in view of Diego [de] Holguín, who is a
member of council, having gone to San Salvador to serve there as mayor, names as his replacement Francisco de Arévalo."

58. Díaz del Castillo, as rendered by Alfred P. Maudsley, in Mackie (1924, 121). Maudsley
may have meant to say "the valley of the *one*-eyed" (Spanish "tuerto"), not "the valley of the
cross-eyed" (Spanish "bizco") in reference to Panchoy.

59. Díaz del Castillo, as rendered by Alfred P. Maudsley, in Mackie (1924, 122).

were constructed out on the plain were the preferred accommodation. Iximché, we must remember, was a stronghold that could be laid siege to as much as defended. Luján and Cabezas interpret Díaz del Castillo's description to mean that the Spaniards stationed themselves at Xepau.[60] And second, not one but two attempts "to make peace" went unanswered. The Kaqchikel rebellion was far from over.

A very brief passage in the *Memorial de Sololá* conforms to the timeline: "During the course of this year [March 29, 1526, to June 2, 1527] our hearts had some rest. So also did the kings Cahí Ymox and Belehé Qat. We did not submit to the Spaniards, and we were living in Holom Balam."[61]

From their refuge at Holom Balam ("Head of a Tiger") in the mountains near Iximché, the Kaqchikel leaders could look back on over two years of resistance with some sense of achievement, if not outright success. Their strategy, in the parlance of modern warfare, was to have mounted a guerrilla insurgency, waged in the terrain they knew best, the hills and the forests, not on open ground or valley floors where they had witnessed other groups defeated. Having fought at close quarters alongside the Spaniards—at Atitlán, Izcuintepeque, and Cuzcatlán, as well as throughout K'iche' country—they had taken notice and learned, and so knew the enemy well. Kaqchikel hearts, however, were not to be at rest for long.

FROM ONE BROTHER TO ANOTHER

If Cortés and Alvarado, metaphorically speaking, were brothers in arms, blood tied the latter to half-a-dozen close relatives—full brothers Gómez, Gonzalo, and Jorge, and full cousins Diego, Hernando, and yet another Gonzalo. Alvarado's namesake, confidant, and right-hand man, Pedro de Portocarrero, was also a relation, as well as the future husband of his daughter, Leonor. The Alvarados saw the conquest of Guatemala, and the wealth that could be derived from it, as a family affair, no one more than Pedro de Alvarado, undisputed leader and patriarch.[62]

60. Luján Muñoz and Cabezas Carcache (1993, 58).
61. Recinos and Goetz (1953, 126).
62. See Sherman (1969) for a meticulous reckoning of Alvarado's estate and his voracious appetite for wealth and power.

Even though the Kaqchikels were still in revolt, and other parts of Guatemala not yet penetrated and therefore beyond Spanish control, Alvarado decided that his top priority was to return to Spain and secure recognition for his accomplishments to date, and Crown approval of more to come. In August 1526 he left for Mexico on the first stage of a mission that would not see him back in Guatemala until April 1530, an absence of three years and eight months. On his departure he named Portocarrero and Hernán Carrillo, not his brother Gonzalo, as interim commanders until such time as he could arrange for another of his brothers, Jorge, to arrive from Mexico as captain general and assume the reins of subjugating and then governing Guatemala with formal authority to do so.

Jorge de Alvarado's role in the conquest of Guatemala has long been overshadowed by that of Pedro, though important correctives, bit-by-bit, have helped set straight the historical record.[63] Jorge arrived in Olintepeque in March 1527 with a massive army made up of between five and six thousand native allies, "Central Mexican conquistadors" in the words of Asselbergs.[64] Among them was a contingent from Quauh-quechollan, a town near Puebla in Mexico that paid tribute to Jorge in goods, services, and warriors. Its members made their own "conquest narrative" in the form of a pictographic account that "tells the experiences and military achievements" of "the 1527–30 conquering campaign under [Jorge] Alvarado's banner." Depicted on a painted cotton cloth measuring 235 by 325 centimeters is the new "base camp" that Jorge set up at Chij Xot near Comalapa, "from which site his army waged war against the Kaqchikel."[65]

<hr />

63. Kramer (1994, 46) deserves credit for being the first to point out that "[Pedro de] Alvarado's contribution to the conquest of Guatemala has certainly been overemphasized and exaggerated," she reckons, "in an attempt to make him a national hero and to compensate for scant documentary evidence." Her pioneering efforts helped Asselbergs (2004), Matthew (2004, 2007, 2012), Van Akkeren (2007), and Restall and Asselbergs (2007) develop their cases for placing Jorge, not Pedro, among those at the forefront of the conquest of Guatemala. Kramer's views are shared by Luján Muñoz and Cabezas Carcache (1993).

64. Asselbergs (2004, 87). The dogged work of Matthew (2004, 2007, 2012) bears this out in eloquent detail.

65. Asselbergs (2008, 69). Asselbergs locates the "base camp" as being "in Chimaltenango," the modern-day department of the same name in "central Guatemala." Recinos and Goetz (1953, 126–27) correlate it with Chi Xot, which means "in the comales," and furnish a more specific location in the "mountains facing Comalapa." Though not as exhaustive as Asselbergs (2004), Van Akkeren (2007, 83–140) also offers incisive commentary on the *Lienzo de Quauhquechollan*, his study of it enhanced considerably by color photographs and digital imagery. A pull-out map

The spatial data of the *Lienzo de Quauhquechollan*, a veritable map of the conquest of Guatemala, mesh nicely with the more temporally minded bulletins of the *Memorial de Sololá*, such as this:

> One year and one month had passed since Tunatiuh razed [the city], when the Spaniards came to Chij Xot. On the day 1 Caok [March 27, 1527] our slaughter by the Spaniards continued. The people fought them and they continued to fight a prolonged war. Death struck us anew but none of the people paid the tribute. The thirty-first year after the revolution had almost ended when they arrived at Chij Xot.[66]

Jorge figured, correctly, that the Kaqchikels should be his first and primary target. Though he is not mentioned in the above extract by name, it was his forces, with Pedro de Portocarrero at the helm, that were responsible not only for a renewal but for an intensification of hostilities. Besides "a prolonged war" against the Kaqchikels, Jorge also spearheaded campaigns at Jalpatagua on the Pacific coast, throughout the Verapaz region, and into the Sierra de los Cuchumatanes, where battles were fought at Aguacatán, Puyumatlán, Sacapulas, and Uspantán.[67] In the eyes of many of his contemporaries, testifying in scores of depositions that allude to their own "merits and services to the Crown" as well as to his, it was Jorge, not Pedro, who should be credited with having executed the conquest of Guatemala. It is Jorge whom brother

accompanies both contributions. The Universidad Francisco Marroquín (2007) published a handsome catalog of the exhibition it mounted to celebrate Asselbergs's proper recognition of the *lienzo*, hitherto "never identified correctly" and "generally presumed" to represent "a region in the neighborhood of Quauhquechollan" near the Mexican city of Puebla in the state of the same name. A second English-language (2008) as well as Spanish-language (2010) edition of Asselbergs's groundbreaking work are now available, the latter enhanced by dozens of reproductions in color. Illustrations from the *Lienzo de Quauhquechollan* are also featured in the *Atlas histórico de Guatemala* (Luján Muñoz 2011, 75–80), including one (illustration 47) in which Jorge de Alvarado is identified as leading the expeditionary force against the Kaqchikels.

66. Recinos and Goetz (1953, 126–27). The "thirty-first year after the revolution" refers to a thwarted attempt by the Tukuché branch of the Kaqchikels to assume political control at Iximché on May 18 or 20, 1493. "The event was considered so important," Borg (2003, 19) writes, "that Cakchiquel history, as recorded in *The Annals of the Cakchiquels*, is calculated forward from this date."

67. Kramer (1994, 66) documents each of these forays with painstaking reference to primary sources that hitherto had escaped scholarly attention. Asselbergs (2004, 15), Van Akkeren (2007, 81), and Restall and Asselbergs (2007, 57) acknowledge the debt for their own research, and pay her a special vote of thanks. See also Luján Muñoz (2011, 83–84).

Gonzalo, treading a fine line, chooses to invoke in one of his letters to the king. "Jorge de Alvarado," he declares, "was one of the persons who most principally served Your Majesty in the conquest and pacification of Guatemala," a claim that Jorge himself saw fit to elaborate.[68]

Three years after Pedro's defeat of the K'iche's at Utatlán, the Spaniards, largely because of sustained Maya resistance, had yet to settle on a location suitable for the construction of a city that would function as their capital. Jorge moved ahead on that front too, founding Santiago in Almolonga (meaning "to spring from the fountain") at the foot of Agua volcano, a place known to the Kaqchikels as Bulbuxyá, on November 22, 1527.[69] "During this year, while we were busy with the war against the Spaniards," the authors of the *Memorial de Sololá* register, "they abandoned Chij Xot and went to live at Bulbuxyá," adding that while "the war continued . . . none of the people paid the tribute."[70] Within two months, however, Spanish gains and Kaqchikel capitulation in at least one locale changed that, for the very next entry in the *Memorial de Sololá* states: "Here in Tzololá, on the day 6 Tzíi [January 12, 1528] the tribute began. Heavy suffering we endured to free ourselves from the war."[71]

Was it perhaps considered more prudent now to abandon a guerrilla war, fighting as fugitives in the hills with all the deprivations it entailed, and pay the price of peace by furnishing tribute, no matter how burdensome? An alliance so unbearable that it lasted a mere six months had given rise to a rebellion, one little recognized and not taken sufficiently into account, already in its fourth year. Would it be possible, somehow,

68. Gonzalo's praise of Jorge comes from Asselbergs (2010, 139), citing the "Probanzas del capitán Gonzalo de Alvarado," in Gall (1967, 68). Kramer (1994, 63–84) devotes an entire chapter of her monograph to "The Government of Jorge de Alvarado, 1527–1529"), basing her portrayal of Pedro's brother's prominent role in the conquest on a wealth of unpublished archival material. For further contemporary testimony, see also statements scattered throughout the voluminous contents of AGI, Justicia 291. Jorge's own record of his "merits and services to the Crown," dated February 26, 1534, may be found in AGI, Guatemala 41, and has been transcribed by Asselbergs (2004, 272–73) and translated from Spanish into English by Restall and Asselbergs (2007, 57–59). The Universidad Francisco Marroquín (2007) edition of the *Lienzo de Quauhquechollan* maps out "la ruta de la conquista" of the forces led by Jorge de Alvarado "escena por escena," based on the detailed "lectura" and "interpretación" of Asselbergs (2004, 127–81 and 183–204.)

69. Recinos and Goetz (1953, 127) and Luján Muñoz and Cabezas Carcache (1993, 58).

70. Recinos and Goetz (1953, 127).

71. Recinos and Goetz (1953, 127–28).

for hostilities to end and a new accord to be struck? Cahí Ymox and Belehé Qat struggled with their dilemma for two more years, until word reached them that Tunatiuh was back in their midst. A time of decision arrived with him.

CHAPTER 3

RETURN AND SURRENDER

Jorge de Alvarado, in the years he was charged with governing the kingdom (1527–29), secured more of Guatemala than when his brother Pedro first ruled (1524–26). It is surely no accident, however, that it was upon Pedro's return from his first sojourn in Spain that Cahí Ymox and Belehé Qat, the two men most identified with Kaqchikel resistance, chose to surrender. As leaders molded in a Mesoamerican tradition that emphasized the forging of treaties and strategic, geopolitical thinking, they well understood that it was no small feat fending off the second-in-command until his superior was once again on the scene. A moment of historic import is recorded in the *Memorial de Sololá* rather matter-of-factly, but with characteristic poignancy nonetheless:

> During the course of this year [1530] the kings Ahpozotzil [Cahí Ymox] and Ahpoxahil [Belehé Qat] presented themselves before Tunatiuh. Five years and four months the kings had been under the trees, under the vines. The kings did not go for their pleasure; they were prepared to suffer death at the hands of Tunatiuh. But the news came to Tunatiuh. And so, on the day 7 Ahmak [May 7, 1530], the kings went forth and they went toward Paruyaal Chay [San Andrés Izapa]. Many lords joined them. The grandsons of the chiefs, the sons of the chiefs, a great number of people went to accompany the kings. On the day 8 Noh [May 8] they reached Panchoy [near Santiago in Almolonga]. Tunatiuh rejoiced in the presence of the chiefs when he saw their faces again.[1]

---

1. Recinos and Goetz (1953, 128–29). Otzoy (1999, 189) records the duration of resistance as having lasted "1,900 days" and interprets the "great number of people" who accompanied Cahí Ymax and Belehé Qat as doing so "to protect them." Maxwell and Hill (2006, 278) opt for "[f]ive years and four twenty-day months" and "[m]any people went as companions of the lords." They

In a deft analysis of Mesoamerican timekeeping, Ruud van Akkeren attributes the surrender of Cahí Ymox and Belehé Qat to the fact that it "coincided with the end of a calendar cycle of fifty-two years, one that had begun in 1478, another year of great change as that was when the Kaqchikels had founded their capital of Iximché." He states that the Kaqchikels believed "time would begin again" and that the close of a cycle of such significance "was a moment of great fear."[2] Whether it was belief, foreboding, or other factors, alone or in combination, that prompted capitulation on the part of the Kaqchikels, we have firsthand evidence from a number of individuals who were in agreement about the pivotal role played by soldier and interpreter Pedro González Nájera in the surrender.

Our source is a petition lodged in 1564 by González Nájera's son, Juan Calvo Nájera, who lobbied the Crown for recognition and assistance on his father's behalf, presenting testimony from six other persons besides himself: two Spaniards and four Indians, all of whom vouch that González Nájera not only "furnished arms and horses" but also, because of his command of Náhuatl, served as an "interpreter in the conquests and pacification of Guatemala" under Pedro de Alvarado. The son's appeal—his father is "in need of being provided for, and entitled to such provision"—hinges on González Nájera's having put his bravery, language skills, and trustworthy reputation to the ultimate test in convincing Cahí Ymox (referred to in variant spellings as Sinacán or Sinacam) and Belehé Qat (referred to in equally variant spellings as Sequechul or Sacachul) to lay down arms and make peace with Pedro de Alvarado. One witness, Juan Núñez, "a [Guatemalan] Indian who hails from San Juan de Nagualapa" and who also served as an interpreter, states that "from these parts the said Pedro González Nájera accompanied the said Pedro de Alvarado to Spain and returned with him when he came back the first time, married to Doña Francisca de la Cueva." The sojourn in Spain had no negative effect on González Nájera's ability to communicate in Náhuatl, which he did to maximum effect when his patron and namesake, Pedro, presented him with a challenge that had thus far stumped the considerable efforts of Jorge de Alvarado:

---

prefer the following wording: "The lords did not wish to go; their deaths were determined by Tunatiw. Their message was presented before Tunatiw. Just then, Tunatiw was happy with the lords when he saw them again."

2. Van Akkeren (2007, 78).

to pursue leads that would see González Nájera, "with certain danger to his person," taken to Cahí Ymox and Belehé Qat's hiding place, negotiate with them there in good faith, and "having rid the said Saca-chul and Sinaca of their fears," escort them from their hiding place to a face-to-face meeting with Pedro de Alvarado. The risk of failure, and what that could mean, was surely not lost on the "go-between," whose own father, Alonso, had been killed by rebellious Indians in Jumayte-peque the year before.

In his deposition, Nicolás López de Yrrarraga, a high-ranking member of the colonial administration, confirms that "the said Pedro González Nájera had indeed gone to Castile" with Alvarado and that, on their arrival back in Guatemala, "a good part of the province was [still] at war, even in the vicinity of the [capital] city," where "evil, threatening fugitives, seeing that there were so few Spaniards in towns like Ystalavaca [and] the province of Chumaytlán [Puyumatlán] and other areas, had risen up and killed them." Like the other witnesses called upon, López de Yrrarraga furnished his testimony on December 6, 1564, three and a half decades after the incidents described had taken place. While he could recall that "a Spaniard named Bartolomé Núñez and the conquistador Francisco García had been killed during the uprising," he added, "others whose names I cannot remember lost their lives too." What remains clear in the mind of López de Yrrarraga, however, is that "the said *caciques* Sacachuil and Sinaca were the most prominent lords of almost all the land" and that "never had they wanted to come to peace or serve under Your Majesty when Jorge de Alvarado was governor, nor when Francisco de Orduña took office after him." It was "Pedro de Alvarado's diligence" that saw him arrange for his messen-gers and those of Cahí Ymox and Belehé Qat to go back-and-forth bearing gifts, until González Nájera finally brokered a deal, assisted in his labors by "a Kaqchikel Indian called Juan, who at present lives in Suchitepéquez." The intermediaries are reported to have traveled "for one or two days to where the said *caciques* came out of hiding with many of their people, so many that the said Pedro González Nájera could not help but feel afraid."

López de Yrrarraga stresses in his testimony that nothing he relays is hearsay, but on the contrary, events he witnessed firsthand. "I saw with my own eyes," he declares, "Pedro González Nájera enter the city, and I was present when Alvarado received the *caciques* warmly, [instructing]

González Nájera to tell them in Mexican [Náhuatl] and the [interpreter] Juan in Kaqchikel that no harm would befall them, that they should serve Our Lord God and Your Majesty." Another disclosure of López de Yrrarraga corroborates what the *Memorial de Sololá* states about the Kaqchikel lords arriving with their sons by their sides. "With Don Jorge, the son of Sacachul there, and a son of Sinaca's too, the rebellion ceased to be." When other dissident groups learned of the capitulation of Cahí Ymox and Belehé Qat, they apparently followed suit, "coming down from the mountains and resettling their towns, which allowed the land to be divided up and gold and silver deposits sought, something that had not been possible up until then." Established "along the banks of rivers in Cahuastlan [Acasaguastlán] and those of the towns of Gueguetenango [Huehuetenango]," successful mining operations ensured a noticeable increase in the size of "His Majesty's share of the takings." The actions of Pedro González Nájera, in brief, were of direct benefit to the welfare of the Crown, which could surely help him out in his hour of need.[3]

3. Juan Calvo Nájera and others to the Crown, December 6, 1564, in AGI, Patronato 58-1-4 ("Información de los méritos y servicios de Pedro González Nájera," 1565). To support what he himself says about his father, Calvo Nájera is joined by Nicolás López de Yrrarraga, "alguacil mayor de la audiencia real"; Juan Fernández Nájera, an experienced interpreter who, like López de Yrrarraga, held important administrative positions in both the "audiencia real de la Nueva España y de la Audiencia Real de los Cofines"; "Don" Antonio de Mendoça, who is said to be a former "conquistador" from "Ynaoquichula [Quauhquechollan] junto a la Puebla en la provincia de Tazcala [Tlaxcala] en la Nueva España"; Juan Gómez, another Mexican lord, originally from Tlaxcala but now a "vezino desta ciudad," a resident of Santiago de Guatemala; "Don" Francisco de Alvarado Arévalo, also (like Gómez) an "yndio principal" from Tlaxcala; and Juan Núñez, an "yndio vecino de San Juan de Nagualapa desta provincia de Guatemala." Identical copies of the same deposition may also be consulted in AGI, Patronato 66-1-3 ("Probanza de Pedro González Nájera," 1564) and AGI, Patronato 59-1-3 (Juan Calvo Nájera, "Sobre los méritos y servicios de su padre," 1549). Kramer (1994, 90–91) records that when Alonso González Nájera, father of Pedro González Nájera and grandfather of Juan Calvo Nájera, was killed with "some other men" at Jumaytepeque in September 1529, they may also have been "eaten by the Indians." Asselbergs (2004, 161–62) offers a "possible reading" of a forested scene in the *Lienzo de Quauhquechollan* (figure 72, p. 161) as being "the unknown hiding place of the two most powerful Kaqchikel lords, Sinacan and Sequechul." Complementing her reading of AGI, Patronato 58-1-4 with that also of Patronato 59-1-1 ("Probanza de los méritos y servicios de Cristóbal Lobo," 1549) and Patronato 60-5-6 ("Probanza de los méritos y servicios de Francisco de Utiel, 1556), Kramer (1994, 67) writes: "Jorge managed to discover the whereabouts of the Cakchiquel rulers Sinacam and Sequechul and led a campaign to Pochutla (present-day Pochuta in the department of Chimaltenango) in search of them. The Spaniards endured severe hardship on the journey, clearing paths with their own hands and wandering for days without food. Although it appears that they managed to defeat the Cakchiquels in their hilltop redoubt, the Spaniards were unable to capture the rulers, who remained in hiding until 1530 when they eventually surrendered to Pedro de Alvarado."

Whether or not assistance was afforded to the penurious Spaniard—Alvarado's former "paje de lanza," literally "the page who carried his lance," was also said to be "very poor and sick, burdened with grown-up sons and daughters, yet to be wed"—we cannot say. No relief was forthcoming, we know, for the two rulers whom González Nájera swayed to resist no more. If resistance was waged at a cost, the price of surrender proved even higher.

The Fallout of Capitulation

Whatever arrangements Cahí Ymox and Belehé Qat sought that would favor them and their people as a result of surrender made little impact on Alvarado. He may have "received the *caciques* warmly," but that had no bearing on what happened next. Not even an impressive show of numbers, to say nothing of the pomp and ceremony that accompanied the arrival of the Kaqchikel kings at Santiago in Almolonga, deterred him from his course. Alvarado had come back from Spain even more empowered than before he left, having been elevated to the status of "Adelantado," most emphatically "supreme governor," on December 18, 1527. He "rejoiced in the presence of the chiefs" in the way he knew best: by demanding crippling amounts of bullion and services, extreme even by his rapacious standards. The Kaqchikel authors record:

> During this year [1530] heavy tribute was imposed. Gold was contributed to Tunatiuh; four hundred men and four hundred women were delivered to him to be sent to wash [for] gold. All the people extracted the gold. Four hundred men and four hundred women were contributed to work in Pangán [site of the Spanish capital] on the construction of the city, by order of Tunatiuh.[4]

"All the people" meant precisely that. Alvarado's terms of surrender decreed that members of the nobility should labor and pay tribute as

---

4. Recinos and Goetz (1953, 129). Otzoy (1999, 189) words the tribute as being "terrible," not merely "heavy." He also states that "all the [city] lots" on which the Kaqchikels had to work "had been portioned out to their respective owners," which Recinos and Goetz overlook. Maxwell and Hill (2006, 279) word the tribute levy as a "frightening" amount. Once again, the figure "four hundred" implies "a great many," not a precise number. See chapter 2, note 26.

much as the common folk. The ruling was not only demeaning but fatal in the case of Belehé Qat:

> During the two months of the third year which had passed since the lords presented themselves, the king Belehé Qat died; he died on the day 7 Queh [September 24, 1532] while he was washing [for] gold.[5]

The death of Belehé Qat, far from being cause for regret to Alvarado, afforded him another opportunity to assert his authority. Rather than wait for the Kaqchikels to name Belehé Qat's successor, the Adelantado intervened and picked someone himself. Although his choice was a son of Belehé Qat, the very "Don Jorge" who was alongside his father when he surrendered to Alvarado, custom and protocol were thrown to the wind in a show of intimidating heavy-handedness:

> Immediately after the death of [Belehé Qat], Tunatiuh came here [to Sololá] to choose a successor to the king. Then the lord Don Jorge was installed in the government by order of Tunatiuh alone. There was no election by the people to name him. Afterwards Tunatiuh talked to the lords and his orders were obeyed by the chiefs, for in truth they feared Tunatiuh.[6]

It all proved too much for Cahí Ymox, who fled the Spanish capital of Santiago in Almolonga and sought solace, according to the *Memorial de Sololá*, in the ruins of the old court at Iximché:

> Seventeen months after the death of Belehé Qat, the lords had to recognize as king Don Jorge. . . . During this year [1533] the king Cahí

5. Recinos and Goetz (1953, 129). When Belehé Qat succumbed, Otzoy (1999, 189) says that his death occurred "40 days" as opposed to "two months" *before* the third anniversary of his and Cahí Ymox's turning themselves in to Alvarado. Maxwell and Hill (2006, 280) concur with Recinos and Goetz, stating "[f]orty days *into* the third year since the lords presented themselves, the lord B'eleje' K'at died."

6. Recinos and Goetz (1953, 129). Otzoy (1999, 189) opts for "no hubo Consejo," implying there was no meeting of leaders who would choose the new king, rather than there being "no election." Maxwell and Hill (2006, 8) believe that "Don Jorge," whose Kaqchikel name was Kab'lajuj Tijax, "was probably a son of B'eleje' K'at, though this is not specifically stated." They word the succession (p. 281) as having taken place as follows: "Immediately, Tunatiw came out to install the lord's replacement. That was when lord Don Jorge [Kab'lajuj Tijax] entered lordship, just by word of Tunatiw, without any council deliberations. 'He will rule immediately!' said Tunatiuh to the lords. His decree was accepted by the lords. In truth, Tunatiw was frightening."

Ymox, Ahpozotzil, went away and went to live in the city. The desire
to go away came to the king because the tribute was imposed on the lords
as well as on everyone else, and therefore the king had to pay it.[7]

What Cahí Ymox did next has never been ascertained. The *Memorial
de Sololá*, inexplicably, makes no reference to him for another seven
years. Resorting to the use of circumstantial rather than direct evidence,
Daniel Contreras argues that Cahí Ymox fomented a second Kaqchikel uprising, perhaps with even more widespread impact than the
first. His hypothesis is not well known, though Francis Polo Sifontes
was inspired by it and indeed may be considered the most enthusiastic
advocate of the notion.[8]

A SECOND KAQCHIKEL UPRISING?

Contreras initially presented his argument in a short, little-cited article
published in 1965, reiterated it in 1971 in a source equally (if not more)
difficult of access, and reprised it four decades later, stating "so disgusted
was Sinacán [Cahí Ymox] with the new way of life that he was obliged
once again to take up arms against the Spaniards."[9] The source Contreras draws upon is the chronicler Francisco Vázquez, who retrieved
pertinent data from the *Libro segundo de cabildo*, the second book of
minutes of the city council of Santiago, which spans the years 1530 to
1541. Until recently given up as lost—Contreras and Polo Sifontes both
stated that to be the case as far as they and other scholars knew[10]—the
whereabouts of this important document, and the *Libro tercero de cabildo*,

7. Recinos and Goetz (1953, 130). Otzoy (1999, 189) has Cahí Ymox leaving to "reconocer
la ciudad [y] separarse porque vio rebajada su jerarquía hasta casi compararse a los demás
señores—reacquaint himself with Iximché and [thereby] distance himself on account of his status being lowered to that of the other lords." Maxwell and Hill (2006, 282–83) word things quite
differently. "In this year when the lord Kaji' Imox, Ajpop Sotz'il, paid tribute," they state, "lord
Kaji' Imox lived in another town. From the lord's own heart came the desire to pay the tribute.
Then the lords contributed all the tribute equally, and the lord brought it."

8. Polo Sifontes ([1977] 2005, 81–85). Borg also picks up on the Contreras hypothesis, first
in her doctoral dissertation (1986, 36) and subsequently in a book chapter (2003, 36) in the volume she edited with Nance and Whittington (2003).

9. Contreras (1965; 1971; 2004, 70).

10. Contreras (2004b, 62) and Polo Sifontes ([1977] 2005, 84).

too, have now been established.[11] While we await the transcription of the *Libro segundo de cabildo* to read its contents in full, we can dip into it and see how close Vázquez's distillations are to the original. His inclusion of five key entries in his massive colonial history, all dealing with native insurrection, allow us to speculate on whether or not three of the entries, certainly one, allude to Cahí Ymox and a second Kaqchikel rebellion.[12]

The first *cabildo* excerpt predates the flight of Cahí Ymox from Santiago in Almolonga, but it contextualizes succinctly the situation in which the Spaniards found themselves. "We note the following," Vázquez writes, "dated November 1 and April 14, 1531, in the said *Libro de cabildo,*" and paraphrases its contents thus:

> On account of his leaving to make war on Indians who have risen in revolt, the Adelantado [Pedro de Alvarado] names Francisco Zurrilla of the royal treasury his delegate. This is [preceded by mention of] Captain Diego de Alvarado and his troops who, having returned exhausted and destroyed from wars waged in the service of His Majesty, need to be made welcome and extended care and attention.[13]

The campaign from which soldiers led by Diego de Alvarado, Pedro's cousin, "returned exhausted and destroyed" we know from other reports to have been fought to the northeast of Kaqchikel country in Teculutlán, today Alta and Baja Verapaz, territory originally believed to be a source of gold. There the Spaniards had founded San Jorge, in the hope

11. The two *Libros de cabildo*, and other documentary treasures besides, are part of the impressive holdings of the Hispanic Society of America in New York. See Kramer, Lovell, and Lutz (2011) for fuller discussion.

12. In addition to having had the good fortune to come across the two *Libros de cabildo*, for which we are indebted to Sebastián van Doesburg and John O'Neill, we have also had occasion to consult a rare early edition of Vázquez's work (1714–16) at the John Carter Brown Library in Providence, Rhode Island, which also houses a first edition of Remesal (1620) and several colonial-era manuscripts, among them a "Vocabulario copioso de las lenguas cakchikel y jiche" of unknown date and provenance. Transcription of the *Libros de cabildo* is being headed by the ever resourceful Jorge Luján Muñoz of the Universidad del Valle de Guatemala, assisted by Edgar F. Chután and Wendy Kramer.

13. Vázquez ([1688] 1937, vol.1, 39). His original Spanish runs: "[P]or causa de ir a la guerra sobre los indios alzados, el señor Adelantado nombra por su Teniente al Contador don Franciso Zorrilla. Y en el 14 de abril del mismo año se había dicho cómo volvió el Capitán Diego de Alvarado y sus escuadrones, desbaratado y destrozado, de las guerras en servicio de su Majestad, y se pidió les diesen acogida, y los cuidasen."

that the city they envisioned would serve as a center of colonization. They had to abandon San Jorge and environs after barely a year, not only because of native unrest at Cobán, Tactique (Tactic), and Tecosist-lán (Rabinal), but also on account of the lure of Peru: the Verapaz, by contrast, turned out to be "barren land" of paltry prospect.[14] Omitted from Vázquez's summary of the *cabildo* log is mention of the difficulty Diego's men encountered in being "made welcome and extended care and attention," for the hospitality of their fellow Spaniards, "brothers in Jesus Christ," left much to be desired. It is stated that "many city residents do not wish to receive the troops" and in fact "spurned them from their homes." In a move designed not to have the beleaguered soldiers "become vagrants," any Spanish resident found to act in such an uncharitable way would incur a "fine of twenty gold pesos," levied so as to help the city council meet the expenses associated with providing assistance.[15]

Dated (according to Vázquez) April 21, 1533, the second extract may well have had in mind the campaign to root out Cahí Ymox, as it coincides with the period when he was at large. It runs:

> Two captains, Diego de Rojas and Pedro de Portocarrero, listed with others of the regiment, have been named to lead the war against the Indians, which is considered a matter of urgency.[16]

14. San Jorge and its Verapaz hinterland, after initial high expectations, are considered "barren land" in the "Probanza de Luis de Soto," composed in Mexico in 1533 and housed in the Real Academia de la Historia in Madrid (Kramer 1994, 104). Excerpts from De Soto's deposition may also be consulted in the Real Academia de la Historia in Madrid (Colección Muñoz, tomo A 106, fol. 322v). Kramer invokes, from Sáenz de Santa María (1964, 207–208), Bishop Marroquín's incisive remarks when writing to the King on August 17, 1545, twelve years later. Despite the fact that, within a year of his first going there, Diego had installed in Verapaz "one hundred Spaniards," this occurred "during the time when the call of Peru was heard, and the call was so loud that captain and soldiers all deserted this land." Marroquín adds: "Because the mind of [Pedro de Alvarado] here [in Guatemala] was fixed on higher stakes, best forget all about this remote corner."

15. *Libro segundo de cabildo* (hereafter *LSC*), Hispanic Society of America (hereafter HSA), Hiersemann 418/239, fol. 13v. In flowery Spanish without accent marks, the minutes of the city council run: "Viene a esta ciudad Diego de Alvarado de la guerra y traie muchas gentes de la dicha guerra que vienen muy desbaratados"—Vázquez lifts this striking word directly—"e tienen necesidad de . . . aposentar en casas de los vecinos . . . donde les den de comer por que no mendiguen pues vienen de servir a sus majestades e por la caridad a los proximos y hermanos en jesu cristo de vida . . . e les requiere con el mandado de los dichos senores que los reciban en sus casas e les den . . . sostenimientos necesarios so pena en qual quier que los no quisiere recibir los que le fueren echados caya en pena de veynte pesos de oro para los gastos deste consejo."

16. Vázquez ([1688] 1937, vol. 1, 39). His original Spanish runs: "Se hace mención de haber nombrado dos Capitanes para las guerras, que fueron Diego de Rojas y don Pedro de Portocar-rero, y que se habían puesto en lista hasta los del regimiento, por la urgencia de las guerras, que les daban los indios."

Both Rojas and Portocarrero, seasoned commanders, had fought against the Kaqchikels during the previous decade, so they would have been reasonably familiar with the terrain in which Cahí Ymox had taken refuge.[17] The pair were good choices for such an important mission. The entry in the *Libro segundo de cabildo*, which is dated four days later than Vázquez states, is considerably more expansive and imparts a palpable sense of crisis. Besides confirming that Rojas and Portocarrero were the ones chosen to lead the campaign, it mentions how their recruitment efforts were being frustrated by the unwillingness of their "fellow Spaniards" to rally to the cause, the council minutes registering that "instructions to serve in the said wars are not being obeyed." Rojas had apparently drafted a "copia," an emergency petition listing the names of eligible combatants, to which council members took great exception, being "upset and put out by it," declaring adamantly that "in no way can Spanish residents be signed up for anything without the *cabildo*'s sanction." Minutes recorded the following day, April 26, make clear the council's intentions "to do what is lawful and appropriate for the good governance of the city."[18] The *cabildo*, despite Rojas and Portocarrero's being "named to lead the war against the Indians," clearly believed that Rojas had overstepped his bounds by taking measures that it believed fell under its power to decide. All might soon be lost, but due procedure (dear to the hearts of Spanish bureaucrats when it suited them) must be followed.

The third *cabildo* excerpt, Vázquez informs us, carries the dates March 2 and 21, 1534, when Cahí Ymox still roamed free but by which

17. Recinos and Goetz (1953, 127) and Kramer (1994, 41).

18. *LSC*, HSA (Hiersemann 418/239, fols. 50v and 51). The key parts of these minutes, in colorful Spanish without accent marks, run: "[E]s que no obedescan los dichos mandamientos para yr a dichas guerras." Juan Peréz Dardón, general attorney, rose to his feet to inform council that, quite recently, it had been brought to his attention that "el Capitan Diego de Rojas hizo cierta copia de gente para la guerra e que los vecinos desta ciudad por ella fueron apercibidos e que algunos dellos o lo mas se agraviaban e agraviaron dello por tanto que pide e requiere a sus mercedes que manden que no se pueda hazer copia en que en ninguna manera los vecinos pueden ser encabezonados para cosa alguna sin que se haga la tal copia en este cabildo para que los vecinos vayan a las guerras." Part of the entry for April 26, in response to what Peréz Dardón had to say, reads: "[D]ixeron que visto su pedimiento que en ausencia del señor gobernador ellos en el caso haran lo que sea justicia e convenga al buen regimiento de esta ciudad." The *Diccionario de autoridades* (1726) lists no fewer than eight different historical uses of the word "copia," the last of which applies here: "socorro bastante de algúna cosa necessaria para algun fin." Though the guardians of "the Castilian language," working under the patronage of King Philip V, mention "copia" in relation to the last rites "quando hai peligro de muerte," they declare, "hai precepto del fin [de] este peligro en algún otro tiempo de la vida."

time Pedro de Alvarado, restless and on the lookout for more promising horizons, had set sail for Peru. His ambition was to wrest control of part of the Spanish conquest there from Francisco Pizarro and Diego de Almagro. The venture would all but ruin him, as it certainly did the lives of thousands of Kaqchikels pressed into building the armada in the years prior to its departure, or lost in a treacherous passage across the Andes in Ecuador, for the Adelantado took on the voyage many Mayas who never made it back to Guatemala.[19] Vázquez relays that Alvarado again appointed his brother Jorge to govern in his absence:

> Unable to be present in the city, the Adelantado names Jorge de Alvarado as his delegate. Frequent sorties are necessary: war must be waged on account of the Indians who each day rebel and refuse to pay tribute.[20]

19. Recinos (1952, 133–55), Sherman (1969, 206 and 210), and Oudijk and Restall (2007, 36–37). For his account of the discovery and conquest of Peru, the chronicler Pedro Cieza de León (1518–55) interviewed and recorded the experiences of survivors of the era, Indians as well as Spaniards. "Because at the time the Adelantado Don Pedro de Alvarado, governor of Guatemala, decided to come to Peru," Cieza ([1553] 1998, 260–61) writes, "I want to relate the reason for it, according to what I learned from some of that land who came with him." The reason, he claims, had to do with the pilot, Juan Fernández, a firsthand observer, telling Alvarado "great things about the treasures of Quito, in addition to those of Cuzco." Aware of Spaniards having arrived and laid claim before him, "Alvarado decided," recounts Cieza, "to take people and horses from his governance to occupy what he could of the land outside the boundaries designated for Don Francisco Pizarro." The Adelantado's expedition to Peru in 1534–36 warrants fuller investigation than it has received up to now. Borah (1954, 134) considered the subject "marginal" to what he was then researching, but deemed it "intensely interesting" nonetheless. When Alvarado set sail from the port of La Posesión, close to Realejo in Nicaragua, Borah (1954, 10) records that "he had with him approximately 450 Spanish soldiers, of whom 260 were horsemen, 100 were crossbowmen and arquebusiers, and the rest foot soldiers armed with sword and shield. Some of these men were recruited in Spain, but most of them were recruited in Central America." Though the Adelantado himself did not—he was itinerant and insatiable to the end—"virtually all of the men he took with him remained in Peru." Of Alvarado's doomed attempt to cross the Andes by an ill-advised route, Cieza ([1553] 1998, 331–37) has left us a vivid description, part of which runs: "[W]hen they entered the snow-covered passes, huge snowflakes were falling from the clouds, which bothered them so much that they did not dare to raise their eyes to see the sky because the snow would burn their eyelashes. The Indians whom they brought—natives of the province of Guatemala and some of Nicaragua, and others that they had captured in the kingdom—could not move their feet [and] being in such difficulties they despaired. . . . Night fell with great darkness, which was another extreme torment. . . . Many groaned and all chattered their teeth. . . . The next day, as best they could, they climbed the mountains without seeing the sun or the sky or anything other than snow. . . . There were many who out of exhaustion leaned against some rocks and ledges that were in the snow, and as soon as they rested, they froze to death and expired in such a way that they looked like scarecrows. . . . Fifteen Spaniards and six Spanish women died in these snows, and many Blacks and more than three thousand Indian men and women of those who had gone."
20. Vázquez ([1688] 1937, vol.1, 39). The original Spanish runs: "por lo cual no puede estar de asiento en la ciudad, y que por eso nombra Teniente suyo a Jorge de Alvarado. . . por causa de los indios que de cada día se alzan contra el real servicio."

Jorge is recorded as having appeared before the city council to confirm his brother's designation of him as acting governor. His powers, in theory at any rate, were somewhat constrained, it being stated that "he is not authorized to remove Indians [held as a tributary award] from anyone." It is also stated that "in his absence or the event of his death, the reins of government will be passed to Francisco Zurrilla."[21]

One year later, on January 4, 1535, the fourth extract Vázquez furnishes once more pertains to when Pedro de Alvarado was in Peru. He was about to return to Guatemala, having negotiated with Pizarro and Almagro the conditions upon which he would not contest their dominion by force of arms, sealed with an exchange in his favor of a hundred thousand pesos.[22] Three and a half months before the Adelantado next set foot in Santiago, its *cabildo* took note of widespread insurrection:

Many towns on the coast, as well others closer to the capital city, like the ones of San Salvador, have refused to pay tribute and have rebelled against the Spaniards. War is in the offing. So as to avoid what happened in previous years, when more than twenty Spaniards were killed, Gonzalo Ronquillo should sally forth as leader with a band of men, since Jorge de Alvarado is engaged in waging other wars, and the Adelantado, at present, is not in Guatemala. These and similar rebellions are occurring all too often.[23]

The city council minutes identify one of the groups Jorge is fighting as "los chirrichotes," responsible for the killing of "many Christians." Fear of a "general uprising" is expressed in a tone of evident concern,

21. *LSC*, HSA (Hiersemann 418/239, fol. 64). "[E]l dicho Jorge de Alvarado," the original Spanish entry states, "no pueda quitar yndios a ninguna persona e que en su absençia de la governaçion e por su fallesçimiento tenga el mesmo cargo de teniente el comendador francisco çurrilla."

22. Recinos (1952, 150–52) and Sherman (1969, 210). The deal was struck, Recinos says, on August 26, 1534, in Riobamba, and included Alvarado's ships—he names six—along with "all the artillery and other arms they carried, [Indian] slaves, horses, and personal equipment." Sherman states that only five vessels changed hands and that Alvarado "was cheated in the transaction," finding out later "that the precious metals in which he had been paid were liberally mixed with copper." One can well imagine the Adelantado's displeasure at finding that out.

23. Vázquez ([1688] 1937, vol.1, 39). The original Spanish runs: "[M]uchos pueblos de la costa, así de los términos de la ciudad, como de los de San Salvador, se alzaron contra el real servicio y contra los españoles; y se previenen de guerra, y porque no suceda lo que años pasados que mataron a más de veinte españoles, atento a estar en otras guerras el Teniente Jorge de Alvarado, y ausente de la Gobernación el Adelantado, vaya con gente y por caudillo, Gonzalo Ronquillo. Y esto mismo y semejantes rebeliones se dicen con bastante frecuencia."

the capacity to safeguard Spanish lives and property stretched to the limit, with no relief in sight.[24]

Some good news, however, either awaited Alvarado upon his arrival back in Guatemala or soon thereafter: the capture of Cahí Ymox and his associate Quiyavit Caok, which Polo Sifontes states took place "in the vicinity of Comalapa around 1535."[25] The two leaders were imprisoned in Santiago, never to be released.

Despite the insistence of the city council and royal officials that he stay put and deal with alarming native unrest, within a year Alvarado was off again, this time to neighboring Honduras, over which he had always harbored pretensions; control of its Atlantic littoral and vast interior, he well understood, was critical to any successful development of Guatemala. The besieged and now relieved governor of Honduras, Andrés de Cereceda, voluntarily handed him the reins of government. With the troops he had brought with him from Guatemala, Kaqchikels and other indigenous groups again well-represented, Alvarado secured limited but strategic territory and founded two cities, San Pedro de Puerto Caballos (today San Pedro Sula) and, through the efforts of Juan de Chávez, Gracias a Dios. Though most of Honduras remained unconquered, Alvarado considered he had done enough there to be able to return to Spain, the debacle of Peru notwithstanding, and enhance his reputation, hoping to be granted further dispensations from the Crown. In August 1536 he set sail from Puerto Caballos with yet another ambitious project ruling his mind and absented himself from Guatemala for three more years as he plotted its execution.[26]

24. *LSC*, HSA (Hiersemann 418/239, fol. 72v), with the original text reading "los yndios estan casi alçados [y] en la dicha costa mato veinte españoles o mas e hizo otros muchos daños que a todos son notorios, el remedio de lo cual es que luego e con mucha brevedad salgan españoles e bayan a lo remediar e apaciguar y el magnífico Señor Jorge de Alvarado teniente de gobernador e capitan General a cuya carga es (fol. 73) el probeimiento de la guerra es absente y esta en la guerra [contra] los chirrichotes que . . . se levantaron contra S[us] M[ajestades] e . . . mataron muchos Cristianos y si el dicho señor Capitan no lo remediara con la breve salida se recreciere alzamiento general." The word "chirrichote" means "ignorant" or "foolish" and may have been used in reference to groups of rebellious Q'eqchi' Mayas.

25. Polo Sifontes ([1977] 2005, 81). The source or sources that allow Polo Sifontes to make the assertion "sin duda" (without doubt) are unfortunately not disclosed. Contreras (1965, 42–45; 1971, 24–27) documents his hypothesis with clarity, precision, and careful citation of references, especially his identification of the Kaqchikel lord Quiyavit Caok as being an "Ahpoxahil aceptado por los indios," a ruler accepted by his people, who he argues fought alongside Cahí Imox, was imprisoned with him following their capture, and accompanied him to the gallows.

26. Recinos (1952, 158–64).

VIGNETTES OF THE VANQUISHED

One reason behind Alvarado's decision to leave Santiago in Almolonga was simply not to be there when the royal judge, Alonso de Maldonado, arrived from Mexico to conduct yet another legal inquiry into the Adelantado's activities and dealings, above all his notorious mistreatment of the native population.[27] Besides this duty, Maldonado was charged (see chapter 8) with the unenviable task of establishing law and order in a land that hitherto had experienced anything but. He applied himself diligently and is remembered appreciatively in the *Memorial de Sololá*:

> [After] Tunatiuh departed for Castile, making new conquests [along] the way [in Honduras] . . . on the day 11 Noh [May 16, 1536] President Mantunalo [Maldonado] came to alleviate the sufferings of the people. Soon there was no washing of gold; the tribute of boys and girls was suspended. Soon also there was an end to the deaths by fire and hanging; the highway robberies of the Spaniards ceased. Soon the people could be seen traveling on the roads again, as it was before the tribute commenced.[28]

Maldonado managed to work well with Bishop Francisco Marroquín, despite the cleric's stubborn defense of Alvarado's criminal comportment. When the Adelantado finally showed his face again, it was Maldonado's turn to pay him the same compliment that he himself had received three years earlier and leave forthwith for Mexico. The dynamic was not lost on the authors of the *Memorial de Sololá*. "Tunatiuh came to Panchoy [Santiago]," they record, "and at once the lord Mantunalo [Maldonado] departed."[29]

In fact, Maldonado overlapped with Alvarado at least a month and was in attendance when the Adelantado appeared before the city council on September 16, 1539, to inform its members of his new (and upgraded) royal credentials, which included being reappointed governor of Guatemala for a further seven years. Alvarado had put in to Puerto Caballos

27. See Vallejo-García Hevia (2008) for full disclosure of Maldonado's findings and Alvarado's defense of his actions.

28. Recinos and Goetz (1953, 130–31). Both Otzoy (1999, 189) and Maxwell and Hill (2006, 284–85) word this passage similarly.

29. Recinos and Goetz (1953, 132). Maxwell and Hill (2006, 287) share the sense of immediacy; Otzoy (1999, 190) does not.

on Good Friday, lingering five months in Honduras to resolve jurisdiction of the province with another contender, Francisco de Montejo.
He also arranged the conveyance of men and material across Honduras
to Guatemala for what was to be his last great exploit: the construction
of a second armada that would cross the Pacific to the Spice Islands
and the mainland beyond—as the first armada was supposed to do—
in the greatest feat of conquest of all. It was a scheme paid for, as
before, at native expense, especially by Alvarado's Kaqchikel tributaries,
whose unpaid labor in assorted and related activities saw the relatively
tranquil years of Maldonado's administration replaced once more by
egregious excess.[30]

On May 19, 1540, the Adelantado once again presented himself
before the city council of Santiago, naming Francisco de la Cueva his
replacement as governor of Guatemala in view of his imminent departure. No mention is made of Beatriz de la Cueva, Francisco's cousin,
whom Alvarado had married in Spain after the untimely death of his
wife Francisca—his second betrothal to a member of such an illustrious family, for Beatriz was the sister of his late wife. A direct transcription from the minutes of this meeting constitutes a fifth such item
that Vázquez lifted from the *Libro segundo de cabildo*, as Fuentes de
Guzmán did also, no doubt on account of the manifest preoccupation
expressed by the city fathers about what might occur in Guatemala
during yet another lengthy absence on the part of Alvarado:

> Your Lordship holds as prisoners Cinacán [Sinacán or Sinacam] and
> Sachil, kings of Guatemala. Your Lordship is about to set sail with
> his armada. Because these Indians have always been rebellious, it is feared
> that their being kept alive will incite others to rebel, and that this may
> trigger an uprising, one from which the country could be lost. City
> council pleads with His Lordship to take them with him as part of the
> fleet. Alternatively, if there is reason to do so, then punish them. Were
> they to remain here, should they escape from prison, which they
> could easily do, there may be another revolt that would prove a great
> disservice to Our Lord God, as well as to His Majesty, exacerbating
> the war fatigue of the Spaniards, and bringing about their deaths.[31]

30. Recinos (1952, 174–86).
31. Vázquez ([1688] 1937, vol. 1, 39) and Fuentes y Guzmán ([1690–99] 1882–83, vol. 1, 148.
Recinos and Goetz (1953, 133) also record the appearance of Alvarado before the Cabildo de
Santiago, stating their source as "the Municipal Council of Guatemala." Vázquez's Spanish text

Alvarado is reported to have said that he would do what he thought best, with God and the King foremost in mind.[32] He mulled things over and reached a decision one week later, ruling out having two known troublemakers accompany him on his planned expedition. "On the day 13 Ganel [May 26, 1540]," the *Memorial de Sololá* records with chilling precision, "the king Ahpozotzil Cahí Ymox was hanged by Tunatiuh, together with Quiyavit Caok."[33] The execution of other lords soon followed.[34] "Thus were the honorable members of the city council," Contreras assures us, "able to sleep in peace."[35]

---

begins, "[D]espediéndose el Adelantado para ir en su armada al descubrimiento de las islas de la Especería, los capitulares le dijeron:. . . ." He then copies folio 188 of the *Libro segundo de cabildo* (HSA, Hiersemann 418/239) verbatim, indicating that he has done so by resorting to italics: "*que su Señoria tiene presos a Cinacán y Sachil, señores de Guatemala; y que su Señoria se va ahora en su armada, porque estos indios siempre han sido rebeldes, y de su estada en la tierra se temen, que se levantarán y harán algún alzamiento con que la tierra se pierda; y por ende, que piden a su Señoria, que o les lleve en su armada, o si han hecho por que haga justicia de ellos; porque de quedar ellos en la tierra, especialmente si se huyesen de la cárcel, que lo pueden bien hacer, se podía recrecer algún alzamiento de que se recrecería grande deservicio a Dios Nuestro Señor y a su Majestad, y de gran fatiga de guerra a los españoles, y muertes de ellos.*" Fuentes y Guzmán also reproduces this same extract from folio 188 word for word, but with one important exception: he renders "Sachil" as "Sequechul" and misidentifies him as a "señor de Utatlán." We should recall that, according to Contreras (1965, 44–45; 1971, 26–27) and Polo Sifontes ([1977] 2005, 81), the name of the Kaqchikel lord captured in 1535 along with Cahí Ymox was Quiyavit Caok (see note 25, above). Fuentes y Guzmán's error, we should also recall, incurred him the wrath of Ximénez (see chapter 2, notes 33 and 34) and has confounded researchers ever since. Sequechul or Sacachul was the name given by Spaniards to Belehé Qat, who we know (see note 5, above) died panning for gold in 1532. We take Sachil, not to be confused with Súchil, the wife of Cahí Ymox (see chapter 1), to be the name Spaniards gave Quiyavit Caok.

32. Alvarado's words are paraphrased in folio 188 of the *Libro segundo de cabildo* (HSA, Hiersemann 418/239) thus: "[S]u señoria dixo que lo vera e hara lo que mas conbenga al serviçio de dios y de S[u] M[ajestad] e bien de la tierra e paçificaçion della."

33. Recinos and Goetz (1953, 132). They add (133n256) that "although it is not recorded in the manuscript, [Alvarado] undoubtedly did the same to the Quiché king, Tepepul," meaning hanged him. Recinos and Goetz present no evidence to link "the Quiché king, Tepepul" to Quiyavit Caok, which Contreras (1965; 1971) does his best to clarify: The execution took place "[t]hirteen months after the arrival of Tunatiuh." Maxwell and Hill (2006, 287) state: "Two hundred days after Tunatiw arrived, the lord, Ajpo Sotz'il, Kaji' Imox, was hanged." Otzoy (1999, 190) records that the deed was done "two hundred and sixty days" after Alvarado's return.

34. The *Memorial de Sololá*—see Recinos and Goetz (1953, 133)—registers three more hangings. Notice of the first execution runs: "Fourteen months after the king Ahpozotzil [Cahí Ymox] had been hanged, they hanged Chuuy Tziquinú, chief of the city ["*Ahauh Patinamit*, or Lord of Yximché"] because they were angry. On the day 4 Can [February 27, 1541] they hanged him in Paxayá. They took him along the road and hanged him secretly." A second execution, involving two leaders, is worded: "Seventeen days after the lord had been hanged, after Chuuy Tziquinú had been hanged, on the day 8 Iq [March 16, 1541] the lord Chicbal was hanged, together with Nimabah Quehchún, but this was not by Tunatiuh, who had already left. . . . Tunatiuh's lieutenant [Francisco de la Cueva] hanged them." Otzoy (1999, 190) translates the first execution as arising not "because they were angry" but "because they were jealous." Repetition in the Kaqchikel text— the word "hanged" is deployed in close succession four times—is a stylistic point of emphasis used to draw attention to something that the authors considered of utmost importance.

35. Contreras (1965, 45).

Their leaders dealt with once and for all, there would be no third Kaqchikel uprising to match the tenacity of the first or the valor of the second. A peace of the dead ensued, but one from which Alvarado was fated not to profit. He never did reach the Spice Islands, nor even set sail for them, dying on July 4, 1541, from injuries incurred at Nochistlán some ten days earlier, when another combatant's horse fell on him during the Mixtón rebellion in Nueva Galicia in Mexico, where he was drawn into action en route to his intended destination.[36] His death allowed Crown officials more scope to impose royal order and pursue colonial objectives. Alvarado's violent and rapacious ways, however, were to cast a long and oppressive shadow over the lands and peoples Cortés had sent him to conquer.

36. Ida Altman (2010, 147–51) discusses the events and circumstances surrounding what she considers Alvarado's "pointless death" with admirable clarity, including how it was depicted by Theodor de Bry (1595) and the indigenous composers of the Codex Telleriano-Remensis (Quiñones Keber 1995).

PART II

SETTLEMENT AND COLONIZATION

CHAPTER 4

THE EMERGENCE OF
CORE AND PERIPHERY

The death of Pedro de Alvarado by no means signaled an end to wars of conquest in Guatemala, but his demise marked a reduction in the intensity and extent of the fighting. Though his fierce campaigns, and those of his associates, saw Spaniards reach and lay claim to far-flung parts, it was clear to the invaders that the country of the K'iche's and Kaqchikels, and adjacent areas over which these two peoples held sway, were where the possibility of enrichment was greatest. It was no accident that Spanish interest in Guatemala, therefore, was drawn to the lands formerly ruled from Utatlán and Iximché. We focus now on the repercussions of conquest in terms of the goals imperial Spain had in mind for the development of the colony, and how native agency was once again instrumental in modifying what actually came to be. Before we offer empirical findings, some thoughts about historiography and how we might hypothesize post-conquest scenarios are in order.

When Murdo MacLeod first published his socioeconomic history of Spanish Central America, he did so at a time when research on the region figured only marginally in the scholarly imagination.[1] Charles Gibson was quick to recognize that MacLeod's contribution created an "intelligible framework" against which all subsequent studies of colonial Guatemala thenceforth might be measured.[2] MacLeod not only established an "intelligible framework"; he was also prudent enough to concede, a decade later, that what he had mapped out would be refined, modified, and altered by future investigations. "Research on colonial

---

1. MacLeod (1973). The first edition of the book is also available in a rather wooden but service-able Spanish translation (MacLeod 1980). A second English-language edition (MacLeod 2008) has a new introduction that reviews historiographical developments since the time of first publication.
2. Gibson (1974).

Guatemala," he declared, "has hardly begun," predicting that the field would "undergo revision, if not demolition" as "almost limitless" investigative options were pursued.[3] MacLeod's words may seem like a simple matter of common sense, but all too often we approach the study of history as if past events and circumstances could be anchored definitively, not subject to reappraisal as time unfolds.

Our aim here is to take one element of MacLeod's schema and develop it in the light of issues that have arisen since he first formulated his ideas about the nature of colonial experiences in Central America. We focus attention on the geographical divide, in MacLeod's view, between a Ladino "east" and an Indian "west" in Guatemala. Our discussion casts the division observed and explained by him in terms of the emergence of a developed "core" and a less-developed "periphery." We examine, first, the resource base of Guatemala as perceived by imperial Spain, outlining the territorial expanse of a colonial core and a colonial periphery. Next we sketch, for core and periphery, patterns of landholding and settlement, after which we present salient features of economic and social life. We lean heavily for our portrayal on the long-standing interest on the part of one of us (Lutz) in the city and environs of the colonial capital, Santiago de Guatemala, today Antigua, and on the part of another (Lovell) in the rural settings of the Sierra de los Cuchumatanes.[4] While Carol Smith, among others, has contributed much to the theorization of core-periphery relationships in Guatemala, what concerns us most is to ground such concepts in their colonial-period origins.[5]

THE RESOURCE BASE

Spaniards appraised the resource base of Guatemala, as elsewhere in the New World, in accordance with certain needs and desires shaped

3. MacLeod (1983, 189–90).

4. Lutz ([1982] 1984; 1994b; 2005) has written at length on Santiago de Guatemala, Lovell ([1985] 2005; 1990) on the Sierra de los Cuchumatanes.

5. Carol A. Smith (1978, 1987) makes for challenging but rewarding reading. For a critique of our thinking on the matter, see Luján Muñoz (1993; 1995; 2011, 104–108). In the *Atlas histórico de Guatemala*, Luján Muñoz reproduces a color version of our delineation of core and periphery (map 51) before offering two formulations of his own (maps 52 and 53). He argues that it is valid "to distinguish between highland and lowland, and also between predominantly indigenous and non-indigenous regions," but takes us to task for leaning too heavily on MacLeod and, in

by their culture. Theirs was a multipurpose enterprise, one in which spiritual, political, and economic motives were intertwined. They looked at Guatemala through very different eyes than did its native inhabitants, and set to work immediately. Soon after Spanish penetration, the cultural landscape began to change as never before, the process of transformation set in motion by inadvertent as well as planned courses of action.

The mark of imperial Spain, to summarize MacLeod, was traced as follows. Being entrepreneurs, lay Spaniards were drawn to areas where environmental conditions and natural resources would maximize material enrichment. They also preferred, according to George Foster, to settle and live in parts that most resembled their places of origin.[6] For these reasons, early on, colonial Guatemala began to assume a very different appearance to the south and east of Santiago, where greater potential existed for both Crown and private gain, than it did to the north and west of the capital city, where opportunities to generate wealth were slight.

The divide MacLeod identifies does not correspond entirely with "highland" versus "lowland." Such a distinction, while neat and convenient, would in fact be misleading. If we think, cardinally, of territory lying south and east of Santiago as forming the "core" and territory lying north and west as forming the "periphery," this crude binary geography fits our state of knowledge reasonably well. It does so because it enables us not only to accommodate MacLeod's dichotomy but also

---

his view, portraying the periphery exclusively as "Indian" and the core likewise as "non-Indian," which we take pains *not* to do. "Only the capital of the Kingdom, Santiago de Guatemala, and its surrounding area," he maintains, "can properly be considered the core." Luján Muñoz (2011, 132) emphasizes his point by having the Corregimiento del Valle, as depicted by Fuentes y Guzmán (1690–99) in the *Recordación florida*, not merely featured in the *Atlas histórico de Guatemala* but adorn its cover. We thank Todd Little-Siebold (personal communication) for his critique of our exposition, echoing his insistence that "the complex ethnic landscape of Guatemala does not respond to any easy geographic division" and agreeing that change over time is difficult to convey, save "from pueblo to pueblo, not core vs. periphery." What we lay out is mindful of the fact that "much of the *Oriente* was majority indigenous even into the twentieth century"—see map 154 in the *Atlas histórico de Guatemala* (Luján Muñoz 2011, 295) for evidence of this—but nonetheless acknowledges that Ladinos became a more conspicuous presence there than in other parts of Guatemala from the late seventeenth century on. This phenomenon is shown by Luján Muñoz (2011, 158–59) in map 87 and map 88 of the *Atlas histórico de Guatemala*.

6. Foster (1960) examines at length the cultural values, material preferences, and social origins of early Spanish settlers in the Americas. See also Sanchíz Ochoa (1976) and Altman (1989). MacLeod ([1973] 2008) takes issue with the views, in particular, of the former.

to elaborate upon it by identifying highland and lowland regions within both the core and the periphery.

Thus defined, the heart of the core was always the colonial capital and its surrounding jurisdiction, the Corregimiento del Valle, largely coterminous with the present-day departments of Sacatepéquez, Chimaltenango, and Guatemala. The core, however, extended beyond this heartland into the eastern highlands (present-day Jalapa and Chiquimula), the eastern lowlands (present-day El Progreso and Zacapa), and the southern lowlands that stretch along the Pacific coast from Soconusco, in present-day Mexico, to Sonsonate, in present-day El Salvador. The periphery incorporated a vast swath that stretched from the Sierra de los Cuchumatanes (in present-day Huehuetenango and El Quiché) past the Sierra de Chamá (in present-day Alta Verapaz) to the Sierra de Santa Cruz (in present-day Izabal) as well as the northern lowlands drained by the Río Ixcán, Río Xaclbal, Río Chixoy, Río Sarstún, and the upper tributaries of the Río de la Pasión (see map 1).

The resource base of the core attracted the attention of Spaniards, as it had their K'ich'e and Kaqchikel predecessors, much more than the resource base of the periphery. Consequently, Spanish colonists settled first in and around the valleys of Almolonga and Panchoy, where (in addition to Mesoamerican staples) wheat could be grown and cattle raised: bread and beef, to the conqueror, were more palatable than corn tortillas and the native fowl (*gallinas de la tierra*) we know today as the turkey. Thereafter, with their African slaves, Spaniards spread south and east into lower-lying *tierra templada* and *tierra caliente*, lands where the climate ranged from warm to hot, where soils were generally fertile, and most important of all, where cash crops such as cacao, cochineal, indigo, sugarcane (primarily for the preparation of cane liquor, or *aguardiente*), and tobacco could be cultivated. A sustained European presence, together with accelerated rates of indigenous depopulation, saw a more Ladino Guatemala emerge in these parts, a region inhabited by *castas*, people of mixed Maya, Spanish, and African descent, who lived alongside native communities that held their ground against newcomer encroachment. Limited commercial options in the periphery, by contrast, meant that Spaniards there, as well as Africans and *castas,* were fewer in number; native inhabitants, even at the nadir of the demographic collapse (see part IV) that accompanied conquest, always constituted the majority of the population. Maya peoples and their distinct ways survived the

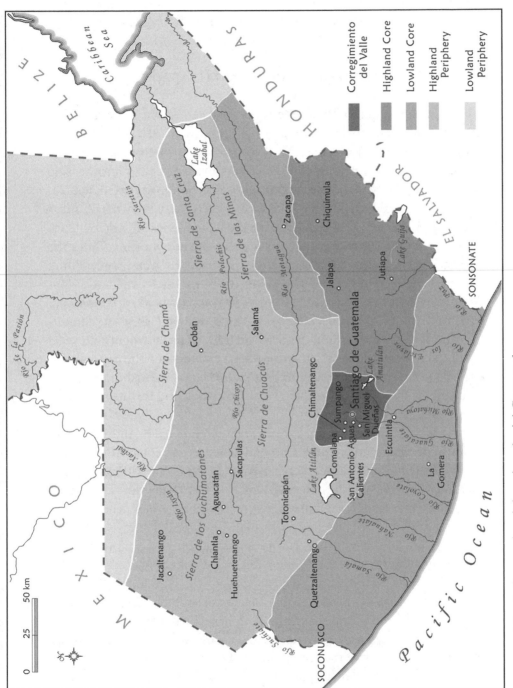

MAP 1. Core and periphery in colonial Guatemala.

Legend:
Corregimiento del Valle
Highland Core
Lowland Core
Highland Periphery
Lowland Periphery

MEXICO
BELIZE
HONDURAS
EL SALVADOR
SONSONATE
SOCONUSCO
Caribbean Sea
Pacific Ocean

Lake Izabal
Lake Güija
Lake Atitlán
Lake Amatitlán

Río Sarstún
Río de la Pasión
Río Xaclbal
Río Ixcán
Río Chixoy
Río Polochic
Río Motagua
Río de los Esclavos
Río Paz
Río Michatoya
Río Guacalate
Río Coyolate
Río Samalá
Río Nahualate
Río Sucbiate

Sierra de Santa Cruz
Sierra de Chamá
Sierra de las Minas
Sierra de Chuacús
Sierra de los Cuchumatanes

Zacapa
Chiquimula
Jalapa
Jutiapa
Cobán
Salamá
Chimaltenango
Santiago de Guatemala
Sumpango
San Miguel Dueñas
San Antonio Aguas Calientes
Comalapa
Escuintla
La Gomera
Totonicapán
Sacapulas
Aguacatán
Chiantla
Huehuetenango
Jacaltenango
Quetzaltenango

0 25 50 km

81

biological and cultural onslaught of conquest to produce, especially in the far north and west, an Indian Guatemala that endures to this day.[7]

LANDHOLDING AND SETTLEMENT

The lure of the highland core led Spaniards to found there a capital city from which to govern. Santiago was founded in the Valley of Almolonga in 1527, but it was destroyed by mud slides that swept down the slopes of Agua volcano in 1541, resulting in a search for another site for the capital city. The new capital, known as Santiago de Guatemala, was established a little north of the former one (today known as Ciudad Vieja) in the Valley of Panchoy, with the forced labor of nearby Kaqchikel communities responsible for most of the heavy lifting. Since the distance between the old and new capitals was not great, landholding patterns changed very little as a result of the move. By the late 1520s, Spanish residents, or *vecinos*, had received grants of land in Almolonga, Panchoy, and neighboring valleys. On these "milpas," they settled indigenous slaves who were instructed on how to grow wheat and tend cattle. They were also expected to provide residents of the capital with grain, meat, fruits, and vegetables, in addition to furnishing Spanish households with fodder for their horses and firewood for their kitchens and living quarters.[8]

After Indian slavery was abolished, around 1550, an expanding Spanish population then moved beyond Santiago and environs into other parts of the highland core. In these parts, around Amatitlán, Chimaltenango, Comalapa, and Sumpango, more wheat farms were established and, in warmer terrain, rudimentary sugar mills or *ingenios*. These estates

---

7. The validity of this assertion, and of our core/periphery designations in general, is nowhere better illustrated than in Luján Muñoz (2011, 292–93), which renders the distribution, by department, of indigenous and non-indigenous populations according to the national census of 1981. Map 153 clearly reveals, three centuries after the first evidence of it was manifest, an "Indian" Guatemala lying to the north and west of a dividing line, and a "Ladino" Guatemala lying to the south and east. See also MacLeod ([1973] 2008, 308; 1983, 193–203). For a discussion of the importation of black slaves into Guatemala and their subsequent incorporation into colonial society, see Lutz (1994a, 79–112); Herrera (2003, 112–32); and Lokken (2013). On the emergence of *casta*, or mixed race populations, see Lutz (1993; 1994a); Lokken (2000; 2008); and Luján Muñoz (2011, 153–62).

8. Lutz ([1982] 1984, 39–41 and 55–61. See also Luján Muñoz (2011, 91–92), which includes an attractive rendering (map 43) of the "milpas de vecinos españoles" around 1530.

certainly encroached on native holdings but, with the indigenous population in precipitous decline throughout the sixteenth century, a decreasing amount of land was necessary to support it.[9]

Appropriation of fertile tracts in the highland core, however, does not mean that the landscape became one of exclusive Spanish settlement. Most landowners actually lived in Santiago and arranged for *castas* and less well-heeled Spaniards to administer their estates. Criollos, people of Spanish descent born in the Americas, also owned rural properties but were not the dominant elite. Land was cheap and the returns from working it relatively modest. The research of Stephen Webre shows how economic power in Guatemala, by the late sixteenth century, came to be held by peninsular Spanish newcomers, colonists who arrived with ample capital and with well-placed connections. Their ranks, Webre demonstrates, were replenished by other peninsular arrivals throughout the seventeenth and eighteenth centuries.[10]

While better-off Spaniards lived in Santiago, several towns in the highland core began to be settled during the sixteenth century by *castas*, free blacks, and non-elite Spaniards. These people were employed in trading activities that supplied the capital, but they also engaged in the transport of commodities between the highland core and the lowland core, which lay farther south and east. When native numbers, after a century or more of decline, began finally to stabilize and then to grow, with population recovery came increased pressure on land resources. The end result, especially in some communities near Santiago, was landlessness and loss of indigenous identity, or ladinoization. We can only surmise that this process shifted eastward by the end of the eighteenth century with the decision to relocate the colonial capital, following a series of disastrous earthquakes, to the present site of Guatemala City. Once again native labor was responsible for the bulk of construction, but this time it was drawn from communities far and wide, not just those in closest proximity.[11]

Contemporaneous with the process of settling beyond the immediate vicinity of Santiago was a gradual occupation, by Spaniards and their African slaves as well as by free *castas*, of the lowland core, a region

9. Lutz (1981). See also Luján Muñoz (2011, 130–41).
10. Webre (1980, 1981). See also Palma Murga (1986) and Santos Pérez (1999).
11. Langenberg (1979, 1981) and Zilbermann de Luján (1987). See also Luján Muñoz (2011, 116–17).

that today includes the *boca costa*, or Pacific piedmont, the Pacific coastal plain, and the Oriente. As in the highland core, on the most suitable of these lands Spaniards established haciendas and *ingenios*. Native depopulation throughout the lowland core, however, left even more land available for Spanish exploitation. Its use tended to be more extensive than intensive. *Estancias*, or cattle ranches, were set up, but in many parts the animals roamed wild. Far more communities in the lowland core than in the highland core, in spite of Crown rulings on who could reside in them, came to have growing numbers of poor Spanish and *casta* populations. These people worked on nearby estates, hunted cattle for hides and tallow, indulged in the manufacture and sale of clandestine liquor, and, most persistently of all, sought to seize control of indigenous cacao production.[12]

The economic geography of cacao is intriguing. So long as Indians survived, most of the groves that grew it remained in their hands. But Spaniards, not native producers, were the ones who profited most from the sale of cacao, whether as traders or recipients of tribute. Though Indians migrated from highland to lowland areas in order to harvest cacao, always an important item of tribute, production declined as indigenous communities along the Pacific coast thinned out or, in some cases, disappeared altogether.[13]

Cacao depended heavily on year-round native labor and was most often grown on native land. The other major export crop of the colonial period, indigo, was cultivated, harvested, and processed for export on Spanish holdings known as *obrajes de tinte añil*. Indians, supposedly protected by law from being compelled to work in *obrajes*, produced this valuable and much-sought dye while working alongside African slaves and *castas*. Unlike other crops, *xiquilite*, the hardy grass from which indigo is derived, could be conveniently grown in conjunction with the raising of cattle. With labor demands being less, indigo replaced cacao in the seventeenth century as the preeminent export earner for entrepreneurially minded Spaniards. These two cash crops did much to gear the resource base of the lowland core to the booms and busts of an export economy. At the same time, however, vast tracts south and east

12. MacLeod (1983, 193–203). For a discussion of cacao and its production in Central America during pre-Columbian and early colonial times, see Bergmann (1958, 1969) and Luján Muñoz (2011, 91 and 133–35), especially map 42.
13. MacLeod ([1973] 2008, 87 and 1985, 58). For Soconusco, see Gasco (1987, 1991); for Izalco, see Fowler (1991).

of Santiago were worked far less ambitiously, producing grains, cattle and other livestock, tobacco, and sugarcane for local consumption. These activities did not make many people rich, but they made possible Spanish and *casta* settlement of sizable areas of the lowland core.[14]

Landholding and settlement patterns in the periphery differed quite markedly from those that prevailed in the core. To portray the periphery as devoid of commercial potential would not be accurate. Scattered throughout the highland zone, around Quetzaltenango, Totonicapán, and Huehuetenango, for example, were pockets of fertile land where wheat grew well and cattle thrived, two options always conducive to arousing Spanish interest. More important, though, than these admittedly modest ventures in mixed farming was the emergence in the seventeenth century of ranching, especially the raising of sheep, mules, horses, and cattle on the open meadows of the Sierra de los Cuchumatanes above Chiantla and Aguacatán. Here Spaniards and criollos, by shrewd, strategic purchases, amassed properties that by the eighteenth century constituted some of the most sizable haciendas in all Central America.[15]

What is important to realize, however, is that Spanish acquisition of land was not attained necessarily at native expense. Indians who lived near Spanish towns obviously lost out. So also did those whose lands bordered the large Cuchumatán ranches, although it must be recognized that these operations came into being on alpine pastures never fully utilized as part of the aboriginal economy. Maya communities in the highland periphery simply did not have to contend with the intensity of Spanish pressure that was exerted on land in the colonial core, primarily because of a relative lack of exploitative options. Furthermore, Indians who lived in the far north had the additional advantage of occupying and farming, if only on a temporary basis, the sparsely settled terrain of the lowland periphery. This practice was not without risk, for in these remote parts lived hostile groups like the Lacandones and Chol Manchés, who raided far and wide. We still know very little about what went on in the lowland periphery, save that it constituted a zone of refuge, an open frontier whose rainforests lay well beyond the reach of Spanish control. Highland peoples (Ixil, Q'anjob'al, and

14. MacLeod ([1973] 2008, 191–92) and Luján Muñoz (2011, 136–37). See also Feldman (1985) and Fowler (1987).

15. Lovell ([1985] 2005, 118–39). For more detailed "highland periphery" scenarios, those of Alta and Baja Verapaz in particular, see Sapper ([1936] 1985) and Bertrand (1987). For similar treatment of "lowland periphery" locations, see De Vos ([1980] 1993) and Jones (1983, 1989, 1998).

Q'eqchi' Mayas) would periodically migrate to fish, hunt, gather, and farm there. The land base of indigenous communities in the highland periphery, in theory protected by a legal system that natives quickly learned to engage, was often not encroached upon, even if certain Old World animals, plants, fruits, and vegetables altered the complexion of what was grown and now grazed on Maya fields.[16]

Much more tampered with in the periphery, but in the end with mixed results, were patterns of settlement, discussed at length in our next chapter. The domestic arrangements in place when Spaniards first arrived, with populations considerably more dispersed than nucleated, suited neither lay demands for efficient provision of tribute nor the Church's concern with conversion to Christianity. By the mid-sixteenth century, the ambitious task of resettling scattered groups in more accessible locales was well under way, led in the highland periphery (as in the highland core) by friars of the Dominican, Franciscan, and Mercedarian orders. More than their secular brothers to the south and east, friars of the regular clergy charged with the evangelizing mission of *congregación* saw their efforts constantly undermined. Judged purely on the evidence of the number of towns and villages founded—some three hundred throughout Guatemala by 1600—*congregación* left a lasting imprint on the landscape.[17] All over the periphery, however, centripetal movement brought about either by missionary zeal or fiscal urge ran counter to sensible centrifugal tendencies on the part of the natives. For various reasons—to flee from an outbreak of disease, to escape the demands of officialdom, to cultivate ancestral land—Indians resisted the nucleation imposed on them, steadily repopulating distant places they or their predecessors had been moved from. The hand of the conqueror certainly left its mark, but not always in the manner envisioned by imperial design.[18]

ELEMENTS OF ECONOMIC LIFE

The economy of the highland core was based at the outset almost exclusively on the exploitation of native labor, which was furnished by

16. Borah (1983, 40–43) and Lovell ([1985] 2005, 128–29). See Luján Muñoz (2011, 164–72) for an elegant cartographic synthesis, six maps in all, of Lacandón disruptions and intrusions, and Spanish efforts to deal with them.
17. Van Oss (1986, 31–32) and Luján Muñoz (2011, 120–25).
18. Lovell ([1985] 2005; 1990).

indigenous slaves or provided under terms spelled out (see part III) in specific grants of *encomienda* as *servicio personal* (personal service). Much of this changed after 1550, when President Alonso López de Cerrato abolished both Indian slavery, concentrated in and around Santiago, and *servicio personal*, much more widespread throughout the jurisdiction over which he presided. Natives who lived in barrios (districts) within the capital or in pueblos (towns) within the core henceforth paid tribute in cash and foodstuffs, and Spaniards took them on under the favorable hiring arrangements—for the Spaniards, that is—of *repartimiento* and *servicio ordinario*, or "normal labor service."[19]

Some Indian pueblos held in *encomiendas* remained in private hands, but more and more in the core were taken over by the Crown. This was especially true of cacao-rich pueblos, over which royal officials ultimately wrested control from once-powerful *encomenderos*. By the late sixteenth century, a situation had arisen whereby the Crown exercised its authority over core *encomiendas*, allowing those of the periphery, valued at much less, to remain in individual hands. The cacao boom, however, was by then long past its peak.

Individual Spaniards and the Spanish Crown received tribute from all married adults, both women and men, and from widows, widowers, and single persons over sixteen and less than fifty-six years of age. These categories remained unchanged, except for minor adjustments, until the 1750s, when women were declared exempt from payment.[20] Paying tribute may not have been overly burdensome for some communities, but under Spanish rule Indians had to meet any number of other fiscal obligations, some legal, others decidedly less so. One exaction peculiar to the core, levied on those who lived around Santiago on lands owned by Spaniards, was the *terrazgo*, a system whereby rents were paid on house plots and adjacent fields, or *milpas*. In addition, all native communities, whether in the core or the periphery, had to fulfill fiscal and labor obligations to the Church.[21] Though Spanish bureaucrats aspired to enrich themselves at the expense of their indigenous subjects, this was not always easy to achieve, especially if the area to be administered was located in the highland core, where the watchful eyes of higher,

---

19. Sherman (1979) remains our best work in English on forced native labor in the sixteenth century. It also exists in Spanish translation (Sherman 1987).

20. Lutz ([1982] 1984, 191). See also Cook and Borah (1971, 275–76).

21. Lutz ([1982] 1984, 102–105); MacLeod ([1973] 2008, 314–15); and Van Oss (1986, 85–89). See also Rubio Sánchez (1982) and AGI, Contaduría 971A and 971B.

less corrupt authorities might prevail. Serious abuse of office occurred in the lowland core, where government representatives such as *alcaldes mayores* and *jueces de milpa* sought to procure, by whatever means necessary, a share in the cacao trade.[22]

When Spaniards in the lowland core were not extracting payments and bribes directly, they devised other ways to exploit the indigenous population. One was simply to overlook, for a suitable fee, consistent violation of laws governing native labor, such as its illegal deployment in *obrajes de tinte añil*. Similarly, *jueces repartidores* in the highland core, charged with overseeing labor contracted under the terms of *repartimiento*, could ignore (again for a price) the illegal hiring of Indians by a Spanish farmer, or *labrador*. At the same time as they enriched Spaniards, these abuses made life even more difficult for the local population.[23]

Repartimiento in the highland core, even without its chronic excesses, placed a heavy burden on native communities. From the mid-sixteenth century on, Indians here were hard pressed. They were ordered to work at various tasks: they farmed, tended flocks and herds of animals, hauled loads, helped to build houses, baked bread, or cleaned streets in the capital city. The topic is still in need of detailed, systematic analysis, but evidence indicates that some Indian pueblos had to provide up to one-quarter of their male population at any given time to work for a token wage of three to five *reales* per laborer each week. The amount paid inched upward over time, but was seldom commensurate with the value of labor expended. In the highland core, *repartimiento* obligations were in force up to forty-nine weeks per year, the only periods free of the duty being Holy Week, the days around Christmas, and the time during which celebration of a town saint occurred. This meant, effectively, that able-bodied males were obliged to work away from home as much as twelve weeks each year. Little is known about the use of *repartimiento* in the lowland core, except for its use in lead mining in Chiquimula.[24]

Agricultural labor in the lowland core appears to have involved the use of cash advances, including debt peonage, more than outright coercion. Such a strategy encouraged natives from both the core and

22. Sherman (1979, 197–98) and MacLeod ([1973] 2008, 76, 210, 240).
23. MacLeod ([1973] 2008, 186–89, 209, 295, 313) and Luján Muñoz (1988, 61–66).
24. Lutz ([1982] 1984, 339, 356); MacLeod ([1973] 2008, 261); Sherman (1979, 191–207); and Pinto Soria (1987, 33–37).

the periphery to abandon their communities and their tributary obligations in order to work on Spanish-owned estates. These migrations
served to promote further miscegenation among an already diminished
indigenous population.[25]

We still know relatively little about native systems of production
and exchange, with the notable exception of cacao. Indians appear to
have operated with relative freedom when they dealt in inexpensive items
such as corn, vegetables, and firewood. When trading in more desirable
or expensive items, say cacao or cotton cloth, they soon ran into trouble,
including even the outright theft of their merchandise. In Santiago,
Spanish authorities attempted from time to time to protect native
merchants who arrived in the capital from shakedowns and forced sales
at the hands of African and *casta* middlemen, or *regatones*, who ventured out from the city to meet incoming traders. *Regatones*, however,
were often in the employ of Spanish bosses, or *patrones*. For the Indians,
the only practical precaution against this looting was to travel in groups
and hope that a show of numbers might dissuade potential thugs and
robbers from mounting an attack. The safest course of action, if not
the most profitable, was to trade in inexpensive products with low
resale value.[26]

The few Spaniards who sought wealth and prosperity in the periphery
did so by concentrating their energies on two main activities: mining
and ranching. The extraction of silver was never as profitable as the
operations set up in Honduras in and around Tegucigalpa. However,
it yielded earnings not to be scoffed at, both for private individuals who
first organized mining activities in the early sixteenth century (see chapter 7) and for the local clergy, who benefited from the proceeds later on.
Silver from mines near Chiantla was used to decorate church altars
throughout Guatemala. Ranching—again focused on Chiantla, where
annual fairs featuring prize heads of livestock attracted buyers from all
over New Spain—brought handsome returns for the handful of families
who dominated the enterprise, and must also have generated tangible
returns for the Crown in the form of taxes. *Repartimiento* drafts from
nearby communities supplied the mines and ranches with necessary

25. MacLeod (1983, 193–95) and Luján Muñoz (2011, 156–62).
26. Lutz ([1982] 1984, 338).

labor, but there is evidence also that the tending of livestock for Spanish *hacendados* carried with it the risk of debt peonage.[27]

Mining and ranching appear to have been conducted for the most part within the boundaries of colonial law, but not so the practice of forced purchase known as the *reparto de efectos*. By this means, government officials and even parish priests would require natives to buy from them goods they could neither afford nor had obvious need of. A related abuse was to distribute loads of raw cotton and demand that it be worked, without pay, into thread and cloth. The finished item was later sold at market, with profits accruing to the distributor, not the producer.[28] Involvement with *reparto de efectos* was not restricted to Spaniards who presided over native charges in the periphery, but extant documentation suggests that distance from responsible bureaucracy in the capital was correlated with a greater incidence of the practice.

The above labor practices aside, most Indians in the periphery dealt only indirectly with Spaniards as participants in a tribute economy. Twice each year native communities were required to furnish, either for *encomenderos* or the Crown, stipulated amounts of locally and regionally available products. These were then auctioned off, with cash benefits passed on to the appropriate recipient. Indian tribute in Guatemala always amounted to a significant portion of total Crown revenue. Miles Wortman reckons that the tribute accounted for more than 80 percent of revenues collected by the Audiencia de Guatemala during the first half of the eighteenth century.[29] Only after demands for tribute had been met could Indians marshal their energies toward the mundane but vital chores of existence, especially the cultivation of corn, upon which all family and group survival ultimately depended.

ELEMENTS OF SOCIAL LIFE

The social life of any collective is difficult to depict without invoking case particulars that depart significantly from, and in the end call into question, general patterns and processes. Indigenous groups in Guatemala

27. Lovell ([1985] 2005, 106–107, 121–26).
28. Ibid., 108–11.
29. Wortman (1982, 145). See also Solórzano (1985, 99).

are no exception. We find it hard to imagine, for instance, that what Adriaan van Oss calls "hermetic" Indian society was ever commonplace in colonial Guatemala, least of all in the core.[30] This does not mean, however, that native communities in the core were obliterated by Spanish intrusion. We perceive, above all else, marked spatial variation in how the impact of colonialism registered on Indian mores and was subsequently manifest. In both the core and the periphery, certain factors helped determine the preservation or decay of native welfare. These factors include: (1) the survival, after the disastrous epidemics and demographic decline of the sixteenth century, of a viable population base, which ensured that a community could maintain itself and eventually recover; (2) the extent of Spanish encroachment on community land; (3) the ability to maintain control of sufficient *terrazgo*-free agricultural lands to support community numbers; (4) the capacity to obtain new lands, which often pitted one community against a rival, adjoining one; (5) the size of Spanish and *casta* populations living either within an Indian pueblo or close by; and (6) the option of exploiting local craft skills or a raw material base, which would lessen dependence on earning a living outside the community. Other key variables, of course, pertain to the physical environment   altitude, soil characteristics, and rainfall conditions, especially the extent to which these influenced whether or not land could produce crops or commodities sought by Spaniards or criollos. In communities where some combination of the above elements operated in their favor, Indians could adapt and survive, despite often overbearing pressures. Where conditions worked against them, native communities under such threats withered and even disintegrated. Some specificity is called for.

In Santiago, for instance, its Indian barrios and some of its *milpas*, with only small surviving populations by the late sixteenth century, faced radical changes. There were agricultural land shortages, excessive labor and fiscal demands, and incursions into their living space by *castas*. San Lucas Cabrera, for instance, struggled through the seventeenth century only to breathe its last gasp and die as an indigenous community in the eighteenth. Its closeness to Santiago had much to do with its transformation. Other core communities, including San Lorenzo Monroy, were farther away from the capital city and managed to maintain

30. Van Oss (1986, 75).

a viable indigenous population base. But San Lorenzo was affected by Spanish pressure on its land and by the burden of *terrazgo* payments, which jointly contributed to its gradual ladinoization.[31]

By contrast, San Lorenzo's neighbor to the northwest, San Antonio Aguas Calientes, situated near the northern shore of Lake Quilizinapa, survived remarkably well. When Indian slaves belonging to Juan de Chávez were emancipated around 1550, their former *patrón*, before departing for Spain, bequeathed to them the lands upon which San Antonio stood. This good fortune, among other things, meant that no *terrazgos* had to be paid. San Antonio thus grew in size and preserved its strong Kaqchikel identity, which lingers still.[32]

San Miguel Dueñas, on the southern shores of Lake Quilizinapa, fared differently. Around Dueñas, which lies at a lower altitude than San Lorenzo, sugarcane can be grown. Spaniards encroached, settled African slaves, and exacted *terrazgos* from surviving Indians. The slave contingent became a nucleus of free mulattoes who, over time, came to be considered Ladinos. Good land, the Dueñas experience indicates, was a blessing if it could be retained but a curse if it prompted an interest on the part of Spaniards, which in the long run resulted in dispossession.[33]

Indigenous communities in the lowland core, in aggregate, did not fare nearly as well as their counterparts in the highlands. Early on, disease took a heavy native toll. Later, seventeenth-century epidemics of more tropical than temperate Old World origin ravaged the survivors of the first waves of pestilence. These lowland communities, furthermore, occupied terrain on which cash crops could be grown. Already weakened by disease, they suffered even more with Spanish and *casta* takeover of their productive fields. Land acquisition was followed by piecemeal settlement of the countryside, Spanish and *casta* residence within indigenous communities, and the founding of exclusive Spanish-*casta* enclaves like La Gomera and Villa de la Concepción de las Mesas. The intensity

31. Lutz (1981). Annis (1987, 24) doubts the importance of San Lorenzo's lack of land as a cause of its ladinoization, arguing that loss of land dates to the late nineteenth and early twentieth centuries with the advent of coffee cultivation. Study of colonial landholding patterns in the valleys of Almolonga and Panchoy, however, suggests that loss of land was well advanced by the end of the eighteenth century. See also Dakin and Lutz (1996) and Luján Muñoz (2011, 91–92).

32. Lutz (1981) and Annis (1987, 28).

33. Lutz (1981) and Annis (1987, 24).

or degree of miscegenation varied from place to place, but the trend overall was the irreversible creation of Ladino Guatemala. Indians certainly survived in these parts but often had no recourse but to rent properties from newcomers who had usurped native resources.[34]

Any evaluation of the nature of Maya social life must inevitably address Eric Wolf's celebrated model of the closed corporate peasant community, discussed in more detail in chapter 5. One thing that debate on the subject tends to overlook, however, is that Wolf envisioned peasant communities in Mesoamerica as forming a cultural continuum with "closed" and "corporate" attributes at one end. His model, in other words, allows for situations in which communities can be less "closed," less "corporate," than is often assumed. In the Guatemalan context, we might best regard indigenous communities as social units regulated by systemic triggers that cause "closure" under pressure but permit "opening" in its absence. Imagined thus, native communities, in the periphery as well as the core, vary internally along an "open–closed" axis, their character at any given time dependent on the interplay of the variables identified above.

EFFORTS AND OUTCOMES

Attempts by the Spanish Crown to create, throughout its American dominion, "republics" of Spaniards that would exist harmoniously alongside "republics" of Indians are widely acknowledged to have failed. In Guatemala, the policies of segregation that inspired the concept of *las dos repúblicas* had little to do, according to Magnus Mörner, with making the "strong Indian character" of what we delineate as the periphery and the "quite clear division" between it and the core. Rather, asserts Mörner, "more likely is the division, historically considered, due to a relative lack of economic stimuli" and what he terms a "self-conscious attitude" on the part of indigenous inhabitants. Mörner concedes, nonetheless, that "segregationist legislation served the Indians as a legal resource through which to strengthen their resistance against intruders." He concludes that "Indian aversion" was "more effective than the letter of the law in driving out undesirable outsiders," even if "segregationist legislation"

34. MacLeod ([1973] 2008, 229); Luján Muñoz (1976; 2011, 153–62); and Pinto Soria (1980, 43).

conformed to, and served to reinforce, a "spontaneous attitude."[35]
While we agree with Mörner that segregation, even to the north and
west of Santiago, failed miserably as a protective policy, one could argue
that parts of the periphery, at least to the untrained eye, resembled what
the Spaniards had in mind when they spoke of a *república de indios*.
By contrast, Hispanicized and proletarianized parts of the highland core,
and virtually all the lowland core, suffered a near complete cultural
transformation. In many instances, disease and miscegenation heralded
the total destruction of native society and the birth of a *casta* society.
In other instances, even close to Santiago and at higher altitudes in
the Oriente, Maya communities sometimes held out against shattering
odds, up to Independence and beyond.[36]

The validity of general propositions notwithstanding—the Indian
"west" and Ladino "east" as delineated by MacLeod, the closed corporate peasant community as theorized by Wolf, the notion of a colonial
core and a colonial periphery articulated here—we must always, when
studying Guatemala, be prepared to live with anomalies and exceptions,
no matter how much they cut against the grain of established thinking.

How decisive a role, overall, did Spanish prerogatives play in the
survival or destruction of Maya culture? While acknowledging the intent
of enlightened legislation like the New Laws, as well as the efforts at
reform of individuals like Alonso de Maldonado, Francisco Marroquín, Alonso López de Cerrato, and Diego García de Valverde, all of
whom we discuss in later chapters, the conscious vision of imperial Spain,
we believe, was tempered significantly. Economic marginality in the
Spanish scheme of empire, along with the unforeseen variable of Old
World disease and crucial ecological factors such as altitude, climate,
and soil fertility, influenced colonial experiences more profoundly than
did social blueprints like "the two republics." We must not forget, as

35. Mörner (1964, 150–51).
36. For an account of indigenous experiences in the Oriente, see Fry (1988). We thank Todd
Little-Siebold (personal communication) for sharing with us findings from his perusal of documents in the Archivo General de Centro América (hereafter AGCA), which indicate that "the
indigenous population [of the Oriente] constituted probably seventy to eighty percent of the
[region's] total population in the eighteenth century." He points out, drawing on official census
returns, that "towns such as Camotán, Jocotán, Olota, and others in the region remained over
ninety percent indigenous in 1921, and have significant indigenous populations today." See also
Luján Muñoz (2011, 255–60 and 284–98), especially maps 133, 134, 147, 154, 155, and 156.

Carlos Fuentes insists, always to distinguish in Latin America between the "real country" and the "legal country."[37] Under Spanish rule, Maya peoples in Guatemala inhabited the former, not the latter terrain, forging there forms of community resolutely their own.

37. Fuentes ([1985] 2001, 33).

CHAPTER 5

CONGREGACIÓN AND THE
CREATION OF PUEBLOS DE INDIOS

O ur argument in this chapter is twofold: First, important socio-
spatial continuities link preconquest, colonial, and present-day
Maya communities in Guatemala. Second, native reaction to the policy
of forced resettlement known as *congregación* is key to understanding
how, throughout the colonial period, Indians maintained a sense of
identity and affiliation with old places of abode after being moved to,
and ostensibly acculturated in, new ones.

Coming to grips with what community means is perhaps best achieved
by working back from the present to the past. The *municipio*, or town-
ship, has generally been regarded as the key socio-spatial unit in Guatemala, especially in the western highlands. Sol Tax, in a classic essay on
the subject, deserves much of the credit for bringing the characteristics
of *municipio* organization to our attention.[1] Tax was in no doubt as to
why the concept of *municipio* was so important. *Municipios* in Guatemala, he asserted, constitute "the basic ethnic divisions and cultural
groups into which the country is divided," from which he reasoned that
ethnographic research "must begin with studies of the cultures of individual *municipios*."[2] In Tax's day—his findings date back to 1937—
Guatemala was made up of 353 *municipios*, some 290 of which lay in
the highlands. Lowland *municipios*, then as now, run larger in area but
are usually less populous than those of the *altiplano*. Tax reckoned that
most highland *municipios* were from 100 to 250 square kilometers in
extent, with populations ranging from 1,000 to 5,000 inhabitants.[3] By

1. Tax (1937).
2. Ibid., 425.
3. Ibid., 425.

the close of the twentieth century, the regional or provincial govern-
ments of twenty-two *departamentos* administered 326 *municipios*, most
of which are still to be found in the highlands, but with populations
now considerably in excess of the minimum and maximum limits
encountered by Tax (table 1).

All *municipios* contain a *cabecera*, or head town, which bears the
same name as the *municipio* itself. The *cabecera* is traditionally the hub
of community life, whether the inhabitants of the *municipio* actually
live there or in surrounding *aldeas* (villages) or *caseríos* (hamlets). Tax
identified two main *municipio* types: "town nucleus" (clustered settlement) *municipios* and "vacant town" (dispersed settlement) *municipios*.
Most residents of "town nucleus" *municipios*, he observed, lived in the
cabecera and walked from their homes to outlying fields in order to
perform the labor essential for the upkeep of agricultural holdings. In
contrast, Tax depicted families living in "vacant town" *municipios* as
very much rural based, residing near or adjacent to their fields and
paying a visit to the *cabecera* only in order to go to church, to attend
market, or perhaps to register a birth, marriage, or death. When the term
"pueblo"—literally "people" or "town"—is used to denote origin or
identity, it can mean *cabecera* but it may also refer to the entire collective unit known as *municipio*.[4]

Tax lived and worked in Guatemala long enough to be convinced
that "progress in the study of Guatemalan ethnology depends upon a
prior recognition of *municipios* as the primary (and possibly final) ethnic
units in which it is involved."[5] From the standpoint of present-day issues,
and in the light of animated debates about Maya identity on the part
of diverse constituencies, not least Mayas themselves, what is most
striking about Tax's discussion is its failure to address the fundamental
question of origins. To be fair to Tax, this oversight was not a trademark peculiar to his brand of research alone. In the Mesoamerican
context, most anthropology was then practiced (as much still is) in a
decidedly ahistorical manner, with community studies often set in a
timeless ethnographic present. Grappling with the ethnographic past,
what a later generation was to call ethnohistory, figured only minimally
(if at all) in the investigative process. Tax's essay drew, in the fashion

4. Ibid., 427–31.
5. Ibid., 444.

and training of the times, almost exclusively on field observation. Indeed, one of a mere three footnotes informs the reader that his analysis is based "on sixteen months' field work."[6]

More serious contemplation, if not explicitly of *municipio* origins then at least about Maya cultural evolution in general, begins with a pivotal essay published by Oliver La Farge in 1940.[7] Since then, the topic has been addressed by a number of scholars, not without generating marked differences of opinion. La Farge concedes that his formulation is based on little historical research, is derived mostly from firsthand knowledge of one remote part of the Maya realm, and is best considered "guesswork" to be challenged and revised rather than an absolute "truth" to be defended and upheld.[8] He attributes a good many features of contemporary Maya culture to "a new tide of intervention in Indian life" that occurred in the late nineteenth century under the banner of liberal reform, a conclusion with which David McCreery finds himself in agreement.[9] La Farge's reckoning is also supported by the work of Robert Wasserstrom, who writes that Maya communities in central Chiapas "remained quite homogeneous in both their internal structure and their position within the colonial order." Wasserstrom goes so far as to assert that "only after independence, it seems, and in fact toward the end of the nineteenth century, did such towns acquire the distinct ethnic identities which later fired the imaginations of anthropologists."[10]

In contrast to these views, Charles Wagley suggests that the *municipio* may represent nothing less than "a continuation of the basic societal unit" of preconquest times.[11] For Chiapas, Wagley's speculation is bolstered by the findings of George Collier, who contends that Maya communities there "endured as ethnic entities throughout the colonial period to modern times, often with significant continuities in their internal organization."[12]

Perhaps the most celebrated rumination on Maya cultural development is Eric Wolf's notion of the closed corporate peasant community, touched on in our previous chapter. His ideas were first put forward as

6. Ibid., 425.
7. La Farge (1940).
8. Ibid., 282.
9. McCreery (1990; 1994).
10. Wasserstrom (1983, 6).
11. Wagley (1969, 55).
12. Collier (1975,157).

a theoretical proposition, then fleshed out in narrative, empirical form, and subsequently (decades later) revisited as an intellectual construct that Wolf himself felt the need to clarify.[13] Wolf initially thought of Mesoamerican communities as having originated under conditions of cultural refuge from a fusion in the course of the seventeenth century of indigenous and European ways. He argued that such communities evolved so as to guarantee "a measure of communal jurisdiction over land" and in order to "restrict their membership, maintain a religious system, enforce mechanisms which ensure the redistribution or destruction of surplus wealth, and uphold barriers against the entry of goods and ideas produced outside the community."[14] The closed corporate peasant community, Wolf believed, is not so much "an offspring of conquest" as the result of "the dualization of society into a dominant entrepreneurial sector and a dominated sector of native peasants."[15] While the socio-spatial characteristics of the closed corporate peasant community obviously have undergone "great changes since the time it was first constituted," Wolf believed that "its essential features are still visible."[16]

For Carol Smith, the concept of *municipio* and the notion of closed corporate peasant communities are inextricably linked, if not synonymous. She writes:

> In the western highlands the classic form of the closed corporate peasant community gradually emerged around the *municipio*. The *municipio* was not an indigenous institution, nor did it closely resemble any indigenous institution. It was a colonial administrative unit—the lowest-level political unit and the unit subject to tribute and labor levies. The *municipio* was also the lowest-level unit in which the Spanish clergy operated. As many have noted, then, this community, centered on the *municipio*, was a novel structure, meeting the needs of both the colonial administration and the peasants subject to that administration.[17]

While Smith acknowledges the importance of *municipios*, she observes also that their emergence "did not eliminate other, more elementary,

13. Wolf (1957; 1959, 203–56; and 1986).
14. Wolf (1957, 6).
15. Ibid., 8.
16. Wolf (1959, 214–15).
17. C. A. Smith (1984, 198–99).

units" known as *parcialidades*.[18] Smith advances the idea that *municipios* were composed of several *parcialidades*, which she defines as "endogamous kindreds holding rights to corporate property and usually ranked in relation to each other."[19] She suggests, furthermore, that *parcialidades* were "rarely recognized by the colonial or other Guatemalan states" and that, as social units dating back to preconquest times, they experienced throughout history "a more stable existence" than did *municipios*.[20]

TOWARD RECONCILIATION

All these views, it seems to us, have varying degrees of applicability and worth. Most certainly, all explain or illuminate certain aspects of Maya settlement and culture. No one single proposition, however, can possibly fit every case of how Maya communities were forged. What is needed, we feel, is greater sensitivity on the part of researchers to the temporal and geographical specificity of their findings. A statement Carl Sauer made decades ago continues to apply. "Good regional geography," he wrote, "is finely representational art,"[21] by which we take him to champion attention to detail while not shying away from measured and meaningful generalization.

The term "municipio" may have come into circulation during colonial times, but our archival sources have yet to confirm that. Its adoption as formal administrative rhetoric more definitely dates to the nineteenth century.[22] It belongs, in other words, more to independence than to imperial parlance. The *municipio*, therefore, was not a "colonial administrative unit," as Carol Smith would have us believe. During the colonial period what we identify today as *municipios* were called "pueblos de indios" or simply "pueblos"—"Indian towns" or simply "towns" in the territorial

18. Ibid., 199.
19. Ibid., 199.
20. Ibid., 200.
21. Sauer ([1956] 1963, 403). Wolf (1986, 326) may have had Sauer's very words in mind when he was taking stock of "the vicissitudes of the closed corporate peasant community," for he notes "that the overly generalized interpretations of the mid-1950s need to be qualified by much variation both in geographical space and in historical time."
22. Gall (1978, vol. 2, 707).

sense defined above.[23] Most of these "towns" were founded as units of settlement in the sixteenth century by members of the regular and secular clergy engaged in the evangelizing mission of *congregación*. Adriaan van Oss estimates that "by 1600 more than three hundred towns and villages had been founded and subjected to the church, representing about two-thirds of all towns founded during the entire colonial period."[24] He records ninety-five "towns" in existence by about 1555 (table 2). However, a well-known archival source—the *tasaciones de tributos*, or tribute assessments, compiled between 1548 and 1551 by President Alonso López de Cerrato—suggests that this number was likely closer to 150 (table 3).

The tribute assessments Cerrato carried out, which we examine in detail in chapter 10, reveal two correlations relevant to our discussion. First, throughout the assessments the term "pueblo" is equated with the term "encomienda," the latter being a system of taxation by which individual Spaniards or the royal treasury received tribute, in goods and services, from designated native communities (see chapter 6 for elaboration). Recipients of tribute, known as *encomenderos*, traded *encomiendas* and made deals relating to them as if they were titles of property, not titles of privilege.[25] While, in principle, the *encomienda* had nothing to do with land or landholding—it was conceived as an institution of economic exploitation, not a territorial construct—in actual practice *encomiendas* took on geographical characteristics. Indians were identified as living within *encomienda* boundaries and so, over time, *encomiendas* came to be thought of as spatial units as well as alienable entitlements.

A second correlation is significant. Of the 150 pueblos or *encomiendas* that conform to the 170 assessments made by Cerrato, almost all of those identifiable as Guatemalan settlements are today *municipios* (table 3). Place names may differ in spelling, then to now, but present-day

23. Martínez Peláez ([1970] 2009, 225–73).
24. Van Oss (1986, 45). His efforts to map town foundation and the establishment of parish administration are most worthy, but Luján Muñoz (2011, 121–23) charts the process into the seventeenth and eighteenth centuries much more effectively. Luján Muñoz himself (2003, 53) subscribes to a slightly different periodization, reckoning that "by 1555 to 1560, save for isolated instances, the foundational cycle of *pueblos de indios* had run its course, even though the rationale behind it, so alien to indigenous culture, had to be constantly enforced." See also Sáenz de Santa María (1972).
25. See, among many examples, an item of correspondence in AGI, Justicia 285, which relates to an exchange of *encomienda* privileges in the 1530s between Antón de Morales and Cristóbal Salvatierra.

nomenclature is discernible in past variations. Archival evidence thus indicates that about one-third of all Guatemalan *municipios* can be traced back at least to the mid-sixteenth century, registered as *encomiendas* by Cerrato. When the population of Guatemala began to grow dramatically in the late nineteenth century, Guatemalan law made it possible for any inhabited place with two hundred people or more to qualify for *municipio* status.[26] This development occurred during a period when liberal desires to transform Guatemala into a "coffee republic" triggered unprecedented seizure of indigenous land and led to intensive exploitation of indigenous labor.[27] *Municipios* that were created or reconstituted in this way—that is, in response to demographic pressure and state intrusion—may be why La Farge, McCreery, and Wasserstrom, among others, favor the late nineteenth century over preceding times as the crucial period in community genesis. Certainly by the time the first national census was carried out in 1880, a total of 323 *municipios* had come into existence.[28]

It is possible, then, to correlate *municipios* in Guatemala with *pueblos de indios* that were held in *encomienda* as far back as the sixteenth century. But what guided imperial logic to create *pueblos de indios* in the first place? Might certain settlement features of preconquest Guatemala have affected what *pueblos de indios* in colonial Guatemala came to look like, and how they operated as social communities? Answers to these questions, and further discussion of the debates outlined earlier, lie in appreciating the dynamics of *congregación*.

CONGREGACIÓN AND COMMUNITY

By the mid-sixteenth century, Spanish hegemony put Maya peoples in Guatemala under increased pressure to conform to imperial designs and expectations. A fundamental element in the Hispanic vision of empire was to organize space and control population movement by the establishment of *pueblos de indios*. Begun in earnest in the 1540s, *congregación* brought together scattered groups of often no more than

26. See Solombrino Orozco (1982, 28), pertaining to a decree passed by the legislative assembly of Guatemala on September 28, 1836. For population trends in Guatemala from earliest times to the present, see Lovell and Lutz (1994).

27. See Cambranes ([1985] 1996) and McCreery (1994).

28. *Censo nacional de población* (1880).

a dozen households, resettled them away from their old mountain homes in church-dominated centers, and converted them to Christianity.[29] The language of the project at times borders perilously on the romantic, as the following extract from the Laws of the Indies illustrates:

> With great care and particular attention we have always attempted to impose the most convenient means of instructing the Indians in the Holy Catholic Faith and the evangelical law, causing them to forget their ancient erroneous rites and ceremonies and to live in concert and order. . . . [S]o that this might be brought about, those of our Council of [the] Indies have met together several times with other religious persons . . . and they, with the desire of promoting the service of God, and ours, resolved that the Indians should be reduced to villages and not be allowed to live divided and separated in the mountain and wildernesses, where they are deprived of all spiritual and temporal comforts, the aid of our ministers, and those other things which human necessities oblige men to give one to another. . . . [V]iceroys, presidents, and governors [are] therefore charged and ordered to execute the reduction, settlement, and indoctrination of the Indians.[30]

The *pueblos de indios* created by *congregación*, as the former term makes explicit, were supposed to be *Indian* communities, from which all non-Indians, save for a few Crown officials, were banned. Why segregation was deemed necessary is again spelled out in the Laws of the Indies:

> Spaniards, negroes, mulattoes, and mestizos are prohibited from living in reductions and Indian villages, for experience has shown that certain Spaniards who deal with Indians, or who live and move among them, are troublesome individuals, being thieves, rogues, and gamblers, people given to doing no good, who cause the Indians, harmed and offended, to take flight and abandon their towns and territories. Furthermore, negroes, mulattoes, and mestizos, besides treating Indians badly, make use of them, setting a poor example, exhibiting unwholesome customs and idleness, as well as other faults and vices, all of which can corrupt and pervert the goals we desire concerning their advancement, salvation, and repose.[31]

29. Martínez Peláez ([1970] 2009: 225–73).
30. As rendered by Simpson (1934, 43).
31. *Recopilación de las leyes de los reynos de las Indias* ([1681] 1973, vol. 3, 200). This four-volume edition of the Laws of the Indies makes fascinating reading.

Indians not only were required to live segregated from non-Indians but also were supposed to live in self-contained groups, each "reduction" in theory constituting a single, ethnically homogeneous unit. The Laws of the Indies, once more, are quite explicit:

> We command that in the Indian villages there shall be no Indian from another reduction, on pain of a hundred lashes, and the *cacique* [lord] shall give four pesos to the church each time he permits it. In consideration of how important it is that Indians shall not live outside their reductions, we order and command that the governors, judges, and justices of every province shall not give permission for it, except in some rare case, such as that of an orphan, on pain of three years' suspension from office and a fine of five hundred ducats. . . . [J]udges [are to ensure that] Indians . . . be returned to their villages at the expense of the guilty.[32]

From the *Memorial de Solalá* we have firsthand Maya evidence of *congregación* in action:

> During the eighth month after the landslide [September 11, 1541] there came to our church the Fathers of Santo Domingo, Fray Pedro de Angulo and Fray Juan de Torres. They arrived from Mexico on the day 12 Batz [February 10, 1542]. The Fathers of Santo Domingo began our instruction. The Doctrine appeared in our language. Our fathers Fray Pedro and Fray Juan were the first who preached the word of God to us. Up to that time we did not know the word nor the commandments of God; we had lived in utter darkness. No one had preached the word of God to us.[33]

The Kaqchikel chronicle continues:

> In the fifth month of the sixth year after the beginning of our instruction in the word of Our Lord God, the houses were grouped together by order of [Governor] Juan Roser [Rogel]. Then the people came from the caves and the ravines. On the day 7 Caok [October 30, 1547] this city [Tzololá] was founded, and all of the tribes were here.[34]

32. As rendered by Simpson (1934, 45).
33. As rendered by Recinos and Goetz (1953, 134–35).
34. As rendered by Recinos and Goetz (1953, 136).

Conversion may have been the spiritual motive behind *congregación*, but *pueblos de indios* were not created solely to instruct people who "had lived in utter darkness"—they also helped Crown officials and *encomenderos* collect tribute and functioned as centralized pools of labor which, controlled effectively, could be drawn upon for all sorts of ends. Severo Martínez Peláez asserts bluntly that, institutionally, *pueblos de indios* were "prison camps with municipal functions."[35] Of all the ventures jointly orchestrated by the Church and the state, few more than *congregación* reflect the symbolic interplay of the cross and the sword.

It is difficult even to estimate how many native families were caught up in the process of *congregación*. The Cerrato *tasaciones*, carried out while *congregación* was still in progress, pertain to many of the *pueblos de indios* that had been founded by 1548–51, focusing on what goods and services the Indians living in them were required to provide. As demographic indicators, however, these tribute records are highly problematic (see chapter 10). Conservatively, at least forty to fifty thousand indigenous households, perhaps one-quarter of a million people, must have moved from one location to another over the preceding five or six years.

That Indians *had* to be moved, either by persuasion or by force, was something the bickering factions within the colonial regime could agree upon: native settlement patterns in the highlands were decidedly more dispersed than nucleated, with what little urbanization as had developed prior to the arrival of the Spaniards restricted usually to defensive, hilltop locations, not the least conducive to efficient administration and at odds with Spanish notions of civilized town life.[36] Our knowledge of preconquest living arrangements is still scant, but from the work of Robert Carmack on the K'iche' we have evidence of a social structure that was, in his words, "a complicated integration of rank, descent, territoriality, hierarchy, and quadrachotomies."[37] Within this rather elaborate configuration, one unit—the *chinamit*—has emerged as more important than any other in grasping how Maya families who were "congregated" in *pueblos de indios* successfully engaged in what Nancy Farriss calls acts of "strategic acculturation."[38]

35. Martínez Peláez ([1970] 2009, 231).
36. Borhegyi (1965).
37. Carmack (1977, 6).
38. Farriss (1983, 34).

Chinamitales, which Spaniards referred to as *parcialidades* or *calpules*, have been identified by Robert Hill and John Monaghan as exhibiting four main socio-spatial characteristics:

First, they held land and other natural resources (water, forests, salt wells) as a corporate unit, with members occupying a shared and well-defined territory or space. Second, each *chinamit* was an endogamous group, with membership based on birth in the group. Third, members of *chinamitales* assumed collective responsibility for individual actions or deeds. And fourth, members of a *chinamit* took part, according to their age and gender, in group-defined economic specialization.[39] Judith Maxwell and Robert Hill state that "[t]wo or more *chinamitales . . .* commonly confederated themselves in an *amaq',*" thereby occupying "contiguous territories" and "making peaceful alliances practical and beneficial" at a higher level of sociopolitical organization.[40]

Like Hill and Monaghan, whose thinking on the matter clearly influenced Carol Smith, we consider the importance of the *chinamit*, or *parcialidad*, to be underestimated. Focusing attention on the *parcialidad*, to employ the Spanish designation, allows us to examine the success or failure of *congregación* as first, a process of imposed cultural change, and second, a process of displacement and resettlement. Such a focus also enables us to reconsider the applicability of Wolf's portrayal of the Mesoamerican peasant community as both "corporate" and "closed."

Unfamiliarity on the part of missionaries with the discrete nature of *parcialidades* often resulted in several of them being brought together in the hope of forming a single *pueblo de indios*. Once gathered at the site of a *congregación*, however, unrelated *parcialidades* often preserved their aboriginal identity by continuing to operate socially and economically as separate components rather than merging to form one unified body. Far from being the placid, harmonious entities that the Laws of the Indies conjure up, many *pueblos de indios* turned out to be a mosaic of *parciali-dades* that touched but did not interpenetrate, that coexisted but did not always cooperate. In the province of Totonicapán and Huehuetenango alone, a seventeenth-century source records nine *pueblos de indios* being made up of some thirty-one *parcialidades*, each of which was assessed

39. Hill and Monaghan (1987, 24–42).
40. Maxwell and Hill (2006, 4). Beyond the *chinamit* and the *amaq'* was the *winäq*, "the highest level of late pre-contact socio-political organization in the Maya highlands," the equivalent of a "people" or "nation" in English.

individually for purposes of paying tribute (table 4). Scores of other *pueblos de indios* were organized internally in this same fashion, too many not to call into question Wolf's assertion that *parcialidades*, some of which survive to this day, "remain the fascinating exception to the general rule that territoriality in one community and common participation in communal life have long since robbed such units of any separatist jurisdiction they may at one time have exercised."[41]

Closer examination of what took place in one specific *pueblo de indios* throws into even sharper relief just how different the outcome of *congregación* could be from what clergy and bureaucrats originally conceived. The case of Sacapulas, a town founded in the highland periphery, may not be entirely representative, but it is instructive.

PARCIALIDAD AND PUEBLO: THE CASE OF SACAPULAS

Sacapulas, today a *municipio* in the department of El Quiché, lies on the south bank of the Río Negro or Chixoy, a river to the north of which rise, covered in thorny chaparral and cactus, the front ranges of the Sierra de los Cuchumatanes. Archaeological investigations undertaken by Ledyard Smith show the area to have been occupied on the eve of Spanish conquest in typical protohistoric fashion. Several fortified hilltop sites, home of the elite, defended the land around and below, where the common people lived, hunted, and farmed.[42] These sites, Hill and Monaghan contend, can be associated singly or in combination with a particular *amaq'* or certain *parcialidades*.[43]

Contradictions in the documentary record make it difficult to determine exactly when Sacapulas came into existence in its early colonial form. Francis Gall, citing the *Popol Vuh*, informs us that Sacapulas was once called Lamak or Tuhal and that, prior to Spanish arrival, it lay some twenty-eight kilometers northeast of its present location at a place called Magdalena.[44] Warfare and destruction, another source tells us, resulted in people being displaced from Magdalena and relocated, sometime after 1530, in four different *pueblos de indios*—Chalchitán, Cunén, Uspantán,

41. Wolf (1959, 220).
42. A. L. Smith (1955).
43. Hill and Monaghan (1987, 63–75).
44. Gall (1983, vol. 3, 135). See also Recinos (1950b, 171).

and Sacapulas.[45] Writing in the late seventeenth century, Francisco Vázquez claimed that Sacapulas and many other *pueblos de indios* were established, from 1545 on, by the Franciscan missionary Gonzalo Méndez.[46] An eighteenth-century chronicler, Francisco Ximénez, mentions that Méndez was responsible for "converting to the Catholic Faith" two groups that later formed part of Sacapulas: the *parcialidades* San Francisco and Santo Tomás.[47] Writing in the early seventeenth century, Antonio de Remesal records that Fray Gonzalo worked throughout the area until about 1553, when Dominicans asserted ecclesiastical authority over their Franciscan counterparts by building a convent at Sacapulas that served as the administrative hub of all Dominican proselytism for the next hundred years.[48]

Sacapulas was shared in two equal parts by *encomenderos* for much of the sixteenth century. Our earliest record of it as an *encomienda* is 1534, when Antón de Morales exchanged his right to half the tribute of Sacapulas for one-half that of Acasaguastlán, a *pueblo de indios* lying some two hundred kilometers to the east.[49] In Cerrato's time, fifteen years or so later, Cristóbal de Salvatierra and Alonso Páez each received tribute payments, mostly locally produced salt, from eighty heads of households, indicative of a total population of perhaps eight hundred people.[50] The two *encomenderos* did not get along, either with each other or with Cerrato. Their complaints against Cerrato had to do with the measures he took to curb *encomendero* abuse. Salvatierra, described unflatteringly in one document as a "ladrón" and "bebedor de sangre"—a "thief" and "drinker of blood"—was a vociferous critic of the reformist president; Páez, for his part, claimed that Cerrato's intervention had decreased the worth of his share of Sacapulas, along with that of three other *pueblos de indios*, to a paltry 150 pesos per year.[51] Prior to the Cerrato reforms, Indian tributaries were required to haul loads of salt from Sacapulas one hundred kilometers southeast, over rugged terrain, to Santiago

45. "Títulos territoriales de Chalchitán y Aguacatán," cited in Gall (1983, vol. 3, 135).
46. Vázquez ([1688–95] 1938, vol. 2, 32).
47. Ximénez ([1715–20] 1929, vol. 1, 191).
48. Remesal ([1619] 1966, vol. 2, 259–61).
49. AGI, Justicia 285, "Pleito sobre el pueblo de Acasaguastlán" (1564).
50. AGI, Guatemala 128, "Las tasaciones de los pueblos de los términos y jurisdicción de la ciudad de Santiago de Guatemala" (1548–51), fol. 71.
51. AGI, Justicia 301, "Residencia de Alonso López de Cerrato" (1555) and Patronato 68-2-3, "Información de los méritos y servicios de Juan Páez " (1568).

de Guatemala, where their *encomenderos* resided. This service was commuted on January 13, 1550, to an annual levy of fourteen *xiquipiles* of cacao.[52] Meeting this demand, however, also entailed a long and exhausting trek, for the principal cacao source closest to Sacapulas lay in the *tierra caliente* of Suchitepéquez far to the south.

The most striking social feature about Sacapulas was its marked and persistent heterogeneity. Passing through town in 1631, Captain Martín Alfonso Tovilla observed:

> The pueblo of Sacapulas is divided into six *parcialidades*, each of which constitutes a unit known as a *calpul*. When the missionaries congregated them, as each had only a small population, they brought four or five [*parcialidades*] to each pueblo in order to create a larger [settlement]. In this way each *parcialidad* maintained the name of the place it came from. And the lands that they possessed they still cultivate today in order to grow corn and meet other [subsistence] needs.[53]

Over a century and a half later, Tovilla's observation was validated by Andrés Henríquez, then serving in Sacapulas as parish priest. In connection with litigation over land rights and boundaries, Henríquez testified in 1786 that the *parcialidad* known as Magdalena, "like the other five of this pueblo was, and were, small settlements congregated by royal order to form the pueblo of Sacapulas."[54] By sifting through the archival records that relate to Sacapulas, Hill and Monaghan have been able to correlate preconquest *chinamitales* with congregated *parcialidades* that functioned as distinct intra-community units throughout the colonial period and beyond (table 5).

The earliest evidence we have that *congregación* at Sacapulas did not result in the social "melting pot" espoused by imperial rhetoric dates to 1572, when the six *parcialidades* split along *amaq'* lines into two rival

---

52. AGI, Guatemala 128, "Las tasaciones de los pueblos de los términos y jurisdicción de la ciudad de Santiago de Guatemala" (fol. 71). A *xiquipil* is a measure of 8,000 cacao beans.

53. Tovilla ([ca.1635] 1960, 218). The Spanish text reads: "Está este pueblo de Çacapulas dividido en seis parcialidades, y en cada una de ellas hay una cabeza a que llaman calpul . . . porque cuando los padres los juntaron, como ellos tenían pequeñas poblaciones, traían cuatro o cinco a cada pueblo que hacían para que fuese grande, y así cada parcialidad de aquellas se quedó con el nombre del pueblo de donde vinieron. Y las tierras que tenían por suyas las gozan hoy y gozarán para hacer sus milpas y demás menesteres."

54. AGCA, A1, leg. 6037, exp. 53258.

factions self-identified as "foreigners" and "natives." At issue, primarily, was the running of the pueblo's horse herd, but other related concerns soon arose. Three "foreign" *parcialidades*—the Coatecas, Sitaltecas, and Zacualpanecas—lobbied for (1) division and control of community funds, (2) the right to elect their own civil representatives, and (3) legal recognition that the lands they had been moved from still belonged to them.[55] Concessions on all counts suggest that Indians learned, early on, how to lobby successfully in a court of law. Equally important is to recognize that the colonial regime could, and in this case actually did, accommodate native preferences, even when they clashed with other plainly stated imperial objectives.

The supremacy of *parcialidad* over pueblo at Sacapulas continued throughout the seventeenth century, with each social group responsible for paying its own tribute.[56] So long as the stipulated amounts were furnished on schedule, allowing tribute to be paid by *parcialidad* likely mattered little to Spanish recipients. Much more problematic, however, was the arrangement whereby *parcialidades* held and operated land. Toward the end of the colonial period, when the population began to grow, it was inevitable that land disputes would take on a *parcialidad*-versus-*parcialidad* dimension.

The last quarter of the eighteenth century was a time of bitter feuding at Sacapulas, with each *parcialidad* seeking to maximize control over land in the immediate vicinity of the pueblo (table 6 and map 2). Spanish attempts to resolve the conflict only exacerbated it, since certain proposals ignored traditional divisions and allocations. Particularly controversial was the proposal to redistribute resources so as to place the salt works owned by *parcialidades* Santiago and San Sebastián within the confines of the *ejido*, or common land, and thus also at the disposal of rival neighbors. The people of Santiago and San Sebastián objected to the plan and entered into litigation (in the end successfully) to guard the salt works against all encroachment, but especially from *parcialidad* San Pedro.[57] The *parcialidad* San Francisco also became embroiled in a long legal tussle with Santo Tomás, primarily over efforts by the

55. AGCA, Al, leg. 5942, exp. 51995.
56. AGI, Contaduría 815, "Razón de las ciudades, villas y lugares vecindarios y tributarios de que se componen las provincias del distrito de esta Audiencia" (1683) and AGCA, A3.16, leg. 1601, exp. 26391.
57. AGCA, Al, leg. 6025, exp. 53126 and Al, leg. 6037, exp. 53257.

latter to limit the access of the former to fertile irrigable land in the Río Negro valley.[58]

Wolf's "corporate" delineation of community, then, does not fit the splintered case of Sacapulas, nor that of many other Guatemalan communities established as *pueblos de indios* as a result of *congregación*. Elías Zamora is most insistent on the point, stating categorically that "pueblo and community were not analogous concepts. In most instances, *parcialidad* descent structures defined the limits within which each Indian perceived community to lie, considering members of other descent groups as strangers even though they lived in the same pueblo."[59]

Just as notions about the "corporate" nature of community need to be reconsidered, so also does our thinking about how "closed" *pueblos de indios* must have been, as territorial units at any rate. Highland pueblos on the Pacific side of the continental divide were often formally associated with "estancias" or "rancherías" in the piedmont zone some distance below. These lowland settlements were considered an integral part of the community, where perhaps only a few families resided permanently. All *pueblos de indios*, under colonial law, were entitled to a communal allocation of land, the *ejido*. As well as working *ejido* land, which usually lay close to the pueblo center, Indians returned to plant fields farther away in the hills and mountains near the dwellings they had been moved from. Tovilla commented on this tendency when he passed through Sacapulas early in the seventeenth century, but the movement back and forth, by then, must have been long-established practice. Returning to grow corn on ancestral land not only made good agricultural sense; it also served to lessen the impact of acculturation in new places of residence by affirming important ties with old ones. This behavior would eventually see settlement patterns in the countryside preserve their "dispersed" preconquest essence while at the same time taking on a "congregated" conquest appearance. Few Spaniards understood native habits in this way, but two exceptions were the Dominican friars Tomás de Cárdenas and Juan de Torres, whose eyewitness account of *congregación* furnishes unique insights into the process.

58. AGCA, A1, leg. 6021, exp. 53084; A1, leg. 6060, exp. 53305; and A1, leg. 6042, exp. 53327.
59. Zamora (1985, 171). He states: "[D]urante el primer siglo de la colonia, pueblo y comunidad no eran conceptos análogos. En la mayoría de las ocasiones las estructuras de parentesco definían los límites dentro de los cuales cada indígena percibía su *comunidad*, considerando a los miembros de los demás grupos de parentesco como extraños aunque habitaran en el mismo pueblo."

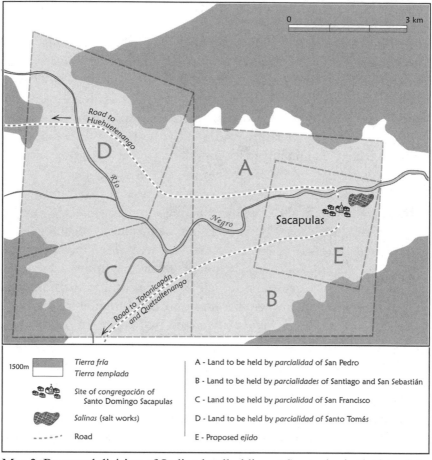

MAP 2. Proposed division of Indian landholding at Sacapulas in the late eighteenth century. Source: Archivo General de Centro América, A1, leg. 6025, exp. 53126, and leg. 6040, exp. 53305; Lovell [1985] 2005, 136.

On December 6, 1555, Cárdenas and Torres wrote to King Charles V from the Dominican convent at Sacapulas to express their views on a number of matters, among them the tremendous obstacles working against effective *congregación* in the area for which they were responsible. They speak of difficulties imposed by the physical environment, pointing out that "this part of the sierra is among the most rugged and broken to be found in these lands, where there were settlements of only eight, six and even four houses and huts tucked and hidden away in gullies and ravines where, until the arrival of one of us, no other Spaniard had reached."[60] While conducting missionary work earlier that year, the friars had stumbled across "idols in abundance, not just concealed but placed out in the open as they had them before they were baptized."[61] The friars are of one mind about the play of forces they were up against. "What is certain," they remark stiffly, "is that Indians would never have tried to do this had it not been for their confidence in the ruggedness of the terrain, thinking that no one could reach there who might disturb or destroy their evil living."[62] To critics who observe that *congregación* is conducted forcibly, that it shifts families from one place to another against their will, the friars contend that "there is no sick person who does not find the taste of medicine unpleasant."[63] In this sense Indians are "like children" and so "one must do not what pleases them but what is best for them."[64] Cárdenas and Torres cut to the quick of the matter when they comment on why native families might resist and resent being resettled: "Among all these Indians," they declare, "there is not one who wishes to leave behind the hut passed on to him by his father, nor to abandon a pestilential ravine, or desert some inaccessible craggy rocks, because that is where the bones of his forefathers rest."[65]

DE-CONGREGATION, DISPERSAL, AND FUGITIVISM

The words of the friars, suffused with foreboding, intimate that the work they are engaged in, and the grand vision of which it forms part, will in the end amount to little. Certainly Pedro Ramírez de Quiñones, a high-ranking Crown official, was under no illusions when he wrote to the Council of the Indies a year after Cárdenas and Torres had voiced their concerns:

60. AGI, Guatemala 168, Fray Tomás de Cárdenas and Fray Juan de Torres to the Crown (December 6, 1555). The friars write: "[P]orque aquel pedazo de sierra es de lo más fragoso y áspero que hay en estas tierras, donde había poblaciones de hasta ocho y seis y aun de cuatro casas o chozas, metidos y escondidos por las barrancas donde hasta uno de nosotros ningún otro español aportó."

61. Ibid., the precise words of the friars being, "muy grande copia de ídolos, no sólo escondidos pero en públicas casas como los que tenían antes que fuesen baptizados."

62. Ibid., the friars declaring that "nadie aportaba allá que les pudiese perjudicar ni estorbar su mal vivir."

63. Ibid., the friars asserting that "no hay enfermo a quien las medicinas no sepan mal."

64. Ibid. "Son como niños," is how the friars word it, "y como tales cumple hacer no lo que más les agrada sino lo que más les cumple."

65. Ibid. Cárdenas and Torres state: "[E]ntre todos estos indios ninguno hay que quiera dejar la casilla que su padre le dejó, ni salirse de una pestilencial barranca o de entre unos riscos inaccesibles, porque allí tienen los huesos de sus abuelos."

There is great disorder among the Indians in matters that relate to their government and administration. Things are chaotic, lacking proper direction. Grave public sins abound. What is most of concern is that their actions go unpunished, without redress, because they are not brought to the attention of the *audiencia*. In most *pueblos de indios* people live much as they wish to, or can, and since the *audiencia* cannot arrange for visitations to be made, we, its officers, cannot vouch for one-tenth of the territory over which we have been placed in charge.[66]

From the native leaders of Santiago Atitlán, held accountable not only for the actions of pueblo residents but also for those of people living in outlying *estancias*, we hear of "rebellious Indians" in the latter settlements "who wish to remain outside our authority and who disobey our orders concerning what tribute should be paid."[67] The *principales* and *caciques* of the pueblo were giving testimony in 1571. Similarly, the years between 1575 and 1578 witnessed "many Indians" near Santiago de Guatemala "move about, in hiding, from one place to another," a strategy they resorted to "in order to avoid paying not just their own tribute but also that part deemed still to be owed by deceased relatives."[68] Around the same time, there was talk of the virtual disintegration of *congregación* in parts of the Verapaz, where "*parcialidades* and entire families leave to live idolatrously in the mountains."[69] Two sizable *pueblos de indios*—Santa Catalina and San Lucas Zulbén—were said to have been abandoned almost completely by 1579, only five years after the Bishop of Verapaz himself had supervised the process of *congregación*. At Santa María Cahabón, formerly congregated Indians abandoned

66. AGI, Guatemala 9A, Pedro Ramírez de Quiñones to the Council of the Indies (May 20, 1556). The Spanish text reads: "[E]n los pueblos de los naturales hay gran desorden en lo que toca a la policía. Hay muy poca orden entre ellos, ni justicia. Pecados públicos hay entre ellos muy grandes. Y lo más es que son sin castigo, porque no viene a noticia de la audiencia. En los más pueblos de indios viven cada uno como quiere o como puede y como la audiencia no puede enviar visitadores no pueden cumplir de visitar la décima parte del distrito."

67. AGI, Guatemala 53, *Principales* and *caciques* of Santiago Atitlán to the Crown (February 1, 1571). The Spanish text reads: "[H]ay en nuestras estancias algunos yndios rebeldes que quieren estar fuera de nuestra subjeción y no obedecer nuestros mandamientos en recojer el tributo."

68. AGI, Guatemala 10, President Pedro de Villalobos to the Crown (October 5, 1575) and Fiscal Eugenio de Salazar to the Crown (March 15, 1578).

69. AGI, Guatemala 163, Fray Antonio de Hervias, Bishop of Verapaz, to the Crown (1583). His exact words are "que se ivan las parcialidades y familias enteras a los montes y tierras de ynfieles a vivir y idolatrar."

tributary life altogether and settled among unconquered Lacandón and Chol Manché groups on the other side of the frontier.[70]

A century or so later, after the Bishop of Guatemala, Andrés de las Navas, had twice toured his jurisdiction and heard disturbing reports from parish priests about lawlessness, idolatry, and tribute evasion, he prepared a thick dossier that leaves little doubt about how much the grip of *congregación* had become undone. One entry from it is particularly concise. Not far from San Juan Sacatepéquez it was reported that Indian families "who neither hear Mass nor confess their sins" had lived in makeshift settlements called *pajuides* "for upward of twenty years, dwelling there under the pretext of growing corn."[71] Calls by the authorities to re-congregate such wayward folk met with few lasting results. Native families drifted away from the *pueblos de indios* they were supposed to inhabit, a drift that was triggered and sustained by a mix of cultural preference, ecological sense, and material circumstance.

If it is difficult to estimate the numbers involved in the centripetal thrust of *congregación*, it is impossible to approximate how many took part afterwards in the decision (for whatever reason) to abandon their designated *pueblos de indios*. Certainly by the late seventeenth century, centrifugal movement had been significant enough that Fuentes y Guzmán could write with persistent exasperation of "wild and uncivilized" Indians occupying secluded areas some distance from town centers.[72] When he drew a map of the Corregimiento of Totonicapán and Huehuetenango, the chronicler saw fit not only to locate on it some forty different *pueblos de indios* but also to depict numerous satellite "ranchos" where native families lived far removed from the greedy clutches of *encomenderos* and the watchful eyes of parish priests (figure 1). Fuentes y Guzmán's view of spatial and cultural dissolution was echoed toward the end of the eighteenth century by Archbishop Pedro Cortés y Larraz in his aptly named "moral-geographic" description. "Because Indians live like fugitives in the mountains," he bemoaned when writing about Nebaj,

70. AGI, Guatemala 51, Francisco de Miranda to the Crown (March 1579) and Guatemala 163, Juan Fernández Rosillo, Bishop of Verapaz, to the Crown (March 20, 1600).

71. AGI, Guatemala 159, Bishop Andrés de las Navas, et al., "Testimonio de los autos hechos sobre la perdición general de los indios de estas provincias y frangentes continuos que amenazan su libertad" (1689).

72. Fuentes y Guzmán ([1690–99] 1972, vol. 3, 26). The chronicler singles out the "indios agrestes y montaraces" of San Juan Atitán.

FIGURE 1. *Corregimiento* of Totonicapán and Huehuetenango (Fuentes y Guzmán, 1690–99).

116

"all sorts of wrongs occur."[73] The situation was no better in Huehue-tenango, where the archbishop reckoned, "not even one in three families may be considered town residents."[74] In the parish of Cuilco, Cortés y Larraz notes wearily, "very few families live in towns and almost all out in the wilderness among their cornfields, which is what Indians prefer, to dwell alone in the mountains."[75]

Geographically, then, Maya communities in colonial Guatemala were often disparate and non-contiguous, seldom compact and neatly bounded. Physically and symbolically, their centers may have been identi-fiable in the form of church towers rising above Christian burial grounds, as rendered cartographically in the scores of maps accompanying both Fuentes y Guzmán's and Cortés y Larraz's (figure 2) vivid reports. Beyond the confines of a central Spanish grid, however, their edges were blurred and dissolved into more open, ancestral horizons.

THE PRESENCE OF THE PAST

Throughout highland Guatemala, a striking arrangement of towns per-sists, in each of which the presence of a Catholic church and a central plaza is conspicuous. Closer inspection reveals that towns where Mayas predominate are often divided into barrios, or districts, in which subtle differences of language, dress, occupation, or ceremonial activity may be observed. Where Ladinos are the dominant town-dwelling group, the surrounding countryside is often populated by natives living in more dispersed units of settlement. This pattern of "town nucleus" and "vacant town" municipios was very much in evidence during the first half of the twentieth century, when Sol Tax and other anthropologists were engaged in ethnographic field work. Important findings emerged from the research of Tax and his associates, but the issue of community origins and change over time was somehow overlooked.

73. Cortés y Larraz ([1768–70] 1958, vol. 2, 48). The archbishop states: "[P]or hallarse los indios fugitivos en las montañas, resultan muchos daños."
74. Cortés y Larraz ([1768–70] 1958, vol. 2, 117). The parish priest of Huehuetenango, Félix Fernando Rosel, informed the archbishop that "no existe en los pueblos aún la tercera parte de sus familias."
75. Cortés y Larraz ([1768–70] 1958, vol. 2, 137). The archbishop states: "[V]iven en los pue-blos muy pocas familias y cuasi todas en los despoblados y milperías; lo cual es conforme a la inclinación de los indios, que apetecen vivir en los montes y solos."

FIGURE 2. Parishes of Santiago Atitlán, San Pedro La Laguna, Sololá, and Panajachel (Cortés y Larraz, 1768–70). Courtesy Archivo General de Indias, Ministerio de Educación, Cultura y Deporte, Spain.

Much of what is visible in the cultural landscape reflects the workings of the idealistic mindset of imperial Spain, and native reaction to it, in colonial times. Through *congregación*, hundreds of *pueblos de indios* were created, "Indian towns" that formed the embryos of future *municipios*. These "Indian towns" came into being as "congregations" of displaced people who were resettled, by force if necessary, so that the spiritual and material goals of empire could more readily be attained. *Pueblos de indios* were not just where Maya peoples were supposed to become Christians. They were also *encomiendas*, tribute rewards for the Crown and for privileged Spaniards. While *congregación* operated at many levels as a powerful instrument of Hispanization, native subjects resisted acculturation either by flight or by regrouping within *pueblos de indios* around preconquest lineage structures referred to by Spaniards as *parcialidades*. Many of these *parcialidades* survive today as barrios in "town nucleus" *municipios*.

Colonial-period *pueblos de indios* were often heterogeneous communities that functioned, internally, quite differently from how Eric Wolf imagined them. As the findings of Anne Collins demonstrate at Jacaltenango, however, Wolf's notion of the "closed corporate peasant community" is still a useful one to bear in mind when conducting ethnohistorical research.[76] But the "corporate" nature of community must be examined critically, period by period, place by place, and not be regarded as an all-encompassing proposition. So also, at least geographically, must the "closed" dimension of community be reappraised, for the nucleation of *congregación* was followed soon thereafter by a process of dispersal in which preferences for rural, not town life, were reasserted. In repopulating the countryside, the *parcialidad* again figured prominently, this time as the key to social identity at the village or hamlet level. While the destruction wrought by civil war in the second half of the twentieth century has had a devastating impact on Maya culture and community life, age-old arrangements endure.

76. Collins (1980).

PART III

LABOR AND TRIBUTE

CHAPTER 6

THE BIRTH OF THE *ENCOMIENDA*

Communities in collision, communities in collusion. *Calpul* or *parcialidad*, barrio of a *pueblo de indios*—or the entire town itself. Pre-Columbian in essence, yet created by colonialism, above all, by the policy of *congregación*. Understanding the meaning of "community" in Guatemala is no easy matter and would not be complete without taking into account the *encomienda*, an institution that played a key role in formalizing relationships of power and consolidating conquest culture. Until quite recently, little attention had been paid to *encomienda* origins in Guatemala, even though Spaniards introduced it almost immediately as a means of controlling native populations and exploiting their resources. The history of the *encomienda* is complex, but it remained, throughout the sixteenth and seventeenth centuries, a device whereby Spaniards or their criollo offspring received tribute in labor, goods, or cash from native groups entrusted to their charge. *Encomiendas* were not grants of land but, rather, entitlements to enjoy the fruits of what the land and its people could provide, whether the fruits in question were prized items such as gold, silver, salt, and cacao or more mundane produce like corn, beans, and chili peppers.

It has long been thought that, because of unstable government and prolonged native resistance, early grants of *encomienda* in Guatemala were few in number and of little consequence. Thanks to the efforts of Wendy Kramer, we can now state that the opposite is true. The *encomienda* in Guatemala dates from 1524, the year that Pedro de Alvarado led the first incursion into lands south of Mexico. Conquest and the distribution of *encomiendas* thus went hand in hand. By 1549, when the New Laws promulgated under Charles V began to be enacted by President Alonso López de Cerrato, the *encomienda* already had a turbulent quarter-century history. Prior to Kramer's investigations, scholars of colonial Guatemala, Francisco de Solano and Salvador Rodríguez Becerra among them, focused discussion of the *encomienda* on the years of Cerrato's presidency, from 1548 to 1555.[1] This tendency may be explained by the fact that a well-known record of *encomiendas*, and the individuals who held them, dates to the time when Cerrato held office. Tribute assessments carried out earlier, in the 1530s and early 1540s, are mostly considered to be missing, except for fragments we have located sporadically over the years.

Cerrato and his assistants recorded tribute information while simultaneously seeking to moderate the amount of goods and services that *encomenderos* were supposed to receive. They did not, however, carry out a *repartimiento general*, a survey or inventory that might redistribute the spoils of conquest in an orderly, systematic fashion. Cerrato did grant some *encomiendas* and reallocated others that fell vacant after their holders died; cases like these, however, are relatively few. Unfortunately, nowhere in the tribute assessments drafted by Cerrato is there any statement as to how long a particular community, or group of communities, had been held in *encomienda*, nor by whom these awards were originally granted. However, titles to *encomiendas* held by the son or heir of a *conquistador*—a fact almost always noted—indicate the existence of earlier titles, often dating back two generations prior to Cerrato's arrival. His tribute assessments are an invaluable source for studying the *encomienda* at mid-century, but they should not be considered the beginning of the institution in Guatemala. They represent, rather, a record from which to extrapolate when reconstructing the historical geography of earlier times, a quality well recognized by John Bergmann in his innovative work on cacao cultivation.[2]

For some time now, we have searched in Spanish and Guatemalan archives for sources that contain information on the places listed in the Cerrato assessments, which record tribute information on 170 communities held in *encomienda* by ninety-three different *encomenderos* (see chapter 10). Because of political clout or favoritism, some *encomenderos* were granted two or three awards because one was deemed insufficient for their needs. Although we initially concerned ourselves with the establishment

1. Solano (1974) and Rodríguez (1977).
2. Bergmann (1958; 1969).

of *encomienda* chronologies and the elaboration of settlement histories, it became apparent that the best way to improve our knowledge of the institution was through study of individual *encomenderos*. It therefore became necessary to gather information on the family background and social connections of these recipients. All of this lured us into a labyrinth of colonial paperwork, the nature and contents of which it makes sense to discuss before summarizing our findings.

THE SOURCES

Information on *encomenderos* before Cerrato held office comes from various sources. Perhaps the most useful for our purposes are *probanzas de méritos y servicios*, documents in which conquerors or their descendants petitioned the Crown, seeking recompense for services rendered. Also very useful are *pleitos*, or lawsuits, between Spanish residents over rights to *encomienda*.[3] The correspondence of governors, treasury officials, high-ranking clergy like Bishop Francisco Marroquín, and the *cabildo* or city council of Santiago de Guatemala furnish additional data.[4] These sources yield considerable information, especially about unexplored or unsuspected aspects of what precisely the *encomienda* in Guatemala constituted prior to Cerrato's presidency. We restrict the following remarks, however, to *probanzas* and *pleitos*.

Probanzas were designed to serve either as a record for posterity or as a petition to the Crown. Social background and contribution to conquest and colonization are usually described in detail. In most cases a petitioner sought compensation for his services to the Crown in the form of an *encomienda*. Often the petitioner already held an *encomienda* and would note that he had received scant reward in consideration of his many services and the quality, or *calidad*, of his person. In some instances the petitioner, or his descendants, would argue that an *encomienda* had been unfairly removed and had been granted to a relative or follower of the governor then in charge. The petitioners, and witnesses who testified on their behalf, describe at what juncture a governor had

3. Sanchíz Ochoa (1976) makes good use of this documentation. For a critique of its strengths and weaknesses, see MacLeod (1998).
4. Sáenz de Santa María (1964) and Suñe Blanco (1984).

awarded the grant and why the grant was awarded in the first place. In addition, many *probanzas* contain information on how long an *encomienda* had been held, and whether it had been removed or reconfirmed under subsequent governors. Because the first Spanish colonists were obsessed with the prospect of acquiring supplementary or more lucrative *encomiendas, probanzas* almost always contain some reference to economic potential and, in certain instances, specific locations. By compiling a record of the names of men who received awards, as well as the places associated with them, it is possible to trace *encomienda* succession in detail and to determine what native settlements figured, over time, in the distribution process.

Governors involved in the allocation or reallocation process routinely had formal documents drawn up at the time they awarded *encomiendas*. These records, called *cédulas de encomienda*, have survived in some cases and are an additional source of information. A typical *cédula* lists the date, the name of the settlement(s) held in *encomienda*, the name of the recipient, and the name of the governor who made the award. The *cédula* was often included in legal correspondence as definitive proof that the petitioner or his heir held, or once had held, a certain settlement, or settlements, in *encomienda*. The text frequently notes the name of the person who held previous title and for what reason the *encomienda* became available for reallocation. Many *cédulas*, for example, record that *encomiendas* fell vacant because of the death or absence of the former owner, as a result of the former recipient being awarded a new, often better *encomienda*, or because the holder was said to be mistreating Indians.

Though fewer in number than *probanzas, pleitos* sometimes contain the richest and most revealing data. These documents are housed in the Justicia section of the Archivo General de Indias in Seville, a part of the archive few researchers have had the time or inclination to explore.[5] *Pleitos* usually contain documents that duplicate much of the information found in *probanzas*. They are primarily concerned, however, with rival claims. *Encomenderos* would either be involved in litigation against each other or would be pressing charges against a governor over the removal of a grant. Claimants would seek to discredit one another by the presentation of testimony that might damage or ruin reputations. Fascinating details, therefore, come to light regarding the

5. Sherman (1979) was a notable exception.

activities of governors and *encomenderos* alike. These sources disclose both how the granting of *encomiendas* was used by governors as personal leverage and to what extent *encomenderos* ignored Crown directives regarding the proper treatment of their native charges. Valuable testimony concerning *encomienda* succession may be found in these documents. *Pleitos*, unlike the majority of *probanzas*, also occasionally provide detailed information on the size, location, and tribute-paying capacity of indigenous communities.

THE FINDINGS

On the basis of our work in the archives, we are now able to identify and locate more than half of the communities listed in the tribute assessments compiled by Cerrato, something that long frustrated and eluded us. We can now also describe, in detail, when many of these communities were first assigned and held in *encomienda*, as well as document when and under what circumstances they reverted to the Crown or were passed from one colonist to another. This information is distilled in table 7, which shows the vital statistics of awards by governorship; some one hundred communities were granted as *encomiendas* between the beginning of conquest in 1524 and the arrival of more stable royal government in 1548. In an attempt to convey how often *encomiendas* could change hands in these early years of intrigue and flux, table 8 reconstructs the succession of grantors and holders of Chichicastenango, eleven recorded permutations between 1526 and 1549. The experience of Chichicastenango, by no means unique, reflects the propensity of one governor to alter or modify the decisions of his predecessor, and indicates how unstable and temporary early *encomienda* privileges could be.

A KEY FRAME OF REFERENCE

Our discussion above gives some idea of the data that can be extracted from *probanzas* and *pleitos*, little-known or little-used sources that shed light on both the distribution of communities held in *encomienda* and the history of *encomienda* succession. Initially, the tribute assessments carried out when Cerrato was president of Guatemala served as our organizational benchmark. We now know that there is abundant, untapped documentation on earlier years. Consequently, the tribute assessments compiled by Cerrato serve more as a vital checklist, a key frame of reference, rather than an exclusive register for early *encomienda* arrangements. Even in the absence of comprehensive tribute rolls for the first quarter-century or so after conquest, *encomiendas* can be effectively traced through individual documents prepared by *encomenderos* themselves. Kramer, elsewhere, has pursued this topic at length.[6]

Having taken note of the sources and hinted at the richness of their contents, we now turn, by way of providing a detailed example, to examining what they can tell us about the operation of *encomienda* at the local level.

6. Kramer (1994). Her pioneering work is appreciatively featured in Luján Muñoz (2011, 88–90), especially map 41 and table 3, which are based on her figure 1.1 (Kramer 1994, 20) and appendix A (Kramer 1994, 237–40).

CHAPTER 7

ALVARADO, ESPINAR, AND THE
BOOTY OF HUEHUETENANGO

Few Spaniards mustered the courage to confront Pedro de Alvarado as Juan de Espinar did. Allegedly at one time a lowly Spanish tailor, Espinar saw his prospects change dramatically on October 3, 1525, after he received title from Alvarado to the *encomienda* of Huehuetenango, the most lucrative award of native goods and services in the Sierra de los Cuchumatanes. Not content with what he had been given, Espinar sought to increase his quota of labor and tribute by manipulating native families in areas beyond the confines of his award. He set their houses on fire, thus forcing former occupants to abandon their homes and take up residence closer to the central reach of his *encomienda*.

Though Espinar's actions were unlawful, what the *encomendero* did was later legalized and, indeed, became established practice in the enforcement of *congregación* (see chapter 5). After several communities had been burned to the ground, an inquiry into the affair unveiled Espinar's trickery and wrongdoing, thereby furnishing Alvarado with what seemed to be legitimate grounds for stripping him of his assets. Thrown in jail and put on trial, Espinar managed to escape and flee to Mexico. There he presented his version of events to court authorities and was acquitted of the charges laid against him on a legal technicality: Alvarado, apparently, did not have the authority to remove Huehuetenango from him at the time when he did so, while the case was being contested. The *encomienda* was given back to Espinar, who returned to Guatemala to plot his revenge. Reinstated but incensed, he filed suit against Alvarado for damages and loss of income during the ten- to twelve-month period when his privileges had been revoked. The lawsuit (*pleito*) between the two men, in which Espinar records in meticulous detail just how much Huehuetenango was worth to him, draws on the testimony of Indians as well as Spaniards and thus affords a unique glimpse of the reward and burden of *encomienda* during its early period of operation.

THE STAKES

Prior to the stabilizing presence in Guatemala of educated, professionally trained, Crown-appointed administrators, conquerors themselves set the requirements for what goods and services they expected to receive from the native communities they held in *encomienda*. It is no surprise that this kind of information went undocumented, for the amount of tribute and the variety of services furnished often exceeded reasonable limits, by far. We know, from fleeting references, of several sources that may contain such information, but these have not yet come to light. It is for this reason that uncovering data relating to the operation of *encomienda* in and around Huehuetenango soon after it was conquered is exceptional. Our principal source is the correspondence from the lawsuit mentioned above.[1] Such entangled court cases occurred frequently in the period immediately following conquest. Bickering was exacerbated in the Guatemalan case, as we noted in the previous chapter, by the constant reassignment of *encomiendas* on the part of those individuals charged with governing the colony between 1524 and 1536 (see table 7). It was, in fact, the reallocation of Huehuetenango, which in 1530 Alvarado authorized be removed from Juan de Espinar and given to Francisco de Zurrilla, one of Alvarado's business partners and the colony's chief accountant or *contador*, that triggered the *pleito* we examine. Our examination, however, requires beforehand a brief sketch of preconquest and conquest-period history in the Huehuetenango region in order to illuminate certain incidents referred to later on.

PRECONQUEST HUEHUETENANGO

Archaeological and ethnohistorical evidence indicates that, by the mid-fifteenth century, the Huehuetenango region had fallen under the political

---

1. The *pleito* may be found in AGI, Justicia 1031. Unless indicated otherwise, this is the source of all direct quotations we refer to throughout this chapter. Kramer (1994, 201–25) mines this *legajo* for her purposes, too.

and tributary jurisdiction of the K'iche's of Gumarcaah.[2] The precise extent of K'iche' control, however, is not clear. While strong all across the south, K'iche' influence appears to have been less pronounced in the north and west, where small Mam chiefdoms held out against the expansionist aims of their neighbors. The secession of the Kaqchikels from the K'iche's, which occurred around 1475, led to civil war between the two groups, a development that weakened the rule of Gumarcaah over subjugated peoples. At least three Cuchumatán groups then asserted their independence, for the native chronicle known as the *Título de Santa Clara* exhorts the K'iche's to be on guard against the Agaab people of Sacapulas, the Balamiha people of Aguacatán, and the Mam people of Zaculeu.[3] Certainly by the time the Spaniards arrived in Guatemala in 1524, the Mam of Zaculeu were treated by the K'iche's more as allies than as vassals, Alvarado himself observing that the Mam ruler, Caibil Balam, was received with great ceremony and respect at Gumarcaah.[4]

The primacy of Zaculeu in immediate preconquest times is unequivocal, even if the nature of its political hold over surrounding communities is as difficult to establish as the spatial range of its domination. We are told that warriors from Cuilco and Ixtahuacán fought alongside the Mam against the Spaniards at Zaculeu, so its sphere of influence extended at least fifty kilometers to the west. Northward, also, it commanded allegiance and affiliation, perhaps as far as Todos Santos and even beyond, for it was from these parts that a relief force is said to have descended to assist Caibil Balam during the Spanish siege of Zaculeu in 1525.[5]

CONQUEST OF THE MAM

Spanish penetration of the Huehuetenango region began in 1525, when Gonzalo de Alvarado led an expedition against the Mam. Alvarado had been informed, so Fuentes y Guzmán tells us, that Mam country was "great and rich" and that "abundant treasures" would be among the

2. Carmack (1973).
3. Recinos (1957, 197). See also Luján Muñoz (2011, 53–59).
4. See Woodbury and Trik (1953, vol. 1, 10).
5. Woodbury and Trik (1953, vol. 1, 16–19).

spoils of victory.[6] Alvarado set off early in July 1525 with a party of forty cavalry, eighty infantry, and two thousand indigenous auxiliaries. Assisted by another contingent of several hundred natives who served as pack bearers, the party proceeded first to Totonicapán, which functioned as military and supply headquarters for the campaign. After a brief encampment at Totonicapán, the party then journeyed north, entering Mam country proper. In the days that followed, Alvarado's men defeated two sizable Mam armies—one from Mazatenango, the present-day San Lorenzo, and the other from Malacatán, the present-day Malacatancito—before marching on toward the *cabecera* of Huehuetenango, which they found abandoned. Having heard of the Spaniards' approach, Caibil Balam had ordered the evacuation of Huehuetenango and had retreated with his forces to the nearby stronghold of Zaculeu, where Mam forces awaited the enemy.

The task confronting the Spaniards was formidable, for Zaculeu exhibited a distinct air of impregnability. Though located on an open plain, the site was surrounded by ravines on all sides but one, and further protected by a man-made system of wall and ditches. A reconstruction of the fortress as Fuentes y Guzmán imagined it to be appears in the *Recordación florida*. While the chronicler's drawing is certainly fanciful, it nonetheless imparts a sense of Zaculeu as a safe and secure redoubt (see figure 3). Inside its defenses Caibil Balam is reported to have gathered six thousand warriors, which means that the Spaniards and their native allies were outnumbered by some two to one.

By early September, however, Gonzalo de Alvarado had steered his men successfully through two armed engagements. During the second clash, eight thousand warriors are said to have come down from the mountains to the north in an attempt to break the siege laid to Zaculeu following the first confrontation. On both occasions, victory on the part of the invaders is attributed to the murderous impact of Spanish cavalry on native foot soldiers. Following a second defeat on the field of battle, the Mam never again ventured outside their stronghold, where they were effectively cornered until Caibil Balam surrendered a month or so later.

6. Fuentes y Guzmán ([1690–99] 1969–72, vol. 3, 110). The chronicler's precise words are "grande y rico" and "muchos tesoros," something of an exaggeration. For a detailed reconstruction of the conquest of the Mam and their Cuchumatán neighbors, see Lovell ([1985] 2005, 58–66, 178–81, and 202–204).

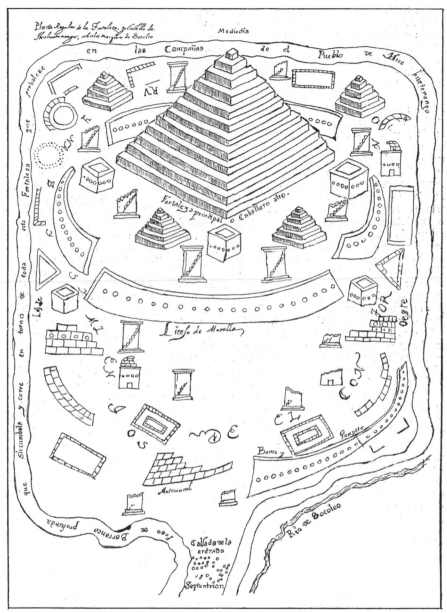

FIGURE 3. Mam fortress of Zaculeu (Fuentes y Guzmán, 1690–99).

Satisfied that the subjugation of the Mam had been accomplished, Gonzalo de Alvarado left for Spanish headquarters, at that time located in or near Iximché, with news of his triumph.

The fall of Zaculeu in October 1525 meant that Spanish rule was considered to prevail throughout the territory where the Mam had once held sway. In his account of the conquest, Fuentes y Guzmán talks in exalted tones about the valor of Gonzalo de Alvarado, whose own account of the conquest (alas no longer extant) the chronicler leaned on heavily. Using Fuentes y Guzmán as a historical source is often problematic, but the chronicler makes it clear in this case that he was working directly from Gonzalo de Alvarado's firsthand descriptions.[7] Alvarado's account may likewise have been imperfect, weighted perhaps in his own personal favor, but the fact remains that Fuentes y Guzmán's filtered version is the best source we have for the conquest of the Mam. Fuentes y Guzmán singles out the role played in the campaign by Antonio de Salazar and Gonzalo de Solís. Salazar is credited with maintaining the siege of Zaculeu when Alvarado led other Spaniards into battle against the relief force that attacked from the north. After Alvarado's departure for Iximché, Solís was left in command of Spanish and allied troops stationed in the *cabecera* of Huehuetenango. To Solís fell the task of conducting a reconnaissance of those communities either subject to, or aligned with, Zaculeu. Any one of these three prominent conquerors might be expected to have been awarded the *encomienda* of Huehuetenango for the part each played in bringing the natives to heel. But that dividend, the right to exact unspecified goods and services from native communities in the newly conquered land, fell to Juan de Espinar, a Spaniard whose name has passed without mention in the story so far.

FROM TAILOR TO MAN OF SUBSTANCE

The documents are silent about Juan de Espinar's place of origin—he may have come from Segovia, as did one of the Spanish overseers he hired—so nothing is known of his family background. This is hardly surprising, given that Espinar would have had no wish to dwell on what appear at best to have been humble roots; it is difficult, generally speaking,

7. See Sáenz de Santa María (1969).

to identify the place of origin and family background of many of Guatemala's conquistadors. A few of them, like Espinar, were of lower social standing and for reasons of pride chose not to disclose where they were born or who their families were, standard refrains in most depositions prepared by first conquerors and their offspring when they sought recognition from the Crown. Men who included facts of this kind usually had something they felt they could boast about. In her study of the *hidalgos*, or noblemen, of Guatemala, Pilar Sanchíz notes that the intense longing among Spanish residents to become *hidalgos* spread even to non-conquerors, tradesmen, and laborers. Sanchíz, however, is able to add but little to our knowledge of either the regional or social origins of Spanish residents, observing only that, in spite of vociferous claims to "hidalguía," likely only a very few "hidalgos peninsulares" ever made it to Guatemala.[8]

Espinar was awarded Huehuetenango by Pedro de Alvarado in 1525. He held the *encomienda* until 1530, when Don Pedro saw fit to strip him of the privilege. Although no reference is made of it, we assume that Espinar must have served under Gonzalo de Alvarado, for he gained control of Huehuetenango around the time the Mam surrendered at Zaculeu.[9] Huehuetenango was then a prize catch, but there were other *encomiendas* of comparable size or even larger with which notable Spaniards could be rewarded, *encomiendas* held by such men as Pedro and Jorge de Alvarado, Pedro de Portocarrero, Pedro de Cueto, Sancho de Barahona, Diego de Rojas, and Bartolomé Becerra. Huehuetenango was returned to Espinar in 1531, and though he no longer had the usufruct of some neighboring towns, his *encomienda* continued to be substantial.[10]

Unlike most of his contemporaries, Espinar was prepared to make the most of what Guatemala had to offer. He states with obvious pride that, since the time of the conquest, he had never traveled outside of Mexico or Guatemala, a thinly veiled slight about the mobility of the men he had fought alongside of, many of whom left the area disappointed

8. Sanchíz Ochoa (1976).
9. Formal title to the *encomienda* of Huehuetenango is dated October 3, 1525. Even though it appears that Zaculeu did not actually capitulate until toward the middle of the month, the Spaniards by early October must have felt confident of victory. We have testimony, from Espinar himself, of his having served not under Gonzalo but under Jorge de Alvarado for three years when he led campaigns of conquest during brother Pedro's absence (AGI, Guatemala 41, fol. 77, "Sobre los méritos y servicios de Jorge de Alvarado," February 26, 1534).
10. AGI, Justicia 295.

with what they had to show for it, seeking greater enrichment elsewhere.[11]
There was none more restless in this regard than Espinar's adversary,
Pedro de Alvarado.

Two chroniclers make mention of Espinar, but are unable to tell
us very much. The reason he attracted their attention is because of the
money Espinar is known to have made in Guatemala. Bernal Díaz del
Castillo claimed that he remembered when, at the time of the conquest of Mexico, Espinar disembarked in Villa Rica from Spain and the
Canary Islands, noting that he went on to become a wealthy resident of
Santiago de Guatemala.[12] Fuentes y Guzmán also notes that Espinar
became a wealthy man, but depicts his lot prior to his exploitation of
silver mines near Chiantla, which lies at the foot of the mountains a
little to the north of Huehuetenango, as one of dire poverty. He describes
Espinar, before fortune smiled on him, as a "miserable subject, with a
wife and many children but with no means to feed so many mouths," a
man so poor that he was forced to carry "in the manner of the Indians"
the wheat he took to the local mill to be threshed. The chronicler, yet
again, may be confusing fact with fancy; archival sources at our disposal
say nothing about Espinar having been so impoverished. One document
records him as fathering an "hija natural" who married the son of Juan
Peréz Dardón.[13] We also have evidence that Espinar profited considerably from placer gold mining along the Río Malacatán south of Huehuetenango, an enterprise he became involved in soon after the conquest.
Espinar may indeed have played a role later on in the exploitation of

11. AGCA, A1.29, leg. 4678, exp. 40244.
12. Díaz del Castillo ([1632] 1968, 284).
13. Fuentes y Guzmán ([1690–99] 1932, vol. 3, 99–101). We take "in the manner of the Indians"
to mean that Espinar was reputed to have carried wheat by tumpline, the traditional human means
of haulage throughout Mesoamerica, still practiced today. Fuentes y Guzmán goes so far as to
claim that dire economic circumstances at one time forced Espinar and his family to live not in a
house in Chiantla or Huehuetenango but in a cave up in the mountains near his subsequent for-
tuitous discovery. "This cave is admired with wonder," Fuentes y Guzmán informs us, "on account
of its giving shelter and sustenance to the man who later was able to give those very things to so
many others." According to the chronicler, Espinar stumbled across Chiantla's famous silver
deposits while on his way to buy some cows with five hundred pesos of borrowed money. Fuentes
y Guzmán's "rags to riches" tale ends with Espinar going back to Spain, where he died, guarding
all the while the secret of his discovery's whereabouts. Plans on the part of Espinar to return to
Guatemala to exploit the mines further, in the chronicler's account, thus came to naught. The
pleito we examine allows us to tell the story of Juan de Espinar quite differently from Fuentes y
Guzmán. Evidence of Espinar's having fathered an "hija natural" who went on to marry the son
of Juan Pérez Dardón comes from AGI, Guatemala 116.

silver mines within the boundaries of his *encomienda*—a mural in the parish church at Chiantla certainly promotes this image—but by then he was already a man of some means. A fellow conqueror, Francisco López, made the unsolicited remark as early as 1539 that Espinar "has very fine *haciendas* and makes a good living from them."[14] Years later, President Cerrato also remembered that Espinar had "good Indians," implying an ample or sufficient number at his disposal.[15] Espinar himself reveals little, concerned in one deposition with simply telling the Crown that he was a conqueror of Mexico and a first conqueror of Guatemala.[16] It meant a great deal to him to establish that he owned a rather fine horse, the feeding and grooming of which entailed significant expenses, a feature pointed out by others, too.[17]

Besides his soldierly deeds and his owning a horse, nothing about Espinar's standing prepares us for the award of such a prime *encomienda*. We must bear in mind that he was neither a member of the Alvarado clan nor one of its favored cronies. Don Pedro, the original grantor, was himself hard pressed to explain why Huehuetenango landed in the hands of such an unworthy recipient. In 1530, the only explanation he could offer runs as follows:

> As a result of continuous warfare in the region, the distribution of *encomiendas* has been irregular. Consequently, there are men like Espinar to whom the captains, to placate the appetites [of their soldiers], have given disproportionately large *encomiendas*, while others who deserve better end up with very little.

It is to Alvarado's prying into Espinar's background that we owe some specific evidence as to who the *encomendero* of Huehuetenango may have been.

There was certainly no love lost, as time unfolded, between Pedro de Alvarado and Juan de Espinar. Indeed, we have on record Alvarado's

14. AGCA, Al.29, leg. 4678, exp. 40244.

15. AGI, Justicia 301.

16. AGCA, Al.29, leg. 4678, exp. 40244.

17. The witness Hernando de San Cristóbal states that Espinar "served in the conquest on foot and on horseback," suggesting a rise from more lowly to higher status. Ignacio de Bobadilla recorded that Espinar was "among the first conquerors of this province of Guatemala" and that in the conquest he had seen him serve "with arms and horses." Bobadilla also noted that, on occasion, "he had a servant." Pedro de Paredes, a witness for Pedro de Alvarado, knew of Espinar having served "in the war of conquest of this province and in that of Tututepeque."

own admission that he considered Espinar his "mortal enemy." The hostility between the two men dates from the time of governor Francisco de Orduña's inquiry of 1529–30, when Espinar presented damaging testimony against Alvarado. Upon Don Pedro's return to Guatemala in 1530, he set his sights on Huehuetenango as a way of getting back at Espinar for speaking out against him; Alvarado saw it as an appropriate reward either for himself or one of his followers. Long accustomed to getting his way, he was unprepared for Espinar's refusal to relinquish his *encomienda*. Even though Don Pedro had originally granted Huehuetenango to Espinar, changed conditions in the former's own fortunes and the influx of new colonists made it necessary to usurp or divide large *encomiendas* held either by members of the first conquering expedition or distributed by Jorge de Alvarado in 1528. Besides, reports that Espinar had mistreated Indians, and had burned several of their towns in order to get them to relocate closer to Huehuetenango, provided Alvarado with what he thought was ample justification for the removal of *encomienda* privileges.

Don Pedro had this to say about the man he regarded as having been rewarded well above his station:

> Espinar is a person of low standing and menial occupation, someone who has survived by plying his trade as a tailor. His Majesty orders that tradesmen of the mechanical arts should not be granted Indians but, rather, that they should practice their trades so that they benefit newly settled lands and kingdoms. Indians should be granted to the members of the nobility and persons of status, not to tradesmen like Espinar.

For most men, Alvarado's scorn would have been sufficient cause to back down. Espinar, however, stood firm. Although careful always to minimize his knowledge of a manual skill, he was not ashamed of the fact that, blatant prejudices aside, he had once earned a living making garments. Don Pedro and his supporters also tried to belittle Espinar by accusing him of gambling away huge sums of money; Pedro de Portocarrero observed haughtily that "one would almost think it was his profession." Gambling, however, was so common a habit among Spanish settlers that this accusation likely did little to erode Espinar's reputation. Indeed, he lost especially large sums to Alvarado himself, four thousand pesos on one occasion, two horses on another.[18] Gambling debts evidently forced Espinar to make excessive demands on his Indians. His stubborn nature and his staunch belief that *encomienda* rewards should rest purely on military service and seniority in the region help explain how he was able to frustrate Alvarado's attempts to appropriate or reassign Huehuetenango for any significant length of time. Thus, regardless of his inauspicious past and his growing infamy as a Spaniard who abused Indians, Espinar argued that Huehuetenango was his from the time of its first assignment and should continue to be so.

THE SPANISH REWARD

Juan de Espinar held the *encomienda* of Huehuetenango from 1525 until his death in the early 1560s, with one ten- to twelve-month hiatus from 1530 to 1531. For more than thirty-five years, many of them fraught with uncertainty, a combination of tenacity, political savvy, and being on the alert, together with a toughness that drifted, no doubt, into unabashed cruelty, made him *the* force to be reckoned with in Huehuetenango. Espinar also had keen business instincts, controlling the sale of tribute and developing an elaborate infrastructure of mining and agricultural activities. Detailed land titles that cover his tenure as *encomendero* have yet to be located. It seems safe to assume, however, that by virtue of the power he wielded, Espinar could use the land much as he pleased, even though, in theory, *encomienda* had nothing to do with proprietary rights. For example, he owned a pig farm next to the *cabecera* of Huehuetenango and laid claim to enough land to raise large quantities of corn and beans, which he stored for consumption throughout the year.[19]

About ten kilometers to the south of Huehuetenango, along the course of the Río Malacatán, Espinar was fortunate enough to be one of the first Spaniards to exploit local deposits of gold. Good fortune for Espinar proved to be a heavy burden for local inhabitants. There is

18. AGI, Justicia 295. Alvarado justified his own indulgence by claiming that because the men who paid him a visit "had nothing else to occupy their time, as there is little to keep one busy in these parts," he had no choice but to entertain them by gambling with them.

19. See Lovell ([1985] 2005, 118–39) for a fuller discussion of Spanish and native landholding patterns in the region. On the often close link between *encomienda* and *hacienda*, of which this appears to be a good example, see Lockhart (1969) and MacLeod ([1973] 2008, 129–30).

no record to show that he actually owned the gold deposits. Rather, he laid claim to them, as did other Spaniards in the area. Since he held the largest *encomienda* close to the placer streams, he took advantage of his position to sell food supplies to other Spaniards who had gangs of indigenous slaves, or *cuadrillas*, working there. While his *encomienda* gave him a foothold in the region and supplied him with foodstuffs, cloth goods, and labor services, it was panning for gold that made him a rich man.

Espinar claimed in his litigation with Alvarado that he earned approximately nine thousand pesos a year from his mining operations and another three thousand pesos from his agricultural enterprises. These earnings might lead one to think that the rewards accruing to Espinar from his *encomienda* were secondary, because, after all, he was an entre- preneur, not a feudal lord. That conclusion, however, would be mis- leading. In the case of Espinar, and many other *encomenderos* as well, the two roles were intertwined. Without the booty from his *encomienda*, and all the other perks that a rapacious *encomendero* could enjoy, Espi- nar's mining and agricultural pursuits might never have been more than modest operations.

While it is difficult to chart the course of Espinar's fortunes through- out his lifetime, we are on reasonably solid ground in assuming that the most profitable years occurred prior to the mid-sixteenth century. Native populations were at their highest levels in the first decades after conquest. Population decline (table 9) set in quickly and precipitously. Espinar lived long enough to see his *encomienda* shrivel to a fraction of what it had been when he was initially awarded it. One factor that affected its size was that during the first five years of tenure—until 1530—Espinar held not only the *cabecera* of Huehuetenango but also a handful of other communities he lost the right to later on, when they were granted to other Spaniards.

Added to the woes of a shrinking population and territorial erosion, the enforcement of the New Laws (1542) under President Cerrato (1548–55) brought restrictions on the amount of tribute collected and the numbers of Indians given in personal service, and the abolition of most forms of indigenous slavery.[20] Also, involvement in gold panning in the Río Mala- catán probably did not provide as lucrative a payoff in the 1540s and

20. Sherman (1979, 129–52).

1550s as in earlier decades: native numbers and prospecting for gold, MacLeod has pointed out, declined at roughly the same time.[21] These developments must have made Espinar's later years somewhat less prosperous. Even as his fortunes waned, however, his canny use of native labor and native tribute allowed him to live well, right up to the time of his death. Measured solely in terms of the number of tributaries, Espinar's *encomienda* in the mid-sixteenth century was the eleventh largest in a list of more than ninety entitlements, not including those of the Crown.[22]

Espinar did not run this impressive operation, especially the panning of gold, by himself. He had native servants (*naboríos*) who worked exclusively in the mines, a Spaniard who served as a mining expert, a foreman (*mayordomo* or *calpixque*), and several pig herders (*pastores*) in Huehuetenango. To the south, whether Santiago's capital site was Almolonga (1527–41) or Panchoy (after 1541), Espinar ran a household that would have been provided for by a staff of native workers. By 1530, possibly even earlier, he was a council member (*regidor*) on the body (*cabildo*) that governed the most important city in Central America. That year we have a record of his sharing living quarters in Santiago with Francisco de Arévalo while his own house was under construction. As well as a residence in the capital, Espinar owned agricultural lands nearby. On them he likely settled indigenous slaves, who would be joined by groups of *encomienda* Indians to produce wheat and other foodstuffs, both for domestic consumption and sale at market.[23]

THE INDIAN BURDEN

Litigation between Juan de Espinar and Pedro de Alvarado, especially Espinar's decision to press for damages and loss of income during the ten- to twelve-month period when Alvarado reallocated Huehuetenango to Francisco de Zurrilla, provides the earliest data we have found on the tribute obligations of a Guatemalan *encomienda*. We compare in table 10 the proceeds for 1530–31, when Zurrilla held Huehuetenango, and eighteen years later, in 1549, when Espinar had long since regained control.

21. MacLeod ([1973] 2008, 60–61, 110–11).
22. AGI, Guatemala 128.
23. AGI, Justicia 1031; Arévalo (1932, 34); and Lutz ([1982] 1984).

Circumstances had clearly altered over time. First, the *encomienda* of Huehuetenango in the early 1530s consisted of the population of the *cabecera* itself plus the inhabitants of at least four outlying communities. In 1549, the *encomienda* contained only the *cabecera* and one subject town, Chiantla. Second, the total number of tributaries dropped from an estimated 2,000 to 2,500 to five hundred during these two decades (table 9). Third, stricter enforcement of Crown laws, especially regarding native labor, must have eventually reduced the burden on the surviving population. Because of lack of data between the early 1530s and the late 1540s, we are forced to speculate about the fate of Huehuetenango's Indians in the interim.

Espinar's loss of towns and tributaries surely signaled harder times for the natives who remained under his charge. As the components of his *encomienda* dwindled, Espinar no doubt would have wished to continue his mining operations, maintain an acceptable level of income, and consolidate his status in Santiago society. In short, if the year under Zurrilla was exacting, even more difficult times quite possibly lay ahead.

On the other hand, the year that Zurrilla held Huehuetenango might well have been an unusually demanding one. Zurrilla took advantage of the opportunity to direct considerable native resources toward supporting the mining operations he and Pedro de Alvarado ran, deploying 120 to 200 *indios de servicio* to this end. He also owned outright, from his days in Mexico, a second *cuadrilla* of 100 Mixtec slaves. To the feeding and clothing of these laborers we must add an unknown quantity of goods and services given to Alvarado for the Indian slaves belonging to him, for they worked the same gold deposits as the slaves of Zurrilla. Forty other *indios de servicio*, along with honey, fowl, and cloth, were sent to Zurrilla's house in Santiago and the estate he owned nearby. Most other goods and services—reed mats, foodstuffs, and the labor of men and women—were used to support Indian slaves and the Spanish mining expert. We lack information on precise tribute schedules, but if payment followed the pattern used in subsequent periods, then one-half would have been furnished in June and the other half in December. Juan, a native lord of Huehuetenango, stated that each time tribute was paid to Zurrilla he counted the items and turned them over to the foreman, also a Spaniard, who distributed the items between the mines and Santiago. Most of the crops harvested would have been furnished in the December payment. In his litigation with Alvarado, Espinar claimed that he had 3,000 *fanegas* (4,500 bushels) of corn and 300 *fanegas* of beans and chili peppers stored at Huehuetenango, which vanished during the time Zurrilla held the *encomienda*. Likewise, Espinar's 600 pigs disappeared, although Zurrilla denied any responsibility.

If we believe the testimony of several witnesses, Zurrilla and Alvarado were even more rapacious in their exploitation of Huehuetenango than was Espinar. While we know with hindsight that Zurrilla only held the *encomienda* for ten months to a year, he could not have known that he would hold it so briefly, so it makes no sense that he extracted its worth as quickly as possible. On the other hand Zurrilla—unlike Espinar—did not intend to stay in a backwater like Guatemala all his life. Neither Zurrilla nor his partner Alvarado, who was ever anxious to amass large sums of cash to finance his foreign ventures, seems to have acted as if preserving the *encomienda* and its population was the sensible thing to do.

Espinar claimed, and found witnesses to support him, that the population of Huehuetenango declined by half during the brief period Zurrilla was *encomendero*. Apart from attrition due to disease, numbers fell because Indians fled to the mountains to escape the clutches of Zurrilla's administrators. In an unidentified town subject to Huehuetenango, the natives were said to be "very hostile and did not want to serve, running off always into the wilds. Sometimes Indians from the *cabecera* [together] with the Spaniard working as foreman went to look for them. They would bring them back forcibly, as prisoners, and make them work. [Zurrilla] had them put in chains so that they might labor at the mines, as did [the Indians] from the other towns." Native resistance, perhaps more passive than in the subject town just mentioned, also occurred in the *cabecera*. When two high-ranking leaders of Huehuetenango did not cooperate with Zurrilla in mobilizing labor, he ordered that they be sent before Alvarado in Santiago. It was said by one witness that Zurrilla "arranged that a lord and a lord who was a translator be punished."

Another witness, Luis de Vivar, testified that he had heard it said that Indians from Huehuetenango had been mistreated, perhaps even killed, when they refused to serve Zurrilla and Alvarado. Vivar stated that when Espinar arrived back in Guatemala in 1531 he found that native leaders, like Espinar himself, had been jailed, charged with both allowing fugitive behavior and engaging in it themselves. Among those jailed was Coatle, the lord of Chiantla. Vivar alleged that Coatle subsequently fled to escape from Espinar, who was himself not averse to dealing with Indians harshly.

In his defense, Espinar's attorney stated that when his client had mis-treated Indians, "it was a long time ago, when the natives were uncivilized and half at war, and [because] they did not want to feed or support the slaves that their *encomendero* had in the mines, on account of which some of them [slaves] died of hunger." Espinar himself made no bones about such abuse: "I put them in chains to scare them so that they would serve me," he declares bluntly, adding for good measure, "the Indians of these provinces, especially those of Huehuetenango, are so incorri-gible, evil, and rebellious that it is hardly a crime to threaten and beat one of them." Ignacio de Bobadilla, on the other hand, noted that on two occasions he had written letters on Espinar's behalf, with instruc-tions for his foreman to give native inhabitants more corn, if they were in need, even though they had received their regular supplies. This suggests that, while certainly no saint, Espinar was understandably concerned about the welfare of his charges; it was their toil, after all, that guaran-teed his prosperity. These two factors, indigenous well-being and keeping up the flow of gold, appear to have been instrumental in the decision in January 1530 to raze to the ground several of Huehuetenango's subject towns, perhaps the most startling revelation offered by the documents at hand.

FIRE IN THE MOUNTAINS

It was an extreme, self-serving act, the motives of which are not at all easy to discern. We conclude, however, after sifting through the evidence, that it was Juan de Espinar himself who was behind the burning of four or five Indian settlements. He acted, we reckon, in tandem with the lords of Huehuetenango and perhaps also with the lords of the burned towns themselves. Why events unfolded as they did calls for us to take into account, once again, the nature of preconquest relations.

Contradictions, gaps, and inconsistencies abound. The record states, for instance, that Mam communities west and north of Huehuetenango, as well as the *cabecera* itself, began to pay tribute to the K'iche's of Gumarcaah following K'iche' expansion into the region by the early fif-teenth century. Not only was tribute collected, but the conquering K'iche's are also said to have displaced local populations from lands they tilled around Zaculeu, forcing them to move farther north and west to colder,

less fertile upland locations. As K'iche' influence declined in the late
fifteenth century, Huehuetenango began to enjoy increasing independence. However, smaller Mam communities in outlying areas—each with
its own plaza and temples, the witnesses report—are said to have remained
loyal to Gumarcaah. Atitán, Chiantla, Chimbal, and Niquitlán chose
not to recognize the authority of Huehuetenango and Zaculeu, and
kept their ties to Gumarcaah. Running counter to this line of reasoning,
though, is evidence that, after the Spanish conquest, the leaders of Huehuetenango ordered the people of these same places to pay tribute to
Juan de Espinar, a command the rulers of the subject towns obeyed.
This apparent willingness suggests that Huehuetenango exerted at least
some control over these outlying communities. Justified or not, the lords
of Huehuetenango referred to non-elite inhabitants of the subject settlements as "our commoners." The links between the subject towns and
Huehuetenango are indicated by their involvement, mentioned earlier,
in Mam efforts to defend Zaculeu against Spanish attack in 1525.

If the second of the two scenarios outlined above is the one that
prevailed, it becomes more understandable why, in early 1530, under
orders from Espinar and the lords of Huehuetenango, families in several
mountain towns (see table 11) burned their houses—having presumably
first removed their personal possessions and food supplies—and abandoned both home and community to move a relatively short distance
to the plain surrounding Zaculeu. Espinar tried to cover up his involvement in the plot by telling the then governor, Francisco de Orduña, that
the Indians had burned their towns because they had risen up in arms
against the Spaniards. Meanwhile, Espinar persuaded native leaders
to proceed with the destruction and flee with their dependents so that
Spaniards (who he claimed would be passing through the region on
missions of conquest) would not see them. Afterwards, those who fled
were to come and live near Zaculeu, also referred to in the documents
as Zacualpa Huehuetenango. Cotoha, a ruler of Huehuetenango, testified that a native messenger of Espinar's told the lords that his master
had said that "everyone should go down to the plain and gather together
so that the Christians could not divvy them up." The same witness said
Espinar had ordered that the towns be burned quickly, before informants
of Governor Orduña could see them, for if they did not act in haste
the Spaniards would kill them.

Espinar's principal motive in torching communities was related to his fury over what he saw as an intrusion onto his turf by two other Spaniards, García de Salinas and Juan Niño. These men had laid claim to Atitán and Chimbal (claimed by Salinas), and Niquitlán (claimed by Niño).[24] In order to counter the case made by them—that he was usurping *their* towns—Espinar plotted with his allies, the lords of the *cabecera* of Huehuetenango, to burn the subject towns and resettle their inhabitants elsewhere. Because a grant of *encomienda* was tagged to the production and labor of a specified number of tribute payers, and not the lands on which tributaries lived, by this move Espinar effectively eliminated the population base of his adversaries while simultaneously augmenting his own. Espinar's actions served to bolster not only his own authority but also that of the lords of Huehuetenango.

When Orduña investigated the matter, it turned out that the Indians of the subject towns were *not* in rebellion but, rather, were simply following Espinar's instructions. The *encomendero*'s motives were thus ones of unabashed greed, the desire for optimal enrichment. They also indicate a spitefulness and sense of outrage against what he saw as the impertinence of Salinas and Niño. To these must be added his wish to protect the network of interests that he had developed in the environs of Huehuetenango within a scant five years of conquest.

Indigenous motives are less obvious to grasp. Throughout the lawsuit, there is evidence of a congruence of interests between Espinar and the native lords of both *cabecera* and outlying towns. Even though the solution chosen—to raze entire communities—was a radical one, inhabitants of these places had legitimate complaints about where they lived. Indian witnesses complained that locations in the mountains were unhealthy and excessively cold, and that agricultural conditions there were inferior to those of the more level plain around Zaculeu. By contrast,

24. Espinar refers to García de Salinas and Juan Niño as "enemies of mine who have endeavored to dispute with me [my rights] over the aforementioned towns." Our evidence that these three towns were in contention is admittedly more circumstantial than direct. Atitán (San Juan Atitlán) and Chimbal (Santiago Chimaltenango) were considered one *encomienda* when President Cerrato assessed them for tribute in 1549; see AGI, Guatemala 128. At one point in the proceedings, Niño volunteered detailed testimony on Niquitlán (San Pedro Necta), suggesting more than just a passing acquaintance with the community. He notes that, while paying a visit there, he found the *cabecera* of Niquitlán to be a burned-out shell, a place devoid of people. Niño then journeyed one league in order to sleep "at some other places, for they were inhabited." The people living where Niño ended up, however, took off when they caught sight of him. Niño records that he did not observe any men.

the same witnesses noted that they, their families, and their children now lived in warmer, more hospitable locales.[25]

Equally important, the return to the plain, after the displacement caused by K'iche' conquest, relocated people closer to better land for growing corn; Olín, a lord of Huehuetenango, testified that the Indians of the burned towns now lived in the vicinity of Zaculeu, where cornfields were attended to devoutly. Without exception, all the witnesses spoke favorably of moving from higher to lower elevations. Even the lords mentioned this as a factor, which suggests that Huehuetenango in the late 1520s may have been in a different location from the modern city of the same name.

Another reason given for burning the towns was that the region was "no longer at war," meaning that disruptions caused by K'iche' and then Spanish conquest were over. Testifying in 1530, Olín stated that the main justification for setting fire to part of the old *cabecera* and moving closer to Zaculeu was that hostilities had ended; by implication, people could move to less-defensible, open terrain. If the plain could be farmed more rewardingly and was a more agreeable place to live, this was beneficial for all concerned. On the negative side, the subject towns, and especially their leaders, must have lost some autonomy, for they were now under the thumb of the lords of Huehuetenango and, through them, Espinar. Whether or not advantages accrued to ordinary people, burning and resettlement was a boon for the *encomendero* and for the native elite who were his accomplices. In short order, the scattered population of some half-dozen towns was successfully moved. Regrouping the region's labor pool must have taken pressure off Huehuetenango's own population while at the same time increasing the productivity of Espinar's varied enterprises in agriculture and mining.

Though the strategy had spin-offs for everyone, the main beneficiary was Juan de Espinar. Unfortunately for him, the matter came to the attention of Francisco de Orduña, whose investigative findings were passed on to Pedro de Alvarado. Alvarado, in turn, used the disclosures to his advantage. This resulted, about eight months after the incidents occurred,

25. Because of the conspiracy between Espinar and native leaders to tell Spanish authorities the same, agreed-upon story, it is difficult to separate indigenous concerns from those voiced by the *encomendero* himself. The problem is compounded by Espinar's threats to harm, perhaps even kill, anyone who disclosed what he was doing. Added to the confusion of motives is the difficulty, at this early date, of accurate translation from Mam to Spanish, and vice versa.

in Espinar's forfeiting his *encomienda* and the collapse of his related enterprises. It also resulted in Espinar's imprisonment, flight from captivity, and escape, albeit temporarily, to Mexico. After Francisco de Zurrilla's one-year tenure as *encomendero*, Espinar was reinstated. The spoils that he and his native allies once enjoyed, however, were much depleted. Excessive exploitation by Zurrilla caused Huehuetenango's population to fall precipitously. Furthermore, when Espinar regained control of Huehuetenango, the *encomienda* by that name no longer included Atitán, Chimbal, or Niquitlán, which were apparently ceded to Zurrilla.[26] The parts of Huehuetenango that remained under Espinar's entitlement incorporated only the *cabecera* itself and nearby Chiantla. As a consequence, Espinar's economic power and the influence of native elites suffered a sharp decline.

By 1536, when Espinar's claim against Alvarado came before the courts, Huehuetenango as a Spanish reward was well past its peak. Moreover, of the ten thousand pesos Espinar demanded as compensation, he received only six hundred. The Indian burden, however, had yet to be lifted. That same year, 1536, Alvarado again left Guatemala for Spain. During his absence, the Crown at last took steps to curb the excesses of *encomenderos* by formalizing the process of levying tribute.

26. AGI, Justicia 295.

CHAPTER 8

MALDONADO, MARROQUÍN, AND THE REGULATION OF EXCESS

The cunning, at times malevolent, behavior of Juan de Espinar was that of an ambitious man intent on making himself undisputed master over the lands and peoples entrusted him as *encomendero*. Yet Espinar's orchestrated exploitation of Huehuetenango, if we are to believe Bartolomé de Las Casas, was not exceptional, for the Defender of the Indians claimed that Guatemala was where the worst abuses of the *encomienda* system took place, quite a thing to assert even if we are prepared to accept at face value only a fraction of what Las Casas has to say.[1] It was to curb such excesses that the Crown undertook to draw up legislation governing the amount of goods and services *encomienda* obligations should entail. Moves toward regulation in Guatemala date to 1535. That year, in response to *reales cédulas* issued in 1533 and 1534, Alonso de Maldonado (at that time an *oidor*, or judge, in the Audiencia of New Spain) wrote to Pedro de Alvarado (then governor of Guatemala) about the legal requirement to have controlled and systematic *tasaciones de tributos*, assessments of tribute, levied on native communities.

Maldonado had been notified by the Crown to leave Mexico in 1535 to serve as acting governor in Guatemala during Alvarado's anticipated absence in Spain. No small amount of tension already existed between the two men, for they held very different views about what constituted effective government, especially the extent to which Guatemala should be subject to the jurisdiction of Mexico. Their differences soon came to a head over the issue of tribute assessment.[2] Alvarado's reaction to

1. Las Casas ([1552] 1982). See also Sherman (1979, 182–84).
2. For evidence of the impending conflict between Alvarado and Maldonado, see AGI, Patronato 180-1-64. An abstract of the controversy surrounding the *tasación* may be found in the Real Academia de la Historia (hereafter RAH), Colección Muñoz A 107.

Maldonado's mandate instructing him to regulate the payment of tribute—that of outright opposition—was typical of the veteran conquistador, who preferred to recognize no authority other than his own and who regarded Guatemala as little more than his personal estate.³ Maldonado, following royal orders, stated his position as follows:

> Given that, for the Indians of Guatemala, there are no levies or controls in place as to what they have to furnish and pay in tribute to those persons who hold them in *encomienda*, and in view of the need to preserve them for posterity, it is a good thing that these Indians be regulated and assessed as to what they are to give and contribute to those within whose *encomienda* they live and to whom they are entrusted. . . . [The King] therefore [orders] that all persons holding Indians in *encomienda* in the Province of Guatemala see to it that they be assessed and evaluated with tribute payment in mind within the next thirty days, under penalty of ignoring the order and placing oneself above the authority of His Majesty.⁴

The time had come, Maldonado made clear, to put the house in order. His pronouncements to that end, however, did not go over well with Alvarado, who considered them intrusive, misguided, ill-informed, and counter-productive, at odds with Guatemalan realities very different from the situation in which Spaniards found themselves in Mexico. The Adelantado, angered and dumbfounded, thought it best to deal with the situation by writing to the King directly. He fired off a testy rebuke, part of which runs:

3. For biographical treatment of Alvarado, see Kelly (1932); Barón Castro (1943); and Recinos (1952). García Añoveros furnishes both a biography (1987b) and a critical study (1987a) of sources dealing with him. Concerning his considerable estate, see Sherman (1969). Maldonado, when sent to Guatemala in 1535, was instructed to conduct Alvarado's *residencia*, the second such investigation into the conquistador's affairs, which inevitably led to heated exchange between judge and defendant; see AGI, Patronato 275-1-19 and Patronato 180-1-64, "Autos hechos sobre la tasación de los indios" (1535). An exhaustive study of the *residencia*, which includes a full transcription of court records by Julio Martín Blasco, is undertaken by Vallejo García-Hevia (2008). We deal with Alvarado and his reckless ways at length in part I.

4. AGI, Patronato 180-1-64, "Autos hechos sobre la tasación de los indios" (1535). The document states: "[P]orque en esta provincia de Guatemala los indios de ella no están tasados ni moderados en lo que han de dar y tributar a las personas que los tienen encomendados y para la conservación y perpetuidad de los indios de esta provincia conviene que los indios de ella se moderen y tasen en lo que han de dar y contribuir a las personas en quien están encomendados y depositados, por tanto . . . que todas las personas que tuvieron indios encomendados en esta provincia de Guatemala los traigan. . . a tasar y moderar dentro de treinta días primeros siguientes, so pena que se pronunciará por vaco y se pondrá en cabeza de Su Majestad."

Because I am governor of this Province of Guatemala, in His Majesty's name, being governor means that the Very Revered President and *oidores* of the Royal Audiencia of Mexico neither then nor now can interfere in any way with my governing. . . . And even if His Majesty has indeed ordered that tribute assessments be levied on the Indians of New Spain, it does not follow that the Indians of Guatemala have to be assessed, because Guatemala is a jurisdiction in its own right, distinct and separate from the jurisdiction of Mexico and the said New Spain, as is well known. . . . And if His Majesty were best served by having the Indians of Guatemala assessed for tribute, His Majesty would send me the order [himself], as he has sent me other such commands and royal decrees, I who govern by His mandate. . . . And because, as governor of Guatemala, I have [already] assessed and regulated the tribute-paying capacity of Indian towns and their inhabitants, I am prepared to do so once again, should the opportunity arise and if I consider it in His Majesty's best interest to do so. . . . Guatemala is not yet completely conquered or pacified; the Indians of these parts are ferocious and unruly, and number more than the Spaniards who live here. The greater part of the year is taken up waging war on them, conquering and pacifying them to benefit His Majesty. . . . Also, because Guatemala is [such] a wild and rugged [country], traversed by mountains, sierras, and ravines, its tribute potential is paltry and limited, and so the Indians do not furnish Spaniards with gold, silver or blankets, as do the Indians of New Spain, only corn and chili peppers, and even these in small quantities, what the Indians want to give voluntarily, without the use of force. . . . If the said tribute assessment were carried out, Spanish residents would be unable to sustain themselves here and, out of pure necessity, would have to abandon Guatemala and search for a living in other parts. This would result in an Indian uprising and native repossession of the land, which in turn would make it difficult to reconquer and pacify, given that I and [other] Spaniards and captains who have fought alongside me for seven years or more [are still hard pressed]. For these reasons, each and every one of them, I therefore request, [indeed] implore Your Majesty to withdraw and reconsider the said order, for to carry out tribute assessments in this province and jurisdiction would not be to His Majesty's advantage.[5]

5. AGI, Patronato 180-1-64, "Autos hechos sobre la tasación de los indios" (1535). The document states: "[P]orque yo soy gobernador de esta provincia de Guatemala, por Su Majestad, y siendo gobernador no se pudieron ni pueden entremeter el Muy Reverendo Presidente y oidores

It made no sense, Alvarado contended, to talk of regulating tribute by establishing schedules and setting quotas when there were still Indians in parts of Guatemala who had yet to be conquered. What most infuriated him was that men "who have fought alongside me for seven years or more" would have their *encomiendas* declared vacant and placed in the hands of the Crown if they failed to comply with the new measures "within the next thirty days." What kind of out-of-touch world were the King and Maldonado living in?

Maldonado, however, was neither persuaded nor impressed by Alvarado's reasoning, and was in no two minds about the fundamental cause of the problem: unwillingness on the part of *encomenderos* to put down roots and make a long-term commitment to remaining in Guatemala, as Juan de Espinar had done:

> What is best in this jurisdiction in order to protect the Indians in it and to have them treated well is that the said tribute assessment and regulation be conducted, as His Majesty demands. This is more a necessity here than in Mexico, because in Mexico almost all the [Spaniards] have settled down and have no intention of returning to Castile. Rather, these people wish to stay put, and so each of them endeavors to lighten

---

de la Audiencia Real de México en cosa alguna de mi gobernación. . . y porque aunque por S[u] M[ajestad] se haya mandado tasar los indios de la Nueva España, no por eso fue visto mandar que se tasen los indios de esta gobernación de Guatemala, por ser como es gobernación por sí, distinta y apartada de la gobernación de México y de la dicha Nueva España, como es notorio . . . y porque si S[u] M[ajestad] fuera servido que se tasen los indios de esta gobernación de Guatemala, S[u] M[ajestad] me enviara a mandar, como a su gobernador, por expreso mando suyo, como me ha enviado a mandar otras cosas por sus Provisiones Reales . . . y porque yo, como gobernador de Guatemala, tengo tasados y moderados los pueblos e indios de ella, y estoy presto a volverlos a tasar, habiendo oportunidad, cuando me pareciere que conviene al servicio de S[u] M[ajestad] . . . y porque esta tierra y provincia de Guatemala no está acabada de conquistar ni pacificar, y lo más del año, por ser los indios y naturales de ella bravos e indomables, están los españoles que en ella viven en la guerra sobre ellos, conquistándolos y pacificándoles al servicio de S[u] M[ajestad] . . . y porque esta dicha provincia, asimismo, es muy recia y áspera de montes, sierras y barrancas, y muy estéril y flaca de tributos y mantenimientos, porque los indios de ella no dan a los españoles oro ni plata ni manta, como los indios de la Nueva España, salvo maíz y ají, y eso muy poco, y lo que los indios les quieren dar de su voluntad sin premia ni fuerza alguna . . . y porque si la dicha tasación se hiciese los vecinos españoles no podrían sostenerse en esta gobernación y de pura necesidad se habían ir de ella a buscar de comer a otras partes, y sería dar causa a los indios y naturales de ella se levantasen luego y se alzasen con la tierra, la cual sería mala de volver a conquistar y pacificar según el largo tiempo que yo y los españoles y capitanes que conmigo anduvieron en la guerra estuvimos en la conquistar y pacificar que fueron siete años y más, por las cuales razones y por cada una de ellas pido y suplico a V[uestra] M[ajestad] mande revocar y reponer el dicho pregón . . . para hacer la dicha tasación, pues no conviene al servicio de S[u] M[ajestad] que se haga en esta provincia y gobernación."

the load of their Indians as much as is possible. Here it is the opposite; the majority of Spanish residents [wish] to return to Castile, amassing monies to that end and not [in the least] concerned with native welfare but [rather] getting as much as they can out of the Indians, in order to fulfill promptly their desire to leave for Spain. They do not object to the reasons that the Governor [Alvarado] puts forward in his efforts to prevent the said tribute assessment from being carried out, nor oppose him from alleging that I am insisting that it be done, whereas I am ordered to do so by His Majesty. . . . It is against His Majesty's rulings in his Royal Decree, for there is no impediment to conducting the tribute assessment of the Indians in your jurisdiction. It seems clear that the Governor can rule as he sees fit and I can get on with conducting the said tribute assessment, without one of us contradicting the other.[6]

Instead of amassing wealth ruthlessly, so as to return esteemed, if not exalted, to Spain, *encomenderos* should cooperate with the authorities and make do with their lot. That way, Maldonado contended, things could be made to work for the betterment of all. Alvarado, once he read or was informed of Maldonado's remarks, could not have failed to see in them an indictment of his own actions and behavior.

Other Spaniards besides Alvarado refused to see any merit in Maldonado's position, among them Rodrigo de Sandoval. Writing to the King on behalf of the *cabildo* of Santiago de Guatemala, Sandoval echoed Alvarado's point of view:

I ask and beseech that the said proclamation to carry out tribute assessments be revoked, because it is not in His Majesty's interests to have

6. AGI, Patronato 180-1-64, "Autos hechos sobre la tasación de los indios" (1535). The document states: "Que lo que más conviene en esta gobernación para [la] conservación de los indios de ella y su buen tratamiento es que la dicha tasación y moderación se haga como S[u] M[ajestad] lo manda y esto es más necesario aquí [en Guatemala] que en México porque en México casi todas las personas están de asiento y no tienen intención de se ir a Castilla sino permanecer en la tierra, y así cada uno procura relevar sus indios en todo lo que puede . . . [A]quí [en Guatemala] es lo contrario porque la mayor parte de los vecinos . . . están de camino para Castilla en allegando dineros para se poder ir a ella y así no tienen respeto a la conversión de los indios sino a sacarles todo lo que más pueden para más presto poder cumplir su deseo [de] irse a España y no obstan las razones por que el S[eño]r Gobernador se alegan para impedir que la dicha tasación se haga ni menos le obsta decir que yo soy parte para hacer esta tasación, pues tengo mandado de S[u] M[ajestad] para hacerla . . . y que es contra lo que S[u] M[ajestad] tiene mandado por su Real Cédula, porque ningún impedimento se le pone en su gobernación con hacer la tasación de los dichos indios como parece claro que él puede gobernar en todo lo que pareciese que conviene y yo hacer la dicha tasación y no contradice lo uno a lo otro."

such a thing done [here] in Guatemala, for the reasons stated by Governor [Alvarado]. . . . It would result in our losing control over this land, and in the Spaniards who have taken up residence here leaving to seek sustenance elsewhere.[7]

Opposition from powerful quarters, then, meant that Maldonado had to proceed with caution. Not without vested interests himself, he saw fit to denounce them in almost everyone else. Not until Maldonado worked alongside the first bishop of Guatemala, Francisco Marroquín, did they muster sufficient resolve to overcome the resistance of Alvarado and the *cabildo* of Santiago, thus eventually enabling the *tasaciones* to be carried out.[8] Since these *tasaciones* have long been considered lost or destroyed, we were most pleased to locate several of them in the course of our research.[9] Given their historical value, we think it important to transcribe them in full and comment (as in the case of Huehuetenango

7. AGI, Patronato 180-1-64, "Autos hechos sobre la tasación de los indios" (1535). The document states: "Pido y suplico a . . . revocar y reponer el dicho pregón . . . para hacer la dicha tasación pues no lo conviene al servicio de S[u] M[ajestad] que se haga en esta provincia y gobernación de Guatemala por las razones dichas y alegadas por el Señor Gobernador [Alvarado] a que se refiere porque sería dar causa a que la tierra se perdiese y los españoles que en ella viven y moran la dejasen y se fuesen a buscar de comer en otras partes."

8. For a summary of Maldonado's career, and details of accusations concerning abuse of office, see MacLeod ([1973] 2008, 83, 86, 113, 116, and 129) and Sherman (1979, 129–30 and 136–41). Maldonado's *residencia*, taken by Alonso López de Cerrato, may be found in AGI, Justicia 299A. For a biography of Marroquín, see Sáenz de Santa María (1964). This book is very much a laudatory tribute. MacLeod ([1973] 2008, 104 and 108) is more critical of the bishop, considering him "mild and compromising," too much an apologist for Pedro de Alvarado's blatant excesses. Sherman (1979, 162–63) also views Marroquín as the champion of compromise and moderation. See also Rodríguez Becerra (1977, 117–18).

9. Rodríguez Becerra (1975, 246) states: "We have word that tribute assessments were carried out during the early years of conquest, but unfortunately none of these documents has survived or at least been located as of now." Carmack (1973, 137–38) writes: "I have been unable to find tribute records on the Guatemalan Indians for the 25 years following the conquest. . . . Both Marroquín and Maldonado took tribute censuses before 1540, but unfortunately the records are no longer available." We have located seventeen *tasaciones* undertaken by Maldonado and Marroquín, relating to twenty-one *pueblos de indios*, in the course of our work in the Archivo General de Indias in Seville. Six of the *pueblos de indios* referred to in the *tasaciones* are located in present-day Guatemala, the other fifteen in neighboring El Salvador. These *tasaciones* form part of a seven-folio *traslado*, a copy made from the original, both found in AGI, Indiferente General 857. Three other *tasaciones*, one of which is most likely an original, may be found in AGI, Patronato 70-1-8. The original, in an appalling state of disrepair, actually bears the signatures of Marroquín ("Epicopus Cuahtlmalensis") and Maldonado. AGI, Justicia 286 contains two *tasaciones*, for Jumaytepeque in Guatemala and Tacuba in El Salvador, which may be attributed to the initiatives of Maldonado and Marroquín. Another *tasación*, for Santiago Atitlán in Guatemala, may be found in AGI, Justicia 295, among documents pertaining to Alvarado's *residencia*.

in the previous chapter) on the nature, amount, and frequency of the goods and services that Indians were expected to provide. First, however, we offer a few more observations about the process of tribute assessment itself.

The *tasaciones*, begun after a royal edict was issued on February 23, 1536, were undertaken in the years between 1536 and 1541. On May 10, 1537, Bishop Marroquín wrote to the King informing him that he had compiled "the register covering the entire extent of the jurisdiction," claiming also (surely with exaggeration) that he knew "all the towns [in question], each and every one," and had "conversed and communicated with [their inhabitants] as best one can."[10] The following eighteen months or so must have been busy ones indeed, for by January 20, 1539, Marroquín could inform the King:

> With the tribute assessment now carried out in most areas—we, the Governor [Maldonado] and I, will divide up what is left to do at the end of this month—considerable progress has been achieved. We have given the Indians to understand that they have God in Heaven, the King on Earth, and a Governor and Bishop who act in the name of Your Majesty in their defense and assistance, all of which conforms to an order that Your Majesty sent to this effect and in all of which they are instructed fairly well each day they are taught.[11]

Marroquín and Maldonaldo involved themselves in the hard work of traveling throughout Guatemala in an attempt to ensure that just and realistic assessments were carried out. They appear to have enjoyed a good working relationship, for Marroquín states:

> In truth, during the entire time that Licenciado Maldonado was here, nothing came between us, for he behaved more like a judge than a

10. Bishop Marroquín to the King, May 10, 1537, in Sáenz de Santa María (1964, 128). Marroquín states that "yo tenía hecha la matrícula de todos los pueblos, porque los conosco todos, uno a uno, y muchas veces he platicado y comunicado lo que cada uno puede."

11. Bishop Marroquín to the King, January 20, 1539, in Sáenz de Santa María (1964, 141). The original text reads: "[C]on la tasación que se ha hecho, en la mayor parte della (y para lo que queda nos partiremos en fin deste mes el gobernador [Maldonado] y yo) ha recibido grande beneficio, y se va conociendo, y sobre todo habérseles dado el entender que tienen Dios en el cielo y el rey en la tierra, y que tienen gobernador y obispo en nombre de Vra. Magt. para su defensa e amparo. [Y] todo lo demás conforme a una cédula que Vra. Magt. [e]nvió para este efecto y en todo están medianamente instruidos y de cada día se instruyen." Marroquín's letter is summarized in RAH, Colección Muñoz, A 108.

governor, and so we were able always to agree, having decided to conduct the tours of inspection together; I say this because it is my desire to fulfill my duties as protector and thus ease Your Majesty's mind. One should know that this is necessary, in order to make it clear that [my duties] are about protection, and [also to make it clear] to whom this applies. This is, and should be, my responsibility, with which no one should interfere nor should be able to interfere, and in which neither the law nor the governor should hinder me.[12]

Even though the bishop and the acting governor attempted to do the most thorough job possible, Marroquín had no doubts that what they achieved was less than perfect and, as such, would be the subject of controversy, if not the target of criticism. He wrote to the King spelling out a couple of recommendations:

Two very vital points that I have forgotten are that Your Majesty shall order that (1) after the tribute assessment has been carried out, the governor should not add to it, nor delete anything [from it], nor grant permission that the obligation be suspended without consultation and determining whether [or not] it would be advantageous, for everything collected would flow down that drain; and (2) it should be stated clearly what has to be given and what can be given every year or two, for each day one finds out whether or not this is possible—a statement to that effect is necessary.[13]

In hindsight, Marroquín expressed reservations almost six years later, stating that "the tribute assessment that Licenciado Maldonado and I

12. Bishop Marroquín to the King, January 20, 1539, in Sáenz de Santa María (1964, 145). The original text reads: "[V]erdad que en todo el tiempo que ha estado aquí el licenciado Maldonado no ha habido entre nosotros diferencia, porque se ha tenido más por oidor que gobernador, y a esta causa siempre ha habido conformidad; y porque siempre habemos andado juntos en la visitación; digo esto porque deseo hacer mi oficio de protector como descargue la conciencia de Vra. Mt.; que esto se conozca es menester se aclare que cosa es ser protector y a que se extiende; y que en lo que es o fuere a mi cargo no se entremeten ni puedan entremeter, ni me impedir la justicia, ni el gobernador."

13. Bishop Marroquín to the King, January 20, 1539, in Sáenz de Santa María (1964, 147). The original text reads: "Olvidado se me habían dos punctos muy esenciales y es que Vra. Magd. mande que hecha la tasación el gobernador no pueda añadir, ni quitar cosa alguna ni dar licencia para quebrantar la tasación, sin que se consulte y se vea si conviene que sería un desaguadero por do[nde] se saliese todo lo coxido; ansimismo en las tasaciones no puede haber claridad, ni lo que se debe y puede dar en un año y dos, cada día se descubre la posibilidad o falta; es menester declaración para esto."

carried out could not be done with full and complete knowledge."[14] Much earlier, in fact, he had to endure "ugly and shameful words" from *encomenderos* who felt wronged by the *tasaciones* and who caused great "commotion and uproar" on finding out about them.[15]

Alvarado's departure for Spain in 1536 and Maldonado's governorship of Guatemala during the three years Alvarado was away apparently signaled a marked improvement in the native lot. There was no more panning for gold, the *Memorial de Solalá* informs us, nor deployment of child labor, both welcome reprieves.[16] By August 10, 1541, the assessment procedure had been completed. Marroquín alludes to the fact in a letter he wrote that day to the King. In the same letter, Marroquín tells of hearing about the death in Mexico of Pedro de Alvarado the month before, and surmises quite correctly that with the conquistador's demise Guatemala would undergo further changes:

> On my way home from finishing the tribute assessment for this province, which has been most advantageous, I received correspondence from the Viceroy with the saddest news possible, that of the death of the Adelantado Don Pedro de Alvarado. I fear that Your Majesty has lost his best and most loyal servant in these parts. I, for one, had great [affection] and love for him, for he had no equal. I suspect that with his death things will change here, most of all in [how] Guatemala and its jurisdictions are governed.[17]

After Alvarado's death, Maldonado was appointed president of the Audiencia de Guatemala, a post he held from 1543 until 1548 and one in which he was supposed to implement the New Laws of the Indies for the Good Treatment and Protection of the Indians.[18] Under Maldonaldo's presidency, another effort was made to assess the tribute-paying capacity as fairly and accurately as possible; records exist of three *oidores*—Diego de Herrera, Pedro Ramírez de Quiñones, and Juan Rogel—having

14. Bishop Marroquín to the King, March 15, 1545, in RAH, Colección Muñoz, A 111.

15. Bishop Marroquín to the King, March 27, 1539, in Sáenz de Santa María (1964, 148–49). His precise words are "[p]or cartas desa cibdad he sabido el alboroto y escándolo que ha nacido. . . . Palabras feas y desvergonzadas me escriben."

16. Recinos and Goetz (1953, 130–31). See chapter 3, note 28, for elaboration.

17. Bishop Marroquín to the King, August 10, 1541, in Sáenz de Santa María (1964, 164). Marroquín's letter, written from Chiapas, where the bishop had travelled in order to complete the *tasación*, is summarized in RAH, Colección Muñoz, A 109.

18. MacLeod ([1973] 2008, 390) and Sherman (1979, 129–32 and 136).

undertaken the task.[19] We have managed to locate only fragments of these *tasaciones*.[20] When they heard about these new assessments, *encomenderos* reacted with clamorous indignation to the quotas imposed by them, especially the ones carried out in Chiapas by Rogel:

> The said tribute assessment is very much in favor of the Indians and to the detriment of [us] Spaniards, who are ruined by it. The Spanish residents of Chiapas in particular lament the assessments undertaken by Licenciado Rogel [in his capacity as] *oidor*, assessments that he carried out without ever having seen the Indians or their towns and having no idea as to what they are able to furnish.[21]

It was not, however, until Alonso López de Cerrato succeeded Maldonado as president of Guatemala in 1548 that tribute assessments reflecting the New Laws were systematically enforced.

THE TRIBUTE ASSESSMENTS OF MALDONADO AND MARROQUÍN

The *tasaciones* transcribed below constitute little more than a handful of those Maldonado and Marroquín compiled, for we know that the two men visited many other communities throughout Central America with the goal of tribute assessment in mind.[22] While, in terms of present-day geography, only seven Guatemalan pueblos are represented, they include some of the most highly prized *encomiendas*, held by several of the most illustrious, or infamous, of conquerors. Utatlán, the K'iche' capital known as Gumarcaah before the conquest, paid tribute to Cristóbal de la Cueva;[23] Momostenango and Comalapa were in the hands of

19. Rodríguez Becerra (1977, 118).
20. The documents in question may be found in AGI, Patronato 70-1-8 and Justicia 286.
21. Taken from Rodríguez Becerra (1977, 118), citing AGI, Justicia 299A. The document states: "[L]a dicha tasación fue muy provechosa a los indios e a los españoles muy dañosa y que están destruidos por ella y que especialmente los vecinos de Chiapas lloran de la dicha tasación a causa que el Licenciado Rogel, oidor, la hizo sin ver los indios ni los pueblos ni saber de cierto lo que podían dar."
22. Rodríguez Becerra (1977, 117). As early as 1532, Marroquín appears to have been particularly influential in having tribute assessments carried out in neighboring El Salvador; see Gall (1968), Fowler (1987, 1989), and Amaroli (1991) for fuller discussion.
23. Cristóbal de la Cueva took part in the conquest of Mexico and Guatemala. For a summary of his services to the Crown, see AGI, Patronato 70-1-8 and Recinos (1952, 158–60).

Juan Pérez Dardón;[24] Jumaytepeque, which was always closely associated with Tacuba, in present-day El Salvador, furnished goods and services to Francisco de la Cueva, as did San Martín Sacatepéquez and Ostuncalco, which were also linked together;[25] and Santiago Atitlán was shared between Pedro de Alvarado and Sancho de Barahona.[26] Only one *tasación* carries a date, that of Santiago Atitlán, which was assessed on March 16, 1537. We can, however, assert with confidence that the others also belong to the *tasaciones* carried out between 1536 and 1541 by Maldonado and Marroquín.

Given their importance, we now make a record of these *tasaciones*, commenting town-by-town on their contents and implications. As with our discussion of Huehuetenango in chapter 7, we compare and contrast the tribute levies of Maldonado and Marroquín with those decreed by Cerrato a decade and a half later. To avoid exaggerating the burden that *tasaciones* represented for the native communities in question, we err on the side of caution; we assume, for example, that in most cases labor requirements under "servicio ordinario" (normal labor service) were imposed for forty-nine and not fifty-two weeks annually, taking into account the three weeks for which Indians were excused from such services later on. These were (1) Semana Santa, or Holy Week; (2) the week during which a town's patron saint and feast day were celebrated; and (3) a week at Christmas. We begin with Santiago Atitlán (see table 12), followed by San Martín Sacatepéquez and Ostuncalco (table 13), Jumaytepeque (table 14) and Tacuba (table 15), Comalapa (table 16), Momostenango (table 17), and Utatlán (table 18).

We close with excerpts from the tasaciones and an evaluation of what, comparatively, the tribute burden represented for these eight communities.

[Santiago] Atitlán

The tribute assessment of the Indians of Atitlán, held in *encomienda* by the Adelantado Don Pedro de Alvarado and Sancho de Barahona,

24. Juan Peréz Dardón took part in the conquest of Mexico and Guatemala. For a summary of his services to the Crown, see AGI, Patronato 70-1-7 and 75-2-5.

25. Francisco de la Cueva was the son-in-law of Pedro de Alvarado. He first arrived in Guatemala upon the return of his father-in-law in 1539. For a summary of his services to the Crown, see AGI, Patronato 60-5-3 and Recinos (1952, 183–228).

26. Sancho de Barahona arrived in Guatemala with Pedro de Alvarado after the conquest of Tututepeque. Barahona's relationship with Alvarado was often stormy, the result of the latter's moves to appropriate Barahona's half of Atitlán either for himself or his brother Jorge. See AGI, Justicia 295.

was carried out on March 16, 1537. Every year the Indians are to give 1,000 *xiquipiles* of cacao, 500 to each *encomendero*. They are to provide each *encomendero* with fifteen Indians to serve in the city [Santiago in Almolonga], and every fifteen days they are to provide each *encomendero* with 40 Indian mantles, striped, and twenty doublets and loincloths. Every year they are to provide each *encomendero* with 100 pairs of sandals; and every fifteen days [they are to give] to each *encomendero* fifteen fowl (ten Spanish chickens and five native turkeys) and fifteen *cargas* of corn, one [*carga*] of beans, one [*carga*] of chili peppers, one [*carga*] of salt, and a jug of honey. Every Friday they are to provide each *encomendero* with forty eggs and a *carga* of crabs; and every year sixty reed mats [to each *encomendero*] and the same amount of gourds. These amounts are for this year only, because the Indians claim that they are exhausted and that the tribute assessment should be adjusted to what they are able to give. The Indians are not obliged to give any more [than the above amounts], nor is any more to be taken from them under pain of [the *encomenderos*] forfeiting their Indians altogether.

This assessment is a clear-cut case of excess in the extreme, which we attribute to the fact that one of the *encomenderos* involved is none other than Pedro de Alvarado himself, though Sancho de Barahona was also a very powerful man. Together, Alvarado and Barahona were fortunate beneficiaries indeed, nowhere more graphically noted than in the *tasacion*: the tributaries themselves "claim that they are exhausted" and that the levy placed on them "should be adjusted to what they are able to give." Women as much as men would have been hard pressed to meet the community quota, be it an article of clothing or an item of foodstuff.

By the time of the later Cerrato assessment in 1549, Alvarado had been dead for some eight years. With Alvarado gone, his half of Atitlán was taken over by the Crown. Barahona was by then also deceased, but his share of Atitlán had been assumed by his son, also called Sancho. Cerrato reduced the tribute levy considerably, eliminating all goods save cacao, which was to be delivered in quantities that were actually 20 percent more than those demanded twelve years before. During this period, however, Atitlán lost at least a third of its population.[27]

27. Based on a tributary count of 1,400 for 1545 and a count of 1,000 for 1549; see MacLeod ([1973] 2008, 131) and AGI, Guatemala 128, respectively. Atitlán's population would have been much larger in 1537 than it was in 1545, as this entire period was one in which devastating epidemics claimed thousands of lives; see Lovell ([1992] 2001, 71–72).

Since the town controlled extensive territory from the highlands around Lake Atitlán to the Pacific piedmont, furnishing such large quantities of cacao was not as difficult a challenge as it would have been for communities without Atitlán's ecological advantage. MacLeod observes that the town functioned as "the cacao trading point" between the coast and Santiago de Guatemala.[28] Nonetheless, 1,200 *xiquipiles* of cacao was a sizable amount for any one community to supply. MacLeod estimates that one *xiquipil* (a unit of 8,000 cacao beans) weighed 16.6 pounds, so Atitlán's annual tribute of the crop weighed in at about 20,000 pounds, some ten tons.[29] Meeting this requirement would have taxed the resources of even a well-endowed community, especially when its population was in precipitous decline.

[San Martín] Sacatepéquez and Ostuncalco

Every 70 days [the Indians] are to give 100 *xiquipiles* of cacao plus 400 pieces of cotton cloth of good measure and twenty bedcovers, as well as twenty pieces of ornamental cloth of the type they usually give, and twelve baskets of salt. [Every 70 days they shall furnish] provisions for the pig farms, having planted cornfields for [this purpose]. On certain days and holidays they are to bring honey, chickens, quail, and eggs, and clothes for the swineherds. [The Indians] need not give anything more [than this], save for some food for the *calpisque* who lives there [and whose job it is to oversee the swineherds].

San Martín Sacatepéquez and Ostuncalco are located in what is today the department of Quetzaltenango.[30] Their combined tributary population in 1549 was estimated at two thousand, making the jurisdiction the largest *encomienda* in Guatemala in the mid-sixteenth century. It must have been even more populous in 1538 when held by Francisco de la Cueva, whose cousin, Beatriz de la Cueva, was Pedro de Alvarado's wife.[31] After the deaths of Alvarado and Doña Beatriz, who were killed within months of each other in 1541, De la Cueva married Doña Leonor,

28. MacLeod ([1973] 2008, 117).
29. Ibid., 70.
30. San Martín Sacatepéquez was formerly known as San Martín Chile Verde; see Gall (1962, vol. 2, 197) for a summary of its history and municipal administration. Several communities in different parts of Guatemala carry the indigenous name Sacatepéquez, hence the need to identify the town in question as precisely as possible.
31. See Kramer (1994, 152).

Alvarado's *mestiza* daughter from a union with a Tlaxcalan noblewoman; she became his principal heir. Even before the benefit of these family ties became a reality, Don Francisco was influential enough to receive and retain this prestigious *encomienda,* as well as others discussed below.

How did De la Cueva's native charges fare when he was their *encomendero*? A number of items furnished him in 1538 were left unspecified as to quantity and frequency of delivery. These included corn, to be fed to Don Francisco's pigs, as well as honey, quail, chickens, and eggs. Not spelling out what specific amounts were to be delivered is a feature of most of these early *tasaciones*, Atitlán being a notable exception.

Apart from a 40 percent reduction in the amount of cacao he received, De la Cueva appears to have enjoyed a steady allocation of tribute between 1538 and 1549, including an allotment of Indians for "servicio ordinario."[32] This provision is quite striking, given that most *encomenderos* forfeited the privilege under Cerrato.

Jumaytepeque

[The Indians] are to grow wheat, and to that end they shall receive assistance from the people of Tacuba. The said wheat should be brought to this city [Santiago in Almolonga] along with six Indian workers to serve their [*encomendero*] when they are not bringing in the harvest. Each Sunday [they shall] give two fowl, one a Castilian chicken and another a native turkey, and give [to the *encomendero*] the honey and beeswax that he needs, in addition to some sandals for [his] slaves as well as cultivating the cornfields as they should do.

Tacuba

Each year [the Indians] are to plant their plots with chili peppers and black beans and harvest forty *xiquipiles* of cacao and bring to [their *encomendero*'s] house the chili peppers and [all] the salt he needs. They should also supply him, at all times, with the labor of nine Indians for work in this city [Santiago in Almolonga]. It is in Jumaytepeque that Indians [from Tacuba] are to help cultivate the wheat fields. They shall carry the said wheat to this city. When these Indians come to help cultivate the fields, they should not come to the city to serve, [but] should bring the wheat to the city in the dry season. They are also to give 100

32. Like Santiago Atitlán, San Martín Sacatepéquez and Ostuncalco had relatively easy access to cacao from lands they held on the Pacific piedmont; see Zamora (1985, 345–46) and Diego de Garcés, Alcalde Mayor de Zapotitlán, to the Crown, AGI, Guatemala 52 (1560).

pieces of cotton cloth, 60 *huipiles*, and 100 loincloths. Every Sunday
they shall give five fowl, three native turkeys and two Castilian chickens, and deliver the honey and beeswax they wish to provide for [the
encomendero's] house, as well as some leather sandals for his slaves.

Jumaytepeque is still part of Guatemala, but Tacuba now lies in neighboring El Salvador.[33] The *encomiendas,* though distinct entities, had
also been held jointly, prior to De la Cueva's entitlement, by Sebastián
del Mármol. Mármol had been granted Jumaytepeque and Tacuba in one
of the first *encomienda* distributions in the late 1520s and held them
until his death in 1540.[34] We know that the early *tasaciones* transcribed
and translated here were carried out in Mármol's time, the late 1530s,
because they are identical to ones we have found for the period when
he was still *encomendero.*

Jumaytepeque's native inhabitants had to plant, cultivate, harvest,
and thresh a planting (*sementera*) of wheat of unspecified size, assisted
by nine Indians from Tacuba. We know from another source that Jumaytepeque was required to plant twenty-five *fanegas* of wheat for Don
Francisco who, in turn, was responsible for having the wheat field plowed
with his oxen. De la Cueva had a "morisco" work for him who was seen
"on numerous occasions" with a team of pack animals, bringing wheat
to the capital city from Jumaytepeque; Tacuba was again to provide
men to help with the wheat harvest.[35] By 1549, Jumaytepeque's planting
of wheat had been reduced to six *fanegas*, less than one-quarter the
amount planted in earlier times.

Once again, quantities of many items of tribute—honey, beeswax,
and sandals—are left unspecified, while quantities of chickens and turkeys
are spelled out. By 1549, honey, beeswax, and sandals were no longer

33. By 1770 Jumaytepeque, then called Jumay, was part of the Parish of Los Esclavos, a Chortí
Maya community in the present-day department of Santa Rosa; part of Tacuba, the Parish of
Aguachapan, was a Pipil-speaking town. See Cortés y Larraz ([1768–70] 1958, vol. 1, 51–56 and
63–67) for further information. At odds with Cortés y Larraz's information on the language
spoken in Jumay, Alonso Crespo, Justicia Mayor of the Partido of Escuintla, informs us in the
"Relación geográfica de las provincias de Escuintla y Guazacapán, 1740," that the Indians of the
town are administered by a secular priest who deals with them in Xinca; see Luján Muñoz (2006,
12) and Gall (1981, vol. 2, 447).

34. See Kramer (1994, 155).

35. See AGI, Justicia 286 ("Juan Rodriguez Cabrillo sobre Jumaytepeque y Tacuba, 1542–1568").
The original states: "[V]io a un morisco de Don Francisco muchas vezes en tiempos diversos con
una harria traer trigo y dezia que hera de la sementera de Xumaytepeque."

required, and the number of chickens was reduced. A small planting of 1.5 *fanegas* of corn, which is not listed in the 1538 document, was included for the first time in a *tasación* dating to 1544, as well as being a requirement of the Cerrato assessment in 1549.

Tacuba, unlike Jumaytepeque, paid forty *xiquipiles* of cacao to De la Cueva in 1538 and twice as much, eighty *xiquipiles*, in 1549. In the 1544 *tasación*, Tacuba gave seventy *xiquipiles* of cacao and a tribute item unique to this town—"henequén," or maguey fiber, four *cargas* of it annually.[36] In 1538 specific numbers of chickens and turkeys were ordered delivered to the *encomendero*'s house in Santiago, and a smaller amount in 1544, but fowl were no longer part of the 1549 levy. Likewise, specific amounts of handwoven clothing are listed in the 1538 document but omitted from the assessment eleven years later. The earlier *tasación* made Tacuba inhabitants vulnerable to abuse, as they were required "to bring to [their *encomendero*'s] house" the chili peppers and salt he needed in addition to "the honey and beeswax they wish to provide." These items of tribute had been pared down by 1544, when Indians were told rather vaguely that they "should give the foodstuffs that they want to give," and were gone from the list by 1549.[37]

Labor obligations also changed between 1538 and 1549, to native advantage. In 1538, both Jumaytepeque and Tacuba were required to supply Indians under terms of "servicio ordinario," but by 1549 the requirement no longer applied.[38] What did remain was a demand for manpower, in the case of Tacuba, twenty laborers twice a year, each stint for four days, to assist with the wheat harvest at Jumaytepeque. That this unusual joint tribute obligation between two discrete settlements survived the Cerrato reforms at mid-century is testimony to the enduring influence of the early *encomienda* grants and of the Alvarado family ties.

Comalapa

Each year [the Indians] are to provide [their *encomendero*] with 80 *cargas* of salt, 50 *fanegas* of chili peppers, 100 *fanegas* of black beans, 300 *cargas* of lime, and bricks and tiles for his house. They are also to

36. AGI, Justicia 286. MacLeod ([1973] 2008, 166) writes: "Henequen [is] the fiber from which *xarcia* or caulking for ships was obtained." It is also used to make rope or twine.
37. AGI, Justicia 286, in which the original states, "que den la fruta que ellos quisieran dar."
38. Once again, in the 1544 levy the *servicio ordinario* component was decreased, but not abolished.

give him fodder for his livestock, repair the stables, and furnish reed mats for his house, as well as honey and quail and other necessities, providing him [also] with 50 Indian laborers for the city [Santiago in Almolonga]. When [the Indians] come to work [in the city] they are to bring eight native turkeys and eight Castilian chickens and plant wheat and a large cornfield. If they are unable to produce [at least] 2,000 *fanegas* [of corn], they need to supplement the amount. And they are to give 60 *xiquipiles* of cacao. They are [also] to give 400 pieces of cotton cloth of the kind they are accustomed to giving.

None of the other *encomiendas* discussed here suffered the dual disadvantages that befell Comalapa, a Kaqchikel-speaking community in what is today the department of Chimaltenango. It lay in close proximity to the Spanish capital, first at Almolonga and later at Panchoy, and it was held by the mighty Juan Pérez Dardón. Both these factors left Comalapa open to onerous exploitation.

The *tasación* for 1538 has an array of tribute items (honey, quail, wheat, reed mats, tiles, and bricks) unspecified as to amounts due. At the same time, the *tasación* states in specific detail the number of units of a variety of other foodstuffs, cotton cloth, and lime to be delivered annually. The most demanding of the obligations was that Comalapa had to provide 2,000 *fanegas* (3,000 bushels) of corn, apparently planted, cultivated, and harvested on Indian communal lands. If the specified amount was not delivered, any shortfall had to be compensated for, presumably from the Indians' own supplies. Tribute payers in Pérez Dardón's other prize *encomienda*, Momostenango, also had to contend with this requirement. In addition, Comalapa had to furnish sixty *xiquipiles* of cacao.

In 1538, Pérez Dardón enjoyed a large allotment of fifty laborers, sent weekly from Comalapa to the Spanish capital to work in nearby fields. By 1549, despite Pérez Dardón's position of authority, the amount of tribute owed was much reduced and simplified. Gone were demands for turkeys, black beans, chili peppers, cacao, and all the building materials.

Comalapa had to pay a vast amount of salt, eighty *cargas* (240 bushels); however, this item had been reduced to fifteen bushels annually by 1549.[39] Comalapa had a long and continuous association with *salinas*

39. MacLeod ([1973] 2008, 468) reckons that a *carga* measured two *fanegas*, one *fanega* being the equivalent of 1.5 bushels.

(salt pans) on the Pacific coast, an association that dated back to pre-Hispanic times and that lasted well beyond the sixteenth century.[40] In an assessment for 1562, for instance, it is noted that Comalapa boasted "many salt and cotton merchants" whose commercial beat covered much of the Pacific coast.[41] The fall in the salt levy may have been due to native depopulation in lowland areas, even though traders were still active.

Between 1538 and 1549, Pérez Dardón's use of native labor fell by some 60 percent. By September of the latter year, Cerrato had ordered that Pérez Dardón's twenty remaining "indios de servicio" be substituted by an annual payment of 150 gold pesos. This was generous compensation compared to what was awarded other *encomenderos* without Pérez Dardón's connections and, in the end, constituted an additional burden for the Indians of Comalapa.

Momostenango

> Every fifteen days [the Indians] are to send 30 workers to the city [Santiago in Almolonga]. When they come to work they should bring ten turkeys and provide all the fodder and necessary care for the pigs and all the other livestock [there], as well as planting cornfields. If they do not manage to produce [at least] one thousand *fanegas*, they shall supplement the harvest by giving 60 *xiquipiles* of cacao. When they bring the turkeys, they shall also bring some quail with them, and whatever game they wish to give. [They should also] furnish honey, reed mats, pots, jugs, and clay griddles for making tortillas. Every Sunday they are to give [their *encomendero*] one *carga* of salt and another of chili peppers. They should also harvest the wheat.

Momostenango, a K'iche' community in the western highlands, like Comalapa, was assigned to Juan Pérez Dardón. As with Comalapa, the *tasación* for Momostenango contains a number of items, left unspecified as to amounts payable; other items such as corn, turkeys, salt, cacao, and chili peppers were spelled out in terms of quantity and frequency of delivery.

40. See, for example, "Autos de los indios de Comalapa, sobre que don Miguel Casique les impide la labranza de sus sales," AGCA, A1, leg. 6064, exp. 53974 (1601); and "Autos que siguen diferentes indios del valle de esta ciudad, salineros en la costa de Esquintepeque," AGCA, A1, leg. 4119, exp. 32636 (1675).

41. The original states "[h]ay muchos mercaderes tratantes en sal e algodón," and comes from the observations of Francisco del Valle Marroquín in the "Tasación y cuenta de Comalapa" (1562), cited in Kramer, Lovell, and Lutz (1986, 357–94, especially 382–83n51).

By contrast, as we have noted before, Cerrato's later *tasación* was more precise and allowed fewer loopholes for abuse. Also, chickens were now substituted for turkeys while wheat, fodder, and pottery were struck from the list. Other items, including corn, salt, and chili peppers, were sharply reduced. At sixty *xiquipiles* annually, however, the levy of cacao remained the same.

Pérez Dardón's connections and status, as in the case of Comalapa, did not protect him from losing significant labor privileges, which were cut from thirty Indians per fortnight in 1538 to seventeen in May 1549. By October 1549, Cerrato had removed twelve of the remaining seventeen Indian laborers who had to travel the long distance from Momostenango to Santiago de Guatemala, stipulating that Momostenango instead pay forty *xiquipiles* of cacao. Pérez Dardón was left with only five Indians of "servicio ordinario" status to work a cattle *estancia* near Momostenango, a sizable attrition that likely reflects not only reformist zeal on Cerrato's part but also a significant fall in native numbers from outbreaks of disease.[42]

Utatlán

[The Indians] are to give ten *xiquipiles* of cacao and twenty skirts and twenty pieces of cloth and forty Castilian chickens and whatever honey and salt and chili peppers they wish to give, in addition to some reed mats for [the *encomendero*'s] house, and [the labor] of ten Indians.

During the time it was held in *encomienda* by Cristóbal de la Cueva, Utatlán's days of grandeur as the capital of the K'iche' kingdom had long passed.[43] De la Cueva held two other towns along with Utatlán from as early as 1530.[44] In the mid-1530s he was involved in the ongoing conquest of neighboring Honduras, during which his reputation for heavy-handedness was commented on. One royal official and acting governor, Andrés de Cereceda, who had earlier complained of the "harsh treatment" of the Indians of Honduras, wrote a letter to the Crown in which he states: "Because [De la Cueva] was not given the Indians he asked for

42. Carmack (1995, 425, appendix 3) reckons that the population of Momostenango in 1524 was around 10,000, a figure that fell to 2,700 in 1550. The latter figure is based on a Cerrato tally of 450 tributaries, with a population-to-tributary ratio of 6:1.
43. See Carmack (1981) for a detailed account of the rise and fall of Utatlán.
44. Kramer (1994, 115, table 6.2).

[to serve as human carriers], incensed, he ordered that six hundred or more of them be gathered together; he had all of them murdered."[45] Whether or not De la Cueva behaved with similar brutality toward his charges at Utatlán we cannot say.[46]

In 1538 Utatlán was ordered to pay specific quantities of cacao, chickens, and cotton cloth. As with other *tasaciones*, items such as honey, salt, chili peppers, and reed mats were left unspecified, allowing De la Cueva ample opportunity to demand as he pleased. Certainly an allocation of only ten Indians to serve as his laborers seems insignificant when one considers De la Cueva's high rank as one of Alvarado's most trusted lieutenants.

With the death of Alvarado three years or so after the tribute assessment of 1538 was levied, his era of influence came to an end. De la Cueva was appointed royal factor, a position in the treasury, at some point in the 1540s.[47] William Sherman notes that, in 1544, Maldonado arranged the marriage "[of] his bastard daughter to don Cristóbal de la Cueva."[48] Even though, in theory, his government position prevented him from enjoying the privileges of *encomienda*, De la Cueva managed to hold on to Utatlán and several other towns throughout the 1540s. The fact that his father-in-law was president likely did his prospects no harm. After Cerrato replaced Maldonado, however, De la Cueva lost his *encomiendas*; neither he nor Utatlán appears in the tribute assessments drawn up by Cerrato and his clerks between 1549 and 1551. Writing to the King in early 1550, Cerrato observes that "Factor Cristóbal de la Cueva has been off [in Spain] for some time."[49] It was likely during his absence that Utatlán was reassigned to the Crown, which is recorded as holding the community by 1553, when Cerrato undertook to review the tribute payments of selected towns. Surely to the relief of its inhabitants, Utatlán's tribute was reduced significantly.

45. The original reads: "Porque no le dieron los indios que pidió para las cargas, con maña hizo juntar 600 indios o más en un pueblo y todos los hizo matar juntos en una casa"; see "Carta al rey de Cereceda sobre las incidencias ocurridas con D. Cristóbal de la Cueva sobre asuntos de gobierno," AGI, Guatemala 39, August 31, 1535, folio 9, from a transcribed summary in the Ruben Reina Collection, Box 3, American Philosophical Society, Philadelphia, Pennsylvania. We thank Laura Matthew for providing us with this reference.

46. See Lovell and Lutz (2001) for elaboration.

47. Kramer (1994, 254) describes a "factor" as "a royal official charged with collecting rents and tribute owed to the Crown."

48. Sherman (1979, 136–37).

49. AGI, Guatemala 9A (Cerrato to the Crown, January 26, 1550).

Weighing the Burden

Several features stand out in terms of appreciating the burden that these *tasaciones* represented for native communities, but we draw attention to four: (1) how the demand for cloth fell heavily on women in particular; (2) the implications of planting crops with a targeted levy in mind; (3) the sheer hard work, to say nothing of time management, involved in meeting quotas; and (4) the geographical challenge, variable from town to town, of actual delivery.

The daily round for Maya women in Guatemala can be exacting: they give birth to babies; they raise children and take care of husbands as well as elderly parents or in-laws; they grind corn to prepare the *masa* dough for making tortillas, which they serve to accompany the two or three meals they prepare each day; and they fetch water to wash the clothes they make from the cloth they weave. Attending to these routine family chores would have been challenging enough, even without the extra duty of supplying quantities of woven cloth, or getting hold of the necessary raw materials beforehand. Looking back, it must have seemed at times all too much, especially when one views the obligation to produce cloth in the context of a life hounded by the trauma of conquest and outbreaks of sickness.

Tributary obligations involving the planting of crops meant that Indian men had to set aside parcels of land that might otherwise be used to feed their families. If productivity was an issue, as it surely must have been, then communities would have to forfeit using their best fields for local consumption. How much land was needed, as in the case of Comalapa, to harvest two thousand *fanegas* of corn is not easy to calculate, but based on what Charles Gibson has to say about the Valley of Mexico, we reckon that some 180 acres would be designated for this purpose.[50]

By 1549, when Comalapa was required to supply Pérez Dardón with the harvest from a planting of ten *fanegas* (fifteen bushels) of seed corn, we calculate that this would have required some 90 to 105 acres, based on six to seven acres per bushel of seed corn. The planted acreage would have yielded 700 to 1,250 *fanegas,* more or less half of what Comalapa was required to pay eleven years earlier. This constituted a notable investment in labor deployed to prepare the *milpa* in the first place, then provide and

50. See Gibson (1964, 324–29) for a basis of comparison.

plant the ten *fanegas* of seed in question, then weed, tend, and finally harvest the crop. Again, we must appreciate that Comalapa's population, as did that of neighboring communities, dropped in size between the early and mid-sixteenth century. While this downward trend surely made land available, it was toward the end of this period, around 1550, that Spaniards began to lay claim to land to raise wheat, precisely in towns like Comalapa, which lay close to Santiago. Indians would soon be called upon to work on *labores de pan llevar*, wheat farms, established to grow the Spanish staple on holdings once owned and cultivated by native communities.[51]

An integral part of tribute in the late 1530s was the provision of labor, an exacting requirement that, for the most part, was curtailed when Cerrato reassessed what each town should render its *encomendero*. Besides stipulated periods of labor, however, tribute items implied an expenditure of time and effort. So, too, did the actual delivery of tribute, reasonably straightforward if the *tasación* stated that goods were payable in a town and would be collected there. It was another matter entirely if Indians had to deliver the tribute in question to their master's abode in the capital city: no matter the quantity (grains and building materials), the difficulty (quantities of fowl, crabs, sometimes fish), the fragility (eggs), the weight (loads of cacao) or the distance, compliance was expected, even (as in the case of Jumaytepeque) when delivery meant a trek of some fifty kilometers, with all the logistical challenges the long haul entailed. While Maldonado and Marroquín were able to temper the free-for-all of the Alvarado years, not until Cerrato was installed as president did the regulation of excess in Guatemala become a government priority.[52]

---

51. See Lutz ([1982] 1984, 356 and 389) for further discussion.

52. Orellana (1995, 102–104) concurs that, in relation to Escuintla in particular, Cerrato's presence helped ease the Indian load. She writes: "In general, the taxation was heavy, but as Cerrato reduced tribute in most areas it is clear that the burden must have been even heavier in the early post-conquest years. Alvarado took much in tribute from his *encomiendas* before his death in 1541, and Escuintla was one of his holdings."

PART IV

DYNAMICS OF MAYA SURVIVAL

CHAPTER 9

AT FIRST CONTACT

No debate has generated as much controversy in colonial-period literature as the one surrounding the size of Native American populations at the time of contact with Europe. A dichotomy of opinion may be said to exist between those who claim that native numbers were prodigious—at least in Mesoamerica and parts of the Andes—and those who claim that native numbers were scant. Related to the controversy of population size is the issue of population decline in the wake of European intrusion. The proponents of substantial contact populations maintain that, following newcomer penetration, there was a marked decrease in native numbers. Conversely, the proponents of small contact populations tend to dismiss the idea of massive demographic collapse, though they do acknowledge that attrition did occur.

In a critique as polemical as the debate itself, David Henige has labeled the two camps "high counters" and "low counters"; he examines the evidence in such a way as to leave little room for moderate positions in between.[1] Henige, who asserts that all such exercises are "forlorn attempts to answer a thoroughly unanswerable question," is especially dismissive of the work of "high counters," among whose ranks he includes two of us.[2] He contends that "at the heart of the high counters' enterprise is an ensemble of assumptions," the most spurious of which are (1) "that early European observers could count or estimate large numbers closely; (2) that they wanted to do just this, reckoning precision a virtue; (3) that they actually did so; and (4) that these counts were transmitted into and through the written sources accurately."[3] These assumptions,

---

1. Henige (1998).
2. Ibid., 9 and 318, fn. 20.
3. Ibid., 6.

in Henige's mind, render the population estimates advanced by "high counters" of dubious worth if not completely useless. Singled out for close scrutiny by Henige is the research of the "Berkeley School," particularly the work of Woodrow Borah and Sherburne Cook. One of us, elsewhere, has responded at some length to what Henige has to say, disagreeing with his argument on moral as much as scholarly grounds.[4]

In order to provide a framework against which our examination of Maya population history may later be considered, we will summarize the salient features of the Berkeley thesis. We note, however, that a volume edited by William Denevan contains a thorough discussion not only of the findings of the Berkeley School but also of its methodology.[5] Furthermore, by presenting an equally detailed critique of the anti-Berkeley position, Denevan succeeds in establishing a reasonably balanced view of the debate, a balance none too apparent in Henige's dissection.

Concerning the credibility of contemporary testimony, and as an antidote to Henige's views, we first note the following appraisal by Cook and Borah:

> Much of our information on Indian population in the years immediately preceding and following the Conquest comes from the conquerors themselves. Some information represents their efforts to determine the nature of the people and country they were entering. Other information arises incidentally from their reporting of what they did and of the hazards they overcame. Spanish reporting of the period of the Conquest has been impugned on two grounds: First, that the Europeans of the sixteenth century could not handle statistical operations or concepts of larger numbers; second, that all explorers and conquerors in a new land tend to exaggerate. If one reflects upon the complexity of European commercial and administrative techniques in the sixteenth century and upon the variety of motives and the rivalries among explorers and conquerors, a more defensible view would be that the Europeans could count and that a tendency to exaggerate in some would be balanced by a tendency to minimize in others. On the whole, we do better to receive gratefully the fragments that have come down to us and to apply the normal canons of textual examination and comparison.[6]

The classic Berkeley School inquiries relate to central Mexico. There, according to Cook and Borah, native populations dropped from 25.2

4. Lovell (2002).
5. Denevan ([1976] 1992).
6. Cook and Borah (1971, 7).

million in 1518 to 1.075 million in 1605, a fall of more than 95 percent in scarcely four generations.[7] In scores of articles and books, the two scholars document a demographic collapse of staggering proportions. In their final collaborative endeavor, they distill the essence of their research into one succinct sentence. "We conclude," Cook and Borah write, "that the Indian population of central Mexico, under the impact of factors unleashed by the coming of the Europeans, fell, by 1620–1625, to a low of approximately 3% of its size at the time that the Europeans first landed on the shore of Veracruz."[8]

The factors "unleashed" by European penetration arise from the conquest, subjugation, and exploitation of native societies by a materially better-equipped invasion force. The myriad forms of this encounter, from an indigenous point of view, may be regarded as "culture shock" of catastrophic dimensions. It is now quite certain, however, that the principal cause of aboriginal depopulation was not massacre and mistreatment at the hands of conquering Europeans, the infamous Black Legend, but the introduction of an array of Old World diseases to which Native Americans were immunologically defenseless. The fall of the central Mexican population to 3 percent of its level at first contact in the course of one hundred years is therefore critically linked to native vulnerability to diseases such as smallpox, typhus, measles, and mumps. Though Cook's death in 1974 prevented him and Borah from completing a planned study of disease outbreaks in sixteenth-century Mexico, such an inquiry was subsequently undertaken by Hanns Prem, who was able to conduct his research drawing on Borah's expertise.[9] Prem's research on central Mexico, as well as that of dozens of scholars for other parts of the Americas, supports considerably more than it negates the Berkeley thesis of disease-propelled demise, though it must be stressed that epidemics operated in conjunction with other, decidedly non-biological, forces in the erosion of indigenous lives.[10] Denevan states that "as the quality

7. Borah and Cook (1969).

8. Cook and Borah (1979, 102).

9. Borah writes in the preface to the third volume of *Essays in Population History* (Cook and Borah 1979, v): "A fourth inquiry, to identify the epidemics that so devastated the Indian population of Central Mexico during the colonial period, we had planned but not begun; that I have abandoned." Prem ([1992] 2001, 20–48) was able to take up where Cook and Borah left off, furnishing us with an analysis that leans as much on native texts as on Spanish documentary sources.

10. See Newson (1985) for an insightful discussion of key "survival variables." For detailed analyses of the relationship between epidemic disease and native depopulation, see N. D. Cook and Lovell ([1992] 2001).

of the research improves, the trend is toward acceptance of higher numbers."[11] Henige disagrees. For our part, we maintain that, once the general
validity of a process has been established, then the principles under
which it operates may be applied, with care and modification, to situations for which data are not extant. Temporal and spatial lacunae in
the documentary sources for Guatemala require us to extrapolate some
of the findings of Cook and Borah for central Mexico. While a skeptic
like Henige would surely not concur, we believe that such controlled
comparisons can justifiably be made.

Having set a context for this chapter and the ones that follow, we
now turn to three procedures for estimating the population of Guatemala at Spanish contact. The first of these generates two "high" estimates,
the second a "low" one, the third a figure between "high" and "low"
that we consider moderate and in which we place most confidence.

PROCEDURE 1

The first procedure involves multiplying the territorial extent of our
unit of analysis by a factor representing the carrying capacity of the
land at the time of Spanish contact. Given, in terms of present-day political boundaries, that the vast majority of the documentation available
to us pertains to Guatemala south of El Petén and Belize, this part of
the republic constitutes our unit of analysis (some 73,035 square kilometers). Guatemala thus defined coincides closely with the administrative
division known in the mid-sixteenth century as "los términos y jurisdicción de la ciudad de Santiago," which stretched west to the border
with the present-day Mexican state of Chiapas and east to the border
with El Salvador. What we designate in chapter 4 as "lowland periphery"
is excluded from our calculations, though we draw the reader's attention to work in these parts conducted by Jan de Vos, Grant Jones, and
Lawrence Feldman.[12] By way of justifying our exclusion, we point out
that the absence of reliable data led J. Eric S. Thompson to state that,
for what he called the "Maya Central area," including El Petén and Belize,
"an estimate of the population . . . early in the sixteenth century would

11. Denevan ([1976] 1992, 1).
12. See De Vos ([1980] 1993); Jones (1989; 1998); and Feldman (2000).

not be worth considering."[13] Coming from a scholar who knew that area particularly well, we take Thompson's words as good advice.

For central Mexico, the work of Borah and Cook indicates a population density of 49 persons per square kilometer on the eve of the Spanish conquest.[14] Applying that same index for Guatemala, and multiplying it by the region's territorial extent, produces an estimate of 3.6 million. If only the most thickly settled areas of aboriginal central Mexico are considered (that is, excluding the populations that would have inhabited the present-day states of Jalisco, Nayarit, and Colima), the density of occupation rises to 64 persons per square kilometer, generating a contact estimate for Guatemala of about 4.7 million. Both these estimates, however, we believe are too high for two reasons: (1) qualitatively, to assume that population densities for central Mexico can be applied directly to Guatemala fails to take into account significant cultural differences between the Mesoamerican "core" and a Mesoamerican "periphery," particularly with regard to degrees of urbanization, levels of societal complexity, and sophistication of agricultural practices; and (2) quantitatively, archaeological evidence for sizable late Postclassic populations (A.D. 1200–1524) is far greater for central Mexico than for Guatemala.

PROCEDURE 2

The second procedure entails working with data found in the *tasaciones de tributos* compiled between 1548 and 1551 by President Alonso López de Cerrato.[15] The Cerrato *tasaciones*, we observe in previous chapters, contain important information regarding (1) the number of Indian tribute payers; (2) the nature, amount, and rate of tribute payment; and (3) the names of Spaniards to whom tribute was paid. Of the 170 towns listed in the Cerrato *tasaciones* as being "within the limits and jurisdiction of the city of Santiago," thirty-six have no record of how many tributaries they had. The 134 towns for which a number was recorded have a total of 23,769 tribute payers. Multiplying this figure by the same population-to-tributary ratio Cook and Borah employ for the mid-sixteenth

13. Thompson (1966, 31).
14. Borah and Cook (1963).
15. AGI, Guatemala 128, "Las tasaciones de los pueblos de los términos y jrisdición de la ciudad de Santiago de Guatemala" (1548–51).

century, 3.3, produces a population estimate of 78,438. Primarily because of the devastating impact of Old World epidemics, mid-sixteenth century numbers in central Mexico were approximately one-quarter that of the contact period.[16] Applying equivalent rates of depopulation to Guatemala generates a contact-period estimate of 313,752. This estimate, however, we believe is too low, on account of textual flaws in the *tasaciones* themselves and in the manner in which Cerrato had them carried out. These impediments are discussed at length in chapter 10, where we also suggest ways to compensate for them.

Procedure 3

In the third procedure we gather information from studies already conducted for parts of Guatemala and compile a series of subregional estimates for the contact period. These are presented in table 19, with some estimates also offered for the years 1525, 1550, and 1575. Spatial extents are indicated in map 3. Wherever possible, the data shown in table 19 are taken directly from the studies indicated, with minimum statistical manipulation on our part. When, in some studies, tributaries were converted to total population by ratios higher or lower than the ones employed by Cook and Borah, we opted to leave them unadjusted on the assumption that the scholars in question had good reason to select ratios different from what we would have chosen. When, in other studies, tributaries are left unconverted, we convert them to total population by using Cook and Borah's ratios of 3.3:1 for the first half of the sixteenth century and 2.8:1 for the second half of the sixteenth century.[17] We consider that figures arrived at for the mid-sixteenth century, again extrapolating from the findings of Cook and Borah, constitute roughly one-quarter the size of the contact population. When the earliest figures to be recorded date to the second half of the sixteenth century, we take them to represent, once more following Cook and Borah, the population that remained after a process of marked decline of between 75 and 97 percent, and compute back to 1520 accordingly. The estimate for the South Central (Kaqchikel) region is derived for the most part from the Cerrato *tasaciones*;

16. Borah and Cook (1967; 1969) and Cook and Borah (1971).
17. Borah and Cook (1967) and Cook and Borah (1968).

surprisingly, no study on the Kaqchikel (to the best of our knowledge) furnishes contact-period estimates that we consider plausible.[18]

An overall tally of approximately two million, derived by adding up eleven subregional figures, results in what we believe to be our most reliable estimate of the contact population of Guatemala south of El Petén and Belize. There are, however, subregional figures from some studies that contain significant margins of error and that warrant some commentary:

(1) The contact-period estimate for the Southwest, which incorporates much of the present-day departments of Quetzaltenango and San Marcos, is very low. Underestimation here is a consequence of Feldman's study not having taken into account deficiencies inherent in the sources, primarily those of the Cerrato *tasaciones*; we discuss these deficiencies at length in the following chapter.[19]

(2) The contact-period estimate for the Northeast is likewise too low, primarily because this lowland area, according to Thompson, was likely depopulated faster and more drastically than adjacent highland areas. Climatic and altitudinal variation in central Mexico, according to Borah and Cook, had a significant influence on the rate of depopulation, coastal areas being emptied of their inhabitants much faster than upland areas.[20]

(3) The contact-period estimate for the South Central (K'iche') region, culled from studies by Carmack and Veblen, we consider too high. Though the K'iche's were certainly the most powerful group in Guatemala for much of the late Postclassic, by the end of the fifteenth century their hegemony had been successfully challenged by the Kaqchikels. After about 1475, Kaqchikel secession triggered a period of warfare that lasted eleven years. During

18. Luján Muñoz (2011, 57 and 59), basing his indicators on studies by Borg (1999) and Hill (1996), offers estimates of "20,000 to 40,000 inhabitants" for the western part of Kaqchikel country and "12,000 to 16,000 persons" for the eastern part of Kaqchikel country. Both these estimates, we reckon, are much too low.

19. Two of us elsewhere (Lovell and Lutz 1995, 54–59) offer a critical discussion of Feldman's work on the population history of Guatemala.

20. Borah and Cook (1969) distinguish between the demographic experiences of coastal zones (0–3,000 feet), intermediate zones (3,000–4,500 feet), and plateau zones (4,500 feet and above). According to their calculations, if the population of central Mexico in 1568 is assigned a figure of 1.00, then the contact-period population (ca. 1518) of the three different environments, stated in multiples, is: Coast × 47.80; Intermediate × 9.55; Plateau × 6.60.

MAP 3. Demographic regions of Guatemala.

180

this struggle, Kaqchikel forces emerged victorious. The *Memorial de Sololá* recounts:

> When the sun rose on the horizon and shed its light over the mountain, the war cries broke out and the banners were unfurled; the great flutes, the drums, and the shells resounded. It was truly terrible when the Quichés arrived. They advanced rapidly, and their ranks could be seen at once descending to the foot of the mountain. They soon reached the bank of the river, cutting off the river houses. They were followed by the kings Tepepul and Iztayul, who accompanied the god. Then came the encounter. The clash was truly terrible. The shouts rang out, the war cries, the sound of flutes, the beating of drums and the shells, while the warriors performed their feats of magic. Soon the Quichés were defeated, they ceased to fight and were routed, annihilated, and killed. It was impossible to count the dead.[21]

Given that, militarily, the Kaqchikels could more than hold their own against the K'iche's, with no technological superiority to speak of, we surmise that the population base upon which both groups drew may not have differed in size by more than a factor of two. If, as we reckon, a Kaqchikel population of 250,000 at contact is a reasonable estimate, one computed largely on the Cerrato *tasaciones*, then our reading of 500,000 strikes us as a realistic one for the K'iche's. This estimate is notably lower than those put forward by Carmack and Veblen (see table 19). If, however, what we regard as overestimation in the case of the K'iche's is considered alongside what we regard as underestimation in the case of the Southwest and the Northeast, the tendencies cancel each other out. We consider the figure of a little over two million (2,046,500) that emerges at the end of the third procedure to be our most plausible estimate.

A MODERATE POSITION

Three procedures, none of them without flaws, allow us to generate four different estimates for the contact population of Guatemala. These range

---

21. Recinos and Goetz (1953, 103). Luján Muñoz (2011, 54–59) discusses Kaqchikel military might (and territorial expansion) not only in relation to the K'iche's but also the Tz'utujils.

from a low of 313,752 to a high of 4.7 million, with a tally of two
million representing what we consider to be a moderate, more likely figure
between both extremes. Piecing together subregional data to arrive at
a composite regional estimate strikes us as the least risky procedure,
given the complex reality in Guatemala of local variations in culture,
environment, and historical experience. Interestingly, an estimate of two
million for all of Guatemala on the eve of conquest was advanced by
Denevan some time ago. Denevan put forward his estimate, however,
before many of the studies referred to in table 19 were completed; he
attained the figure by what he terms "comparative" reckoning, defined
as "an estimate based on incomplete documentary figures, on other
forms of evidence, and on comparisons with comparable regions with
better information."[22]

The estimate of two million proposed by Denevan and ourselves may
be compared to those advanced by other scholars, among them William
Sanders and Carson Murdy (500,000 to 800,000), Elías Zamora (315,000),
and Francisco de Solano (300,000).[23] While, at first glance, our estimate
and Denevan's appear "high" in relation to the "low" reckoning of these
researchers, closer inspection reveals otherwise, at least in two of the
three cases cited. The key to reconciliation lies in calibrating the scale
of our varying units of analysis. In their work, for example, Sanders and
Murdy restrict themselves to Guatemala's western and central highlands. Zamora is even more spatially specific, focusing his attention on
the colonial jurisdiction known as the Alcaldía Mayor de Zapotitlán,
roughly coterminous with the western part of the country. Both of these
studies, in other words, deal with territory significantly smaller in extent
than the one we deal with. Only Solano's estimate seems conspicuously
low, at odds with Zamora and with Sanders and Murdy as much as with
Denevan and us. Though his unit of inquiry is never spelled or mapped
out precisely, Solano's work pertains to vast areas of Guatemala. Far less
vague is Solano's ideological positioning: at one juncture in his study he
attributes to Borah and Cook "a secret passion," the object of which
is "to blame Spanish action as a direct cause of the massive collapse

22. Denevan ([1976] 1992, 291).
    23. Sanders and Murdy (1982); Solano (1974); and Zamora (1983). For further discussion of
these studies, see Lovell and Lutz (1995, 142–43, 148–49, and 166–67).

of the Indian population in the sixteenth and seventeenth centuries."[24] For some researchers, the Black Legend has yet to be laid to rest.

To end on yet another comparative note, it is worth observing that, if Cook and Borah are correct, then not until midway through the twentieth century did the population of Mexico again reach its contact size.[25] The work of Carl Johannessen and Linda Newson on Honduras indicates a similar trajectory.[26] So, too, does our reckoning, for according to national census statistics, the population of Guatemala in 1880 numbered 1.2 million and in 1950 numbered 2.8 million. An estimate of two million thus fits a demographic pattern of short-term collapse and long-term recovery characteristic of two of Guatemala's neighbors.

Having established a contact-period benchmark, we now turn to providing further details of the population history of colonial Guatemala, especially the fate of native inhabitants in the wake of conquest.

24. Solano (1974, 61). Such a vehement statement calls for us to record and share with readers Solano's precise words, which are "una secreta pasión [para] culpar la acción española como causa directa del descenso masivo de la población indígena en los siglos XVI y XVII."
25. Cumberland (1968).
26. Johannessen (1963) and Newson (1986).

CHAPTER 10

THE CERRATO YEARS

On May 26, 1548, Alonso López de Cerrato took formal charge of the presidency of Guatemala.[1] Prior to his arrival in Central America, Cerrato had served for five years as the Crown's most senior representative in the Audiencia de Santo Domingo, a "High Court" jurisdiction with its seat in the port city of the same name, from which not only Hispaniola but also other Caribbean islands, including Cuba, Jamaica, and Puerto Rico, were governed. An ardent reformer, Cerrato sought to enforce legislation enshrined in the New Laws of 1542–43, specifically those provisions dealing with the abolition of Indian slavery.[2] His reformist tendencies in Santo Domingo and later in Guatemala made him the enemy of many Spanish colonists, whose resentment knew no bounds. William Sherman sums up the man and his mission as follows:

> A dour, dedicated judge who brooked no nonsense, Cerrato set in motion a policy that was seen by the colonists as their complete ruination— that is to say, he was completely intent on enforcing law. His substantial achievement of that goal, in the face of incredible odds, was a landmark in the history of Indian labor in the New World. By 1550 the situation of the Indians was significantly altered because of Cerrato's actions, and their condition was never quite so deplorable as in the past. This is not to say that the high ideals of Spanish legislation were fully realized; indeed, life for the Indians remained that of servitude to their white masters throughout the sixteenth century and beyond. Officials

1. Sherman (1979, 135).
2. The "New Laws of the Indies for the Good Treatment and Preservation of the Indians," promulgated 1542–43, prohibited indigenous slavery, sought to control the operation of *encomienda*, and regulated native tribute payments. See Gibson (1966, 48–67) for a general discussion and Sherman (1979, 129–88) for Central American details.

who followed Cerrato were not his equal in zeal and courage, and the social patterns of the conquest society took further root.[3]

One of Cerrato's first acts as president was to arrange for tribute payments to be reassessed, the third such undertaking for which we have records. These *tasaciones* are a well-known source that many scholars have consulted, for they deal with other regions besides Guatemala, most notably El Salvador, Honduras, Nicaragua, and Yucatán.[4] For purposes of population reconstruction, however, the *tasaciones* are highly problematic, a factor not taken sufficiently into account by researchers who have used them to that end. Cerrato's *tasaciones* must be read and interpreted carefully, with contextual appreciation of the difficult and unstable circumstances under which they were compiled. Here we examine the *tasaciones* as a demographic source, taking their defects into account before using them to generate an estimate for the native population of Guatemala in the mid-sixteenth century.

VITAL STATISTICS

The Cerrato *tasaciones* may be consulted in two different archives. One set of documents is housed in the Archivo General de Indias (AGI) in Seville and dates from 1548 to 1551.[5] Another set, dating from 1553 to 1554, is housed in the Archivo General de Centro América (AGCA) in Guatemala City.[6] The tribute assessments in Guatemala City, some forty-three listings in all, include data on seven communities that do not appear in the *tasaciones* kept in Seville, a much more comprehensive register with 170 settlement listings. The Seville register, therefore, has

3. Sherman (1979, 12). Elsewhere, Sherman (1971) reviews what he considers to be Cerrato's notable accomplishments, though MacLeod ([1973] 2008, 116) regards the president's achievements, on balance, to be "mixed." The friar Francisco de la Parra, writing to the King on July 15, 1549 (AGI, Guatemala 168), speaks highly of Cerrato, stating that "in my opinion he has served Your Majesty well, relieving these poor Indians of serious affronts and injustices, their having previously been treated not as human beings but as animal brutes."

4. Studies based at least in part on the Cerrato *tasaciones* include López de Velasco ([1571–74] 1971); Paso y Troncoso (1939); Barón Castro (1942); Bergmann (1969); Radell (1969); Cook and Borah (1974b); Gerhard (1979); Stanislawski (1983); and Newson (1986; 1987).

5. AGI, Guatemala 128 ("Tasaciones de los pueblos de los términos y jurisdicción de la ciudad de Santiago de la provincia de Guatemala").

6. AGCA, A3.16, leg. 2797, exp. 40466.

attracted more scholarly attention; over the years it has been consulted by a host of researchers, including Lawrence Feldman, Salvador Rodríguez Becerra, and Francisco de Solano.[7] Paleographic difficulties often result in researchers spelling place names quite differently and, our main concern here, in tallying variable aggregates of the tribute-paying population. Each assessment must be examined with utmost caution, and this goes for both the text itself and the key words and figures that appear in the left-hand margin, where numbers representing tribute payers (*yndios*) are penned in Roman numerals below the name of the *encomendero* to whom tribute was paid and the name of the community held in *encomienda*.

To minimize interpretive error on our part, and to serve as an independent check, we enlisted the assistance of a professional Spanish paleographer, Manuel Fuentes Mairena. Following closely his reading of the text, and rechecking his figures against those in our notes and in the original documents, we tally the number of tribute-payers recorded in the Cerrato *tasaciones* in Seville to 23,769 (see table 20). In order to illustrate how each researcher reads the documents differently, we point out that Feldman tallies tributary figures to a total of 20,558, Rodríguez Becerra to 23,660, and Solano to 24,269.[8] Of the 170 AGI listings, some 150 are registered as being held in private *encomienda*; only seventeen are assigned to the Crown. Two communities (Chiquijotla and Malacatepeque) are listed, temporarily, as being vacant and awaiting designation. We locate ninety of the settlements associated with the Cerrato *tasaciones* in map 4, assigning them the numbers listed in table 21. Many spatial designations are approximate and indicate only the general area of the *encomienda*, for no maps have survived to guide us. In addition, several communities have since disappeared or have experienced a marked change in nomenclature. Sixteenth-century spelling of place names varies widely, so we have opted for renderings that most resemble present-day orthography. For numerous communities, we are unable to assign even an approximate location.

From a financial standpoint, how much income was generated by tribute is difficult to calculate, especially for individual concessions. One source in another archive in Spain, the Archivo General de Simancas,

---

7. Feldman (1992); Rodríguez Becerra (1977); and Solano (1974). The work of these three scholars is reviewed in Lovell and Lutz (1995, 59, 138, and 149). See also Kramer (1994).
   8. Feldman and Walters (1980, 75); Rodríguez Becerra (1975, 248); and Solano (1974, 83).

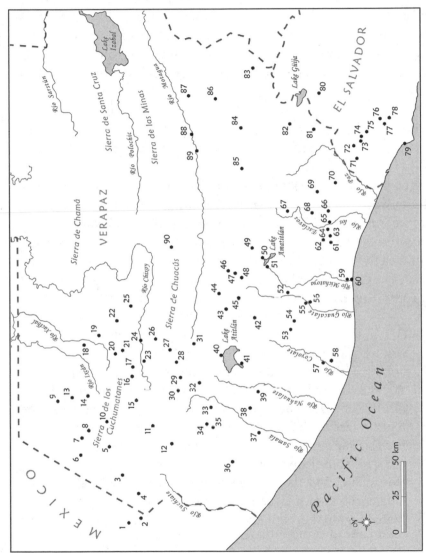

MAP 4. *Pueblos de indios* in the Cerrato *tasaciones* (1548–51). Source: Archivo General de Indias, Guatemala 128, "Las tasaciones de los pueblos de los términos y jurisdicción de la ciudad de Santiago de Guatemala" (1548–51) and Kramer (1994, 20). For the names of numbered towns, see table 21.

which still stores colonial-period documents that in theory should have been dispatched long ago to the Archivo General de Indias in Seville, records a Cerrato-era figure for the Crown's share of the takings: the "tributo de los pueblos de la Provincia de Guatimala" is listed as having generated 8, 205 pesos, a sum roughly equal to that of the 7,259 pesos and 800 pesos that constituted "His Majesty's" share of gold- and silver-mining operations, respectively.[9] Half of what the Crown could expect to gain from its pursuit of empire in Guatemala, in short, was furnished by tribute.

EVALUATING THE SOURCE

Before engaging Cerrato's *tasaciones* as surrogate indicators of population size, we must first evaluate their reliability. Put bluntly, to what extent should we trust them? How accurate (or not) might they be of situations on the ground? What are their flaws and inadequacies? Unlike Solano, who praises their "scientific rigor" and "absolute veracity," we hold that the *tasaciones* have notable deficiencies that need to be borne in mind when consulting them.[10] These are discussed below.

(1) One in five settlements listed in the *tasaciones* do not have any record of their tributary population. Whereas most settlements appear in the left-hand margin of the Seville manuscript alongside the name of the *encomendero* who held them and the number of officially designated tributaries, thirty-six listings have no such register (see table 22). Among them are what we know to have been sizable and lucrative awards, including Acatenango, Jumaytepeque, Totonicapán, and Quetzaltenango.

(2) Not included in the *tasaciones* are entries for several areas of Guatemala known to be populated. Such areas include the Lake Izabal region, parts of the Verapaz, the Pacific piedmont, the

9. Archivo General de Simancas, leg. 6, número 53, "Sumario general de lo que valen todas las Indias a Su Majestad." Though the document is dated 1558, its contents clearly indicate that the accounts in question pertain to Cerrato's time in office.

10. Solano (1974, 77). He writes: "Estas tasaciones serán las primeras noticias sobre población con cierto rigor científico. Son un excelente índice para realizar cálculos, y desde el punto de vista de la historia de la demografía son de una gran importancia, porque los recuentos son absolutamente veraces."

Sierra de los Cuchumatanes, and even pockets of the colonial core (see chapter 4) near Santiago. Given that later records for the same spatial unit, the "términos y jurisdicción de la ciudad de Santiago," furnish detailed information on more than three hundred occupied places, we reckon that the population of as much as one-half of the inhabited area of Guatemala went undocumented.[11] As a point of comparison, for the same period in central Mexico, the famous *Suma de visitas* (1547–51), according to Woodrow Borah and Sherburne Cook, covered only approximately one-half of the territory of New Spain then known to be populated.[12]

(3) The fiscal category recorded in the *tasaciones* is that of *tributarios*, that is, residents of *pueblos de indios* who were expected to pay tribute either to the Crown or to individual *encomenderos*. This category can be equated with married males, since at the time of the assessments other sectors of the native population, theoretically at any rate, were not liable for tribute payment, though they became so later on.[13] The Cerrato *tasaciones*, unlike similar registers undertaken only ten years later, do not record the number of *reservados,* who, for a variety of reasons, were exempt from paying tribute. *Reservados* included children, the elderly, the sick or infirm, members of the nobility, slaves and domestic servants tied to Spanish residents or their households, and individuals involved in some way with assisting the Church.[14] Consequently, it is difficult to know exactly what proportion of the total population *tributarios* represented in the mid-sixteenth century. We return to this question later on.

(4) When Cerrato ordered that new *tasaciones* be undertaken, he relied partly for his information on reports submitted by native leaders rather than on personal inspections carried out by officials of the Crown. In other words, not every settlement recorded

11. See, for example, AGI, Contaduria 973, which contains fiscal records for the years 1624 to 1710. One set of documents in this *legajo* relates to the treasury accounts of the Audiencia de Guatemala for the years around 1710, when 326 settlements are listed as constituting the spatial unit that concerns us.

12. Borah and Cook (1969, 177–78).

13. Newson (1982, 263–65).

14. See, for example, the meticulously detailed *tasaciones* in AGI, Guatemala 45, dating to 1562, which we discuss in chapter 11.

in the *tasaciones* received a visit either from Cerrato himself or from one of the judges working under his supervision. Furthermore, the assistance of experienced clergy, who often knew the locale in which they served much better than any government official, seems not to have been requested. We can well imagine that, in order to reduce the amount of tribute expected to be paid, some native leaders whose counsel was sought would under-record the number of eligible tributaries. Cerrato was certainly criticized for lack of thoroughness and good judgment by several of his contemporaries, two of whom were Bishop Marroquín and Bernal Díaz del Castillo. The latter, in a letter to the Crown, lodged the following complaint:

> Your Majesty should know that everything was carried out contrary to your royal order. [Indian communities] were not visited but rather assessed from the private residences [of Crown officials] according to an unintelligible system . . . and [yet Cerrato] claims that he is sending Your Majesty all the assessments as if they [Cerrato and his judges] were acquainted fully with all the facts and the circumstances surrounding them.[15]

The *tasaciones*, to say the least, caused quite a stir, enraging *encomenderos* who considered them not only financially punitive but also, from their perspective, politically unacceptable.[16] Cerrato routinely lowered the number of Indians liable for tribute. He also reduced the amount of tribute payable and eliminated many of the labor services that had been rendered previously. A veritable furor erupted once the new levies were known, hardly surprising given that the *tasaciones* were among the first in all Spanish America to incorporate the progressive thinking of the New Laws. The text for the pueblo of Cochumatlán (the present-day Todos Santos Cuchumatán) actually records such consternation; below the entry of the *tasación* itself it is mentioned

15. Bernal Díaz del Castillo, quoted in Sáenz de Santa María (1964, 74). The letter reads: "Sepa VM que todo se hizo al contrario de vuestro real mando, porque no se vió cosa de los dichos sino estándose en sus aposentos, se tasó no sé porqué relación y cabeza . . . y dice que envía agora allí a VM todas las tasaciones como si tuviesen experiencia de lo que es cada cosa y las circunstancias dello."

16. Carmack (1973, 138–39) and Sherman (1979, 153–88).

explicitly that Cochumatlán's *encomenderos* "were offended by this assessment," the individuals in question, the sons of Marcos Ruiz and García de Águilar, demanding that they be paid more tribute.[17]

(5) Compared with other Crown officials, Cerrato, so it seems, was content with statistical approximations, for many of his figures are rounded off in units of five, ten, or twenty (see table 20). Diego García de Valverde, for instance, who governed some thirty years later, was more of a perfectionist, assessing tribute-paying capacity down to individual family units, even half-units where appropriate.[18] The figures for most if not all settlements listed in Cerrato's *tasaciones*, therefore, must be considered approximate rather than precise.

(6) Throughout Guatemala, but especially in the central and western highlands, the laborious task of assessing tribute capacity was contemporaneous with the process of *congregación* (see chapter 5). *Congregación*, we observe, did not always unfold according to plan, for Spanish authorities ran into all sorts of difficulties in the course of resettling native families. Fugitivism, for example, we know was common throughout the colonial period, but the tendency to avoid or flee Spanish officialdom altogether must have been especially prevalent during the devastating *gucumatz* or *cocoliztli* epidemic that raged immediately before Cerrato's assessments were carried out.[19] His *tasaciones*, therefore, failed to include those Indians who sought refuge away from *congregaciones* where assessments were focused, whether to escape the effects of disease or to evade the exploitation to which they were subjected while resident there.

These, then, are some of the drawbacks that researchers must deal with when working with the Cerrato *tasaciones*. They remain, nonetheless, our most comprehensive tribute record for the mid-sixteenth century. Having held the source to scrutiny, let us now seek to derive from it an estimate of native population.

17. AGI, Guatemala 128. The text states "estaban agraviados de esta tasación."

18. AGI, Guatemala 10 ("Razón de las tasaciones que se han hecho después que el presidente [Valverde] vino a esta audiencia, de pueblos de su distrito con lo que antes tributaban").

19. MacLeod ([1973] 2008, 19) thinks *gucumatz* or *cocoliztli* was a form of pulmonary plague. See also Lovell ([1985] 2005, 71–72).

DERIVING AN ESTIMATE

By compensating for its defects, we believe it possible to come up with an estimate of the Indian population of Guatemala based on the Cerrato *tasaciones*. Our procedure is as follows:

First, to the tributary population listed in the Cerrato assessments (23,769) we add 20 percent (4,754) for those settlements with no registered number of *yndios* (tributaries) in the left-hand margin of the *tasaciones*. We would prefer to estimate the tribute-paying population for the thirty-six communities in question by using a commodity-to-tributary ratio known to be invariable. This method, for example, was employed by Cook and Borah for the Yucatán component of the Cerrato *tasaciones*, for which a direct correlation can be made between the number of cotton *mantas* requested and the number of tributaries, since each tributary was required to pay one *manta* of cotton cloth each year.[20] The same kind of reasoning was used by Linda Newson for the Honduran component and by David Radell for the Nicaraguan component of the Cerrato *tasaciones*, in which a standardized correlation can be made between corn supplies and Indian tributaries—a quota of one *fanega* of corn for every ten tributaries.[21] We have sought to identify in the Cerrato *tasaciones* for Guatemala an invariable ratio between the number of recorded tributaries and levies of cacao, corn, cotton, salt, wheat, and numerous other items of tribute, but have found no such correlation to exist.

Second, to the above figure (28,523) we add 50 percent (14,262) to allow for under-recording arising because of Cerrato's enlisting native leaders to help formulate assessments, abandonment of communities in the wake of the *gucumatz* epidemic of 1545–48, and fugitivism related to native antipathy to *congregación*. An estimate of 50 percent under-recording is based partly on the existence of more reliable population data for the years following the compilation of the Cerrato *tasaciones* for important Guatemalan communities such as Santiago Atitlán, Comalapa,

20. Cook and Borah (1974, 9 and 16). They define a *manta* as "four *piernas*, or strips of cotton cloth woven on a native loom, each strip three-quarters of a Spanish *vara* [about 33 inches] wide by four *varas* long."

21. Newson (1981, 221) and Radell (1969, 87). A *fanega* is a unit of dry measure of approximately 1.5 bushels or 116 pounds. The area planted with this amount of seed was known as the *fanega de sembradura*.

Huehuetenango, Sololá, and Zumpango (see table 23). Some idea of the extent of under-reporting inherent in the Cerrato *tasaciones*, listed in column one, can be gained by comparing the figures in this column with more reliable figures listed in columns two to five. The figures in column six, expressed as percent change, reflect the difference between Cerrato's enumeration and the earliest post-Cerrato count of the tributary population. Reckoning on the basis of 50 percent under-reporting, we recognize, conceals a significant margin of error, so the figure is approximate. Since available evidence overwhelmingly indicates that native numbers declined substantially between the mid-sixteenth century and 1581, the discrepancies between the 1549 figures and later ones, especially those dating to the 1550s and to 1562, reflect changes in tribute assessment procedures as well as deficiencies inherent in the Cerrato *tasaciones*.[22] It is possible, however, that certain deficiencies may be rationalized (as Borah and Cook demonstrated in their analysis of the *Suma de visitas*) in the light of new material uncovered in the course of future research and advances in our understanding of the Spanish tribute system.[23]

Third, assuming that the figure we now have (42,785) represents roughly one-half of the area of Guatemala south of El Petén and Belize known to be inhabited at the time of the Cerrato assessments, we add a full 100 percent to compensate for spatial lacunae, giving a hypothetical tribute-paying population of 85,570.

Our next exercise is to establish what proportion of the total native population the number of tributaries represents and to convert accordingly. No consensus prevails, but we are fortunate in having several sources at hand that facilitate this task.

Central Mexico again serves as a useful comparison. There, we noted in chapter 9, Borah and Cook reckon a population-to-tributary ratio

22. See, for example, Guatemala 10 ("Razón de las tasaciones") and MacLeod ([1973] 2008, 130–31). An increase in the number of tributaries between 1549 and 1581 does not reflect an increase in the Indian population but rather a change how tributaries were counted. Essentially, some sectors of the native population hitherto granted *reservado* status were later classified as being eligible for tribute in an attempt by the royal treasury to increase revenue. The situation in central Mexico is discussed in detail in Borah and Cook (1960, 54–74). Among those who have interpreted statistical increase as population increase are Barón Castro (1942, 100); Kubler (1942, 615–16 and 623–25); Rosenblat (1967, 70–71); and Spores (1967, 73–75).

23. Borah and Cook (1960, 1–19) and Cook and Borah (1960, 5–6). As yet, we have no study of the Spanish tribute system in Guatemala that approaches the quality of the classic work of Miranda (1952) on Mexico.

(P:T) in the first half of the sixteenth century of 3.3:1 and in the second half of the sixteenth century of 2.8:1.[24] In an elaborate critique of the Borah-Cook methodology, B. H. Slicher van Bath raises these figures to 4.75:1, a ratio also favored by Elías Zamora.[25] Like Slicher van Bath, Sanders rejects certain fundamental principles governing the Borah-Cook methodology, but accepts their population-to-tributary ratio of 2.8:1.[26] Peter Gerhard, on the other hand, declares himself to be "in basic agreement" with Borah, Cook, and the Berkeley School in general.[27] In an earlier study of central Mexico, Cook and Simpson suggest a P:T ratio of 4:1, while Miguel Othón de Mendizábal and Howard Cline put forward 3.2:1 and 2.7:1, respectively.[28] For the Tlaxcala region of central Mexico, Charles Gibson uses a population-to-tributary ratio of 5:1.[29]

For Central America, divergence of opinion is also striking. Murdo MacLeod, Newson, and Sherman all employ a P:T ratio of 4:1, with Newson qualifying what she regards as a conservative ratio by suggesting that a multiplication factor of 4.5 or 5 might be more accurate.[30] For Guatemala specifically, both Veblen and Suzanne Miles use a P:T ratio of 5:1.[31] Carmack suggests two ratios—6:1 for the first half of the sixteenth century, and 5:1 for the second.[32]

Turning to the documentation at hand, we know of tribute assessments dating to 1562 that have survived for eight Guatemalan communities, among them important settlements such as Comalapa, Chimaltenango, Petapa, San Juan and San Pedro Sacatepéquez, and Zumpango.[33] These *tasaciones*, which we discuss in chapter 11, contain significantly more information on the internal composition and structure of the native population than do the Cerrato assessments. In these other *tasaciones*, a tributary is considered a household head and is usually a married Indian male responsible for himself, his wife, and his offspring. Tributary units,

24. Borah and Cook (1967, 719).
25. Slicher van Bath (1978) and Zamora (1983). Other critiques of the Borah-Cook methodology include Henige (1998) and Zambardino (1980).
26. Sanders (1976, 125).
27. Gerhard (1972, 23).
28. Cook and Simpson (1948, 11–13); Othón de Mendizábal, cited in Borah and Cook (1960, 75); and Cline (1956, 115–37), especially page 131, which concerns the *barrio* of San Pedro.
29. Gibson (1952, 139).
30. MacLeod ([1973] 2008); Newson (1986; 1987); and Sherman (1979).
31. Veblen (1977, 495) and Miles (1957, 766).
32. Carmack (1982, 139–40).
33. AGI, Guatemala 45 (1562).

therefore, are nuclear families consisting of seldom more than three or four persons. The old, the sick, the infirm, the widowed, and all others comprising the *reservado* group are meticulously listed, and constitute anything from one-quarter to one-seventh the size of the tributary population (see table 24). Influenced by the content of these *tasaciones*, we reckon that a ratio of 5:1 best reflects the relationship between total population and tributary population in the mid-sixteenth century, a ratio that seems reasonable when viewed alongside those mentioned above. A hypothetical tribute-paying population of 85,570, obtained by our procedure of compensation, thus indicates a total population of 427,850, which we estimate to be the approximate size of the Indian population of Guatemala south of El Petén and Belize around the year 1550.

Viewed in relation to our contact-period estimate of two million, the figure of 427,850 represents native depopulation in the order of 78.6 percent between 1520 and 1550. Demographic decline in the aftermath of conquest, we shall see, was to continue throughout the second half of the sixteenth and into the seventeenth century.

CHAPTER 11

DECLINE BETWEEN REFORMS

For the almost three decades after the initiatives of Alonso López de Cerrato, no records survive of any equivalent attempt to survey Guatemala on a macro scale and generate a register, town by town, of native numbers and tribute-paying capacity. Not until 1578, when Diego García de Valverde arrived to assume executive office, did a royal appointee in the reformist mold of Cerrato commit himself to that end and, by so doing, seek yet again to put a troubled house in order. For the period between Cerrato and Valverde, we have a number of sources of variable statistical worth and, more crucially, of variable geographical extent. One source, for instance, offers us a tantalizing look at the internal composition of eight communities in 1562, furnishing information that, were it available for *pueblos de indios* across the region, would afford us considerable advantage in reconstructing not only Maya population dynamics but native socioeconomic life as well. Such systematic data, alas, have yet to be found. On the other hand, we have located several documents that furnish information on population size beyond the town or district level, in which continued decline is apparent and cause for concern for Spaniards and Indians alike. We review the available sources in chronological order, offering comments on textual content and limitations.

AN APPRAISAL BY JUAN DE ESTRADA (CIRCA 1550)

For roughly the same time that Cerrato served as president, his Spanish contemporary, Juan de Estrada, estimated that 26,000 "indios, poco más o menos" lived in what he termed the "Jurisdicción de Santiago." Estrada's figure exists alongside data for seven other jurisdictions in Central America (see table 25). His summary appraisal may be consulted in the same *legajo*, or bundle of documents, in which we found transcriptions of the *tasaciones de tributos* undertaken in the late 1530s (see chapter 8) by Alonso de Maldonado and Francisco Marroquín.[1] Estrada's figure is close to the number of Indian tribute payers (23,769) recorded for the "términos y jurisdicción de la ciudad de Santiago" by Cerrato, from whose *tasaciones* Estrada's estimate may in fact be derived, rather than calculated independently by other means. William Sherman, certainly no "high counter" with respect to the debate surrounding native population size, considers Estrada's estimate "much too low."[2]

A SAMPLE OF MODEL *TASACIONES* (1562)

Few sixteenth-century sources match the extraordinary detail of the *tasaciones de tributos* recorded by an anonymous Crown official, or more likely a team headed by him, for eight communities in 1562.[3] Five *pueblos de indios* (Comalapa, Chimaltenango, San Juan Sacatepéquez, San Pedro Sacatepéquez, and Zumpango) lie in Kaqchikel-speaking parts of the highlands, three (Petapa, Santa Inés, and San Juan Amatitlán) in Poqomam country. For San Juan Amatitlán, much of the manuscript is actually written in Poqomam, with Spanish summaries scribbled in the margin. Perusal of these documents imparts a palpable sense of their having been composed in meticulous fashion by bureaucrats bent on precision and minute attention to detail, civil servants who must have spent considerable time in the field with local informants rather than dreaming up numbers from their comfortable quarters in Santiago de Guatemala.

The tribute assessments are organized along *parcialidad* lines, the first Indian named being the *cacique*, or clan leader, who is always given the honorific title "Don." After the *cacique* comes his wife and children, with reference made as to whether the offspring still live with their parents or in households of their own. Cropland (*milpa*) is registered, the quantity of chickens (*gallinas de Castilla*) raised also. Then follows an inventory of town residents who are married and pay tribute, along

1. AGI, Indiferente General 857 (ca. 1550).

2. Sherman (1979, 384). It is Sherman who suggests the date of ca.1550 for Estrada's assessment.

3. AGI, Guatemala 45 ("Tasaciones de tributos," 1562).

with a register of their children; any married male still living with his parents is ordered to cut family ties and establish an independent household, refusal to do so punishable by a whipping. If a tribute payer, besides working the land, practices a trade—*ollero* or pot-maker, *salero* or salt-maker, *petatero* or reed mat-maker—this too is noted. These *tasaciones* allow us to appreciate the presence of skilled labor, an indication of the range of pursuits in which commoners were trained by Spanish and native artisans alike.

The tribute assessment for Chimaltenango, a community made up of four distinct *parcialidades*, caught the eye of Sherman when he worked in Seville at the Archivo General de Indias. He marveled at its intricate listing of "carpenters, potters, salt-makers, mat-makers, sawyers, brick-and-tile makers, lime-makers, blacksmiths, cooks, fishermen, sacristans, swineherds, merchants and traders, apprentice teachers in the Church (*teupantlacas*), as well as various kinds of officials."[4] Colonial bureaucrats recorded the names of individuals who, by physical toil, contributed to Chimaltenango's tributary worth and community welfare; but equally important was to make a list of those who, for whatever reason, were deemed exempt from paying tribute. In Chimaltenango's case, besides members of the nobility, this included sixty-five widows and twenty-seven "viejos y enfermos," the elderly and the sick. Among the latter was "one old man who does not pay tribute because he is blind."[5] Orphans classified as "minors" lived with the relatives of their deceased parents, in such instances increasing family size notably.

Just as Sherman was drawn to Chimaltenango, so too has the tribute assessment for Petapa attracted the attention of Jorge Luján Muñoz.[6] Following the categories of the *tasación* itself, he identifies (1) married male tributaries; (2) unmarried male tributaries; (3) married men who served the church as *sacristanes* and so did not pay tribute; (4) older married men who, because of their age, were also exempt from paying tribute; (5) children; (6) widows; and (7) widowers. Of a total of 227 married couples, 154 had children living at home when the *tasación* was carried out. Sixty-five couples are recorded as being "sin hijos," without

---

4. Sherman (1979, 91 and 393).

5. AGI, Guatemala 45 ("Tasación de tributos, Chimaltenango"). The text, dated "20 de febrero, 1562," reads "viejo y ciego no tributa de los malos ojos."

6. Luján Muñoz (1985). Given what he is able to glean from one single *tasación*, the other seven in the series warrant similar assiduous scrutiny.

children, which Luján Muñoz takes to mean that any offspring had either grown up and left home or that the couples in question were young and recently married. Among couples who did have children, 78 had one child, 51 had two, 20 had three, and 4 had four. The total number of children, those up to thirteen or fourteen years of age, was 252. Seventeen widows and seventeen widowers are also registered, giving Petapa a total population of 723. These people lived in 194 houses and farmed 199 plots of land. Some indication of the trying times and circumstances in which the residents of Petapa found themselves is revealed by Luján Muñoz's reckoning that the average number of children per married couple was a mere 1.18, well below the number necessary for the community to sustain itself.

THE BRICEÑO *TASACIONES* FOR VERAPAZ (1566)

Four years or so after the Kaqchikel and Poqomam assessments were carried out, Licenciado Francisco Briceño drew up *tasaciones* for *pueblos de indios* held in *encomienda* by the Crown. Of the documents that have survived, those dealing with sixteen communities in Verapaz are the most noteworthy, even though their information is summary in nature, not nearly as elaborate as the registers discussed above or the census we discuss next.[7] Several scholars, Lawrence Feldman among them, have consulted the Briceño *tasaciones*, especially the data for Verapaz. For the same year as the tribute assessments, 1566, we have a letter dated September 3, in which Tomás de Cárdenas, recently appointed bishop of Verapaz, states: "For the levy made on Saint John's Day [June 24], not quite four thousand tributaries could be accounted for, which leads me to understand that twelve to fifteen thousand 'vecinos indios' live here, with more than sixty thousand in other parts of Guatemala."[8]

Categories exempt from tributary obligations resemble the ones we noted for the Kaqchikel and Poqomam towns. A striking feature

7. AGI, Justicia 332 ("Tasaciones hechas por el licenciado Briceño en la Provincia de Guatemala en los pueblos de su Majestad, 1566").

8. Feldman (1982) and AGI, Guatemala 168 (Tomás de Cárdenas to the Crown, September 3, 1566). The bishop's precise words are "que estas últimas cuentas después de San Juan no se hallaron qtro [cuatro] mil tributarios y déme entender hasta que tenga número de doze a quinze mil vecinos indios [y que en] los más comarcas de Guatemala tienen más de sesenta mil." His figures for Verapaz line up with those of other contemporaries, and his estimate for the rest of Guatemala matches our own calculations from other sources surprisingly well.

of the *tasación* for Santo Domingo Cobán is the disclosure that the provincial capital contains, living among its Q'eqchi' Maya majority, two hundred *vecinos* (adult heads of households) from Chol-speaking Acalá territory, which only recently had been brought under Spanish control. Briceño's *tasaciones* have another notable characteristic, namely that a direct correlation exists between the number of tributaries and the quantity of chickens (one per tributary) and corn (half a *fanega* per tributary) payable to the Crown. Such a rationalization, the earliest indication we have for Guatemala, facilitates analysis and comparison when no actual count of tributaries is recorded in the levy. Also worthy of mention is that certain provisions were made for *caciques* to receive food and services from Crown tributaries, a rare concession. Even though they lack the meticulous house-by-house enumeration of the Kaqchikel and Poqomam assessments, the Briceño *tasaciones* for Verapaz are a most valuable source.

The Verapaz Census of 1570–1571

Enriching the Briceño data for Verapaz is a unique census of the region conducted by its *alcalde mayor*, Pedro de Casa de Avante y Gamboa. This dedicated royal official records that he oversaw the task personally, beginning his labors on November 10, 1570, and ending them on January 31, 1571. The census he produced ranks among the most remarkable sixteenth-century documents to be found in the Archivo General de Centro América; not many researchers, however, have made their way to Guatemala City to consult it. Two exceptions are Murdo MacLeod and Michel Bertrand, though they make use of the document only in passing. The manuscript escaped the attention of André Saint-Lu entirely, for the illustrious French scholar wrote his magnum opus on Verapaz without ever having visited the Guatemala City archive.[9]

9. AGCA, A3.16, leg. 1600, exp. 26371 ("Cuenta de los naturales de todos los pueblos de la Verapaz, hecha por el alcalde mayor Pedro de Casa de Avante y Gamboa, 1570–71"). MacLeod ([1973] 2008, 93) incorporates data from Casa de Avante's census in his table on the tributary population of sixteenth-century Verapaz, as does Bertrand (1982) in his study of part of the region. The classic work of Saint-Lu (1968) on Verapaz has yet to appear in English translation. Two of us (Kramer and Lutz) are engaged in a full-length study and transcription of the Casa de Avante census, with the assistance of Héctor Concohá and Gabrielle Venturi.

Some 107 folios in length, the census was undertaken after native leaders informed Spanish authorities that many of their tribute-paying brethren had died in a recent epidemic and that a new tally should be carried out. The census contains tributary data by household, much like the Kaqchikel and Poqomam *tasaciones*, for fifteen *pueblos de indios*, whose inhabitants are often registered by name. Each town-by-town entry is organized by *parcialidad*, listing *caciques* and their family members first. For Cobán alone, almost thirty *parcialidades* are recorded, the town's total population amounting to some 2,583 men, women, and children. The wife of the *cacique* is identified and their offspring enumerated. Population totals are given for "vecinos vasallos," heads of households deemed to be subjects of the Crown, a figure always greater than the number of tributaries. All male tributaries are listed, along with the names of their wives and the number of their children. Those who enjoyed "reservado" status and thus were exempt from paying tribute are afforded special attention, with mention made (in the case of the infirm or crippled) of their specific ailment, such as "missing one hand." Almost every town has a separate page that lists the names of young men eligible for marriage ("por casar"), with reference as to whether or not "they live with their parents." These male youths were kept track of because they would soon be of age to pay tribute.

Casa de Avante's inspection on occasion reveals minute human details, as in the case of "Elena, single mother of Gasparico, *mestizo* son of the scribe Hernán Núñez, who used to work for my predecessor, Alonso de Paz; Elena lives in La Mungia with the widow of a Spaniard, one Benito Palomo, and her children."[10] The *alcalde mayor* also makes observations about climate, agricultural activities, and crop production, relying on *caciques* for the accuracy of data relayed to him.[11] He lists staples such as corn, beans, and chili peppers; cacao and cotton, too. He notes that green feathers are highly valued, probably alluding to those of quetzal

10. AGCA, A3.16, leg. 1600, exp. 26371 ("Cuenta de los naturales . . . , 1570–71). The original text reads "Elena, moza soltera de esta parcialidad [San Mateo de Xocolo] madre de Gasparico, mestizo [e] hijo de Hernán Núñez [el] escribano que fue de Alonso de Paz, alcalde mayor que fue, está en La Mungia con la viuda mujer que fue de Benito Palomo y sus hijos." Because Spaniards were few and far between in Verapaz at the time, the region being controlled by Dominican missionaries and devoid of *encomenderos*, "little Gaspar" must have been among the first *mestizos* born there. Alonso de Paz was the first *alcalde mayor* assigned to Verapaz. La Mungia was a short-lived Spanish settlement in the eastern lowlands of Verapaz.

11. Carmack (1973, 140) notes that *caciques* were key informants in the compilation of the Kaqchikel and Pokomam *tasaciones* in 1562.

birds that "men hunt for in the hills." Very interestingly, Casa de Avante records the amount of tribute that *caciques* told him they thought their towns should pay in the future, a suggestion most likely made because of declining numbers.

When Bertrand worked with Casa de Avante's tallies, he noted a considerable population decline in San Miguel Tucurú and San Esteban Tamahú.[12] Casa de Avante himself acknowledged a state of crisis; on March 11, not six weeks since filing his first report, he tendered a second, which he called a "relación de los tributarios que han muerto." This document records the death of 109 tribute payers who succumbed to an unknown but virulent disease. Subsequent assessments of the tribute-paying capacity of Verapaz were based on Casa de Avante's observations.

Though he worked closely with *caciques* to obtain accurate statistics, the *alcalde mayor* was well aware of absentees, fugitives, and as yet uncongregated Indians, factors for which he attempted to compensate. A tally of his counts amounts to 13,523 people, of whom he considers 3,329 tributaries and 4,214 "vecinos vasallos." Shortcomings and short-falls notwithstanding, Casa de Avante's figures indicate a population-to-tributary ratio of almost exactly 4:1, allowing us to employ this ratio in cases for which only tributary data are available and thus to generate population totals with greater confidence.

THE "MEMORIA DE PARTIDOS" OF MENDIOLA ARTIAGA (1570)

In correspondence dated December 16, 1570, Licenciado Mendiola Artiaga, an attorney of the Audiencia de Guatemala, enclosed documents concerning "those who benefit from the fruits of the land, by how much and to what value."[13] Artiaga divides his "Memoria de partidos" into four discrete units, each of which corresponds to an ecclesiastical jurisdiction within "el obispado de Guatimala." He records the names of towns,

---

12. Bertrand (1982, 72) states that the "demographic crisis touched not only these two villages, but the whole of the Verapaz." MacLeod (1982, 9) comments that "the year 1571 was a year of dreadful mortality."

13. AGI, Guatemala 394 ("Memoria que envió el licenciado Mendiola Artiaga, fiscal de Guatemala"). The document states "es de los beneficios de aquella provincia y la cantidad y valor de ellos." Artiaga served as a *fiscal* (attorney and prosecutor) in an administration known to abuse Indians by forcing *reservados* to pay tribute when in fact they were exempt from the requirement.

the number of *vecinos* said to inhabit the *partido*, or district, over which the town holds sway, and "how much, in pesos, the clergy can expect to take advantage of."[14] In the listing of towns and districts attended to by secular clergy it is stated categorically that, in terms of the total number of *vecinos*, "in truth there are more" than the 27,500 actually recorded.[15] Dominicans are registered as attending to 10,450 *vecinos*, Franciscans to 11,800, and Mercedarians to 4,900.

By what process and reasoning were these figures arrived at? How much care went into their computation? We must be wary of numbers so consistently rounded off; with only three exceptions, *partido* totals are rendered in hundreds, from a low of three hundred to a high of five thousand. Diocesan authorities and the regular orders might have exaggerated native population size in an effort to convince the Crown to send more recruits to spread the Word of God. The number of priests who served (or were deemed necessary to serve) in secular *partidos* goes without mention. By contrast, in *partidos* administered by religious orders, Artiaga indicates that the Dominicans had the services of two friars, the Franciscans and Mercedarians one apiece. With only one exception, *partidos* attended to by regular clergy are located in the highlands, where travel between *pueblos de indios* was slow and difficult. Moreover, the number of *vecinos* in highland *partidos* is almost always larger than that for lower-lying or coastal *partidos*, where secular clergy preached. Size differentials are consistent with recorded patterns of native depopulation and survival.

When Artiaga's rounded-off figures are compared with more precise and elaborate tribute counts, the exercise is invariably frustrating. On

---

See Dakin and Lutz (1996) for elaboration. Another version of Artiaga's "memoria" is housed among the holdings of the Real Academia de la Historia in Madrid (Papeles del Consejo de Indias, D-95, fols. 311–12). It is discussed in summary fashion by Solano (1974, 86–87), who tallies the number of *vecinos* recorded to 34,900, not including Verapaz, indicative (he contends) of a native population of 151,600. Zamora (1985, 91–92) works with the same version of the source as we do.

14. AGI, Guatemala 394 (1570). The document records "lo que vale de aprovechamientos cada partido para el clero cada un año en el pie del altar." The total number of *vecinos* in each *partido* equals the total number of tributaries and all married *reservados*, a calculation we make based on data for Verapaz provided by Feldman (1982, 305). Carmack (1973, 141) operates on the assumption, as we do, that *vecino* totals are roughly equivalent to tributaries.

15. AGI, Guatemala 394 (1570). The document is worded thus: "[L]os dichos partidos tienen los dichos vecinos a común reputación y realmente tienen más . . . en muchos lugares." Artiaga takes pains to point out that "los dichos aprovechamientos" do not include, among other services rendered, provisions of food ("la comida que les den los dichos yndios") or provisions of fodder and firewood ("la yerba y la leña").

the other hand, when these admittedly convenient subtotals are grouped together in an attempt to generate a global estimate, what emerges in the final analysis is useful, especially in the absence of any better data. How do Artiaga's data help us in the latter regard?

In order to correlate Artiaga's figures with the spatial confines of what is today Guatemala, 12,900 *vecinos* must be subtracted from the secular clergy total to account for *partidos* located in Chiapas, El Salvador, and Honduras (see table 26). A similar reduction of 2,000 *vecinos* applies to the Dominican count with respect to two locations, Cuzcatlán and Los Purulapas, in El Salvador (table 27). Artiaga's data for the Franciscans (table 28) and the Mercedarians (table 29) apply solely to Maya communities in Guatemala. Adjustment in this manner gives a total of 39,750 *vecinos* for Guatemala, excluding Verapaz and unsubjugated or unexplored lands in the rainforests to its north. Artiaga's data, deficiencies notwithstanding, are reasonably compatible with those of another document, the "Memoria de los pueblos," compiled five years later.

THE "RELACIÓN DE LOS CACIQUES" (1572)

Like Artiaga's "Memoria de partidos," the "Relación de los caciques" put together by the Dean and Ecclesiastical Council of Santiago is a religious reckoning, the spatial basis of which spans the entire Diocese of Guatemala, including Indian towns in cacao-producing parts of what is today El Salvador. The document, part of the J. García Icazbalceta Collection, is housed in the Nettie Lee Benson Library of the University of Texas at Austin. A published transcription is available, courtesy of diligent scholarship on the part of Thomas Veblen and Laura Gutiérrez-Witt.[16]

As its title indicates, the manuscript furnishes data from a *cacique* perspective, listing the names of native leaders and those of their wives and family members, with the identity of *encomenderos* who received tribute also revealed. Communities administered by both regular and

16. The "Relación de los caciques y número de yndios que hay en Guatemala, hecha por el deán y cabildo, de orden de Su Majestad, 21 de abril de 1572" is cataloged as Vol. 20, no. 1 of the J. García Icazbalceta Collection. Veblen and Gutiérrez-Witt (1983) not only transcribe the document but also comment on its contents. Solano (1974, 88–92) also engages the source, deriving from it the figure of 30,830 *vecinos*, once again not including native heads of household in Verapaz. Zamora (1985, 93) analyzes it, too, noting "subtle differences" between the "Relación de los caciques" and the "Memoria de partidos" compiled two years earlier.

secular clergy are recorded, Indian *vecinos* again rounded off in the former and stated in precise numbers in the latter.[17] Four notable features are (1) the inclusion of personal details not only of the indigenous elite but of privileged *encomenderos* as well; (2) a list of the priests and friars who undertook the counts; (3) a record of what outlying settlements were part of community jurisdiction; and (4) a register, toward the end of the inventory, of Dominican and Franciscan monasteries, along with the number of friars based in them.

VIANA, GALLEGO, AND CADENA'S "RELACIÓN DE LA PROVINCIA DE LA VERAPAZ" (1574)

Complementing the Briceño and Casa de Avante data for Verapaz is yet another valuable source, one that (besides offering general observations about geography, climate, fauna, and flora) records information on fourteen *pueblos de indios* in the region for the year 1574. The "Relación de la Provincia de la Verapaz" was compiled by Francisco Viana, Lucas Gallego, and Guillermo Cadena, three Dominican friars charged with native conversion and welfare. Like the "Relación de los caciques," it too forms part of the Latin American holdings of the University of Texas at Austin. A transcription of the manuscript has been published by the Sociedad (now Academia) de Geografía e Historia de Guatemala. This transcription has in turn been rendered into English by Lawrence Feldman.[18]

Much of its content refers to the census taken in 1570–71, with Viana, Gallego, and Cadena noting that town populations are smaller than four years before. This they attribute to a lethal outbreak of disease. San Juan Chamelco, for instance, had 555 tributaries on the town rolls for 1570–71, but since then "pestilence has struck, causing everyone to fall sick, and over 600 souls to die."[19] So debilitating was the ravage of disease that fields went untended and unplanted, causing the friars to

17. As with Artiaga's data and that for Verapaz, we take *vecino* totals to include all married male heads of household, the combined sum of those who paid tribute and those who were exempt from it.

18. "Relación de la Provincia de la Verapaz, 1574," in *Anales de la Sociedad de Geografía e Historia de Guatemala*, hereafter *ASGH* ([1574] 1955), and Feldman (2000, 2–17).

19. *ASGH* ([1574] 1955, 24). The text reads: "Ha tenido pestilencia después acá en la cual murieron más de seiscientos almas y toda la gente enfermó."

lament that "as is often the case, great hunger is sure to follow."[20] Indians, we are told, only began to pay tribute in Verapaz in 1561, when the Dominicans could account for 7,000 tributaries. The census of 1570–71 recorded less than half that number, "diminished these past three years [alone] by more than 500, as shown by the count just completed by Dr. Cedeño."[21] Acknowledging their role in the disaster unfolding around them, the friars admit that the policy of *congregación* only exacerbates the situation: inducing Indians to live together in nucleated as opposed to dispersed settlements spreads contagion quickly among the souls they have gathered together to save but whose survival, in fact, their actions only threaten. Women, they record with consternation, die in greater numbers than men, who then leave Verapaz in search of new partners, never to return. In few documents are the scale and reverberation of disease outbreak, demographic collapse, and social disintegration so perceptively, and movingly, articulated. Such awareness, however, was never translated into remedy or redress.

THE "MEMORIA DE LOS PUEBLOS" (1575)

Drawn up by members of the Franciscan Order, the "Memoria de los pueblos" focuses only on Maya communities under the spiritual care of one missionary group. Much of what it states, nonetheless, we believe to have had wider applicability.

Elías Zamora makes good use of the manuscript, housed in the Archivo General de Indias, in his ethnohistory of the western highlands.[22] Like the "Relación de los caciques," the "Memoria de los pueblos" names not only *cabeceras de doctrina* (principal or head towns) but also the *pueblos de visita*, subject towns, under their authority. It further lists the number of inhabitants in each discrete outlying settlement, whereas the

20. *ASGH* ([1574] 1955, 29–30). The text reads: "[Y] así se teme que habrá gran hambre y tras ella pestilencia como suele."

21. *ASGH* ([1574] 1955, 29). The text reads: "[Han] disminuido en estos tres años más de quinientos tributarios, como consta por la cuenta que acaba de hacer el Doctor Cedeño." The total number of tributaries that the Dominicans give for 1571 differs from Casa de Avante's census of the same year, which records 3,329 tributaries. Bertrand (1982, 71), who has also examined these sources, observes that Cedeño recorded 2,445 tributaries in 1574, "which confirms both the data from the 1570–71 census and the information provided by the Dominicans."

22. AGI, Guatemala 169 ("Memoria de los pueblos que la Orden de San Francisco tiene en administración, 1575") and Zamora (1985, 93–94).

"Relación de los caciques" lumps them together. Artiaga in his report combined both *cabecera* and *visita* counts as *partido* totals, making it even more difficult, indeed well-nigh impossible, to disaggregate and discern relative numerical size. The spatial sensitivity of the "Memoria de los pueblos" is perhaps its main asset, but even this feature is not without problems.

Data are presented for the jurisdictions attended to by eight Franciscan convents, from Santiago de Guatemala in the central highlands to Totonicapán and Quetzaltenango in the west, including urban barrios (neighborhoods) around the capital city and far-flung *pueblos de visita* both large and small. Some of the latter lay at lower elevations along the Pacific piedmont and on the coast itself, where struggling, almost extinct villages—one *pueblo de visita* only had four *vecinos*—made salt. Robert Carmack, who also consulted the source, believes that it equates *vecinos* with tributaries.[23] Settlements where a convent had been established have more precise numbers of *vecinos* reported as living there, while *pueblos de visita* where friars reached only occasionally are rounded off, suggesting less familiarity on the part of the missionaries and a concomitant lack of precision. In the case of three *pueblos de visita* close to Franciscan headquarters in Santiago, vecino totals are suspiciously the same, twenty-seven, for all three settlements.[24] While it is advantageous to have data on *pueblos de visita*, the information itself must be scrutinized carefully. Whenever possible it should be evaluated and compared with other relevant material.

THE "DESCRIPCIÓN DE LOS CORREGIMIENTOS" (1575)

On March 15, 1575, Dr. Pedro Villalobos, having served as president of the Audiencia de Guatemala for two years, dispatched to the Crown a

23. Carmack (1973, 141–42).

24. Zamora (1985, 94) makes the valid point that the inclusion of *visita* names affords us a sense of *cabecera* territorial reach. He cautions against taking what is recorded, however, at face value, stating that "vested interest on the part of the Franciscans in demonstrating the importance of the *partidos* they administered may have led them, on occasion, to inflate numbers." Carmack (1973, 141–42) is of the same opinion, observing that another report similar to the "Memoria de los pueblos" was composed in 1581 by Fray Bernaldino Pérez. In the latter report population counts are notably lower, leading Carmack to conclude that, "the good friar appears to have performed the task conscientiously." For comparative purposes, see also AGI, Guatemala 171 ("Fray

summary account of the number of "yndios casados" said to inhabit his "governación." Like Artiaga, he breaks down one ecclesiastical unit, the "Obispado de Guatimala," into four sub-units, each of which is given a figure for the number of "yndios casados" administered either by parish priests or mendicant friars. Villalobos, unlike Artiaga, also has data for Verapaz, "which has fifteen towns with 3,135 married heads of household, attended to by twelve friars from three convents, the seat of the bishopric located in Cobán."[25] Even though his four other tallies are rounded off in thousands, Villalobos must have had abundant documentation at hand upon which to base his estimates, and that is what we consider them to be. His "Descripción de los corregimientos," then, essentially synthesizes ecclesiastical data and is therefore somewhat mistitled, as it does not present information, per se, by *corregimiento*. Villalobos does, however, state that twenty-six *corregidores* serve the Crown as district governors within the confines of the Bishopric of Guatemala "in such a fashion that no town goes without proper administration."[26]

Villalobos records 56,000 "yndios casados" for the "Obispado de Guatimala" and 3,135 for the "Obispado de La Verapaz." The Bishopric of Guatemala, we noted in our discussion of the Artiaga document, includes native populations in parts of Chiapas, El Salvador, and Honduras. Here it is a composite of (1) 30,000 "yndios casados" in 39 *partidos* under the control of secular clergy; (2) 12,000 under Franciscan jurisdiction, "divided up among nine convents that are home to forty-five friars"; (3) 6,000 under Mercedarian care, attended to by twenty-five friars from six convents; and (4) 8,000 under Dominican charge, reached by twenty-five friars from convent quarters in Santiago.[27] If, based on Artiaga, we subtract 13,000 from the Villalobos total of 56,000 "yndios casados" to discount non-Guatemalan heads of household, we generate a figure of 43,000, to which we add the Verapaz count (3,135) for a total

---

Bernaldino Pérez de la Orden de San Francisco sobre que se le dé licencia para llevar religiosos a la provincia de Guatemala y Chiapas, 1581"). Another notable difference between the two reports is that the earlier one includes the names of the *encomenderos* to whom the Franciscan-administered towns paid tribute.

25. AGI, Guatemala 39 ("Descripción de los corregimientos que a de aver en gobernación de Guatemala, 1575"). Sherman (1979, 348) supplies us with the date of March 15.

26. AGI, Guatemala 39 ("Descripción de los corregimientos, 1575"). The texts reads "de forma que ningún pueblo del [obispado] queda sin justicia."

27. AGI, Guatemala 39 ("Descripción de los corregimientos, 1575"). The text for the Franciscan jurisdiction reads "administran 12,000 yndios que están divididos en nueve conventos de 45 frayles."

of 46,135. When multiplied by a factor of four to include other family members, this estimate of "yndios casados" produces a figure of 184,540, which we consider our best reckoning for the Indian population of Guatemala in 1575. No independent corroboration is available, alas, but we do have (for 1570) Artiaga's figure of 39,750 *vecinos* for the equivalent territorial extent of Villalobos's data, not including Verapaz. The two figures certainly do not match, but the difference between them is not vast. An estimate of 184,540 indicates continued decline in native numbers since the time of Cerrato, some 243,310 in all, a fall of 56.9 percent.

DECREES AND DOUBLE STANDARDS

We noted in chapter 4 the gulf between what Carlos Fuentes calls the "real country" and the "legal country" when bureaucratic decrees in Latin America are measured against the results of their application— or *non*-application, as is the case all too often.[28] A striking example of the disconnect between rhetoric and reality is the behavior of Diego García de Palacios, a judge (*oidor*) in the Audiencia de Guatemala in the 1570s, someone in a position of authority intimately involved in government affairs for the period under discussion. As part of what he saw as his professional duties, García de Palacios took it upon himself to spell out, step by step, how to inspect and assess an Indian town for purposes of taxation. It is surely no coincidence that the "Palacios primer" is to be found in the very same bundle of documents that contains the *tasaciones de tributos* drawn up by President Cerrato almost twenty years before.[29] The *oidor*, an astute observer of native customs and traditions, authored a set of guidelines that Crown officials were supposed to follow when carrying out a tribute assessment. A few of his instructions, most likely struck after Palacios became aware of procedural problems in how Cerrato and other Crown officials conducted their assessments, are excerpted below:

28. Fuentes ([1985] 2001, 33).
29. AGI, Guatemala 128 ("Relación y forma que el Licenciado Palacios, Oidor de la Real Audiencia de Guatemala, hizo para los que hubiesen de visitar, contar, tasar y repartir en las provincias de este distrito"). The manuscript does not have a date, but the man responsible for its composition was active in Guatemala throughout the 1570s. García de Palacios would have been pleased to know that, before he put pen to paper, his instructions were followed most reverently by the royal official, or team of them, who carried out the tribute assessments in Kaqchikel and Pokomam communities in 1560–61.

In cases where a tributary count is to be undertaken, it is impera-
tive that experienced Indians must be chosen [to work with], ones
who are familiar with the local residents and the activities of the area
in question.

Tours of inspection [*visitas*] shall be conducted with these experienced individuals, during which all *vecinos* and Indians are to be met.
Going from house to house it shall be determined, for each one, who
the head of household is, along with his wife, their children, as well
as their property and agricultural holdings.

These procedures shall be recorded in such a manner that, on one
side of the folio on which the register is made, each person is listed one
after another, indicating whether they are married, widowed, or unmarried; are children; or are exempt from paying tribute. This facilitates,
at the end of the *visita*, a tally being made of how many persons there
are in total, specifically how many of them are married, widowed, and
so forth.

These dictates are those of an earnest if plodding perfectionist, someone not above the drudgery of having to state the obvious and make it
sound important. At least on one occasion, however, García de Palacios
failed atrociously to practice what he preached, as MacLeod has revealed
with damning erudition.[30]

In 1575, the *oidor* left Santiago for Izalcos, an important cacao-
producing town in what is today western El Salvador, close to the border
with Guatemala. The *encomendero* of Izalcos at the time, Diego de
Guzmán, not only was a renowned abuser of native labor but also a
skilled hand in the art of corruption. He relied, in MacLeod's words, on
the twin tactics of "terror and bribery" to ensure that Indians he abused
remained silent, while any official sent to Izalcos either turned a blind
eye to the situation or believed, for a price, the fabricated stories of
compliance with the law that Guzmán or his cronies fed them.

30. MacLeod ([1973] 2008, 90–91). For his sketch of *oidor* García de Palacios and his tour of
inspection in Izalcos, MacLeod draws (among other sources) on various items of correspondence in AGI, Guatemala 10, as we have done also. What the judge himself has to say may be
read firsthand, translated from Spanish into English by Ephraim G. Squier, with additional
observations by Alexander von Frantzius and Frank E. Comparato, in García de Palacios
([1576, 1860] 1985).

García de Palacios actually went to Izalcos in person to conduct a tour of inspection, but the Indians who tried to meet and speak with him were apprehended and beaten at Guzmán's orders. When, during his brief stay, the *oidor* inquired about the cries he could hear as hefty punishment was administered right outside the house in which he was lodged, he was informed that "an obstreperous vagabond was disturbing the peace." Whether García de Palacios was duped or bought off hardly matters. What is most incriminating is that on his return to Santiago he had no qualms in writing up, in MacLeod's estimation, "a false report of conditions in the province." When held in *encomienda* by Juan de Guzmán, father of heavy-handed Diego, Izalcos had between 800 and 900 tribute payers. Cerrato, according to MacLeod, counted 700, of whom 520 survived when García de Palacios ghosted through. The latter saw fit to ignore all signs of evident decline and wrongdoing: presumably to the great delight of Guzmán the younger, he neither lowered the number of Indians obliged to pay tribute nor reduced the amounts they had to furnish. It was to deal with such flagrant injustices that, in 1578, the Crown dispatched to Guatemala a man who it hoped would prove a more trustworthy, reform-minded president.

CHAPTER 12

THE VALVERDE YEARS

D iego García de Valverde, born and raised in Extremadura, the gritty, sun-baked province in southwestern Spain that bred the likes of Pedro de Alvarado and Francisco Pizarro, hailed from comfortable but modest circumstances in the historic city of Cáceres. His parents, Cristóbal de Valverde and Isabel de Mercado, owned property in Cáceres as well as a vineyard in Pozo Morisco, a fertile stretch of land northwest of the city. Besides Diego, the couple had at least three other sons, one of whom, Francisco, by 1582 had risen to the rank of admiral in the Spanish navy; Francisco at one time also served as governor of Panama. If Diego and Francisco did rather well for themselves, their brother Baltasar stumbled through life with less fanfare: when the time came to prepare his last will and testament, he was unable to sign his name on the documents prepared for him because he was illiterate.[1]

While his brother Francisco carved out a distinguished career for himself at sea, Diego opted for the less glamorous life of a civil servant who stuck to dry land. But best pursue public office, he must have reckoned, in places more exotic than Extremadura. Diego bided his time. When the New World eventually beckoned, he was a married and established man in his forties, degree and education long ago in hand. The *Catálogo de pasajeros*, which lists the names of those bound for the Indies, records his departure for New Granada in 1557 as follows: "Licenciado García de Valverde, from Cáceres, [set sail] with his wife, María de Reinosa; his son, Francisco de Valverde; his nephew, Cristóbal de

---

1. We thank Ida Altman for sharing with us her research findings on Valverde and his family from the Archivo Histórico Provincial de Cáceres, most (but not all) of which may be found more fully contextualized in her book on emigration from Extremadura to Spanish America in the sixteenth century (Altman 1989).

Valverde; and his sister, Catalina de Valverde, a single woman." Seven attendants made the passage across the Atlantic with Valverde and his family—a notable entourage.[2] After his first posting as a *fiscal* (attorney and prosecutor) in the Audiencia de Bogotá, Valverde next served (from 1564 to 1573) as a judge in the Audiencia de Lima. Thereafter he was appointed president of the Audiencia de Quito. When he was assigned as president to Guatemala in 1577, Valverde made his way to Central America as a seasoned administrator with twenty years' experience in the colonies.[3]

We have been unable to locate any *residencia*, a formal evaluation of government service, for the ten years or so that Valverde was in Guatemala (1578–87).[4] What we do have is voluminous correspondence either by him, addressed to him, or about him. Sifting through this documentation allows us, first, to impart some idea of the situation that awaited him upon arrival in Guatemala; and second, to determine if the reforms he undertook of the tribute system helped ameliorate the native lot.

"THOSE ALIVE PAY ALSO FOR THE DEAD"

Valverde's son, Francisco, records that his father was "more than sixty and on the point of death" after the family moved "in excess of one thousand leagues" from Quito to Santiago de Guatemala.[5] The poor health of the president, however, paled in comparison with that of the chronic condition of the land he came to govern. Valverde was appalled by what he found. "When I arrived here," he reflected on April 8, 1584, "I began to appreciate from letters written by parish priests and missionary friars, among others, just how burdened with tribute obligations so many Indians are." The cause of native torment, Valverde singles out, was related to

2. Bermúdez Plata (1946, vol. 2, 276).

3. Altman (1989, 217) differs from Schäfer (1947, vol. 2, 473, 480, 492, and 503); Simpson ([1950] 1966, 197–98); and MacLeod ([1973] 2008, 390) in some of the details of Valverde's career in the Indies. We have followed her reconstruction of dates and postings, however, more than the other three sources cited. Valverde was appointed president of the Audiencia of Guadalajara in 1587 but died before he was able to take office.

4. We have looked for Valverde's *residencia*, to no avail, in the sections of the Archivo General de Indias—Justicia and Escribanía de Cámara—most likely to contain it. It does not appear, either, in the list of such items compiled by De la Peña y Cámara (1955).

5. Francisco de Valverde to the Crown (AGI, Guatemala 10, 1579). Valverde's son reckoned that his father's expenses in moving the family from Quito to Guatemala were "more than 6,000 *ducados*."

the fact "that it has been ten, fifteen, or twenty years since [their towns] have been [properly] assessed for tribute purposes." Not adjusting the register of eligible tributaries to conform to actual population numbers meant that "those alive pay also for the dead." He elaborates:

> Making Indians pay to the maximum degree possible has resulted in their general deterioration and, in many parts, complete destruction. Lands that once were inhabited by many Indians now have none at all, a consequence of excessive taxation. So overburdened are they that some wander off, far from their homes, in a desperate attempt to earn enough to satisfy the demands made upon them. The burden on Indians is such that they spend most of their time, wretched and distraught, trying to find the means with which to pay tribute. Expecting them to meet unrealistic quotas causes their numbers to wither, in some cases until not even one Indian in town is left alive.

The president was especially angered by the "deceit" of *encomenderos* who claimed that it "takes only two months' work" to meet the tribute requirement when in fact it took "six months or more."[6]

Valverde's indignation emanates from every page. In an earlier missive, however, it is his incredulity that is most apparent. On November 5, 1582, he found himself forced to respond to allegations that he and his officers, in essence, were guilty of the very crimes they had worked hard to curb. The allegations were leveled at Valverde in correspondence that had arrived in Santiago de Guatemala from Mexico the month before. One "sinister and slanderous" item in particular had triggered "considerable shock and furor." Somehow the Crown had been led to believe, among a litany of complaints, that the following injustices were rampant:

---

6. Audiencia of Guatemala to the Crown (AGI, Guatemala 10, April 8, 1584). Extracts from the Spanish text read as follows: "Quando el presidente de esta audiencia entró en ella [hace] cinco años comenzó a entender por cartas de sacerdotes y religiosos y por otras vías que muchos indios estavan muy agraviados, aviendo [sido] diez, quinze o veinte años que no les tasavan y que faltaban de los que fueron tasados la mitad y más . . . y cobraban por entero de ellos y sino podían cobrar por entero cobraban quanto podían . . . y que avian cobrado de los vivos por los muertos . . . [T]asar los yndios según su posible[dad] a resultado [en] universal daño de ellos y su total acabamiento . . . [M]uchas provincias están [a]cabadas, asoladas, arruinadas y destruidas, y [en] muchas tierras yermas, donde hubo muchos yndios, no ay solo uno, y esto por cargas de tributos demasiadas, dándoles causa . . . para . . . andar buscando fuera de sus pueblos, desnudos y desarrapados . . . [E]s tanto que ocupen el tiempo y el año en solo pagar el tributo . . . [S]egún las cargas ynmoderadas que tienen de tributo, se van disminuyendo y acabando hasta no quedar yndio en el pueblo."

That *encomenderos* treat Indians just like slaves, selling them to one another as if indeed they were; that many Indians die from the blows and beatings they receive; that many Indian women collapse under their heavy loads; that they are apprehended forcibly on *encomendero* estates, where they give birth and raise children and die from the bites of snakes and poisonous vermin; that Indian mothers allow their children to die rather than have them suffer such servitude; and that some Indians hang themselves while others starve themselves to death.

A royal order (*real cédula*) was issued commanding Valverde to look into these matters and report back to Spain.

In mounting a vigorous defense not only of his record as president but also of his moral character, Valverde relayed to the King and the Council of the Indies that "from the day I first entered this office four years ago, I have taken great pains to punish those who abuse Indians in the manner referred to in the royal order." He emphasized the critical issue that the numbers registered as having to pay tribute did not match current population levels. "What I found here was an urgent need to remedy precisely that," Valverde states, "because there were instances of half and even two-thirds of a town's tributaries having died, leaving those who survive to deliver the full amount of what is stipulated." Indians left alive paid tribute not only for those who were deceased but also had to cover the taxes of those who "had fled town and never returned." Valverde warned that "excesses against the Indians" undermined the welfare of all. In a display of his knowledge of Latin, he reminded the King "unita ut nullus ex vitaliis pro aliensis vita ne suum debitis teneatur"— that "no one has the right, in the human scheme of things, to possess the lives of others, not even the lives of their debtors."

Even though chronically short-staffed—"Dr. Aliaga was very old and very sick when he came here as *oidor,* and died soon after, leaving Dr. Villanueva my sole trustworthy associate"—Valverde made it the High Court's top priority to arrange tours of inspection. "Over the past four years," he discloses, "approximately 150 towns have been reassessed," an exercise that entailed "not only striking from the list of tributaries [the names] of those who have died or absented themselves but also removing certain items difficult to obtain, like fish, honey, and salt, from the payment required." Valverde received strategic assistance in the former regard from members of the clergy, who were instructed "to record in a book the names of people who died, indicating whether or not they were tributaries, which house they lived in and which *parcialidad* they belonged to, and the date they passed away."[7] Furthermore, in a bold attempt to make amends for past misdemeanors, he estimated how much excess tribute had been exacted, and deducted that amount from present and future provisions, meaning that some *encomenderos* received "no payment for one or four or six years."[8]

Murdo MacLeod considers the "long-serving" Valverde "a mild reformer of tributes" who was "liked by most colonists."[9] Our reading of the documents suggests something different: that Valverde was assiduous, indeed tenacious in his reform initiatives; and that, in all likelihood, his desire to impose the rule of law did not go over well with *encomenderos* who preferred a more lax approach on the part of the Crown's highest representative. Valverde clearly had enemies in Guatemala prepared to discredit him in the King's eyes in order to protect their own interests. He alludes to this when he informs His Majesty that "the accounts of the royal treasury are not in good shape, because

7. President Valverde to the Crown (AGI, Guatemala 10, November 5, 1582). Extracts from the Spanish text read as follows: "Otra cédula vinó con las demás . . . siniestra y calumniosa . . . [que] puso admiración a los de esta Audiencia, obispo, prelados de las órdenes y a toda la tierra y causó alguna manera de escándalo y espanto . . . [Era] relación de excesos que en esta tierra había contra los indios, como será que los encomenderos se servían de ellos como esclavos y muchos se vendían de unos en otros; que se mataban muchos a azotes y palos que los cargaban, y muchas indias reventaban con las pesadas cargas; y que en los campos en sus ganados y granjerías les tenían por fuerza, y allí parían y criaban y morían mordidos de víboras y ponzoñosos sabandijas; y que de aquí venía que las indias dejaban a morir sus hijos porque no viniesen a tal esclavonía; y otros indios se ahorcaban y otros dejaban de comer, hasta morirse, con otras cosas de esta manera . . . [L]o que he hecho desde el día que en esta Audiencia entre, con mucho cuidado y demonstración, ha de ser castigado el que excediere . . . [E]n esta tierra hallé, con gran necesidad de remedio, fue lo que la Cédula Real referida dice, que faltaban muchos indios la mitad y las dos partes de tres, y la tercera parte pagaba el tributo de todos los indios que estaban tasados, [incluso] los muertos, ausentes y huidos . . . [E]l Doctor Aliaga llegó muy viejo y muy enfermo y luego murió. [D]espués [he] estado con el Doctor Villanueva, enviando persona de confianza a hacer la cuenta de los indios y otras informaciones y diligencias . . . y de esta manera se han ido retasando en estos cuatro años 150 pueblos, pocos más o menos. Y no solo les ha quitado lo que cabía a los indios pero algunas cosas que pagaban muy pesadas y perjudiciales, como el pescado, miel, sal y otras cosas . . . [S]e proveyó auto en esta Audiencia encargando al Obispo de este obispado y prelados de las órdenes . . . que los sacerdotes que están en las doctrinas tuviesen un libro en que asentasen los muertos y si eran tributarios y como se llamaban y en qué casa vivía y de qué parcialidad era y el día de su muerte."

8. Audiencia of Guatemala to the Crown (AGI, Guatemala 10, April 8, 1584). The Spanish text reads: "Con esta consideración se venía arbitrar lo que podría montar y ser, y según lo que parecía condenávase al encomendero a que no llevase tributo por uno año y por cuatro y por seis, y dando a los yndios por libres."

9. MacLeod ([1973] 2008, 390).

considerable sums have been taken from it." He declares frankly, "I don't know if I will be the one held responsible for this, just as I have been in these other matters, or if treasury officials will be blamed." Valverde had Diego Ramírez, an accountant who dealt with Crown finances, prepare a statement testifying that his salary arrangements were in proper order with respect to how much had been drawn from royal sources, "and that is the pure, transparent truth."[10] He also states at one juncture that he has reason to suspect that a Dominican friar, Bernardo de Almarsa, was involved in the campaign to defame him; the two had quarreled, after which Almarsa bore a lasting grudge.

The president gathered sworn testimony to accompany the defense of his regime, in which he was not only supported but commended by an array of notable clergy. Those who bore witness on Valverde's behalf included the dean of the cathedral, Pedro de Liévano; a teacher at the cathedral school, Francisco González; a friar at the Franciscan convent in Comalapa, Juan de Cija; two Dominican friars, Juan de Santiséban and Juan de Castrón; and two Mercedarian friars, Mateo García and Juan Tresino. All these individuals testified that the flagrant exploitation and violent conduct mentioned in the *real cédula* had neither been instigated nor perpetuated under Valverde's presidency but in fact had been inherited and, by diligent action, redressed.[11]

Were these men, as Valverde claimed of himself, telling "the pure, transparent truth"? What evidence can we turn to that reforms were not just declared but carried out? Was the dire situation in which Indians languished in any way improved?

García de Valverde's
"Razón de las Tasaciones" (1578–1582)

The evidence we draw upon when analyzing Diego García de Valverde's "Razón de las tasaciones" is supported by data available from

---

10. President Valverde to the Crown (AGI, Guatemala 10, November 5, 1582). The Spanish text reads: "V[uest]ra Caja Real no andaba buena, se [ha] sacado cantidad de dinero de ella y no sé si me lo echaban a mi como las demás cosas que se han referido o a los Oficiales Reales . . . [C]ertifico a V. M. que desde el día que entré en esta ciudad hasta el día de hoy no he sacado de V. R. caja un tercio adelantado . . . es pura verdad sin que otro secreto ni cosa haya ni ha habido."

11. Pedro de Liévano et al. to the Crown (AGI, Guatemala 10, November 5, 1582). See Simpson ([1950] 1966, 155–56 and 197–98) for a discussion of Valverde that draws on documentation housed in Guatemalan as opposed to Spanish archives.

other sources. For instance, one document we consulted in Seville, penned on November 10, 1582, corroborates Valverde's assertion that "during the four years that the said President has held office the tribute rolls of 150 towns, more or less, have been reassessed."[12] Working decades ago in Guatemala City, Lesley Byrd Simpson found another Valverde-related manuscript that also cites the figure of "ciento y cincuenta pueblos," 150 towns.[13] We have been able to collect information for half that number, seventy-five tribute notices that refer to some eighty-nine places in total.[14]

Textual problems abound in Valverde's "Razón de las tasaciones," some of which we discuss below. Its most striking and potentially useful feature, however, is that it records two counts of the tributary population: the first predates Valverde's arrival, by what lapse of time never clearly indicated; the second records the number deemed by the new president more suited to present demographic realities. We review, in turn: (1) vital statistics and their spatial compass; (2) data on *pueblos de indios* in Guatemala that allow us to make observations about the Cerrato *tasación* from a Valverde vantage point; and (3) scenarios for seventeen communities that were either barrios (districts) of Santiago de Guatemala or *milpas* (agricultural settlements) in the capital's immediate environs.

Content and Reach of the "Razón de las Tasaciones"

Of the seventy-five entries listed in the "Razón de las tasaciones," forty-seven deal with settlements held in *encomienda* by the Crown—nineteen of them in Soconusco, seventeen in or close to Santiago, and eleven others scattered throughout the *audiencia* jurisdiction. Another twenty-five settlements are held as private *encomiendas* in Honduras and El Salvador

12. AGI, Guatemala 10 ("Información hecha sobre el contenido de dos cédulas reales," November 10, 1582), fols. 1v–2.

13. Simpson ([1950] 1966, 155).

14. AGI, Guatemala, 10 ("Razón de las tasaciones que se han hecho desde el muy ilustre señor Valverde vino a esta audiencia a presidir, con lo que antes tributaban de los pueblos de este distrito, 1582"). On March 20, 1583, Valverde prepared a report, "Relación formada por la Audiencia de Guatemala de todos los pueblos de su jurisdicción y modo de administrar en ellos Justicia," in response to a *real cédula* dated November 13, 1581, in Lisbon (AGI: Patronato 183-1-1). It is only four folios in length but packed with data about administrative matters, among which is a three-page list naming "161 pueblos de indios" that lie within the *audiencia's* jurisdiction. No indication is given, save in a few cases, of the tributary population of these *pueblos de indios*. Zamora (1985, 94–95) also discusses the Valverde tribute assessments.

as well as Guatemala. Three settlements are shared between the Crown and individual Spaniards. The entries are reasonably consistent in stating (1) name of settlement; (2) identity of recipient; (3) what the old, pre-Valverde count was and what items of tribute were paid; and (4) what the new Valverde count is and what items of tribute are to be furnished. Occasional commentary justifies certain measures taken, like not lowering the number of tributaries for the barrio of Utlatecos in Jocotenango "because there has been no decrease in the number of its Indians."

Fifty-six settlements, roughly two out of every three, register fewer tributaries in the new count than in the old, with total numbers falling from 9,976.5 to 7,949, a decrease of a little over 20 percent.[15] Eleven settlements, six of them in Soconusco, record an increase, likely because Indians were brought in from other parts to keep up the production of cacao. Some settlements have the date of reassessment precisely indicated, others not. The first settlement listed, the *estancia* of Santa Úrsula, a sub-unit of Totonicapán, was reassessed as early as December 5, 1578, a week after Valverde formally took office. Not until March 17, 1582, however, did the president and the assistant he relied on most, the *oidor* Villanueva, get around to reassessing Comalapa, the last community accounted for.[16]

The Cerrato and Valverde *Tasaciones* in Comparative Context

Valverde voices repeatedly that the tribute rolls to which he has access have not been reviewed "in ten or fifteen or twenty years." In one communication, dated April 8, 1584, the last assessment is recorded as having been carried out even farther back, when Alonso Lopez de Cerrato was president. Though the disclosure is made in relation to Caluco, the document states categorically that it applies to other communities, too. "As this High Court wants to ascertain how many Indians used to pay tribute," we are informed, "it has looked at past information dating to when this jurisdiction was assessed thirty years ago." Cerrato is mentioned by name, and his assessment procedures criticized. "The High Court cannot understand," it is divulged, "why in Cerrato's time ordinances that are on the statute books were not complied with." Crisis reigned. "We assure

15. MacLeod ([1973] 2008, 130) records the first Valverde tally as 10,027.5 and the second as 7,730. In the case of the Barrio de los Utlatecos in Jocotenango, the entry states explicitly "esta tasación se mandó guardar e cumplir por no aver merma de yndios."

16. AGI, Guatemala, 10 ("Razón de las tasaciones," 1582).

Your Majesty, with pure Christian truth, that if Indians are not released from their labors then none of them will be left alive ten years hence, as is the case in neighboring parts, on account of how exploited they are by their *encomenderos.*"[17]

When he examined the "Razón de las tasaciones," Robert Carmack also observed that Valverde "specifically mentions Cerrato's earlier census, arguing that many years had passed since the count had been made." Carmack then hypothesizes that the first count of tributaries in the "Razón de las tasaciones" represents "a modified version of the original Cerrato figures."[18] This is an intriguing hypothesis, worthy of examination.

In table 30 we have assembled, for thirteen settlements in Guatemala, the three figures in question, one from Cerrato (if given) and two from Valverde. Of the thirteen settlements listed, three (Pazón, Pochutla, and Patulul) do not appear in the Cerrato *tasación* and a fourth (Nestiquipaque) has no indication of its tributary total. This leaves only nine settlements for Guatemala that can be looked at to examine Carmack's hypothesis.

If Carmack is correct, it seems logical to assume (1) that there is some correlation between the Cerrato figures and the first tally of Valverde, and (2) that if the two sets of Valverde figures are reliable, they indicate overall a pattern of decline. With regard to the first assumption, we discern a degree of correlation in three instances, namely Apaneca, Misco, and Huehuetenango, with a margin of error increasing in that respective order. In the other six cases data are either missing or the margin of error is too great to support Carmack's hypothesis. Whether or not the seventy-five settlements for which we have no information conform accordingly is a matter of conjecture. It seems best to conclude, then, that while for some settlements Valverde leaned on Cerrato for his reckoning, for others he did not. With respect to the second assumption, nine

17. Audiencia of Guatemala to the Crown (AGI, Guatemala 10, April 8, 1584). The Spanish text reads: "Queriendo esta audiencia entender por cuántos yndios se tasaba, y ver los autos de la tasa, información del posible y padrón de los indios que tenía el pueblo, nos ha hallado en las tasaciones que de treinta años esta provincia se han hecho. No puede esta audiencia entender que en tiempo de Cerrato que se hizieren dejarse cumplir y hazer lo que las cartas acordadas y dar por forma . . . Y certificamos a V[uestra] M[ajestad] con una verdad pura y cristiana que si no reglan y descargan de estos trabajos que de [h]oy en diez años como ya no [h]ay yndios . . . como [en] las provincias comarcas están desoladas y acabadas [porque] se han sacado muchas provisiones los encomenderos."
18. Carmack (1973, 143).

out of eleven settlements reveal levels of population decline consistent with known incidences in Guatemala and elsewhere in Spanish America. Two settlements (Nestiquipaque and Misco) show a slight increase.

The Barrios and *Milpas* of Santiago de Guatemala

Valverde's data for the barrios and *milpas* of Santiago de Guatemala are also worthy of attention. The *milpas* were founded around 1528 to 1530 by Spanish colonists for their Indian slaves, the barrios some twenty years later by Indian slaves emancipated by Cerrato. Native residents of both rural and urban areas, some three to five thousand in number according to one estimate, had onerous duties to fulfill, even though they were exempt from paying tribute from the time of gaining freedom, in 1549, until 1563.[19] The earliest date to which Valverde's first tally may be assigned, therefore, is 1563, the year that former Indian slaves became tributaries; the latest date would be in the mid-1570s, before Valverde took office.[20]

Other useful evidence is at hand. Between 1570 and 1575, native testimony from the Santiago area tells of an array of vicious Spanish officials, none more notorious than an *oidor* named Valdés de Cárcamo. He and an associate set about insisting that all Indians, without exception, be made to pay tribute—young or old, sick or infirm, noble or commoner. "Everyone pays tribute," laments a scribe for the *milpa* of Santa Ana, "even the blind who cannot see."[21] Spanish abuse reached such extreme levels in 1572 that more than twenty native communities arranged for *memorias*, accounts of their plight, to be recorded in Náhuatl and brought to the attention of the authorities.[22] A lack of response saw Indians, many from the same settlements, lodge similar complaints four years later, when another set of *memorias*, on this occasion penned in

19. Lutz ([1982] 1984, 95, 97, 160, 438–39; 1994, 19–23; Lutz 1996, xxiii–xxiv). The estimate of the number of Indian slaves said to have been emancipated in and around Santiago was given to Christopher Lutz in a letter written to him by William Sherman (January 7, 1972). See also Luján Muñoz (2011, 91–92).

20. In the "Memoria de los pueblos" (1575) discussed in chapter 11, the *vecino* totals for eight of these communities are higher than the first of Valverde's tally. This would suggest that his figures date from some time after 1575 but before 1578, when he arrived in Guatemala. A lethal epidemic (see Lovell ([1992] 2001, 75–78) killed many *vecinos* in 1576–77.

21. "Memoria" 8 in Dakin and Lutz (1996, 37). The Spanish text reads "todos dan tributo, hasta los ciegos que no pueden ver."

22. Dakin and Lutz (1996).

Spanish, was sent to the Crown, seeking redress.[23] Native appeals received a more sympathetic hearing the second time around, which indeed may account for why an administrator with the clout and reputation of Valverde was sent from Quito to deal with the situation.

Seen in this light, we think it likely that Valverde's first tally of tributaries for the barrios and *milpas* of Santiago dates to the mid-1570s. Because those *tasaciones* were inflated by the inclusion of people who should not have been on them, their numbers call into question both the validity of Valverde's initial counts and the veracity with which his later ones reflect native depopulation, especially as a result of the epidemic that raged in 1576–77.[24] Any confident reckoning must await further investigation, as must an appraisal of whether abuse on the part of royal officials, so prevalent in and around Santiago, was common elsewhere. Thus, while we consider the "Razón de las tasaciones" to be a rich and revealing document, its effective use poses many challenges. It is perhaps best engaged on an entry-by-entry basis, with care taken to contextualize the two numerical tallies with events and circumstances, wherever discernible, unfolding at the local or district level prior to Valverde's arrival. Informative though the source most certainly is, we consider it prudent not to try to generate a global estimate of population based on its numerical tallies.

"SECRET JUDGMENTS OF GOD"

How successful, in the end, was Valverde at imposing royal order and reforming the tribute system? Did his decade-long presidency reverse the tide of extreme exploitation and native demise?

The burden of tribute continued, but it appears that the worst forms of abuse that accompanied it were tempered, if not eradicated. We might best sum up the situation by invoking, once again, Simpson's notion that such measures as those taken by Valverde "tamed" the *encomienda*: the beast still roamed the countryside, so to speak, but its claws were clipped and its ferocious appetite restrained.[25] Native numbers, however,

23. Lutz (1996, xi–xlvii).
24. See Lovell ([1992] 2001, 75–76 and Lutz (1994b, 244).
25. Simpson ([1950] 1966).

still declined, for Valverde and indeed the whole colonial project were up against not just human depravity, but epidemiological scourge.

The president himself observed that "besides the deaths that ordinarily occur, there are also times when sickness strikes in the form of smallpox, influenza-like colds, and other diseases, from which many die."[26] Nobody worded it more ominously than one of the witnesses Valverde called upon to defend his honor after the defamations of the *real cédula*. "What causes the Indians to die and to diminish in number," wrote Pedro de Liévano, dean of the cathedral in Santiago de Guatemala, "are secret judgments of God beyond the reach of man." Liévano, however, immediately after attributing native decline to divine intervention, goes on to offer a more earthly explanation based on direct personal experience. "But what I have observed during the time I have lived here is that three or four bouts of pestilence have come from Mexico, on account of which the land has been greatly depopulated."[27] No reformer could do much of anything in the face of sustained epidemic outbreaks among a vulnerable native population.

26. President Valverde to the Crown (AGI, Guatemala 10, November 5, 1582). His precise words are: "[D]emás de las muertes ordinarias vienen algunos tiempos enfermos de viruelas, catarras y otras enfermedades en que mueren muchos."

27. Pedro de Liévano to the Crown (AGI, Guatemala 10, November 5, 1582). The Dean's precise words are: "[E]n lo que toca a morirse los indios e ir en dimunución son juicios secretos de Dios que los hombres no alcanzan y lo que este testigo ha visto en el tiempo que ha estado en estas partes es que desde la provincia de México han venido tres o cuatro pestilencias con las cuales ha venido la tierra en grandísima disminución."

CHAPTER 13

REACHING THE NADIR

Disease outbreaks that caused high mortality among the native population during President Valverde's time in office continued for the remainder of the sixteenth century and beyond. At what juncture native numbers hit bottom and leveled out is not easy to pinpoint. In keeping with the regional variation that characterizes other aspects of colonial life, decline continued longer, or recovery set in sooner, in some areas of Guatemala than in others. Our sources suggest that the nadir was likely reached, in global terms, a quarter of the way through the seventeenth century, after which the situation stabilized. It took another three centuries, we calculate, before Maya numbers reattained their approximate size at first contact.

A mere handful of sources are available for consultation for the years between 1594 and 1664, by which time indigenous demise and the need to replace cheap home-bred workers with expensive black slaves ceased to be a concern for Spanish authorities. Two of the sources come from the Contaduría section of the Archivo General de Indias, another two from the Biblioteca del Palacio Real in Madrid. A fifth is a well-known published source.

THE CONTENTS OF CONTADURÍA 969 (1594–1595)

Though dealing with fiscal data prepared for (or by) the royal treasury, documents housed under "Contaduría" often offer some surrogate indicators of demographic worth. Such is the case with a levy known as the *real servicio*, or the *servicio del tostón*, defined by Sherburne Cook and Woodrow Borah as "a tax of one-half peso levied upon each full tributary

and one-half the rate from each half tributary, whether in an encomienda or royal town."[1] The tax, they tell us, became a standard payment
beginning in 1592; Linda Newson records that it was introduced by
the Crown one year earlier "to help pay the costs of defense" and that
Indians were required to deliver the "capitation tax," in Honduras at
any rate, "in two installments of two *reales*."[2] One *tostón* (four *reales*) is
the equivalent of half a peso, so the number of *tostones* a community
paid in meeting its *real servicio* is equal to the number of tribute payers.
Cook and Borah process information for the *servicio del tostón* in Mexico
most resourcefully, as does Newson for Honduras. Documents in Seville
concerning the *real servicio* in Guatemala, alas, have been so badly
damaged by fire as to make many of them useless; some, however, though
fragile, yield valuable details about population size.

One particularly useful source in the *legajo* filed as Contaduría 969
is rendered in duplicate, allowing us to examine both copies to maximum
effect: data missing in one version show up in the other, and vice versa.
The *servicio del tostón* is listed not town-by-town but district-by-district
in a series of aggregates, "what the native tributaries of these provinces
pay His Majesty [in amounts] of one *tostón* each, for the past year, 1595,
with some left over from 1594."[3] Five tallies for 1594 are registered: the
Corregimiento de Tecoçistlán (247 *tostones*, 2 *reales*); the Corregimiento
de Guaçacapán (2,132 *tostones*); the Partido de Chiquimula de la Sierra
(1,174 *tostones*); the Corregimiento de Quetzaltenango (2,900 *tostones*);
and the Valle de Guatemala (8,709 *tostones*, 1 *real*). Two tallies are recorded
for the Alcaldía Mayor de Çapotitlán, also known as the Provincia de
los Suchitepeques (4,175 *tostones*), and the corregimiento de Totonicapán, the only listing in which the number is notably rounded off (5,000
tostones). Verapaz is conspicuously absent from the Contaduría 969
accounts, but we do have a figure for the *servicio del tostón* of the province
(1,873) from another source in Seville for the year 1596, authorized by
Alonso de Vides, *alcalde mayor*.[4] This figure is a composite of native
tributaries in thirteen towns. Since some towns in Verapaz—San Agustín

1. Cook and Borah (1971, vol. 1, 447).

2. Newson (1986, 291).

3. AGI, Contaduría 969 ("Lo que se a cobrado del servicio que los naturales destas provincias se han hecho a Su Majestad de un tostón cada uno el año pasado noventa y cinco con algunos restos del año noventa y cuatro").

4. AGI, Guatemala 172 ("Relación de la Provincia de la Verapaz"). The document was
signed on December 10, 1596.

and Cahaboncillo, for instance—appear with no number for the *servicio del tostón*, the Vides tally of 1,873 must be considered lower than the true amount. The eight districts for which we have data, gleaned from both sources, add up to 26,210 *tostones*, indicating 26,210 tribute payers. No data at all are available for two administrative units that appear elsewhere in Contaduría records—(Santiago) Atitlán and Tecpán Atit-lán (Sololá). Given that these two districts had sizable populations, the figure of 26,210 *tostones*/native tributaries is therefore underrepresented and deters us from estimating a total population based upon it.

A DOMINICAN *RELACIÓN* AND A FRANCISCAN *MEMORIA* (1604)

Two sources for the early seventeenth century date to 1604, both of them ecclesiastical surveys housed in the Biblioteca del Palacio Real. The first, attributed to Fray Rafael de Luján, is a *relación* of the number of "vecinos" administered by the Dominican Order. The second is an anonymous *memoria* that lists "vecinos" placed under Franciscan care.[5] Francisco de Solano, who also consulted these sources, states that they were composed in response to a call by Count Pedro Fernández de Andrade, president of the Council of the Indies, ordering that "secular and regular clergy spell out the number of *pueblos de indios* they attend to, and how many spiritual charges this involves."[6] While the Dominicans and Franciscans complied with Andrade's decree, we have no record that the Mercedarians and secular clergy did so. In the Luján *relación*, Dominicans are recorded as attending to sixty-seven towns with a total of 17,400 *vecinos*; in the anonymous *memoria*, the Franciscans oversee sixty-six towns and 5,000 *vecinos*. Totals for the number of *vecinos* listed as residents of the "pueblos" administered vary from forty to three. Tallies for vecinos recorded in both documents are all rounded off and range

5. Biblioteca del Palacio Real (hereafter BPR), Manuscript 175 ("Relación de Fray Rafael de Luján" and "Memoria de los frailes menores que hay en la provincia de Guatemala," folios 444–46 and 369–81, respectively).

6. Solano (1974, 106–107). He states that a *real cédula* was sent out in 1603 "a todas las autoridades eclesiásticas indianas—seculares y religiosas—para que especificasen, con todo el rigor posible, el número de pueblos de indios y el de sus habitantes que eran adoctrinados en las misiones a su cargo."

from 200 (Ziquinilá) to 8,400 (Santiago de Guatemala), totaling 29,800—
"roughly 120,000 inhabitants," according to Solano, who adds another
75,000 to compensate for the lack of secular and Mercedarian counts,
without explaining his rationale for doing so. He comes up with an
overall estimate of 195,000. We consider this figure improbable, his
assertion that it represents "an increase of some 60,000 inhabitants
with respect to those alive in 1572" even more so.[7]

THE CONTENTS OF CONTADURÍA 973 (1624–1628)

The contents of Contaduría 973, like those of Contaduría 969, above,
are valuable sources of information for the years spanning 1624 to
1710. We concentrate here on data for the period 1624 to 1628. For each
of those five years, amounts are furnished for the *servicio del tostón*
exacted from native tributaries in the "provincia de Guatemala, Chiapa,
San Salvador, San Miguel y Choluteca." The amounts in question are
as follows:

1624	64,878 *tostones*
1625	66,856 *tostones*
1626	62,381 *tostones*
1627	65,610 *tostones*
1628	65,632 *tostones*

An average of 65,000 *tostones* each year, therefore, was paid by "indios
tributarios" who lived and worked not only in Guatemala but in neighboring Chiapas (including Soconusco), El Salvador, and Honduras.
In dealing with such undifferentiated, aggregate totals, the challenge (as
ever) is to come up with a figure that represents the contribution of
Guatemalan Indians and therefore some indication of how many of
them there were.

Some data are at hand to assist us in a process of elimination
involving the subtraction of non-Guatemalan tributaries. For 1595,
we have assessments from Contaduría 969 for the *servicio del tostón*

---

7. Solano (1974, 108). He writes: "El siglo [XVII] inaugura, pues, con un signo positivo, ofre-
ciendo una elevación con respeto al último de 1572, de 60,000 habitantes en esos treinta y dos años."

of Chiapas and San Salvador: 15,993 and 9,910, respectively. For Soco-nusco, a low assessment of 407 exists in Contaduría 969 for the year 1594. Elsewhere among the contents of Contaduría 973, the forty-eight towns that make up the province of San Miguel in El Salvador are noted as paying approximately one-third the amount delivered by the eighty-four towns of San Salvador. Applying the same ratio of repre-sentation allows us to generate an estimate of 3,300 *tostones*/tributaries for San Miguel, El Salvador. For Choluteca in Honduras, Newson lists "663 indios," citing as her source a "relación geográfica" compiled by the surveyor Francisco de Valverde and dated August 28, 1590.[8] Adding up the figures for Chiapas, San Salvador, Soconusco, San Miguel, and Choluteca gives us 30,273, which allows us some leeway for deducting 30,000 non-Guatemalan tributaries from the 65,000 province-wide enu-meration, leaving 35,000. Multiplying this amount by a factor of 3.5:1, significantly less than the population-to-tributary ratio (P:T) of 5:1 that we used for the mid-sixteenth century, generates a total of 122,500. A lower P:T ratio may be justified on the grounds that epidemic outbreaks after 1550 must surely have lowered average family size as well as having other negative impacts; a population-to-tributary ration of 4:1, the ratio preferred by Solano, generates a total of 140,000. An average of these two totals leaves us with an estimate of the native population of Guate-mala in 1624–28 of 131,250. This we consider to be the nadir, or there-abouts, of the native population in the wake of conquest.

The real worry for Spaniards, of course, whether first-generation set-tlers or their offspring, parish priests or government officials, was that as long as Indian survival was perceived to be in danger, provisions had to be made to ensure that enough hands were available to keep the colony ticking. A scarcity of domestic workers in Guatemala, some thought, might best be dealt with (as elsewhere) by an exotic solution in the form of imported black slaves. As the native population declined, the number of blacks rose, though never as many as in other parts of Central America because of limited economic opportunity and high costs associated with transatlantic procurement. When it became evident that Indians would be around in sufficient quantity to meet the needs of their masters, slave imports began to taper off. Although it is derived from different source

8. Newson (1986, 291). Valverde's "relación geográfica" is housed in the Real Academia de la Historia in Madrid (9/4663).

materials, indeed engages a distinct body of literature and pertains to another discrete set of historiographic concerns, our locating the native nadir in the years 1624–28 coincides with the peak of slave traffic to Guatemala recorded by scholars of the black diaspora.[9]

VÁZQUEZ DE ESPINOSA'S *COMPENDIO Y DESCRIPCIÓN DE LAS INDIAS OCCIDENTALES* (CIRCA 1629)

For Guatemala, the demographic data in book 5 of Antonio Vázquez de Espinosa's magnum opus, the *Compendio y descripción de las Indias Occidentales*, are most disappointing. Nowhere in the thirty-three chapters of otherwise astute and useful observations dedicated to Guatemala do we find the detailed population statistics that the Spanish Carmelite friar recorded for Yucatán or Peru.[10] Scattered here and there are references to "muchos indios de seruicio" attending to the needs of "mas de 1,000 vezinos españoles" in Santiago de Guatemala; Petapa is said to have "mas de 600 indios"; Ciudad Vieja is described as "un buen pueblo de indios." Other mentions of population size are vague or nonexistent, with Vázquez de Espinosa settling for disclosing only how many "pueblos" are to be found in nine *corregimientos*, in addition to the "seventeen pueblos" of Verapaz.[11] At least the dating of his information for Guatemala, as with Yucatán, is relayed precisely, something that Noble David Cook found lacking and therefore problematic in Vázquez de Espinosa's treatment of Peru.[12] Though Vázquez de Espinosa traveled extensively throughout Spanish America making comprehensive studies, he spent less time in Guatemala than in other parts. This shows in his sparse commentary on the native population. Like many who passed through, however, he describes one Guatemalan landscape after another as being a "pedaço de paraiso"—a piece of paradise, "with valleys of beautiful orchards watered by fresh, crystal-clear springs" where the land

9. See Lokken (2013) for an incisive synthesis of research findings to date.

10. Vázquez de Espinosa ([ca.1629] 1948, 116–19, 189–247, and 644–70).

11. Ibid., 198, 201, 206–208, and 218.

12. Though Vázquez de Espinosa's work "contains a wealth of population information," concedes Cook (1982, 79), it "has no chronological meaning." He warns against uncritical use of "a hodgepodge of information that at the outset appears accurate, yet on close examination is highly misleading." Vázquez de Espinosa's data for Yucatán is clearly stated as pertaining to the year 1609.

produces "all year round because of its uniform fertility and benign, spring-like temperatures."[13] In his idealization of landscape, Vázquez de Espinosa turns a blind eye to the relentless exploitation of native labor that made Guatemala seem, in the words of Severo Martínez Peláez, "una tierra milagrosa"—a land of miracles.[14]

DOMINICAN AND FRANCISCAN ASSESSMENTS (1664)

Sixty years after they complied with a *real cédula* calling for them to enumerate the native charges under their care, the Dominican and Franciscan orders did so again. As in 1604, however, no records exist of the Mercedarians and secular clergy having been equally cooperative. Bishop Payo de Rivera consulted with the Audiencia de Guatemala on the matter; the *fiscal* of the High Court, Pedro Fraso, responded with a detailed inventory of Indians under Dominican control, "a number totaling, in all said towns, 17,180."[15] The Franciscans are recorded as having significantly more towns to administer, but with only slightly more native residents, 17,989.[16]

In his manipulation of the data, Solano again uses a population-to-tributary ratio of 4:1 to generate, from the combined Dominican and Franciscan tallies (35,169), a figure of 140,676, to which he again adds (without explanation or rationale) another 75,000—"who we can presume were entrusted to the Mercedarians and the secular clergy."[17] His total of 215,676 inhabitants strikes us as inflated, but we concur that, by the mid-seventeenth century, the native population of Guatemala had stabilized and was already embarked on a slow recovery, the trajectory of which we chart next.

---

13. Vázquez de Espinosa ([ca.1629] 1948, 198, 199, 204, and 206). The original, with specific mention of Ciudad Vieja, Jocotenango, Escuintla, and environs, runs "con muchas fuentes y arroyos de aguas dulces, y cristalinas, con hermosas Guertas . . . todo el año sin diferencia por la fertilidad, buen temperamento, y uniformidad de el . . . es primavera todo el año."

14. Martínez Peláez ([1970] 1998, 106).

15. The source (BPR, Manuscript 2,848) is cited by Solano (1974, 111) as stating "y el número de tributarios de todos los dichos pueblos es de 17,180."

16. BPR, Manuscript 2,848, cited in Solano (1974, 111).

17. Solano (1974, 111). He writes: "[S]e suman 75,000 como presumibles a cargo de mercedarios y seculares."

CHAPTER 14

THE SLOW RECOVERY

The recovery that had set in among the native population by the mid-seventeenth century, though irreversible over the long haul, was also intermittent and subject to episodes of crisis and decline. Global statistics, we stress yet again, often conceal as much as they reveal, especially about demographic change at the local level. It bears reiteration that what holds true for one Maya community in Guatemala may not be replicated by others nearby, on the other side of a river or at the opposite end of a valley. Marked variation, town by town, region by region, is a striking feature of the past, not just the present.

We draw on another rich set of data, seventeen items in all, to document a generally upward trend in indigenous numbers between 1681 and 1812. As with our analyses in the preceding chapters, we advance estimates of native population size only if we deem them reasonable to make.

THE "PADRÓN DE LOS INDIOS TRIBUTARIOS" (1681)

In an attempt to lessen, if not eliminate, the abuses rampant in the operation of forced native labor, the *oidor* of the Audiencia de Guatemala, Jerónimo Chacón y Abarca, called upon clergy to undertake, for the communities they served, a detailed town-by-town tally of the tributary population subject to *repartimiento* recruitment. Chacón y Abarca had plenty of experience to draw upon: before being posted to Guatemala, his responsibilities as an official of the Crown included spells in Santo Domingo and Puebla de los Ángeles in Mexico. He notified priests and missionaries of his intentions in 1680; one year later, the "Padrón de los indios tributarios de los pueblos que estaban bajo la administración de religiosos de la provincia de Guatemala" was assembled. It is housed in the Archivo General de Centro América in Guatemala City.[1]

The census has been consulted by, among others, Francisco de Solano, who distills its contents and comments not only on what the *padrón* reveals but also what it fails to disclose.[2] No data for *pueblos de indios* administered by secular clergy, for instance, are given, meaning that the Oriente again goes unrecorded. Three religious orders are identified as having a pastoral base in twenty-one convents. Dominicans, with twelve convents, attended to ninety-six towns, fifteen in Chiapas and eighty-one in Guatemala. Franciscans, with six convents, attended to fifty-four towns, all of them in Guatemala. Mercedarians, with three convents, attended to eighteen towns, all of them again in Guatemala. Two settlements the Dominicans administered from their convent in Santiago de Guatemala—Santa Ana and Santa Inés Hortelano—appear without any indication of their tributary population; so too do four settlements the Mercedarians administered—San Antón, La Merced, San Jerónimo, and Espíritu Santo. Very few of the numbers for *pueblos de indios* are rounded off, and more than forty register the number of tributaries down to half-units, indicating assiduous head counting, or at least the illusion thereof. No mention is made, however, of the number of "reservados," those who were exempt from paying tribute.

Using a population-to-tributary ratio (P:T) of 4:1, but including the towns in Chiapas in his calculations, Solano generates a population of 132,000 from a tributary base of 32,923. From that same tributary base, we subtract 4,858 for the "indios tributarios" of Comitán (1,613) and Ocosingo (3,245) in Chiapas, leaving us with 28,065 "indios tributarios" for Guatemala—14,854 accounted for by the Dominicans, 12,562.5 by the Franciscans, and 648.5 by the Mercedarians. A population-to-tributary ratio of 4:1 we now consider a fitting one to deploy, as average family size must have increased somewhat from nadir levels a half-century or so before. This conversion factor allows us to generate an estimate of 112,260 Indians in Guatemala, but without including those attended to by the secular clergy. Solano reckons that number to have been around 100,000, a figure he derives from measured comparison. If, in this case, we go along with Solano's reasoning and accept that figure as realistic,

1. AGCA, A3.2, leg. 825, exp. 15207 (1681).
2. Solano (1974, 111–18).

then we arrive at a native population in the vicinity of 212,260. Reflecting an increase of perhaps 80,000 over nadir levels not sixty years before, this is our first reliable indication of population recovery.

THE "RAZÓN DE LAS CIUDADES" (1683)

A fire in the Archivo General de Indias in the 1920s damaged not only the building itself but also documents stored in it. One section of the archive particularly affected was Contaduría. Some papers were destroyed completely; others were badly burned and then soiled by water. Among the latter is *legajo* 815, now a charred batch of documents that contains a comprehensive register for the Audiencia de Guatemala, the "Razón de las ciudades, villas y lugares vecindarios y tributarios de que se componen las provincias del distrito," dated 1683. Lovell spent several weeks sifting through the register, taking copious notes. The *legajo* was delivered for consultation not bound in customary ribbon but in a special box. When opened, the smell and appearance of what lay inside drew the attention of even the most self-absorbed researchers, curious to take a look. Rectangular folios had become oval in shape, singed at the edges, and crisp to the touch. Bits of them disintegrated at the turn of a page, history disappearing after being recorded one last time. It was a unique investigative experience.

Few researchers have examined the source; one exception is the intrepid Linda Newson, who extracted population data for Honduras from it. She laments that "there is no detailed breakdown of the Indian population on a village basis," but is able to retrieve a number (3,676) for the province of Comayagua, of "indios casados que hacen otros tantos tributarios enteros"—married men who are full tributaries.[3] Perusal of documents in Guatemala City allows her to derive a population-to-*casado* ratio (P:C) of 3.3:1, whereas documents in Tegucigalpa suggest 3.6:1 and 4.0:1. These ratios are generated from a sample of thirteen communities. Newson, in the end, settles for a P:C ratio of 3.8:1, at least for the mining areas around Tegucigalpa in the late seventeenth century.[4] Her analysis facilitates, as with Solano in the case above, measured

3. Newson (1986, 292).
4. Ibid., 292–93.

comparison with Guatemala. Regarding the demographic worth of Contaduría 815, however, Solano is assertively dismissive, describing the "Razón de las ciudades" as "entirely useless," which is simply not the case.[5] Among the register's myriad attributes is that, unlike what Newson discovered for Honduras, it does contain a "detailed breakdown" at the local level for many areas of Guatemala.

San Juan Ostuncalco is a good representative example. Its entry as part of the Corregimiento de Quezaltenango reads:

> The town of San Juan Ostuncalco has 368 married Indian males in addition to fifty-three men married to women in other towns; they pay half their tribute here in San Juan Ostuncalco. There are sixteen Indian men [who are] exempt from tributary obligations; fourteen widowers; seventy-two unmarried males; fifty-three married Indian females who live in other towns; two Indian women married to absentees; one Indian woman who is married to a *mestizo* man; forty-eight widows; thirty-three unmarried females; and sixty young men now old enough to be married.[6]

While it is the native population on whom we focus attention, the "Razón de las ciudades," as the mention of an Indian woman being married to a "*mestizo* man" makes clear, also enumerates non-native persons, among them Spaniards, Ladinos, mulattoes, black slaves, and indentured laborers. The data for some administrative units are more meticulous and in a better state of repair than others: Verapaz, "which has twenty-seven pueblos, but with many Indians living outside the province," is well-preserved and documented; so too are the Vicaria de Escuintla, "made up of three pueblos and seven haciendas"; Guazacapán, where (at Atiti-quipaque) "live some Indians known as *naboríos*, who do not pay tribute"; Chiquimula de la Sierra, where (in Asunción Mita) "nine Spanish hacienda owners have fifty-two *mestizo* and mulatto families working on their properties;" San Antonio Suchitepéquez, where the native population (excluding *naboríos*) adds up to 25,825; and Santiago Atitlán,

5. Solano (1969, 300). His precise words are "completamente inservible."

6. AGI, Contaduría 815 (1683). The original states: "El pueblo de Ostuncalco tiene 368 indios casados y 53 indios casados en otros pueblos que pagan medio tributo en este; 16 indios casados con indias de reservadas; 14 indios viudos; 72 indios solteros; 53 indias casadas en otros pueblos; dos indias casadas con ausentes; una india casada con mestizo; 48 indias viudas; 33 indias solteras; asimismo e hecho casar 60 solteros."

"whose fifteen pueblos have 2,394 married Indian males and 430 [or so] widows and widowers."[7] Information on the *pueblos de indios* forming the Partido de Tecpán Atitlán is superbly nuanced, as is the Partido de Totonicapán y Huehuetenango; the latter, as we noted in chapter 5, lists the tributary population for nine *pueblos de indios* by *parcialidad*, thirty-one in all. A singular feature for the Partido de San Antonio Suchitepéquez is that in every town in the province, twenty-five in all, the number of Indian boys, a total of 7,736, is greater than the number of Indian girls, 6,519. Beyond Guatemala, Nicaragua figures prominently; so, too, does Costa Rica, with wonderfully fine-grained details.

A conspicuous omission from the musty remains of Contaduría 815 is data for the areas around the colonial capital, Santiago, which appear not at all. This drawback, among others, makes us hesitant to compute a global estimate of the native population. Region by region, however, and for a glimpse of the now manifest presence of non-Indians, especially *castas*, or mixed-bloods, along the south coast and in eastern Guatemala, the "Razón de las ciudades" is a source of exceptional importance.

THE "GRADUACIÓN DE SALARIOS" (1684)

Unlike the previous document, the "Graduación de salarios" allows us to compute a global estimate for broad territories of Guatemala. We are indebted to Genoveva Enríquez Macías not only for locating the document among the holdings of the Archivo General de Indias but also for transcribing it, contextualizing it, and publishing it in a forum that ensures its accessible consultation beyond the confines of Seville.[8] The document, Enríquez Macías makes clear, is not a census "in the strict sense of the term" but in fact a register of "a new tax, which all towns

---

7. AGI, Contaduría 815 (1683). The original reads as follows: Verapaz has "27 pueblos de indios . . . y se ausente de muchos de estos [porque] viven en diferentes provincias y partidos y reconocen sus pueblos para pagar los reales tributos"; Escuintla "consta tres pueblos y siete haciendas"; Atitiquipaque is where "viven algunos indios que se llaman 'lavoríos' y mulatos sin que ai tributarios que paguen tributo"; Asunción Mita has nine "dueños de haciendas"; and the "quince pueblos" belonging to the Partido de Santiago Atitlán "suman 2,394 indios casados [y] 43[0] viudos y viudas."

8. Enríquez Macías (1989). The full title of the document is "Autos hecho sobre la graduación de salarios que tienen los ministros de esta real audiencia en las condenaciones de penas de cámara, gastos de justicia estrados de ella, a pedimento del capitán Cristóbal Fernández de Rivera, receptor y depositario general de ellas" (AGI, Guatemala 168 [1684]).

were obliged to pay in accordance with the number of tributaries they had." The tax in question "was geared toward paying the salaries of civil servants" (hence the title of the document) involved in a variety of government chores, including legal counsel for the poor, medical services at the state prison, and looking after royal finances. It also covered the costs of religious ceremonies such as those held during Lent, Holy Week, and Corpus Christi. Because the tax was decreed payable on the basis of seven *maravedís* per tributary, or one *tostón* and four *maravedís* per twenty tributaries, then the sums levied for any given settlement or jurisdiction can be commuted accordingly into tribute payers. What makes the "Graduación de salarios" of paramount utility is its extensive spatial coverage—"the most complete we have available," Enríquez Matías informs us—825 units of varying size from every corner of the *audiencia*'s far-flung reach, from Chiapas to Costa Rica, including data on 310 localities in Guatemala.[9]

We calculate total payments made for Guatemala (see table 31) to be 3,025 *tostones*—or (multiplying by four) 12,100 *reales*, the equivalent of (multiplying by 34) 411,400 *maravedís*. This sum commutes (divided by seven *maravedís* paid per tributary) into 58,770 tributaries or, using a population-to-tributary conversion of 4:1, an estimated 235,080 native inhabitants.

FRANCISCO VÁZQUEZ AND FELLOW RELIGIOUS CHRONICLERS (CIRCA 1690)

Studies of colonial Guatemala benefit enormously from the work of four religious chroniclers, three of them Dominican (Antonio de Remesal, Thomas Gage, and Francisco Ximénez) and one Franciscan (Francisco Vázquez). No Mercedarian of repute ever dedicated himself to the glory of recording his order's labors, though Andrés de las Navas (d. 1702) had the academic training but presumably not the inclination to do so. While the four who did put pen to paper made valuable observations about native population dynamics—Remesal, for instance, offers insightful commentary (see chapter 5) on the operation and impact of *congregación*—none of them saw fit to address the matter of demography in an

9. Enríquez Macías (1989, 124–28).

organized and systematic manner, somewhat surprising given the emphasis placed on saving Indian souls. References about population size are scattered throughout their texts, often tantalizingly so. A case in point is the mention by Vázquez that, in 1673, the Franciscans administered in the Provincia de Guatemala "upward of 100,000 souls."[10] Vázquez's reckoning, on its own, is rather flimsy, invoked but left undeveloped rather than backed up with supporting statistics. These, however, are provided by the "Descripción de los conventos de la Santísima Provincia del Nombre de Jesús de Guatemala," which Lázaro Lamadrid includes in his introduction to an edition of Vázquez's four-volume treatise.[11] This document dates to 1689, a few years before Vázquez finished writing, and so complements Vázquez's chronicle nicely. It may well be that the chronicler himself penned the "descriptive and truthful account," for it bears several of his characteristic modes of expression, in addition to recording useful demographic data. Lamadrid tells us that the "Descripción de los conventos" was located by the indefatigable José Joaquín Pardo when he was organizing the Archivo Arzobispal in Guatemala City, an archive that for decades has had restricted access imposed on it.[12]

From the same source, Solano excerpts data for twenty-two "cabeceras" (head towns) and sixty-nine "anejos" (subject towns) that he claims add up to 54,766 "almas de confesión." These "souls of the age of confession," he maintains, "represent some 102,000 individuals," the difference between "souls" and "individuals" accounted for (in the document's own words) "by the great many boys and girls eight years of age or less, who are equivalent in number" to the "almas de confesión."[13] Solano argues that the Dominicans would have attended to roughly similar such numbers,

10. Vázquez ([1688–95] 1944, vol. 4, 329–30). The chronicler's precise words are "más de cien mil almas, que corren cuidado de la religión de Nuestro Padre San Francisco de esta Provincia."

11. "Descripción de los conventos de la santísima provincia del nombre de Jesús de Guatemala, hecha en el año 1689," in Vázquez ([1688–95] 1944, vol. 4, 33–67).

12. Lamadrid in Vázquez ([1688–95] 1944, vol. 4, 33). The document is cited as being filed in the Archivo Arzobispal de Guatemala as manuscript A4-5-3. Its author, most likely Vázquez himself, states: "De todos los informes que se me han hecho (los cuales quedan en el archivo de esta Santa provincia) y de los que yo mismo he visto y atrechado, hago esta relación descriptiva y verídica narración."

13. Solano (1974, 121) and Vázquez ([1688–95] 1944, vol. 4, 464). The wording in Solano reads "54,766 *almas de confesión* de indios naturales con 'los muchísimos niños y niñas de ocho años para abajo, que serán otras tantas almas,' representan unos 102,000 individuos." The quote within the quote is from the "Descripción de los conventos" itself.

and the Mercedarians and secular clergy, combined, likewise, allowing him to advance a figure of 300,000 for the total native population.

This estimate strikes us as excessive, indeed unrealistic under the demographic circumstances that then prevailed and the terms under which the document was drafted. As he does with frustrating regularity, Solano misreads how the text is actually worded. The "Descripción de los conventos" clearly states that the Franciscans in neighboring El Salvador and Honduras as well as in Guatemala had "cincuenta y tres mil setecientos y sesenta y seis [53,766] almas de confesión" under their charge, not 54,766. These "indios naturales," furthermore, were attended to along with "seiscientos y ochenta [680] personas ladinas," a non-indigenous category that, at least in the eyes of the person composing the document, constituted "españoles, mestizos y mulatos"—Spaniards, mixed-bloods, and mulattoes. Most interestingly, the document converts "almas de confesión" into tributaries by a ratio of "one full tributary" being the equivalent of "four or five persons of the age of confesión."[14] Thus 53,766 "almas de confesión" are estimated to be "more or less" 12,000 tributaries, native taxpayers who lived in 125 towns "both large and small" and who were administered by friars based in thirty convents, not twenty-two, as Solano erroneously tabulates.

The *Recordación Florida* of Fuentes y Guzmán (1690–1699)

In addition to the religious chroniclers mentioned above, Francisco Antonio de Fuentes y Guzmán has provided a formidable secular account for those who study colonial Guatemala. A good friend of Friar Vázquez and, like him, a proud criollo, he composed his *Recordación florida* in the decade after Vázquez's work. There are some, like the nineteenth-century commentator Juan Gavarrete, who find the *Recordación florida* "a confused accumulation of exaggerated or unconnected associations" and thus dismiss it entirely as a reliable historical source. Others are more inclined to view both chronicle and chronicler more charitably, even gratefully, as is the case with Severo Martínez Peláez. In his magnum

14. "Descripción de los conventos," in Vázquez ([1688–95] 1944, vol. 4, 64).

opus, *La patria del criollo*, a remarkable edifice in which data from the *Recordación florida* are superbly showcased and critiqued, Martínez Peláez chastises Gavarrete for making such a "simplistic, superficial observation" and for failing to grasp the intrinsic merits of what is an admittedly challenging contribution.[15]

Certainly, from a demographic standpoint, the *Recordación florida* teems with information about the native population, which Fuentes y Guzmán took note of from differing perspectives—as a powerful landlord, as a district governor who was a servant of the Crown, as an influential member of the city council of Santiago de Guatemala, but most of all as an astute observer and recorder of the "patria" he so passionately loved. As the title of his great work perfectly reflects, the problem lies in the chronicler's penchant for "flowery reflection," which in the case of language he uses to denote native populations often results in confusion over which category he means. As Enríquez Macías observes, he moves from providing "summary statements about 'tributarios' or 'vecinos' or 'habitantes' to 'almas de confesión' or 'parishioners' or simply 'Indians,' depending on whether the information Fuentes y Guzmán relays comes from a civil census or an ecclesiastical one." Was he using terminology correctly, she queries, assuming that it is able to be defined accurately in the first place? She discerns "significant fluctuations in the number of residents in every town over the course of the seventeenth century."[16] In his defense, the chronicler confesses that he encountered great difficulties figuring out what the population of any given place actually was "because of, first, not knowing the number of people exempted from paying tribute and, second, not knowing how many infants and children there are."[17] In addition, "Indian leaders don't register anyone they feel like leaving off the tribute list and other such accounts."[18] Perhaps the best approach to working with population data in the *Recordación florida* is to forgo, as Fuentes y Guzmán himself did, any attempt at computing general or global parameters and focus attention on demographic details at the local or district level.

15. Martínez Peláez ([1970] 2009, 78). The motives behind Fuentes y Guzmán's writing the *Recordación florida* the way he did are discussed insightfully by Martínez Peláez, especially pp. 21–26.
16. Enríquez Macías (1989, 123).
17. Fuentes y Guzmán ([1690–99] 1972, vol. 3, 97).
18. Ibid., 299.

The Contents of Contaduría 973 (1710)

One set of documents from the bountiful Contaduría 973 in Seville allowed us to estimate the native nadir at 131,250 for the years between 1624 and 1628 (see chapter 13). Another document from the same *legajo*, for the year 1710, has comprehensive data for the *servicio del tostón*, thus affording us an equivalent tally of Indian tributaries.[19] Information is presented not only in a neat and legible hand but also with exemplary precision: numbers are summarized in tabular form as well as written out for each administrative unit, and data presented of what items besides money (corn, beans, chickens, wheat, and garlic, for instance) were paid as tribute. Mention is also made of what amounts Indians contributed to the upkeep of the royal hospital and strategic fortifications. A global figure of 80,621 *tostones* is recorded for 326 "pueblos y parcialidades," a figure that incorporates the "real servicio de Su Majestad" for four non-Guatemalan units, namely Soconusco (806 *tostones*), Chiapas (16,312 *tostones*), San Salvador (3,464 *tostones*), and San Miguel (985 *tostones*). If we subtract the non-Guatemalan *real servicio* of 21,567 from the global figure, this leaves us with 59,054 *tostones* for the eleven districts that constitute Guatemala (see table 32). Multiplying this number by a population-to-tributary ratio of 4:1 gives us an estimate for the native population of 236,216.

The Contents of Contaduría 977 (1719)

Similar in many ways to the document discussed above, Contaduría 977 (with information for the year 1719) records 58,204.5 *tostones* as constituting the *real servicio* paid by Indian tributaries in Guatemala, indicating a native population (again using a population-to-tributary conversion of 4:1) of 232,818. The total value of tribute, district by district, is also given (see table 33). An entry in the treasury accounts offers an explanation of why resources have been depleted. "Many disbursements have had to be made these past few years," it is stated, "to pay for putting down the rebellion of the Tzendal towns in Chiapas,

19. AGI, Contaduría 973 (1710).

and to maintain a military presence in Ciudad Real [San Cristóbal de las Casas]. Other costs were incurred in mounting a small armada, sent to explore enemy territory [inhabited by] Zambos and Mosquitos, a mission that also included a dispatch of soldiers. Furthermore, because of destruction wrought by earthquakes, tribute exemptions were granted to the provinces of Escuintla, Guazacapán, and San Antonio (Suchitepéquez), and some towns in the Valley of Guatemala."[20] Four non-Guatemalan units—Chiapas (14,210 *tostones*), Soconusco (835 *tostones*), and San Salvador and San Miguel (4,952 *tostones*)—indicate a tributary population in those neighboring districts of 19,997.

THE CONTENTS OF CONTADURÍA 976 (1722–1726)

Though not as complete as other Contaduría sources, a document in *legajo* 976 covering the years 1722–26 also provides data on the *real servicio* and thus the native population obliged to pay it. Ten of the eleven districts into which Guatemala was divided for the levy have amounts furnished for at least one of the years in question. No amount is given for Acazaguastlán, for which we use the amount rendered in 1719 (1,005 *tostones*). For districts that have data for two years (Verapaz and the *partidos* of Atitlán and Tecpán Atitlán), we take the average. Though information is available for forty-seven of the seventy-five settlements spread across the Valley of Guatemala, no aggregate is available. In 1710 and 1719, however, the *real servicio* of tributaries in the district was roughly equal to that of the combined contributions of the *partidos* of Quetzaltenango, Totonicapán and Huehuetenango, and Verapaz. A yearly average of those amounts allows us to generate a surrogate total of 18,528 for the Valley of Guatemala. Adding the district totals together gives us a regional count of 57,038 tributaries, indicative of a native population (once more using a multiplier of four) of 228,152.

20. AGI, Contaduría 977 (1719). The original text states "preceden de las muchas pagas que se [h]an ofrecido hacer en los años pasados, como fueron los gastos de la pacificación de los pueblos sublevados de los Çendales en Chiapa [y el] pago de soldados de guardia que se mantuvieron en Ciudad Real [y también] gastos que se hicieron en la Armadilla que se fabricó para la exploración del enemigo Zambo e Mosquittos y soldados que fueron a ella . . . [además de] perdones de tributos de la Provincia de San Antonio y [los] Partidos de Escuintla y Goazacapan y algunos pueblos del Valle [de Guatemala] por açacimiento [?] de los terremotos."

THE "MEMORIA DE LOS CURATOS" (1750)

The eighteenth century witnessed several attempts by ecclesiastical authorities to record the number of native parishioners to whom they extended spiritual care. Some efforts were more meticulous than others in keeping track of Indian souls. One useful but flawed source is the "Memoria de los curatos, pueblos, curas, doctrineros, coadjutores y feligreses e idiomas de que [se] compone el Obispado de Goathemala," housed in the Real Academia de la Historia in Madrid.[21] Solano worked with this document and reproduced pertinent data from it in tabular form.[22] Nine administrative divisions are identified, with Solano calculating a total of 154,517 for the number of "feligreses" said to inhabit them (see table 34). Solano considers these parishioners "souls who are the age of confession and above" (*almas de confesión*), so the number he calculates would not have included children and infants. Most town-by-town entries are rounded off in units of a hundred; very few—those for towns in the parishes of Chiantla, Cuilco, Malacatán, and San Pedro Soloma are exceptions—impart a sense of having been arrived at by careful counting. A striking feature of the source is its register of Ladinos present—10,786 in total, according to Solano, an admittedly small number but more numerous and widespread than the group's appearance in the "Razón de las ciudades" seven decades earlier.

THE "TESTIMONIO PARA AVERIGUAR EL AUMENTO DE TRIBUTARIOS" (1768–1769)

The title of the unusual document "Testimonio para averiguar el aumento de tributarios," is something of a misnomer. While it documents a rise in the number of Indians who paid tribute across the Audiencia de Guatemala as a whole—11,195 to be precise, between the years 1768 and 1769—it actually contains data indicating that, for Guatemala itself, the tributary population *dropped* by some 2,366, from 61,920 payers to 59,554 (see table 35). Five jurisdictions show an increase, another five a decrease. The fall in numbers is especially noticeable in the Corregimiento de

21. Real Academia de la Historia, Papeles del Consejo de Indias, 9-29-2, Manuscript 6051.
22. Solano (1974, 133–46).

Chiquimula y Zacapa, 1,976, more than the combined rise recorded for Totonicapán, Quetzaltenango, and San Antonio Suchitepéquez. Why this is the case we can only speculate. Was there a localized crop failure, perhaps two or three harvests in a row, resulting in hunger and death? Did some kind of disease strike? Were Crown officials whose job it was to count tributaries simply neglectful of their duties, failing to record properly and not pressuring native leaders to round up fugitives whose names were not on the tribute list? Local variations again make it prudent not to offer definitive regional trends.

The document, to be found in the Archivo General de Indias, was drawn up in response to a royal order of November 8, 1765, part of which plainly states that "numbers are to be compiled every five years and not every three, with the goal of making clear the fluctuation in tributaries."[23] It may well be that, previously, the tributary population in some parts of Guatemala had been enumerated every three years, but this was certainly not the case in most instances. The document's own evidence shows that some counts for Chiquimula dated back to 1749, and for Chimaltenango, to 1754. Regarding the eight barrios of the capital, Santiago, "four have not been enumerated since 1763, and others even longer, since 1752."[24] This did not stop Crown officials from assuming a rather self-congratulatory air, choosing to focus on the *audiencia*-wide increase in numbers, which they attributed to "the zeal with which those appointed by the chief magistrate went about their commissions, not allowing any tributary to evade their reach."[25] This wishful thinking is contradicted by the reports of the commissioners themselves.

Two estimates may be offered, in keeping with the document's recording of both former and revised assessments. Using a population-to-tributary ratio of 4:1, a count of 61,920 tributaries for circa 1760 implies a total population of 247,680; a count of 59,554 tributaries for the year 1768–69 indicates a population of 238,216. Recovery, then, may have set in over the long term, but from time to time, downturns still occurred.

23. AGI, Guatemala 560 (1760–69). The original text observes that "se han de hacer las numeraciones cada cinco años, y no cada tres, y con todo es visible la diferencia a de tributarios que se nota provenida de que quedando las numeraciones de distrito."
24. AGI, Guatemala 560 (1768–69). The original text notes that "de los ocho barrios de esta ciudad, quatro no se havían numerado desde el año de 1763, y otros tantos desde el de 1752."
25. AGI, Guatemala 560 (1768–69). The original text applauds "el celo con que los apoderados del señor fiscal procurariden desempeñar sus comisiones sin permitir ocultación de tributario alguno."

THE *DESCRIPCIÓN GEOGRÁFICO-MORAL* OF
PEDRO CORTÉS Y LARRAZ (1768–1770)

One of the true treasures of Guatemalan historiography, the *Descripción geográfico-moral*, is the result of a tour of inspection undertaken over a period of fourteen months by Archbishop Pedro Cortés y Larraz, who visited almost every corner of the diocese under his charge in three separate excursions between November 3, 1768, and August 29, 1770. The archbishop's summary evaluations, which form the core of two published versions of his work, are based on written responses by parish priests to ten questions put to them by Cortés y Larraz. Weeks or months before a veritable entourage of guides, scribes, interpreters, muleteers, and pack animals arrived in town as part of the archbishop's "on site" as well as "en route" deliberations, local clergy had to contemplate, besides spiritual matters, queries relating to all sorts of social, economic, demographic, and linguistic details about their parishioners. Consultation of the responses of parish priests greatly enriches any analysis of the *Descripción geográfico-moral*, which is precisely the investigative strategy adopted by the scholar who has written most perceptively about the source, Jesús María García Añoveros, also co-editor of one edition of it.[26] What sets the work uniquely apart is the existence of 113 watercolor maps produced by an unknown artist (or perhaps more than one) who accompanied Cortés y Larraz on his rounds. These maps are a joy to behold, exquisite creations that afford a rare, parish-by-parish glimpse of the lay of the land. Neither the edition of Julio Blasco and García Añoveros nor an earlier one by Adrián Recinos[27] reproduces the illustrations with anything like the elegance of the originals, which thrill all those fortunate enough to consult them.[28]

26. García Añoveros (1987c) and Blasco and García Añoveros (2001).

27. Recinos (1958).

28. Martínez Peláez ([1970] 1998) was quite struck when he came across the originals, cataloged in the Archivo General de Indias as "Mapas y Planos de Guatemala" numbers 74 (Petapa) to 186 (Nejapa). Lovell worked with the originals on two occasions, the first in 1978, the second in 2001. The latter consultation called for "extraordinary permission" to be granted from the archive's director, as the policy now in place at the AGI makes it nearly impossible to examine an original document if it has been digitized and is available in electronic format. This policy, understandable to a certain extent, has taken away the unique opportunity (and considerable satisfaction) of working in the Seville archive. The policy did not apply in 1978 or before, a now halcyon, predigital research era. AGI, Guatemala 948 (1771–74) contains the responses of parish priests to Cortés y Larraz's questionnaire as well as the archbishop's synopsis of them, and his own acute

Solano worked extensively with the population data left behind by Cortés y Larraz, but we find García Añoveros more trustworthy in his analysis.[29] His book-length dissection contains thirteen tables that distill information in a clear, accessible, and incisive manner. He takes into account the archbishop's repeated assertions that parish priests, whose sloth, ignorance, and laxity incensed their superior no end, underestimated significantly the number of parishioners they were supposed to serve. To compensate for this lack of thoroughness, Cortés y Larraz amended the statistics sent to him, and so, too, does García Añoveros. The latter arrives at a total population for the diocese of 421,147, of whom 295,805 (70.2 percent) were Indians, 75,324 (17.9 percent) were Ladinos, and some 50,000 (11.9 percent) were Spanish (including criollos), blacks, and mulattoes.[30] Territorially, the Diocese of Guatemala incorporated what is today El Salvador, whose jurisdictions of Sonsonate and San Salvador had native populations of 13,466 and 29,622, respectively. If we deduct the sum of these two figures (43,088) from the diocese total, this leaves us with an estimated 252,717 indigenous inhabitants for Guatemala around the time of Cortés y Larraz's tenure as archbishop.

THE CONTENTS OF INDIFERENTE GENERAL 1525 (1772), THE CENSUS AND "NUMERACIÓN DE TRIBUTARIOS" (1778), AND THE TALLIES OF DOMINGO JUARROS (1800)

Consulting sources cataloged in the Archivo General de Indias as "Indiferente General," a miscellaneous grouping to say the least, can result in delightful surprises as well as hours of tedium. One surprise was the find of early tribute records long considered lost (see chapter 8).

---

observations. A visit to the Hispanic Society of America in December 2010 revealed the existence there of sketch maps that the Hiersemann Catalogue (1913, entry 242) records as "dibujados con la pluma por un agrimensor o ingeniero a principios del siglo XIX." We believe, however, that the sketch maps in question, sixty-nine folios in all, are drafts in black ink for Cortés y Larraz's watercolors, not "drawn by the pen of a surveyor or engineer in the early nineteenth century" but by an artist or team of artists who assisted the archbishop in the late eighteenth century. To date, Luján Muñoz (2011, 71 and 122–24) has had the most success in reproducing color copies of the originals, featuring five of them (illustrations 40, 56, 57, 58, and 59) in the *Atlas histórico de Guatemala*.

29. Solano (1974, 147–72) manipulates the source so as to arrive at a total population for Guatemala of 349,000, of whom he reckons 280,000 were indigenous.

30. García Añoveros (1987a, 197).

Another fortunate discovery in trawling through the contents of Indiferente General was *legajo* 1525, which contains (among other unique
items) an abstract in Spanish and a partial translation of Thomas Malthus's celebrated essay *On the Principle of Population* (1798). By chance,
rather than forethought, we suspect, in the same bundle of documents
as Malthus's essay may be found a hemispheric synopsis entitled "Vista
política de la América española" (see table 36). In it, a figure of 800,000
is given for the population of "Guatemala hasta el Ystmo," which we
take to be the *audiencia* district from Chiapas to Costa Rica's eastern
border with Panama. This figure, rounded off like the other seven that
accompany it, is recorded as reflecting "the size of population, according
to the files of the Secretary of the Council of the Indies, for the year
1772."[31] The *Gaceta de Guatemala* of April 26, 1802, carries the summary of an actual census conducted in 1778, indicating a population of
360,204, which suggests that the thirteen jurisdictions that then constituted Guatemala accounted for between two-fifths and one-half of the
isthmian total.

Indian tributaries in 1778, according to another source in the Seville
archive, amounted to 61,386.[32] This count (see table 37) seems to have
been carried out more carefully than many we have examined, with few
figures rounded off and a commentary accompanying it that rings with
the firsthand veracity of a Cortés y Larraz:

> The inconveniences encountered while carrying out the count are
> considerable. Generally all that may be found to shelter from the
> night is a forlorn town hall, if such a thing exists. There is a total
> lack of places where one can eat, areas devoid of any inhabitants,
> and highways that are extremely tough going, rugged and mountainous,
> some of them impassable even on horseback during the dry season,
> and unable to be negotiated even on foot during the rainy season.
> Passage in some parts is only possible if one is carried on the backs
> of the Indians, with evident risk to life and limb. This is especially

31. AGI, Indiferente General 1525 (1772). The original text is rendered "población según los
registros de la secretaría del Consejo de Indias."

32. "Estado que manifiesta el número de provincias que comprende el Reyno de Goathemala, apoderados fiscales que practicaron la última numeración de tributarios de ellas, sus pueblos, tributarios, naboríos, leguas que andubieron, meses y días que gastaron, todo con arreglo a
los padrones originales," in AGI, Guatemala 560 (1778).

the case during the rainy season, when many rivers cannot easily be forded.[33]

If we increase our population-to-tributary ratio from 4:1 to 4.5:1, to acknowledge growing native numbers, especially children, 61,386 tributaries implies an Indian population of 276,237, almost 77 percent of the census count of 360,204. The priest Domingo Juarros, when composing his *Compendio de la historia de la Ciudad de Guatemala* in the early nineteenth century, also drew upon the census of 1778, amending its tally of the total number of inhabitants for all of Guatemala from 366,611 to 389,385 for 1800 (see table 38). Juarros furnishes statistics that Adriaan van Oss believes date to that year and not 1808, when his work was first published.[34]

THE *NÚMERO DE TRIBUTARIOS* (1806), THE *NUMERACIÓN Y TASACIÓN DE TRIBUTOS* (1811), AND THE *RELACIÓN DE LA POBLACIÓN* (1812)

Tribute assessments from the Archivo General de Centro América complete our trajectory of native population recovery (table 39). The *Número de tributarios*, dated 1806, records 72,897 tributaries, a figure that incorporates additions made to allow for acknowledged under-reporting of "tributarios ausentes" four years earlier.[35] All nine of the jurisdictions into which Guatemala was divided as Independence loomed are also enumerated in a count dating to 1811, the *Numeración y tasación de tributos*; the number of tributaries reported is 70,305. If, once again, we raise our population-to-tributary ratio by 0.5 to 5:1 to reflect further increases in family size, a native population of 351,525 is generated, a figure two to three times the nadir size some two hundred years before.

33. "Numeración de tributarios," AGI, Guatemala 560 (1778). The original text reads as follows: "Las incomodidades en los pueblos . . . son muchas, por que generalmente no se encuentra en ellos más abrigo que un triste cabildo, si lo hay, total escasez de viveres, despoblados, caminos fragosos, ásperos y montuosos, algunos intransitables aún en verano a caballo y en invierno ni a pie, pasando en partes a [h]ombros de indios con evidente riesgo de la vida, especialmente en tantos ríos que las circundan, pues en el tiempo de aguas no permiten el paso."

34. Juarros ([1808] 1981, 56) and Van Oss (1981).

35. AGCA, A3.16, leg. 2327, exp. 34374 (1806).

This estimate may be afforded valuable comparative status when viewed alongside data from the *Relación de la población* of 1812, a document from the Archivo General de Indias that has been analyzed and transcribed by Jorge Luján Muñoz.[36] His assiduous calculations allow us to appreciate shifts in total population for a quarter-century span between 1778 and 1812. These shifts are summarized in table 38, in which the first two columns pertain to the total number of inhabitants and column three to the recorded number of "almas" or souls. Trajectories of recovery and growth embedded in the tallies, slow and intermittent for some 130 years, continued that way for another six decades. Thereafter, as the liberal reforms of President Justo Rufino Barrios transformed Guatemala from a colonial backwater into a coffee republic, Indians and non-Indians alike entered the modern era, with profound implications not only for population size but also for what the vastly increased numbers, especially of indigenous peoples, could expect from how the country's resources were allotted and exploited.

36. Luján Muñoz (2005).

CONCLUSION

In the larger scheme of empire, the "strange lands" that Hernán Cortés deployed Pedro de Alvarado to conquer turned out not to be as "rich" as anticipated, at least in the resources that attracted Spaniards most. That they were inhabited by "many different peoples," however, was emphatically the case. The country that became Guatemala emerged from the clash between Spanish interests and Maya cultures that began five centuries ago; the aftermath of that confrontation reverberates, again and again. No one has evoked a sense of Guatemala's enduring "colonial reality" better than the late Severo Martínez Peláez. "The detailed picture of colonial life I have lavished upon readers," he asserts in *La patria del criollo*, "furnishes them with all the information they need to assess its *current* significance."[1] Substantive new research findings, some of them highlighted here, have come to light in the four decades since *La patria del criollo* was first published, but his sobering assertion still applies. There is little "post-colonial" about present-day Guatemala. Martínez Peláez elaborates:

> In Guatemala, the colonial period does not pertain merely to one era in history, a time in the past when certain events occurred that we call "colonial" in order to denote when they took place. The colonial experience saw the formation and consolidation of a social structure that has yet to undergo revolutionary transformation. To a considerable degree, we belong to the social structure forged during colonial times. We do not need to venture far from the sprawl of Guatemala City to see it everywhere. Colonial reality is our everyday reality.[2]

1. Martínez Peláez ([1970] 2009, 274. Emphasis in italics is Martínez Peláez's.
2. Ibid.

Many factors, environmental and cultural, economic and psychological, foreign and indigenous, at times operating alone but more often in complex combination, shaped the nature of the colonial experience—or experiences, as was usually the case. Above all else, it is the marked variability of what took place across space and through time that we have sought to emphasize. Patterns can be observed, but the dynamics behind their appearance are of infinite nuance.

The trend for some time now in Mesoamerican studies, for the colonial period especially, has been to replace a canon that hitherto stressed Spanish action with one in which native agency, in myriad guise, is afforded priority attention.[3] We applaud this historiographic turn, and indeed hope to have contributed to it, giving indigenous actors center stage in a drama of immense import and consequence.[4] That requisite shift of focus notwithstanding, the power wielded by Pedro de Alvarado, either in making decisions or in undermining, contesting, and ignoring those of others, makes us hesitant not to give him the prominence he warrants. One scholar, Inga Clendinnen, has coined as "ambivalent" the relationships between Mayas and Spaniards in early colonial Yucatán.[5] This was not so between 1524 and 1541 in Guatemala, where the actions of Alvarado were anything but.[6]

During that tumultuous decade and a half, Alvarado was frequently involved and caught up in matters elsewhere. Twice he returned to Spain to attend to personal issues as well as affairs of state. While there he married first Francisca, and then, soon after he was widowed, her sister, Beatriz. He muscled in on the conquest of Peru until a deal with Pizarro and Almagro bought him off. With an army and an armada financed by his rapacious dealings in Guatemala, paid for, for the most part, by the lives of indigenous Kaqchikels, he planned to sail for the Spice Islands, but was killed waging war in Mexico before his intended departure. Yet even when he was physically absent, as he was from Guatemala for

3. See Lovell (2004) for a general discussion and Lovell (2009) for more specific treatment in relation to studies showcased in Matthew and Oudijk (2007). See also, among a now voluminous literature, Asselbergs (2004); Matthew (2012); Restall and Asselbergs (2007); and Yannakakis (2008).

4. See Dakin and Lutz (1996); Lovell (1988, 2000); and Lovell and Lutz (2003).

5. Clendinnen (1987).

6. Sherman (1969; 1983) also stresses the decisive role of Alvarado, stating categorically (1983, 137) that "only rarely has one individual dominated the society of his time and place in the way that Alvarado did in Guatemala." He reinforces his point by adding that "[p]erhaps no other Spanish conqueror left his personal imprint so clearly on a colony as the conqueror of Guatemala."

years on end, Alvarado's clout was heavy, his authority incontestable. Awareness of the views he held instilled fear and apprehension in all those around him, which was palpable in their compliance of surrogate governance. Corruption, impunity, deceit and subterfuge, ruthless exploitation, intimidation by terror, and blatant disregard of the rule of law, hallmarks of Guatemala today, have in Pedro de Alvarado a fertile progenitor. There was nothing ambivalent, in our eyes at any rate, about the conquest of Guatemala, nor about Alvarado's forceful personality in setting the parameters within which subjugation would unfold and Spanish, and later criollo, wealth would be amassed, even in a colonial backwater.

So, while Guatemala would always be, in the memorable words of Pierre and Huguette Chaunu, "the richest of the poor or the poorest of the rich" to the coffers of imperial Spain, its "strange lands" and "different peoples" were subjected to plunder and exploitation that radically altered their circumstances in the wake of Alvarado's invasion.[7] By the late 1540s, within a decade of his death, *congregación* had resulted in the creation of *pueblos de indios*, nucleated settlements established by missionary friars whose goals of orderly assimilation were thwarted by native preference for dispersed modes of living that saw Indians retreat back to the mountains they had been moved from. There, at distances that mitigated the demands of paying tribute and furnishing labor either to an impecunious Crown or insatiable *encomenderos*, indigenous communities regrouped and reconfigured, shaping for themselves a culture of refuge from the culture of conquest imposed on them. Even in areas we delineate in chapter 4 as forming part of the core, Maya ways lived on, all the more so in regions we identify as constituting the periphery, where Spanish prerogatives were challenged, tempered, and at times undone.

By no means is this to suggest that Indians did not bear a heavy burden, and stagger under it accordingly. They most decidedly did, as we spell out in detail in part III. However, the excesses with which, early on, they had to contend began to give way in the mid-sixteenth century to less grueling demands as the terms of *encomienda* were curtailed, expectations reduced, and a semblance of regulation brought to bear on abuse, violations, and misconduct on the part of Spaniards bent on maximizing their privileges. The fortunes of the likes of Juan de Espinar

7. As rendered by MacLeod ([1973] 2008, xiv).

were not the only ones to wane, or the Indians of Huehuetenango alone in being less hounded and oppressed.

Yet native numbers, notable when conquerors and clergymen, tribute collectors and district governors first arrived on the scene to be struck by the extent of human habitation, continued to wither, no matter the intent at redress. We chart, in table 40, estimates of the size of the native population in fourteen instances, from the eve of contact in 1520 to the eve of independence in 1811. The attrition of Indian lives was most precipitous between the years 1520 and 1624–28, falling from around two million to 131,250, a collapse of 93.4 percent. After the first quarter of the seventeenth century, recovery set in, most likely earlier in some areas—including the Valley of Guatemala—than in others. Population size from 1684 to 1768, however, continued to fluctuate, between a low of 228,152 in 1722–26 and a high of 247,680 in 1760. Thereafter, growth was steady and without reverse, although our global estimates surely conceal fluctuations at the local or regional level. Outbreaks of epidemic disease to which native peoples had no immunity were particularly devastating in the sixteenth and seventeenth centuries, but could still wreak havoc among vulnerable communities in the late eighteenth and early nineteenth. Indigenous survival was constantly under threat by outbreaks of sickness, against which little could be done. If remedial action was deemed possible, rarely was it pursued.

"If no efforts are taken to assist these wretched people," wrote the Ladino constable Marcos Castañeda as he contemplated the plight of survivors smitten by typhus fever in the parish of Soloma in 1806, "they will most certainly starve to death, because they did not plant corn in the places where they sought refuge, and so have nothing to live on, this year or next, for it is now too late to plant their fields." Castañeda's appeal to his superiors for assistance and relief—"at the very least the people could be exempted from paying tribute for two of the three years during which they have suffered such calamity"[8]— succeeded only in eliciting a reprieve, not a cancellation.

Such was the colonial order, and against such odds Indians in Guatemala served their Spanish masters.

8. Marcos Castañeda, *comisionado*, to the Alcalde Mayor of Totonicapán and Huehuetenango, AGCA, A3.16, leg. 249, exp. 5036, fols. 2 and 2v (May 5, 1806). The Ladino constable pleads, with Santa Eulalia foremost in mind, "a favor de este curato de Soloma, alcancen el alivio, a lo menos que se les perdone el tributo de dos años que adeudan los del pueblo . . . de los tres de peste [y] calamidades."

APPENDIX

Table 1

DEPARTAMENTOS AND *MUNICIPIOS* IN GUATEMALA

Departamento	Number of municipios
Alta Verapaz	14
Baja Verapaz	8
Chimaltenango	16
Chiquimula	11
El Progreso	8
El Quiché	18
Escuintla	13
Guatemala	17
Huehuetenango	31
Izabal	5
Jalapa	7
Jutiapa	17
Petén	12
Quetzaltenango	24
Retalhuleu	9
Sacatepéquez	16
San Marcos	29
Santa Rosa	14
Sololá	19
Suchitepéquez	20
Totonicapán	8
Zacapa	10

Source: Gall (1976–83).

Table 2

TOWNS FOUNDED IN THE SIXTEENTH CENTURY
BY REGULAR AND SECULAR CLERGY

Order/Type	Towns founded by 1555	Towns founded by 1600
Dominicans	47	82
Franciscans	37	108
Mercedarians	6	42
Secular clergy	5?	104
Total	95	336

Source: Van Oss (1986, 43).

Table 3
TRIBUTE ASSESSMENTS OF ALONSO LÓPEZ DE CERRATO, 1548–51
Total number of assessments = 170

Pueblos or *encomiendas* that are present-day *municipios*	95
Pueblos or *encomiendas* that are settlements (*aldeas* or *caseríos*) within present-day *municipios*	13
Pueblos or *encomiendas* in present-day El Salvador	14
Pueblos or *encomiendas* in present-day Chiapas	6
Disappeared pueblos or *encomiendas*	12
Unknown pueblos or *encomiendas*	11
Total number of pueblos or *encomiendas*	151

Source: AGI, Guatemala 128, "Las tasaciones de los pueblos de los términos y jurisdicción de la ciudad de Santiago de Guatemala" (1548–51).

Table 4
PUEBLOS, PARCIALIDADES, AND *TRIBUTARIOS* IN TOTONICAPÁN, 1683

Pueblos de indios	Parcialidades	Number of tributarios
Totonicapán	San Francisco	320–29*
	San Marcos	—
	San Jerónimo	—
	Pal	—
Chiquimula	Santa María	120–29*
	San Marcos	24
Momostenango	Santiago	224
	Santa Catalina	50
	Santa Ana	40
	Santa Isabel	38
Aguacatán	Aguacatán	64
	Chalchitán	91
	Comitán	4
Sacapulas	Cuatlán	84
	Tulteca	45
	Bechauazar	42
	Acunil	48
	Magdalena	8
Cunén	San Francisco	114
	Magdalena	6
Chajul	San Gaspar	64
	Ilom	30
	Uncavav	9
	Box	3
Cotzal	San Juan	20–29*
	Chil	10
	Cul	28
Nebaj	Santa María	76
	Cuchil	26
	Osolotán	16
	Salquil	10–19*

Source: AGI, Contaduría 815.

*The manuscript was badly damaged in a fire in the archive in the early twentieth century. Figures marked with an asterisk indicate that the last numeral was so charred as to be illegible. In four instances, therefore, only an estimate can be made of the tribute-paying population of the *parcialidad.*

Table 5
CHINAMITALES AND *PARCIALIDADES* IN THE PUEBLO OF SACAPULAS

Preconquest chinamit	Colonial parcialidad*
Ah Canil, Ah Toltecat, and Uchabajá	Santiago and San Sebastián
Beabac	San Pedro
Coatecas	San Francisco
Zacualpanecas	Santo Tomás

Source: Gall (1980, vol. 3, 130) and Hill and Monaghan (1987, 63–75).
*These *parcialidades* exist today, by the same name, as barrios or *cantones* (districts or neighborhoods) within the town or surrounding countryside.

Table 6
PROPOSED ALLOCATION OF LAND AT SACAPULAS, 1775–1800

Parcialidad	Location of holdings	Approximate extent of holdings	Indian tributaries (1794)
San Pedro	North bank of the Río Negro, across the river from the town center.	81 *caballerías**	67
Santiago and San Sebastián	South bank of the Río Negro (including salt works) adjacent to the town center.	72 *caballerías*	141
San Francisco	To the west of land held by Santiago and San Sebastián, predominantly on the south side of the Río Negro.	78 *caballerías*	98
Santo Tomás	To the west of land held by San Pedro, predominantly on the north side of Río Negro along both banks of the Río Blanco.	121 *caballerías*	60

Source: Lovell ([1985] 2005, 127).
Note: See map 2 for a cartographic rendering of the proposed land divisions.
*A *caballería* of land measures about 104 acres or 42 hectares.

Table 7
AWARDS OF *ENCOMIENDA* IN GUATEMALA, 1524–48

Governors, lieutenant governors, and interim governors	Tenure in office	Number of awards granted	Number of recipients (*encomenderos*)
Pedro de Alvarado	1524–26	25	21
Jorge de Alvarado	1527–29	86	56
Francisco de Orduña	1529–30	12	11
Pedro de Alvarado	1530–33	77	45
Jorge de Alvarado	1534–35	7	6
Pedro de Alvarado	1535–36	18	10
Alonso de Maldonado	1536–39	12	8
Pedro de Alvarado	1539–40	7	3
Francisco de la Cueva	1540–41	13	5
Bishop Marroquín and Francisco de la Cueva	1541–42	16	16
Alonso de Maldonado	1542–48	30	20

Source: Kramer (1994, 245).

Table 8
ENCOMIENDA SUCCESSION IN CHICHICASTENANGO, 1526–49

Encomendero	Grantor	Date
Gonzalo de Alvarado	Pedro de Alvarado	before August 1526
Jorge de Alvarado	Jorge de Alvarado	after March 1527
Francisco de Orduña	Francisco de Orduña	August 1529
Ortega Gómez	Francisco de Orduña	November 27, 1529
Pedro de Alvarado	Pedro de Alvarado	April 1530
Pedro de Cueto	Pedro de Alvarado	1533
Jorge de Alvarado	Jorge de Alvarado	after January 1533
Gaspar Arias	Jorge de Alvarado	May 15, 1534
Gaspar Arias	Pedro de Alvarado	June 17, 1535
Ortega Gómez	Alonso de Maldonado	March 1537
Gaspar Arias	(unknown)	before 1540
Son of Gaspar Arias	Alonso López de Cerrato	May 6, 1549

Source: Kramer (1994, 242).

Table 9
POPULATION OF HUEHUETENANGO AND
SUBJECT TOWNS, 1530–31 AND 1548–51

Town	1530–31	1548–51[1]
Huehuetenango (including Chiantla)	2,000–2,500 tributaries	500 tributaries
Santiago Chimaltenango (Chimbal, or Chinbal)	500 *casas*[2]	125 tributaries[3]
San Juan Atitán (Atitán)	—	—
San Pedro Necta (Niquitlán, or Niquetla)	200 *casas*[4]	20 tributaries

Source: Kramer (1994, 222).

[1]All 1548–51 figures are from AGI, Guatemala 128, "Las tasaciones de los pueblos."

[2]Two hundred *casas*, or houses, in the town center, or *cabecera*, and 300 in *estancias*, or outlying settlements (AGI, Justicia 1031).

[3]Santiago Chimaltenango and San Juan Atitán together had 125 tributaries in 1549.

[4]AGI, Justicia 1031.

Table 10
ENCOMIENDA OBLIGATIONS IN HUEHUETENANGO, 1530–31 AND 1549

Item	1530–31	1549
Clothing	800 lengths of cotton cloth 400 loincloths 400 jackets 400 blouses 400 skirts 400 sandals	300 lengths of cotton cloth

Foodstuffs	Unspecified amounts of corn,
	    beans, chili peppers, and salt.
	108–26 large jugs of honey
		Harvest from planting 22.5
		    bushels of corn.
		Harvest from planting 7.5
		    bushels of black beans.
		100 loads of chili
		100 cakes of salt

Fowl	2,268 turkeys	12 dozen chickens
Miscellaneous	400 reed mats	Harvest from planting 6 bushels of cotton.

Labor	Forty Indian men sent to work in
	    and around Santiago de Guatemala
	    in 20-day shifts all year.
	120–200 Indian men sent to work in
	    the gold mines in 20-day shifts all year.
	Thirty Indian women sent to the gold
	    mines each day to make
	    tortillas and prepare food.
		Six Indian men to act as
		    general servants.

Slaves	Eighty male and forty female slaves who worked in the gold mines.	

Source: AGI, Justicia 1031 and AGI, Guatemala 128, "Las tasaciones de los pueblos."

Table 11
SETTLEMENTS BURNED, WHOLLY OR IN PART,
IN HUEHUETENANGO, 1530

Identified places	Unidentified places
Huehuetenango	Amala
Cozumaçutla, Xozumaçutla	
(Santo Domingo Usumacinta)	Mocoga
Chiantla	Esquinel
Atitán*	
(San Juan Atitán)	
Chinbal, Chimbal	
(Santiago Chimaltenango)	
Niquitlán, Niquetla, Necotla	
(San Pedro Necta)	

Source: AGI, Justicia 1031.
*The document refers to Atitán as "Acatepeque en lengua de México" and as
"Muachi [en lengua de] la tierra" but states also that "agora se llama Atitán."

Table 12
ENCOMIENDA OBLIGATIONS IN SANTIAGO ATITLÁN

Item	*Encomenderos:* Pedro de Alvarado and Sancho de Barahona	*Encomenderos:* Spanish Crown and and the youngest son of Sancho de Barahona
	Annual delivery and other arrangements	
	March 16, 1537	May 4, 1549
Foodstuffs		
Cacao	1,000 *xiquipiles*. Unclear as to where tribute is to be delivered, whether in Atitlán itself or, more likely, to Santiago in Almolonga.	1,200 *xiquipiles*, 600 to be delivered on the Feast Day of San Juan (June 24), 600 on Christmas Day.[1]
Castilian chickens	500 (20 every two weeks)[2]	None
Native turkeys	250 (10 every two weeks)	None
Corn	750 *cargas* (30 every two weeks)	None
Beans	50 *cargas* (2 every two weeks)	None
Chili peppers	50 *cargas* (2 every two weeks)	None
Salt	50 *cargas* (2 every two weeks)	None
Honey	50 jugs (2 every two weeks)	None
Eggs	3,920 (80 every Friday)	None
Crabs	100 *cargas* (2 *cargas* every Friday)	None
Clothing		
Striped mantles	2,000 *mantas listadas* (80 every two weeks)	None
Doublets (Sleeveless jackets)	1,000 *xicoles* (40 every two weeks)	None
Loincloths	1,000 *masteles* (40 every two weeks)	None
Sandals	200 *pares de cutaras*	None
Miscellaneous		
Reed mats	120 *petates*	None
Gourds	120 *xícaras*	None
Labor	Fifteen Indian men for each *encomendero* every two weeks, some 750 men annually (375 for each *encomendero*). These laborers are to walk from the south shore of Lake Atitlán over mountainous trails to reach Santiago in Almolonga, serving also as bearers (*tamemes*) in order to carry items of tribute to their *encomenderos*. In addition, on alternate weeks when large groups are not to serve in the capital city, Santiago, crabs and eggs still have to be transported there for delivery to *encomendero* residences.	

Source: AGI, Justicia 295, fols. 706v–707, and AGI, Guatemala 128, "Las tasaciones de los pueblos," fol. 109.

[1]All amounts given are total annual deliveries that were split evenly between the two *encomenderos*. This holds for all items of tribute listed in the *tasación*.

[2]We reckon the number of weeks at 49 per year to allow for 3 weeks during which (at least in theory) Indians were exempt from supplying labor. These fortnightly amounts are multiplied by 25 to give approximate annual totals.

Table 13
ENCOMIENDA OBLIGATIONS IN SAN MARTÍN SACATEPÉQUEZ AND OSTUNCALCO
Encomendero: Francisco de la Cueva

| Item | Annual delivery and other arrangements | |
	ca. 1538	April 30, 1549
Foodstuffs		
Cacao	500 *xiquipiles* (100 *xiquipiles* five times a year).[1]	300 *xiquipiles* (75 *xiquipiles* every three months).[2]
Salt	60 baskets (12 baskets five times a year).	9 *fanegas* (13.5 bushels), based on three *fanegas* being delivered to Santiago every four months.
Corn	Unspecified amount to feed the pigs on lands next to one of the towns.	800 *fanegas* (1,200 bushels) delivered to Santiago.
Food	Unspecified amount for the *calpixque*.[3]	None
Beans	None	30 *fanegas* (45 bushels)
Chili peppers	None	20 *cargas* delivered to Santiago
Honey, chickens, eggs, and quail	Unspecified amounts to be delivered to the *encomendero*'s household on "certain days and holidays."	20 jars of honey[4] 300 Castilian chickens 196 dozen eggs (4 dozen per week, 49 weeks).
Cloth		
Cotton cloth	2,000 pieces of cloth of "good measure" (400 *mantas* delivered five times a year).	1,600 pieces of cloth (400 delivered four times a year).
Bedcovers	100 bedcovers (20 *sobrecamas* five times a year).	32 bedcovers (8 delivered four times a year).
Ornamental/ adorned cloth	100 pieces (20 *paramentos* five times a year).	28 pieces (7 delivered four times a year).
Clothes	Unspecified amount for swineherds, likely made from local cotton cloth.	None
Labor	No specific labor requirements, but the swineherds would have been from one of the towns, and bearers would have been needed to deliver tribute items.	Fourteen Indians each week to look after pigs on lands next to town, and 6 more to serve in Santiago. The *encomendero* is to feed the Indians and teach them the Christian doctrine. Some 980 men thus served annually, based on 20 workers each week for 49 weeks of the year.

Source: AGI, Indiferente General 857, "Algunas tasaciones de los pueblos," and AGI, Guatemala 128, "Las tasaciones de los pueblos," fol. 104.
[1]They are to deliver this amount every 70 days, thus five times a year.
[2]The *tasación* states that the cacao should be delivered to town, likely meaning not hauled to Santiago.
[3]Man in charge of overseeing the Indian swineherds (*porqueros*).
[4]Each jar is to contain two *azumbres*, a liquid measure roughly equivalent to two liters.

Table 14
ENCOMIENDA OBLIGATIONS IN JUMAYTEPEQUE
Encomendero: Francisco de la Cueva

	Annual delivery and other arrangements	
Item	ca. 1538	April 30, 1549
Foodstuffs		
Wheat	Indian tributaries to plant, cultivate, harvest, and thresh a planting of wheat of unspecified size. Indians of Tacuba, another town held by the same *encomendero*, are to assist. Delivery of wheat to Santiago, however, is the responsibility of the Indians of Jumaytepeque.	The *encomendero* is to have land plowed by oxen, after which Indians are to seed, cultivate, and harvest a planting of 6 *fanegas* of wheat (9 bushels). See labor component below.
Corn	A *milpa* (cornfield) is to be planted "como lo solían" ("just as [the Indians] are accustomed to doing") for the *encomendero*'s benefit.[1]	A planting of 1.5 *fanegas* of corn (2.25 bushels). Indians must plant, harvest, and then store the corn in town.
Turkeys and chickens	49 turkeys and 49 chickens annually, meaning delivery each Sunday of one turkey and one chicken.	36 Castilian chickens annually
Honey	Delivery every Sunday of an unspecified amount, "whatever is needed."	None
Miscellaneous		
Beeswax	Every Sunday an unspecified amount of *cera*, "whatever is needed."	None
Sandals	Some *cutaras* for their *encomendero*'s Indian slaves.	
Labor	Six Indians to travel each week with foodstuffs to Santiago, arriving there on Sunday "to serve" their *encomendero*, except "when they are bringing in the harvest." See above entry for corn about the obligation to plant a *milpa* in their town.	Three Indians are to plow the wheat fields for "the time that might be necessary." Each week four Indians are required to work on their *encomendero*'s cattle farm, close to town. The Indians in question are to be fed and instructed in Christianity while serving.

Source: AGI, Guatemala 128, "Las tasaciones de los pueblos," fol. 103v; AGI, Justicia 286; and AGI, Indiferente General 857, "Algunas tasaciones de los pueblos."
[1]This stipulation indicates that the obligation was already in place before the 1538 *tasación* was drafted.

Table 15
ENCOMIENDA OBLIGATIONS IN TACUBA
Encomendero: Francisco de la Cueva

| Item | Annual delivery and other arrangements | |
	ca. 1538	April 2, 1549
Foodstuffs		
Chili peppers	Plant and harvest an unspecified amount.	None
Beans	Plant and harvest an unspecified amount.	None
Cacao	40 *xiquipiles*	80 *xiquipiles*, half on the Feast Day of San Juan (June 24), half on Christmas Day.
Salt	Furnish all that is required.	None
Wheat	See labor requirement below, and also the *tasación de tributo* for Jumaytepeque.	None
Fowl	Three native turkeys and two Castilian chickens are to be delivered to the *encomendero*'s house every Sunday (150 turkeys and 100 chickens each year).	None
Honey and beeswax	Unspecified amount each week	None
Cloth and other items		
Cloth	100 *toldillos* (coarse cotton fabric)	None
Blouses	60 cotton *huipiles*	None
Loincloths	100 *masteles*	None
Leather sandals	Unspecified number for the *encomendero*'s Indian slaves.	None
Labor	Nine Indians every week of the year ("a la continua") for an annual total of 468. During the wheat harvest these laborers are to work in Jumaytepeque; during the dry season, November to May, they are to deliver wheat to the residence of their *encomendero* in the capital city, Santiago.	Twice a year, 20 Indians are to be sent to Jumaytepeque for four days to help weed and harvest wheat.

Source: AGI, Indiferente General 857, "Algunas tasaciones de los pueblos," and AGI, Guatemala 128, "Las tasaciones de los pueblos," fol. 68.

Table 16

ENCOMIENDA OBLIGATIONS IN COMALAPA

Encomendero: Juan Pérez Dardón

	Annual delivery and other arrangements	
Item	ca. 1538	May 10, 1549
Foodstuffs		
Castilian chickens	392 (8 every week for 49 weeks)	18 dozen (216 annually)
Native turkeys	392 (8 every week)	None
Quail	Unspecified numbers	None
Salt	80 *cargas* (160 *fanegas*, equivalent to 240 bushels)	10 *fanegas* (15 bushels)
Beans	100 *fanegas* (150 bushels)	None
Chili peppers	50 *fanegas* (75 bushels)	None
Honey	Unspecified amount	4 *arrobas* of honey, each *arroba* weighing approximately 25 pounds.
Wheat	Unspecified amount to be planted and harvested. See labor component below.	Pueblo to seed a field with eight *fanegas* (12 bushels) of wheat. *Encomendero* to have the land plowed beforehand.
Corn	"At least" 2,000 *fanegas* (3,000 bushels).[1] See labor component below.	Pueblo to plant 10 *fanegas* (15 bushels) of corn on community land and to cultivate, harvest, and store it for the *encomendero* in town.
Cacao	60 *xiquipiles*	None
Cloth and mats		
Cotton cloth	400 *mantas*	300 *mantas*
Reed mats	Unspecified number of *petates* for *encomendero*'s house in Santiago.	48 *petates*
Building materials		
Lime	300 *cargas* of *cal* (600 *fanegas*, equivalent to 900 bushels).	None
Bricks	Unspecified amount of *ladrillos* for *encomendero*'s house in Santiago.	None
Roof tiles	Unspecified amount of *tejas* for house construction.	None
Labor		
(*servicio ordinario*)	Each week, Comalapa is to furnish 50 male laborers to work in Santiago, some 2,450 annually. They are to bring with them the chickens and turkeys specified above, and are to plant wheat and corn near the city.	Each week, 20 Indians are to work either in Santiago or on an *estancia* next to Comalapa, a total of 980 laborers annually. In September 1549 it was decreed that the town should pay 150 gold pesos annually instead of furnishing 20 indios de *servicio* each week.

Source: AGI, Indiferente General 857, "Algunas tasaciones de los pueblos," and AGI, Guatemala 128, "Las tasaciones de los pueblos," folio 116v.

[1]The text is difficult to interpret but appears to state that, should the amount harvested be less than 2,000 *fanegas,* the Indians of Comalapa must make up the difference, presumably from what their own fields produce. The same dictate applied to Momostenango.

Table 17
ENCOMIENDA OBLIGATIONS IN MOMOSTENANGO
Encomendero: Juan Pérez Dardón

| | Annual delivery and other arrangements | |
Item	ca. 1538	May 4, 1549
Foodstuffs		
Corn	Yield must be 1,000 *fanegas* (1,500 bushels).[1] Corn was probably planted on the *encomendero*'s fields close to Santiago.	A planting of 10 *fanegas* (15 bushels). Harvested corn and beans are to be stored in town.
Beans	None	1 *fanega* (1.5 bushels)
Cacao	60 x*iquipiles*	60 *xiquipiles*, half to be delivered (in town) on June 24 (Feast Day of San Juan) and half on Christmas Day.
Wheat	Unspecified amount to be planted near Santiago.	None
Fowl, game, honey	250 turkeys (ten turkeys every two weeks) and unspecified amounts of quail and other game. Unspecified amounts of honey.	12 dozen Castilian chickens and 0.5 *arroba* (12.5 lbs.) of honey.
Salt	49 *cargas* (98 *fanegas*), based on one *carga* of salt delivered each week for 49 weeks.	6 *fanegas* (9 bushels)
Chili peppers	49 *cargas* (98 *fanegas*), based on one *carga* of chili peppers delivered each week for 49 weeks.	6 *fanegas* (9 bushels)
Fodder	When *servicio ordinario* workers come to the city (every fifteen days) they must provide fodder for pigs and tend not only these animals but also other livestock.	None
Miscellaneous		
Reed mats, pottery, cotton cloth	Unspecified numbers of *petates* and an unspecified number of clay pots, jugs, and *comales* (clay tortilla griddles).	10 *mantas* of cotton cloth of a specified size and one dozen large reed mats.
Labor	Thirty *servicio ordinario* Indians every fifteen days (750 workers annually). These workers had a considerable distance to travel, bringing items of tribute with them to Santiago.	At first, 12 Indians were to work in Santiago or on the *encomendero*'s cattle ranch near the capital. On October 2, 1549, Cerrato ordered that this labor be replaced by an annual payment of 40 *xiquipiles* of cacao, half delivered on the Feast Day of San Juan and half on Christmas Day.

Source: AGI, Indiferente General 857, "Algunas tasaciones de los pueblos," and AGI, Guatemala 128, "Las tasaciones de los pueblos," fol. 108. The 1549 source records 450 tributaries for this town.
[1]The text is difficult to interpret but appears to state that if the harvest is less than 1,000 *fanegas,* then the Indians are to make up the difference, presumably from their own supplies of corn. A similar requirement applied to Comalapa.

Table 18
ENCOMIENDA OBLIGATIONS IN UTATLÁN

	Encomendero: Cristóbal de la Cueva	*Encomendero*: Crown
	Annual delivery and other arrangements	
Item	ca. 1538	December 4, 1553
Foodstuffs		
Cacao	10 *xiquipiles*	30 *xiquipiles*
Castilian chickens	40	50
Honey, salt, and chili peppers	Unspecified amounts: "lo que ellos quisieren dar" (whatever they want to give).	None
Cloth and other items		
Skirts	20 *naguas*	None
Cotton cloth	20 *mantas blancas*	None
Reed mats	Some *petates* for their *encomendero*'s house.	None
Labor	10 Indians, but unspecified as to where and what kind of work they are to perform.	None

Source: AGI, Indiferente General 857, "Algunas tasaciones de los pueblos," and AGCA, A3.16, legajo 2797, expediente 40466, "Tasaciones de tributos."

Table 19
POPULATION OF GUATEMALA AT SPANISH CONTACT
(WITH SOME ESTIMATES FOR THE YEARS AROUND 1525, 1550, AND 1575)

Subregion*	ca. 1520	ca. 1525	ca. 1550	ca. 1575
Northwest[1]	260,000	150,000	73,000	47,000
Verapaz[2]	208,000		52,000	
Northeast[3]	17,500			524
Southwest[4]	33,000		8,250	
Totonicapán[5]	105,000	75,000		13,250
South Central (K'iche')[6]	823,000			
Tz'utujil[7]	72,000	48,000	5,600	4,020
South Central (Kaqchikel)[8]	250,000			
East Central (Poqomam)[9]	58,000			14,500
Southeast (Pipil)[10]	100,000		10,230	
East Central (Ch'orti')[11]	120,000			
Total	2,046,500			

Source: Population estimates are taken or derived from information contained in:
[1]Lovell ([1985] 2005, 145).
[2]MacLeod ([1973] 2008, 93) and Sherman (1979, 354–55).
[3]Thompson (1970, 48–83).
[4]Feldman (1992).
[5]Veblen (1977, 497).
[6]Carmack (1968, 77) and Veblen (1977, 497).
[7]MacLeod ([1973] 2008, 98 and 131); Madigan (1976, 178); and Orellana (1984, 142).
[8]AGI, Guatemala 128, and Lutz ([1982] 1984, 81–115).
[9]Miles (1957, 765–66).
[10]Fowler (1989, 151).
[11]Thompson (1970, 48–83).
*See map 3 for delineation of each subregion.

INDIAN SETTLEMENTS AND TRIBUTARY POPULATION IN THE CERRATO TASACIONES, 1548–49

Range of tributaries per settlement

3 to 25		30 to 60		70 to 100		109 to 200		250 to 2,000	
Indian settlement	No. of tributaries	Indian settlement	No. of tributaries	Indian settlement	No. of tributaries	Indian settlement	No. of tributaries	Indian settlement	No. of tributaries
Chicujotla	3	Ystatan	30	Amatenango	70	Amatitan	109	Soloma	250
Amayuca	3	Cuchil	30	Cozumaluapa	70	Xocotenango	120	Moyutla	250
Ystapa	4	Atiquipaque	30	Çacapula	80	Texutla	120	Suchitepeque	286
Coatlan	5	Nancintla	30	Çacapula	80	Chimaltenango and Atitlan	125	Cuylco	290
Miaguatlan	6	Tacolula	30	Xutiapa	80	Alotepeque	130	Luquytlan	300
Utlacingo	8	Nema	35	Malacatepeque	80	Motocintla	138	Tasisco	300
Chipilapa	10	Joxutla	37	Çacapa	80	Chiquimula	150	Chichicastenango	400
Quequel	10	Ozuma	40	Çacapa	80	Tecpan Puyumatlan	150	Chiquimula	400
Acatepeque	10	Uçumacintla	40	Çapotitan	80	Cequinala	150	Yzalco	400
Joanagazapa	20	Xitaulco	40	Maçagua	80	Nytla	155	Guazacapan	400
Quezalcoatitan	20	Tecoaco	40	Cerquil	80	Xilotepeque	160	Tecpanguatemala	400
Amatitan	20	Pacaco and Totopeque	40	Acatenango	80	Chiquimula	160	Mustenango	400
Cacaotlan	20	Citala	40	Conuaco and Totonicapa	80	Mysco	160	Comalapa	500
Oçelutla	20	Vyztlan	45	Queçaltepeque	90	Ataco	160	Xacaltenango	500
Niquitlan	20	Tetechan	50	Gueymango	100	Yçapa	160	Huehuetenango	500
Quiahuistlan	20	Tipiaco	50	Cincacantlan	100	Suchitepeque	160	Xilotepeque	500
Baçaco	20	Gueymango	50	Xocotenango	100	Ayllon	160	Yupitepeque	520
Acaxutla	20	Chandelgueve	50	Cacalutla	100	Amatitan	176	Tecocistlan	600
Comytlan	20	Ocotenango	50	Ycuatlan	100	Çumpango	200	Zacatepeque	700
Caqualpilla	20	Jupelingo	50	Maçagua and Mecameos	100	Aguacatlan	200	Ystalavaca and Zamayaque	800
Queçaltepeque	24	Chalchuytlan	60	Tacuscalco	100	Naolingo	200	Atitan	1,000
Yztapa	25	Yzatepeque	60	Pinola	100	Cazaguatlan	200	Zapotitan	1,000
Yzquine	25	Yzatepeque	60	Atezcatempa	100	Zacualpa	200	Tequepanatitan	1,000
Atiquipaque	25	Colutla	60	Camotlan	100	Queçaltenango	200	Xalapa	1,000
Tepemiel	25	Uçumacintla	60	—	—	Casaguastlan	200	Zacatepeque and Ostuncalco	2,000
—	—	Xicalapa	60	—	—	—	—	—	—
—	—	Cozumaluapa	60	—	—	—	—	—	—
—	—	Xuayoa	60	—	—	—	—	—	—
—	—	Totoapa	60	—	—	—	—	—	—

Source: AGI, Guatemala 128, "Las tasaciones de los pueblos" (1548–51).

APPENDIX

Table 21
PUEBLOS DE INDIOS IN THE CERRATO TASACIONES, 1548–51

Pueblo de indios	Number on map 4	Present-day location	Pueblo de indios	Number on map 4	Present-day location
Motocintla	1	San Francisco Motozintla	Acatenango	42	San Bernabé Acatenango
			Comalapa	43	Comalapa
Amatenango	2	Amatenango	Jilotepeque	44	San Martín Jilotepeque
Cuilco	3	Cuilco	Chimaltenango	45	Chimaltenango
Tetechan	4	Tectitán	Zacatepeque	46	San Juan Sacatepéquez
Niquitlan	5	San Pedro Necta	Zacatepeque	47	San Pedro Sacatepéquez
Vyztlán	6	Santa Ana Huista	Zacatepeque	48	Santiago Sacatepéquez
Xacaltenango	7	Jacaltenango	Pinula	49	Santa Catarina Pinula?
Petatlán	8	Concepción	Petapa	50	Petapa
Yztapalapán	9	San Mateo Ixtatán?	Amatitlán	51	Amatitlán
Cochumatlán	10	Todos Santos Cuchumatán	Malacatepeque	52	(disappeared)
			Cozumaluapa	53	Santa Lucía Cotzumalguapa
Zacapa	11	Sipacapa	Ciquinalá	54	Siquinalá
Comitlán	12	Comitancillo	Ozuma	55	San Andrés Osuna
Tianguisteca (Tecpán Puyumatlán)	13	Santa Eulalia	Masagua	56	Masagua
			Mistlán	57	Santa Ana Mixtán
Zoloma	14	Soloma	Tescoaco	58	Texcuaco
Huehuetenango	15	Huehuetenango	Amayuca	59	(disappeared)
Aguacatlán	16	Aguacatán	Yzapa	60	San Andrés Iztapa
Chalchuytlán	17	Chalchitán (barrio)	Tasisco	61	Taxisco
Ayllon	18	Ilom	Taquelula	62	Tacuilula
Quequel	19	?	Guazacapán	63	Guazacapán
Cochil	20	part of Nebaj	Chiquimula	64	Chiquimulilla
Nema	21	Nebaj	Cinacantlán	65	Sinacantlán
Cozalchiname	22	San Juan Cotzal?	Tecoaco	66	San Juan Tecuaco
Culuteca	23	?	Jumaytepeque	67	Jumaytepeque
Zacapula	24	Sacapulas	Yzuatlán	68	Santa María Ixhuatán
Uspantlán	25	Uspantán	Nestiquipaque	69	Santa Anita
Jocotenango	26	San Bartolomé Jocotenango	Moyutla	70	Moyutla
			Tacuba	71	Tacuba
Xocotenango	27	San Pedro Jocopilas	Aguachapa	72	Ahuachapán
Luquitlán	28	San Antonio Ilotenango	Ataco	73	Concepción Ataco
			Apaneca	74	Apaneca
Chiquimula	29	Santa María Chiquimula	Quezalcoatitlán	75	Salcoatitán
			Yzalco	76	Izalco
Momostenango	30	Momostenango	Tacuscalco	77	Tacuscalco
Yzquine	31	Chichicastenango	Yzalco	78	Caluco
Totonicapa	32	Totonicapán	Acajutla	79	Acajutla
Quezaltenango	33	Quetzaltenango	Masagua	80	Santa Catarina Masahuat
Ostuncalco	34	Ostuncalco	Atezcatempa	81	Atescatempa
Zacatepeque	35	San Martín Sacatepéquez	Mitla	82	Asunción Mita
			Yzquipulas	83	Esquipulas
Coatlán	36	Coatepeque	Xilotepeque	84	San Luis Jilotepeque
Ystalavaca	37	Retalhuleu	Jalapa	85	Jalapa
Zapotitlán	38	San Martín Zapotitlán and San Francisco Zapotitlán	Chiquimula	86	Chiquimula
			Jalapa	85	Jalapa
			Chiquimula	86	Chiquimula
			Zacapa	87	Zacapa
Suchitepeque	39	San Antonio Suchitepéquez	Ozumatlán	88	Usumatlán
			Acasaguastlán	89	San Cristóbal Acasaguastlán
Tecpán Atitlán	40	Sololá	Tecocistlán	90	Rabinal
Atitlán	41	Santiago Atitlán			

Source: AGI, Guatemala 128 (1548–51), and Kramer (1994, 237–40). The order tabulated follows the sequence of "Las tasaciones de los pueblos de los términos y jurisdicción de la ciudad de Santiago de Guatemala."

Table 22
PUEBLOS DE INDIOS IN THE CERRATO TASACIONES
WITH NO TRIBUTARY DATA

Pueblo	Encomendero	Present-day location, with department or country indicated
Petatán	Diego Sánchez Santiago	Petatán, Huehuetenango
Uspantlán	Santos de Figueroa	Uspantán, El Quiché
Nopicalco	Isabel Godínez	Mochixicalanco, El Salvador
Zacatepeque	Francisco de Monterroso	Santiago Sacatepéquez, Sacatepéquez
Nestiquipaque y Cuceltepeque	Cristóbal Rodríguez Picón	Santa Anita, Santa Rosa and Cuceltepeque, unknown location
Coatlán	Juan de León Cardona	Coatepeque, Quetzaltenango
Amystlán	Juan de Ecija	Santa Ana Mixtán, Escuintla
Quezaltepeque	Melchor de Velasco	Unknown location
Çumpango	Juan Álvarez	Sumpango, Sacatepéquez
Yzalco	Juan de Guzmán	Izalco, El Salvador
Teguantepeque	Pedro de Ovid	Disappeared town, Escuintla
Tezcoaco	Pedro de Ovid	Texcuaco, La Gomera, Escuintla
Acatenango	Andrés de Rodas	Acatenango, Chimaltenango
Ozumatlán	Antonio de Morales (deceased)	Usumatlán, Zacapa
Suchitepeque	Hernán Gutiérrez de Gibaja and Hernán Méndez de Sotomayor	San Antonio Suchitepéquez
Jumaytepeque	Francisco de la Cueva	Jumaytepeque, Santa Rosa
Chimaltenango	Antonio Ortiz	Chimaltenango, Chimaltenango
Aguachapa	Bartolomé Marroquín	Ahuachapán, El Salvador
Mascote	Bartolomé Marroquín	San Lucas Sacatepéquez, Sacatepéquez
Comapa	Diego López de Villanueva	Comapa, Jutiapa
Pajacis	Diego López de Villanueva	Patzicía, Chimaltenango
Totonicapa	Crown	Totonicapán, Totonicapán
Acatenango	Gonzalo de Alvarado and Pedro de Zaballos	Nejapa, Acatenango, Chimaltenango
Chancoate	Cristóbal Lobo	Ipala, Chiquimula
Quezaltenango	Crown	Quetzaltenango, Quetzaltenango
Copulco	Antonio de Paredes and Pedro González Nájera	Cubulco, Baja Verapaz
Coatlan	Crown	San Sebastián Coatán, Huehuetenango
Los Yzquipulas	Crown	Esquipulas, Chiquimula
Cozalchiname	Crown	San Juan Cotzal, El Quiché
Cochumatlán	Marcos Ruiz and García de Águilar	Todos Santos Cuchumatán, Huehuetenango
Petapa	Crown	Petapa, Guatemala
Conetla	Gonzalo Ortiz	Near Uspantán, El Quiché
Alotepeque	Gonzalo Ortiz	In Chiapas?
Chicuytlán	Gonzalo Ortiz	Near Uspantán
Bohon	Gonzalo Ortiz	Near Uspantán
Cimpango	Crown	Sumpango, Sacatepéquez

Source: AGI, Guatemala 128, "Las tasaciones de los pueblos."

Table 23
TRIBUTARY POPULATIONS OF EIGHT
GUATEMALAN COMMUNITIES, 1548–82

	1548–51[1]	1550[2]	1562[3]	1582[4]	1582[5]	Percentage Change
(Santiago) Atitlán	1,000				2,166	+116.6
Comalapa	600		980			+63.3
Guazacapán	400				350	-37.5
Huehuetenango	500	570		367		+14.0
San Juan and San Pedro Sacatepéquez	700		740			+5.7
Tecpán Atitlán (Sololá)	1,000	2,037		1,433	1,161	+103.7
Tecocistlán (Rabinal)	600				463	-22.9
Sumpango	200		464			+132.0

[1]AGI, Guatemala 128, "Las tasaciones de los pueblos" (1548–51).
[2]AGI, Guatemala 10, Diego García de Valverde to the Crown (1582).
[3]AGI, Guatemala 45, "Tasaciones y cuentas de los indios tributarios" (1562).
[4]AGI, Guatemala 10, Diego García de Valverde to the Crown (1582).
[5]AGI, Patronato 183-1-1, "Relación formada por la Audiencia de Guatemala de todos los pueblos de su jurisdicción (1582).

Table 24
TRIBUTARIO-TO-*RESERVADO* RATIOS FOR SIX
GUATEMALAN COMMUNITIES, 1562

	Number of tributarios	Number of reservados	Ratio T:R
Comalapa	980	145	6.8:1
Chimaltenango	630	106	5.9:1
Petapa	219	31	7.1:1
San Juan Sacatepéquez	320	80	4:1
San Pedro Sacatepéquez	420	62	6.8:1
Sumpango	464	89	5.2:1

Source: AGI, Guatemala 45, "Tasaciones y cuentas de los indios tributarios" (1562).

Table 25
NATIVE POPULATIONS OF CENTRAL AMERICA
(ACCORDING TO JUAN DE ESTRADA, CIRCA 1550)

Jurisdiction	Native Population ("Indios")
Santiago [de Guatemala]	26,000 "poco más o menos"
Chiapas	15,000 "poco más o menos"
Soconusco	2,000 "escasos"
San[t] Salvador	1,000 "poco más o menos"
San Miguel [El Salvador]	4,000 "poco más o menos"
Choluteca [Honduras]	2,000 "poco más o menos"

Source: AGI, Indiferente General 857.

Note: There is "poca noticia" of Honduras and Nicaragua in Juan de Estrada's missive (see Newson 1986; 1987), but he states that "puede aver en la [provincia] de Nicaragua tres mil indios y en la [provincia] de Honduras seis mil."

Table 26
NATIVE POPULATIONS ADMINISTERED
BY SECULAR CLERGY IN THE BISHOPRIC OF GUATEMALA, 1570

Jurisdictions in Chiapas, El Salvador, and Honduras		Jurisdictions in Guatemala	
Jurisdiction	Estimated number of *vecinos*	Jurisdiction	Estimated number of *vecinos*
CHIAPAS		**GUATEMALA**	
Xoconusco	300	San Luis	400
Huehuetlán	350	Atitipaque	400
Ayutla	350	Taxisco	600
Tianquiztlán	400	Las Yzquipulas	600
Tuxtla	500	Chiquimula	700
EL SALVADOR		Los Cevallos	700
Guaymango	500	Tlequetziapeque	700
Tacuxcalco	500	Yupiltepeque	700
San Salvador	500	Zapotitlán	800
Ataco	600	Guazacapán	800
Locuiltla	600	Chiquimula de la Sierra	800
Heymoco	700	Acazaguastlán	800
Aguachapán	800	Zamayaque	1,000
Naulingo	800	Quetzaltepeque	1,000
Yzalco de Girón	800	Nitla	1,000
Naucalco	1,000	Los Suchitepéques	1,400
Yzalco de Guzmán	1,000		
HONDURAS			
La Chuluteca	400		
Moncagua	600		
Usulutlán	800		
Chapeltique	1,000		
Los Uloas	1,000		

Source: AGI, Guatemala 394, "Memoria que envió el licenciado Mendiola Artiaga, fiscal de Guatemala" (1570).

Table 27
NATIVE POPULATIONS ADMINISTERED BY THE
DOMINICAN ORDER, 1570

Jurisdiction	Estimated number of *vecinos*
Petapa y su visita	1,500
Los Çacatepéques	2,000
Chimaltenango	1,200
Çacapula y su visita	1,500
Tequecistlán (Rabinal)	1,500
Yzquentepeque (Escuintla)	500
Valle de Guatemala	250
Cuzcatlán	1,000
Los Purulapas	1,000

Source: AGI, Guatemala 394, "Memoria que envió el licenciado Mendiola Artiaga, fiscal de Guatemala" (1570).

Table 28
NATIVE POPULATIONS ADMINISTERED BY THE
FRANCISCAN ORDER, 1570

Jurisdiction	Estimated number of *vecinos*
Totonicapán	[más de] 1,000
Quezaltenango	1,800
Tecpán Atitlán	5,000
Atitlán	1,500
Tecpán Guatemala	1,300
Comalapa	1,200

Source: AGI, Guatemala 394, "Memoria que envió el licenciado Mendiola Artiaga, fiscal de Guatemala" (1570).

Table 29
NATIVE POPULATIONS ADMINISTERED BY THE
MERCEDARIAN ORDER, 1570

Jurisdiction	Estimated number of *vecinos*
Huehuetenango	1,000
Çacatepeque	1,200
Amatenango	1,000
Los Mames	1,000
En el Valle [de Guatemala]	700

Source: AGI, Guatemala 394, "Memoria que envió el licenciado Mendiola Artiaga, fiscal de Guatemala" (1570).

Table 30
COMPARISON OF TRIBUTARY COUNTS IN TOWNS THAT APPEAR
IN BOTH THE CERRATO (1548–51) AND VALVERDE (1578–82) *TASACIONES*

Town	Recipient of tribute under Valverde	Cerrato count	Valverde count Old	New
Nestiquipaque	Crown[1]	No number given	148	161
Pazón, estancia de Tecpanatitlán	Crown[2]	Not in Cerrato	315.5	225
San Miguel Pochutla	Crown	Not in Cerrato	57	51
Apaneca	Pedro de Alvarado	100	107	70
Misco	Álvaro de Paz	160	190	195
Tecpán Guatemala	Francisco Marroquín[3]	400	553	301.5
[La Magdalena] Patulul	Francisco Marroquín	Not in Cerrato	140	129
Xilotepeque	Tomás de Salazar[4]	500	366	316
Comalapa	Luis Dardón[5]	600	978	814.5
San Pedro Yepocapa	Juan Calvo Nájera[6]	80?	?	97
Quezaltenango	Crown[7]	400	840	771
Tecpán Atitlán	Crown[8]	1,000	?	1,213
Huehuetenango	Francisco de la Fuente[9]	500	570	367

[1]The Cerrato *tasación* mentions 34 widows, who are to pay one *tostón* and one *gallina de Castilla*. The Valverde *tasación* notes that two widowers are the equivalent of one tributary.

[2]See note 8, below, in which San Bernardino Pazón is mentioned as forming part of Tecpán Atitlán. No separate figure is given for this town.

[3]Mention is made of 301.5 tributaries and fourteen young widows.

[4]Xilotepeque, the present-day San Martín Jilotepeque, was held by Juan de Chávez in Cerrato's time.

[5]A *tasación* for Comalapa dated 1562 (AGI, Guatemala 45) records 980 tributaries, and another dated 1613 (AGI, Guatemala 98) records 508 "indios casados."

[6]One of the towns called Acatenango in the Cerrato *tasación* we believe to be Yepocapa, then held by the Crown and recorded as having 80 tributaries. The Crown may have shared the *encomienda* with Nájera.

[7]The Valverde *tasación* states also that "setenta y una viudas mozas" should each pay four *reales*. Zamora (1985, 105, 114) believes that Quezaltenango was a shared *encomienda* in Cerrato's time. Another source (AGI, Patronato 183-1-1) records that there were 764 "tributarios casados" in 1583.

[8]AGI, Patronato 183-1-1 (1583) records Tecpán Atitlán as having 1,161 "tributarios casados." Valverde does in fact provide a figure for the "old" count (2,037), but he includes outlying settlements that are not included in the "new" count. We have included here, therefore, only the figure that Valverde furnishes for the *cabecera* of Tecpán Atitlán, which we believe was also Cerrato's unit of designation. The text for the "old" count reads "el pueblo de Tecpán Atitlán y sus estancias, que son San Jorge Epanahachel y Çimitabat y San Gabriel y Santo Tomás y San Jerónimo y San Agustín [y] San Juan y San Miguel y San Bernardino Pazón, se tasó por 2,037 tributarios," while the text for the "new" count reads, "tasaron el dicho pueblo y sus estancias en esta manera, el pueblo de Tecpán Atitlán que es la cabecera por 1,213 tributarios y San Francisco Panahachel por 56 tributarios y San Jorge por 111 tributarios y Santo Tomás y San Jerónimo por 53 tributarios."

[9]A total of 570 tributaries is derived by "haciendo de dos viudos y dos solteros un tributario."

Table 31
TOTAL PAYMENTS MADE IN THE *GRADUACIÓN DE SALARIOS*, 1684

Jurisdiction	Number of settlements	Amount paid	Correlation in tributaries	Estimated total population
Valle de Guatemala	75 pueblos	1,095 *tostones*	21,274	85,096
San Antonio (Suchitepéquez)	34 pueblos and *parcialidades*	301 *tostones*	5,848	23,392
Totonicapán (includes Huehuetenango)	72 pueblos and *parcialidades*	334 *tostones*, 3 *reales*	6,504	26,016
Quezaltenango	27 pueblos and *parcialidades*	195 *tostones*, 1.5 *reales*	3,796	15,184
Tecpanatitlán	25 pueblos and *parcialidades*	271 *tostones*, 0.5 *reales*	5,268	21,072
Atitlán	17 pueblos	156 *tostones*, 2 *reales*	3,041	12,164
Verapaz	13 pueblos	282 *tostones*, 2 *reales*	5,489	21,956
Acasabastlán	7 pueblos	32 *tostones*, 3.5 *reales*	639	2,556
Chiquimula	20 pueblos	125 *tostones*, 0.5 *reales*	2,431	9,724
Guazacapán	20 pueblos	129 *tostones*, 2.5 *reales*	2,518	10,072
Escuintla	19 pueblos and *parcialidades*	101 *tostones*	1,962	7,848
Total	329 pueblos and *parcialidades*	3,025 *tostones*	58,770	235,080

Source: Enríquez Macías (1989).

Note: The formula for the amount paid being converted into tributaries and total population is as follows: the number of *tostones* (the total collected was 3,025) is converted into *reales* by multiplying by four, giving 12,100 *reales*. This amount is converted into *maravedís* by multiplying by 34 (411,400). Dividing 411,400 *maravedís* by seven, the amount each tributary was expected to pay, yields 58,770 tributaries, which indicates (using a tributary to population multiplier of four) an estimated total population of 235,080. Some of the amounts paid by jurisdiction have been rounded off.

Table 32
PAYMENTS MADE IN *REAL SERVICIO DEL TOSTÓN*, 1710

Jurisdiction	Number of settlements	Amount paid
Valle de Guatemala	75 pueblos and *barrios*	19,621 *tostones*, 2 *reales*
Totonicapán and Huehuetenango	65 pueblos and *parcialidades*	7,474 *tostones*, 2 *reales*
Quezaltenango	28 pueblos and *parcialidades*	4,151 *tostones*
Verapaz	13 pueblos	6,755 *tostones*
Acasaguastlán	8 pueblos	831 *tostones*
Chiquimula de la Sierra	20 pueblos	3,463 *tostones*
Guazacapán	21 pueblos	2,592 *tostones*, 2 *reales*
Escuintla	19 pueblos and *parcialidades*	1,120 *tostones*, 2 *reales*
Tecpán Atitlán	26 pueblos and *parcialidades*	5,388 *tostones*
Atitlán	17 pueblos and *parcialidades*	2,329 *tostones*, 2 *reales*
Suchitepéquez	34 pueblos	5,328 *tostones*, 2 *reales*

Source: AGI, Contaduría 973, documents of which span the years 1624–1710.

Table 33
PAYMENTS MADE IN *REAL SERVICIO DEL TOSTÓN*, 1719

Jurisdiction	Amount of *real servicio del tostón*	Total value of tribute
Valle de Guatemala	19,785 *tostones*	36,487 *tostones*
Totonicapán and Huehuetenango	7,176 *tostones*	15,123 *tostones*
Quezaltenango	4,320 *tostones*	12,579 *tostones*
Verapaz	6,734 *tostones*	17,952 *tostones*
Acasaguastlán	1,005 *tostones*	3,029 *tostones*
Chiquimula	3,463 *tostones*	6,438 *tostones*
Guazacapán	2,482 *tostones*	7,098 *tostones*
Escuintla	991 *tostones*	4,525 *tostones*
Tecpán Atitlán	5,388 *tostones*	14,430 *tostones*
Atitlán	1,903 *tostones*	8,069 *tostones*
San Antonio Suchitepéquez (Zapotitlán)	4,957 *tostones*	13,428 *tostones*
Chiapas	14,210 *tostones*	33,805 *tostones*
Soconusco	835 *tostones*	4,797 *tostones*
San Salvador and San Miguel	4,952 *tostones*	6,627 *tostones*

Source: AGI, Contaduría 977. Figures are rounded off to the nearest *tostón*.

Table 34
NATIVE PARISHIONERS AND LADINO INHABITANTS
OF GUATEMALA, 1750

Jurisdiction	Recorded number of "filigreses"	Number of Ladinos
Los Amatitanes	21,166	2,550
Chimaltenango	26,610	400
Chiquimula de la Sierra	22,015	4,280
Guazacapán	14,413	100
Suchitepéquez	10,407	420
Sololá	11,144	1,000
Quezaltenango	11,193	1,598
Totonicapán (y Huehuetenango)	22,319	438
Verapaz	15,250	"algunos"*
Total	154,517	10,786

Source: "Memoria de los curatos [del] Obispado de Goathemala" (RAH, Papeles del Consejo de Indias, 9-29-2).
* No number is recorded for Ladino inhabitants of Verapaz, only that "some" live there.

Table 35
TRIBUTARY POPULATION COUNTS, 1768–69

Jurisdiction	Pre–1768–69 count	1768–69 count	Rise or fall
Barrios de Santiago de Guatemala	441	472	+31
Chimaltenango	10,509	9,640	-869
Amatitanes y Sacatepéquez	7,264	6,752	-512
Chiquimula y Zacapa	10,205	8,229	-1,976
Verapaz	9,195	8,865	-330
Totonicapán y Huehuetenango	7,785	8,446	+661
Quezaltenango	3,973	4,528	+555
Suchitepéquez	3,287	3,461	+174
Tecpán Atitlán	6,070	5,807	-263
Escuintla y Guazacapán	3,191	3,354	+163
Total	61,920	59,554	-2,366

Source: AGI, Guatemala 560, "Testimonio para averiguar el aumento de tributarios" (1768–69).

Table 36
POPULATION ESTIMATES FOR SPANISH AMERICA, 1772

Jurisdiction/Territorial extent	Population
Mexico hasta [as far as] California	3,200,000
Guatemala hasta [as far as] el Ystmo [Panama]	800,000
Santa Fé [Nueva Granada] hasta [as far as] el [río] Orinoco	1,200,000
Provincia de Venezuela	600,000
Río de la Plata [Argentina and Uruguay]	800,000
Perú, Chile, Quito [Ecuador]	3,200,000
Isla de Cuba	350,000
Isla de Puerto Rico y demás [other Caribbean islands]	300,000
Total	10,450,000

Source: AGI, Indiferente General 1525, "Vista política de la América española y sumario de su población según los registros de la secretaría del Consejo de Indias" (1772).

Table 37
INDIAN TRIBUTARY POPULATION IN 1778

Jurisdiction	Number of pueblos	Number of tributaries
Barrios de la Ciudad (Neighborhoods of Guatemala City)	8	422
Quezaltenango	25	4,222
Chiquimula	30	8,045
Sololá	31	5,720
Verapaz	14	9,783
Totonicapán and Huehuetenango	48	9,556
Escuintla	26	3,010
San Antonio (Suchitepéquez)	19	3,047
Chimaltenango	21	8,609
Amatitlán	42	8,972
Total	264	61,386

Source: AGI, Guatemala 560, "Estado que manifiesta . . . la última *Numeración de tributarios*" (1778).

Table 38
COMPARATIVE SHIFTS IN POPULATION, 1778–1812

Jurisdiction	Juarros 1778[1]	Juarros 1800[1]	Souls (*Almas*) in 1812[2]
Ciudad de Guatemala	23,434	24,707	37,952
Sacatepéquez	50,786	78,321	46,601
Totonicapán and Huehuetenango	51,272	57,045	88,498
Chimaltenango	40,082	37,623	44,750
Sololá	27,953	28,765	16,558
Quezaltenango	28,563	28,757	28,295
Verapaz	49,585	45,945	45,544
Chiquimula (including Zacapa and Acasaguastlán)	52,423	45,743	65,252
Escuintla and Guazacapán	24,978	25,699	15,283
Suchitepéquez	17,535	16,780	14,304
Totals	366,611	389,385	403,037

Source: Luján Muñoz (2005).
[1]The Juarros figures for 1778 draw upon a census conducted that year, the priest amending them to arrive at population totals for 1800.
[2]A record of the number of Christian souls (*almas*) for 1812 comes from a *Relación de la población* carried out that same year.

Table 39
TRIBUTARY POPULATION IN 1802, 1806, AND 1811

Jurisdiction	Original 1802 count	Number of absentees or *huidos*	Revised 1806 count	1811 count	Estimated Indian population in 1811*
Chimaltenango	8,316	1,888	10,204	8,804	44,020
Chiquimula	7,578	497	8,075	7,094	35,470
Quezaltenango	6,148	206	6,354	7,362	36,810
Amatitanes and Sacatepéquez	10,054	1,928	11,982	9,930	49,650
Escuintla	2,051	410	2,461	3,092	15,460
Sololá	6,860	363	7,223	6,863	34,315
Suchitepéquez	2,558	53	2,611	2,773	13,865
Totonicapán and Huehuetenango	11,803	325	12,128	13,128	65,640
Verapaz	11,311	548	11,859	11,259	56,295
Totals	66,679	6,218	72,897	70,305	351,525

Source: AGCA, A3.16, leg. 243, exp. 4856 (1802); AGCA, A3.16, leg. 2327, exp. 34374 (1806); and AGCA, A3.16, leg. 953, exp. 17773 (1811).
*The estimated Indian population in 1811 (351,525) is obtained by multiplying the number of tributaries (70,305) by a factor of five.

Table 40
NATIVE POPULATION OF GUATEMALA, 1520–1811

	Estimated population size	Comments
ca. 1520	2,000,000	—
ca. 1550	427,850	P:T of 5:1
1575	184,540	P:C of 4:1
1624–28	131,250	P:T of 3.75:1
1681	212,260	P:T of 4:1
1684	235,080	P:T of 4:1
1710	236,212	P:T of 4:1
1719	232,818	P:T of 4:1
1722–26	228,152	P:T of 4:1
1760	247,680	P:T of 4:1
1768	238,216	P:T of 4:1
1768–70	252,717	—
1778	276,237	P:T of 4.5:1
1811	351,525	P:T of 5:1

Source: For sources and rationale, see chapters 9 through 14.
P:T = ratio of total population to number of tributaries.
P:C = ratio of total population to number of *casados*, or married men.

GLOSSARY

Adelantado   Recipient of a royal contract to explore and conquer hostile territory, which carried with it entitlement to govern with supreme authority and to enjoy certain rights and privileges. In Guatemala, a title associated with Pedro de Alvarado.

Aguardiente   Locally made liquor usually distilled from sugarcane, often produced clandestinely to avoid government controls and taxes.

Alcalde   Officer given administrative and judicial duties by the *ayuntamiento* or *cabildo* on which he served.

Alcalde mayor   Chief district officer, either a Spaniard or a criollo, charged with governing an *alcaldía mayor*, a jurisdiction comparable in size to a *corregimiento* or *provincia*.

Aldea   Village, a unit of settlement smaller than and subordinate to a pueblo.

Almas de confesión   Persons of the age of confession who live in a specific parish.

Amaq'   Dispersed, far-flung unit of settlement where commoners lived in preconquest times that was also of social and political import. See also *calpul, chinamit,* and *parcialidad.*

Anejo, anexo   Visita; a settlement with a church, subordinate to a parish center or *cabecera.*

Antigua Guatemala   Literally "ancient" or "old" Guatemala; the name given to Santiago de Guatemala after earthquakes caused serious damage in 1773, prompting civil and ecclesiastical authorities to relocate the capital in what is today Guatemala City.

Arroba   Unit of weight equivalent to eleven kilograms or 25 pounds.

Audiencia   High Court or governing body of a region and, by extension, the name given to the territory of jurisdiction itself. The Audiencia de Guatemala, based in Santiago de Guatemala, governed all of Central America, from the present-day Mexican state of Chiapas to Costa Rica.

Ayuntamiento   Town or city council, synonymous with the term *cabildo*.

Azumbre   Liquid measure equivalent to two liters.

Barrio   District or neighborhood, usually urban, whose residents share a common identity, place of origin, or language.

Caballería   Measure of land, approximately 104 acres or 42 hectares.

Cabecera   Principal town or city of a *municipio* or *departamento*; seat of local government.

Cabecera de doctrina   Indian town with a resident parish priest.

Cabildo   Town or city council composed of various officials elected annually by outgoing members.

Cacique   Hereditary Indian ruler considered a member of the native nobility, afforded certain privileges under Spanish rule not enjoyed by commoners.

Caites   Sandals, originally made of fiber, worn by Indians. Also referred to as *cutaras*.

Cal   Lime ground up to powder form, used as mortar for construction and in the preparation of dough (*masa*) for making tortillas.

Calpisque, calpixque   Person assigned to collect Indian tribute. The term also referred to an overseer or administrator of an agricultural estate. Often a *casta* held this position.

Calpul   Indigenous, clan-like social and territorial unit. *Calpul* is a corruption of the Náhuatl term *calpulli*; synonymous with the Spanish term *parcialidad*. Also referred to as *chinamit*, plural *chinamitales*, several of which constituted an *amaq'*.

Carga   A load of indeterminate size, legally ruled not to exceed fifty pounds but often weighing more, carried by Indian bearers.

Casa   Literally, house; in colonial parlance a household.

Casada, casado   Married person. In terms of tributary status, a married Indian couple (husband and wife) usually paid full tribute.

Caserío   Hamlet, a grouping of houses in a rural area, smaller in size and more dispersed than an *aldea*.

Casta   Person of mixed racial descent.

Castiza, castizo   Offspring of a union between a Spaniard and a *mestizo*.

Cédula de encomienda   Title or certificate that formally registered the date and terms of an *encomienda* grant, the Indians granted in *encomienda*, and the name of the *encomendero* or recipient.

Chinamit   Equivalent of *calpul,* above. A socio-territorial unit associated with certain native lineages.

Choza   Hut, a rudimentary dwelling.

Cofradía   Religious fraternity or sodality. Criollos, Indians, blacks, and certain persons of the middle strata had their own *cofradías.*

Comisionado   Constable; a low-ranking official, often Ladino, who represented government authority in a predominantly indigenous town or district.

Composición de tierra   A way to make legal, through payment to the Crown, the acquisition of land obtained by irregular or unlawful means.

Congregación   Policy of forced native resettlement; by extension, a settlement thus created. Under *congregación,* previously dispersed Indian populations were "congregated" into nucleated centers under the watchful eyes of a parish priest and colonial officials. Also referred to as *reducción.*

Contador   Treasury official assigned to look after the fiscal interests of the Crown.

Corregidor   Government official who administered a *corregimiento*, a position often sought and held by criollos.

Corregimiento   Administrative unit governed by a *corregidor*.

Criollo   In Guatemala, a term used to denote the offspring of Spanish parents. More generally, the designation applies to all persons born in the Americas of European ancestry.

Crónica   Narration of events written either by a lay person or, often the case in Guatemala, by members of a religious order or a secular cleric.

Cuadrilla   Gang of workers in the sixteenth century, often Indian slaves used in mining activities run by their Spanish masters.

Danza de la Conquista   Dance of the Conquest; a dance drama, or *baile*, introduced by Spanish authorities to instruct Indians about the conquest of Guatemala, thereby reinforcing their subordinate status. Associated with the death of the K'iche' ruler Tecún Umán, in man-to-man combat with Pedro de Alvarado in 1524.

Departamento   Administrative and territorial term adopted in the 1820s soon after Guatemala's independence from Spain. At first there were seven departments; today Guatemala has twenty-two.

Doctrinero   Parish priest, who might also belong to a religious order, responsible for attending to Christian duties in the *doctrina* or jurisdiction assigned him.

Ducado   Gold coin, first minted in 1504, worth 375 *maravedís*.

Ejido   Area of common or communal land ceded by the Crown to Indian towns and to Spanish urban centers, used to grow crops, graze livestock, and gather or cut firewood.

Encomendero   Spaniard awarded the privilege of Indian tribute in the form of an *encomienda.*

Encomienda   Grant of Indian tribute in the form of goods and commodities and, especially early in the colonial period, the provision of native labor.

Estancia   Ranch or rural estate dedicated to the raising of livestock, most often cattle, smaller in size than a hacienda.

Fanega   Unit of dry measure of about 1.5 bushels, weighing approximately 116 pounds or 53 kilograms.

Feligreses   Parishioners of the age of confession. See *Almas de confesión.*

Fiesta del Volcán   Celebration of the surrender of Kaqchikel lords Cahí Imox and Belehé Qat to the Spaniards and their Mexican allies, performed to emphasize Spanish victory in conquest and Indian defeat and subordination.

Fiscal   *Oidor* or judge in charge of the financial affairs of an *audiencia.*

Gallina de Castilla   European chicken, introduced with the arrival of Spaniards in the New World.

Gallina de la tierra   Turkey, fowl domesticated and bred in the Americas.

Gucumatz   Indigenous term for a devastating outbreak of sickness that took many native lives in the mid-sixteenth century, an epidemic that may have been a form of bubonic or pulmonary plague.

Hacendado   Owner of a large, rural estate or hacienda.

Hacienda   Large, rural estate devoted to raising crops or livestock; a term used to denote Spanish or criollo-owned properties.

Hidalgo   Member of the lesser Spanish nobility, an untitled nobleman.

Hija natural, hijo natural   Female or male child born outside of formal wedlock, usually recognized by their Spanish or criollo father.

Huipil   Handwoven Indian woman's blouse.

Indio, yndio   "Indian," a term today considered disrespectful or demeaning but in colonial times (and parlance) the name used to describe individual members of Guatemala's indigenous population, commoners and nobility alike.

Indios amigos   Term used to denote various groups of Indian allies who, in the sixteenth century, assisted the Spaniards in large numbers as soldiers and auxiliaries in campaigns of conquest. Sizable contingents of *indios amigos* indigenous to Mexico opted to remain in Guatemala after their military services were no longer required.

Indios de servicio   Indians who were an integral part of an *encomienda* award, obliged to provide personal service on a fixed schedule to their *encomendero*. The practice was formally abolished in the mid-sixteenth century.

Ingenio   Sugar mill, technologically more sophisticated than a *trapiche.*

Juez de milpa   Official appointed to ensure that Indians planted and harvested their corn crop or *milpa*, not only in order to feed themselves but also to pay tribute.

Juez repartidor   Official charged under system of *repartimiento de indios* with ensuring the distribution of Indians for forced labor on agricultural estates.

Labrador   Farmer, a term often used to describe a Spanish owner of a *labor de pan llevar*, or wheat farm.

Ladino   In Guatemala, a term that usually refers to people of mixed descent who have some combination of Indian, African, and Spanish background. A distinct ethnic category from Indian, Spaniard, or criollo, used today in national censuses to denote all persons not considered indigenous Mayan.

Ladrillo   Brick made of baked clay.

Las dos repúblicas   Theoretical division of colonial society into one republic of Spaniards and another of Indians. An exclusionary construct that did not take into account the colonial presence of African slaves, free blacks, mulattoes, *mestizos*, and Ladinos.

Legajo   Bundle of archival documents often covering a specific subject.

Libro de cabildo   Book of city or town council minutes recording official meetings held by members of council. A document of matters discussed, decisions reached, and appointments made.

Manta   Standard-sized piece of woven cloth, usually cotton.

Maravedí   Unit of currency, one thirty-fourth of a *real*.

Masa   Dough made from ground maize, mixed with water and ground lime powder, used for making *tortillas*.

Memoria   Written account of specific events and circumstances, often providing dates around or about a specific subject. At times a narrative addressed to superior authorities, even to the King himself.

Méritos y servicios   Literally, "merits and services," usually recorded as a court document detailing the plaintiff's case, highlighting his loyalty and dedication to the Crown, and corroborated by witnesses testifying on his behalf. See also *probanzas*.

Mestiza, mestizo   Person of mixed Indian and Spanish descent, female or male.

Mestizaje   Race mixture.

Milpa   Plot of lands usually planted with corn and worked by Indians. In the Valley of Panchoy, the Spanish core of Guatemala, name given to Indian settlements founded there by a Spaniard and his indigenous slaves.

Monte   Land covered with scrub, not useful for agriculture but containing resources such as herbs, firewood, and small game.

Mulata, mulato   Strictly speaking, person of mixed black-Spanish descent. In Guatemala, however, the term included in almost all cases those of black-Indian descent.

Municipio   Post-independence successor to colonial-era *pueblo de indios*.

Naboría, naborío   Indian servant (female or male) who worked for Spaniards and was exempt from tributary obligations. In the late sixteenth century, *naboríos* began to pay a special tribute called *laborío*, also paid by free persons of African descent.

Nagua   Underskirt or petticoat made with white cloth.

Negra, negro   Black, a person allegedly of full African descent, slave or free.

Obraje de tinte añil   Indigo dye works, for the most part found along the Pacific coastal plain.

Oidor   Judge who served as a member of an *audiencia*.

Pajuides   Makeshift Indian settlements, established without official sanction in zones of refuge, where inhabitants were free of tributary and labor obligations, as well as the scrutiny of the Church.

Paramento   Adorned, ornamental cloth furnished as an item of tribute.

Parcialidad   Term used by Spaniards to define social units, often divided and resettled as separate entities in the process of *congregación*. Also used to describe ethnic groups that formed part of the same pueblo or, in the case of Santiago de Guatemala, urban barrios.

Pardo   Another term for *mulato*, one often associated with members of the militia.

Pastor   Shepherd.

Peso   A gold or, more commonly, silver coin divided into eight *reales*, hence "pieces of eight."

Petate   Mat woven from reeds, used for sleeping on.

Pleito   Formal complaint made by one person or group against another, invariably contentious in nature and related to some kind of dispute or grudge.

Probanza   Paperwork connected to the declaration of *méritos y servicios*, a certified statement of facts, proof of deeds done and services rendered.

Procurador   Attorney and legal representative of one party who acts before another.

Protector de indios   Crown-appointed attorney charged with preventing harsh treatment of Indians.

Provincia   Literally, "province," a territorial division of similar areal extent as an *alcaldía mayor* and presided over by a governor.

Pueblo de indios   Indian town created by the process of *congregación*.

Pueblo de visita   Smaller Indian town unable to support a resident priest and so visited by one occasionally.

Rancho   Hut (*choza*) or dwelling of a poor person. When *ranchos* are grouped together, they are called a *ranchería*. Traditionally, primitive house with a thatched roof.

Real   Spanish silver coin, worth one-eighth of a *peso*; known in English as a piece of eight.

Real cédula   Royal order or decree.

Real servicio   Beginning in 1593, tax paid to the Crown of one-half a peso, levied on Indian tributaries.

Regatón   Intermediary or middleman who intercepted and accosted Indian traders with a view to stealing their goods or buying them at rock-bottom prices.

Regidor   Alderman who served on an *ayuntamiento* or *cabildo* either in a Spanish city or in a *pueblo de indios*.

Relación   Descriptive account or report on a particular subject.

Repartimiento de efectos   Forced sale of items to Indians (often useless to their way of life and involving payment in cash) by Spanish and criollo officials, undertaken to augment their regular salaries.

Repartimiento de indios   System of draft labor imposed by Spanish law on adult Indian males, obliging them to serve on a rotating basis on predominantly criollo-owned estates. The obligation also pertained to certain urban duties, such as the baking of bread for Spanish and criollo households.

Repartimiento de mercancías   Forced purchase by Indians at unfavorable prices of unwanted merchandise thrust on them by *corregidores* or district governors. Another term for *repartimiento de efectos*.

Repartimiento general   First major distribution of *encomienda* awards carried out by Jorge de Alvarado in March and April of 1528, after the founding of Santiago in Almolonga, today Ciudad Vieja, the year before.

República de españoles   A policy supposedly grouping Spaniards into their own towns and cities, designed to protect Indian welfare. The policy failed for many reasons, primarily because of Spanish dependence on Indian labor. See *república de indios*.

República de indios   The obverse of *república de españoles*: a policy establishing *pueblos de indios* with the goal of protecting Indians from the abuses of Spaniards.

Requerimiento   Literally the "Requirement," a document read aloud in Spanish or a native language prior to military engagement, warning Indians to submit to Crown authority or face immediate attack and certain defeat. Resistance to Spanish presence, in effect failure to follow the terms of *Requerimiento*, resulted in authorized enslavement of the Indian population and their being branded as *esclavos de guerra*, "slaves of war."

Reservado   Indian exempt from tributary obligations because of advanced age, poor health, church service, *cabildo* membership, and (in some cases) having fought alongside Spaniards in campaigns of conquest. A privilege often ignored by Spanish authorities intent on generating revenue.

Residencia   Judicial review and inquiry into the conduct of a Spanish official or representative of the Crown who had completed his term of office or had been removed from it.

Salinas   Salt pans or salt works mostly found along the Pacific coast.

Santiago de Guatemala   Capital city established in 1541 in the Valley of Panchoy after the destruction of an earlier Spanish nucleus, today Ciudad Vieja, in the nearby Valley of Almolonga. Known as Antigua Guatemala after it was badly damaged by earthquakes in 1773, after which the capital was relocated in Guatemala City.

Sementera   Specified planting of grain, usually maize or wheat, often stipulated as part of Indian tribute obligations in early colonial times.

Servicio del tostón   Head tax on top of normal tribute obligations, imposed on all eligible Indian tributaries. See *real servicio*.

Servicio ordinario   Literally "ordinary service"; all manner of obligations imposed on Indians who lived close to Spanish settlements, which required work to de done for little or no compensation.

Servicio personal   Literally "personal service"; the labor component of Indian tributary duties for Spanish *encomenderos*. The obligation was formally abolished under reforms enacted by President Alonso López de Cerrato in the mid-sixteenth century.

Tasación de tributo   Tribute assessment. A head count of an Indian *pueblo* undertaken to determine the amount of tribute deemed payable to an *encomendero* or to the Crown.

Teja   A clay tile used on roofs of public buildings and the houses of Spaniards and criollos. A tile-roofed house symbolized elite status in towns and cities.

Tercio de Navidad   The day around Christmas, six months after the *tercio de San Juan*, when the second half of the annual levy of Indian tribute was due.

Tercio de San Juan   Even though called a "third," the term used for when half the annual tribute was due, furnished by Indians on Saint John's Day, June 24.

Terrazgo   A land-use tax imposed on Indians who, after indigenous slaves were emancipated, worked properties owned by Spaniards. Mostly a per capita levy but at times a lump sum divided among the residents living on the land.

Teupantlaca   Náhuatl term for those who served their local church, literally "those who work in the house of God." Such people were usually exempt from paying tribute.

Tierra caliente Literally, "hot land," located at elevations below 800 meters, either along the Pacific coast or in low-lying parts of the interior.

Tierra fría Literally, "cold land," located at elevations above 1,600 meters.

Tierra templada Literally, "temperate land," located at elevations between 800 and 1,600 meters.

Tinamit In both K'iche' and Kaqchikel, the name given to nucleated, military strongholds where the indigenous elite lived in preconquest times.

Título Literally, "title," more specifically, a term used by Spaniards to describe indigenous documents created, often decades after first contact and conquest, to furnish details, often mythic, regarding places of origin, migrations, wars, and land boundaries.

Tostón Four *reales* or one-half of a peso.

Trapiche Rudimentary sugar mill that used animal power as opposed to water power to grind cane.

Tributario Male Indian, between sixteen and fifty years of age, who paid tribute in goods and commodities twice a year to his Spanish master or to the Crown. Before the mid-sixteenth century, *tributarios* also had to provide labor services.

Tributo Quantity of goods, and also money, paid by Indian adults to individual *encomenderos* and to the Crown.

Tunatiuh "Sun" in Náhuatl, the name first given to Pedro de Alvarado by native inhabitants in Mexico (1519–21) on account of his fair hair and pale complexion. Later used in Guatemala, where it was passed on to Indians who lived there by Alvarado's Mexican allies.

Vecino Resident of settled, well-established towns and cities.

Visita Formal tour of inspection of an ecclesiastical or civil jurisdiction by a high-ranking official.

Xiquilite   Grass-like plant grown especially along Guatemala's Pacific coast. Its leaves, picked and processed, yield the blue dyestuff *añil*, or indigo.

Xiquipil   Of Náhuatl origin, a measure of 8,000 cacao beans.

Zacate   Fodder or hay for animals, especially horses.

Zambo   A person of mixed African and Indian descent.

BIBLIOGRAPHY

UNPUBLISHED MANUSCRIPT SOURCES

Odd as it may sound, after having located, read, and tried to make sense of a pertinent manuscript source, there remains the problem of how to cite it, which at times can be far less straightforward than one first imagines. This is especially the case with archival documents, nowhere more of an issue than when working with materials housed in the Archivo General de Indias (AGI) in Seville. The great Spanish archive is without equal, but even the laudable measures taken to digitize and safeguard its bounty, which afford the possibility of consulting some of the collection without actually having to travel to Seville, do not eliminate the challenge of proper citation. Quite the contrary: the PARES (Portal de Archivos Españoles, http://pares.mcu.es) initiative of the Ministry of Education, Culture, and Sport, which allows researchers access to the AGI and scores of other Spanish repositories, often compounds the difficulty by entering data erroneously, most commonly with respect to date of composition, identity of authorship, geographical coverage, and subject matter. These infelicities are only added to by scanning procedures having been undertaken without due vigilance, meaning that documents, when retrieved electronically, can appear on computer screens so blurred as to be illegible. In other words, despite the enormous convenience (in theory) of online inquiry, nothing can rival working in the Seville archive, or any other for that matter, and perusing documentary evidence "in situ." In some cases, the existence of digitized versions of original sources actually precludes access to the original, as is regrettably the policy currently in place at the AGI (see chapter 14, footnote 28). Furthermore, not all AGI materials that have been digitized—presently estimated at some 7 percent of the archive's holdings— are available for research purposes via PARES. This is the case with holdings in the AGI cataloged under "Mapas y Planos," many of which are not on PARES. The ones that are, alas, are often "maps and plans" of very low resolution, their utility further impeded by a diagonal watermark that covers up cartographic features or that obliterates entirely key words and thus compromises textual understanding.

In compiling our list of unpublished manuscript sources, we have endeavored to record their whereabouts and characteristics as precisely as possible. While document titles are rendered, for the most part, in Spanish, we resort also to English, usually for the sake of clarity or comprehensiveness, when (for example) no title has been bestowed on an item either by the person(s) who first composed it or by anyone responsible for its subsequent handling. Researchers interested in perusing documents for their own purposes, we trust, will have minimal difficulty tracking them down. Patience and perseverance, however, are called for if the source we cite happens to be filed in one of the thick *legajos* (veritable bundles of documents) in the AGI, where making a catalog of contents by folio numbers has not been standard procedure. When it is possible to furnish an exact date, we do so by noting the month, day, and year of composition in that order. This, however, is not always possible; in some instances we have to settle for the year alone, if the data allow. We must also warn that documents available to us when we first started working decades ago in the Archivo General de Centro América (AGCA) in Guatemala City may no longer be extant. The loss of such documentation—see Kramer, Lovell, and Lutz (2011) for further details—represents a tragic pillage of patrimony that makes initiatives such as PARES, human error in entering data notwithstanding, a matter of priority, if not urgency. "What is history," asks a protagonist in J. M. Coetzee's novel *Elizabeth Costello* (2003), "but a story made up of the air that we tell ourselves?" We beg to differ. Oral traditions of all kinds offer valuable and credible testimony. But written texts, maps, and other such sources, if they can be protected and preserved, remain our investigative materials of preference—defects, deficiencies, and all. And subject, of course, always to rigorous scholarly scrutiny.

We extend first mention to the AGI, followed by the AGCA. Thereafter we bring to the attention of readers items that may be found in the Archivo General de Simancas, near Valladolid, in Spain; the Biblioteca del Palacio Real in Madrid; the Biblioteca Provincial in Córdoba, Spain; the Hispanic Society of America in New York City; the Nettie Lee Benson Library at the University of Texas at Austin; the John Carter Brown Library in Providence, Rhode Island; the Real Academia de la Historia in Madrid; and the Special Collections of the University of Glasgow, Scotland. A list of published sources, some of them more readily available than others, follows our inventory of unpublished ones.

Archivo General de Indias

Audiencia de Guatemala

Guatemala 9A
Alonso López de Cerrato to the Crown (1/26/1550).

Pedro Ramírez de Quiñones to the Council of the Indies (5/20/1556).

Guatemala 10
Pedro de Villalobos to the Crown (10/5/1575).

Eugenio de Salazar to the Crown (3/15/1578).

Francisco de Valverde to the Crown (1579).

Pedro de Liévano to the Crown (11/5/1582).

"Razón de las tasaciones que se han hecho después que el presidente [Diego García de Valverde] vino a esta audiencia, de pueblos de su distrito con lo que antes tributaban" (1582).

Diego García de Valverde to the Crown (11/5/1582).

"Información hecha sobre el contenido de dos cédulas reales" (11/10/1582).

Audiencia of Guatemala to the Crown (4/8/1584).

Guatemala 39
Andrés de Cereceda to the Crown (8/31/1535).

"Descripción de los corregimientos que a de aver en gobernación de Guatemala" (1575).

Guatemala 41
Jorge de Alvarado to the Crown (2/26/1534).

Guatemala 45
"Cuenta y tasación de los indios tributarios del pueblo de Chimaltenango, encomendado a Antonio Ortiz" (2/20/1562).

"Tasación y cuenta de los indios tributarios de San Pedro de Zacatepeque, encomendado a Bernal Díaz del Castillo" (3/3/1562).

"Tasación y cuenta de indios tributarios de San Juan Zacatepeque" (3/3/1562).

"Juan Martínez de Landecho, presidente de la Audiencia de Guatemala, sobre tributarios y tributos que se darán a los encomenderos en el pueblo de Comalapa" (7/12/1562).

"Tasación y cuenta de los indios tributarios del pueblo de Petapa y de su barrio de Santa Inés" (1562).

"Tasación y cuenta de los indios tributarios de Zumpango" (1562).

"Tasación y cuenta de los indios tributarios de San Juan de la Laguna Amatitlán, encomendado a Juan Lobo el menor" (1562).

Guatemala 51
Francisco de Miranda to the Crown (3/1579).

Guatemala 52
Diego de Garcés to the Crown (1560).

Guatemala 53
Principales and caciques of Santiago Atitlán to the Crown (2/1/1571).

Guatemala 98
"Tasación de tributos de Comalapa" (1613)

Guatemala 116
Concerning Juan Pérez Dardón (1570).

Guatemala 128
"Las tasaciones de los pueblos de los términos y jurisdicción de la ciudad de Santiago de Guatemala" (1548–51).

"Relación y forma que el Licenciado Palacios, Oidor de la Real Audiencia de Guatemala, hizo para los que hubiesen de visitar, contar, tasar y repartir en las provincias de este distrito" (ca. 1575).

Guatemala 159
Andrés de las Navas et al., "Testimonio de los autos hechos sobre la perdición general de los indios de estas provincias y frangentes continuos que amenazan su libertad" (1689).

Guatemala 163
Antonio de Hervias to the Crown (1583).

Juan Fernández Rosillo to the Crown (3/20/1600).

Guatemala 168
Fray Francisco de la Parra to the Crown (7/15/1549).

Fray Tomás de Cárdenas and Fray Juan de Torres to the Crown (12/6/1555).

Fray Tomás de Cárdenas to the Crown (9/3/1566).

"Autos hecho sobre la graduación de salarios que tienen los ministros de esta real audiencia en las condenaciones de penas de cámara, gastos de justicia estrados de ella, a pedimiento del capitán Cristóbal Fernández de Rivera, receptor y depositario general de ellas" (1684).

Guatemala 169
"Memoria de los pueblos que la Orden de San Francisco tiene en administración" (1575).

Guatemala 171
"Fray Bernaldino Pérez de la Orden de San Francisco sobre que se le dé licencia para llevar religiosos a la provincia de Guatemala y Chiapas" (1581).

Guatemala 172
"Relación de la Provincia de la Verapaz" (12/10/1596).

Guatemala 394
"Memoria que envió el licenciado Mendiola Artiaga, fiscal de Guatemala" (12/16/1570).

Guatemala 560
"Testimonio para averiguar el aumento de tributarios" (1768–69).

"Estado que manifiesta . . . la última *Numeración de tributarios*" (1778)

Guatemala 948
"Sobre la visita general de Pedro Cortés y Larraz" (1771–74).

Contaduría

Contaduría 815
"Razón de las ciudades, villas y lugares vecindarios y tributarios de que se componen las provincias del distrito de esta Audiencia" (1683).

Contaduría 969
"Lo que se a cobrado del servicio que los naturales destas provincias se han hecho a
    Su Majestad de un tostón cada uno el año pasado noventa y cinco con algunos
    restos del año noventa y cuatro" (1594–95).

Contaduría 971A and 971B
Documents related to payments of the "terrazgo" land tax and fiscal obligations to
    the Church.

Contaduría 973
Documents related to payments of the "servicio del tostón" (1624–1710).

Contaduría 976
Documents related to payments of the "servicio del tostón" (1722–26).

Contaduría 977
Documents related to payments of the "servicio del tostón" (1719).

Indiferente General

Indiferente General 857
"Traslado de algunas tasaciones de los pueblos de los tenientes" (1538).
Population figures recorded by Juan de Estrada (ca. 1550).

Indiferente General 1525
"Vista política de la América española y sumario de su población según los registros
    de la secretaría del Consejo de Indias" (1772).

Justicia

Justicia 285
"Pleito sobre el pueblo de Acazaguastlán" (1564).

Justicia 286
"Juan Rodríguez Cabrillo contra Francisco de la Cueva, teniente de gobernador
    por el adelantado Pedro de Alvarado, sobre la posesión de las encomiendas de
    Jumaytepeque y Tacuba" (1542–68).

Documents related to the "tasaciones de tributos" carried out by Diego de Herrera,
    Pedro Ramírez de Quiñones, and Juan Rogel (1543–48).

Justicia 291
Documents related to "los yndios mexicanos, tlaxcaltecas, çapotecas y otros" (1564).

Justicia 295
"Residencia tomada al adelantado Pedro de Alvarado, gobernador de la provincia de
    Guatemala; a su teniente, Jorge de Alvarado; y al contador Francisco de Zorrilla,
    por el licenciado Alonso de Maldonado, oidor de la Audiencia de México" (1535).

Justicia 299A
"Residencia tomada a los licenciados Alonso de Maldonado, Pedro Ramírez de Quiñones,
    Diego de Herrera y Juan Rogel, presidente y oidores de la Audiencia de Guatemala,

y a sus oficiales: Diego de Quijada, fiscal; Martín de Villalobos, alguacil mayor y fiscal; Diego de Robledo, secretario; Juan de Astroqui, escribano; Pedro Méndez, procurador de la ciudad de Gracias a Dios; Vicente Vargas, chanciller de la Audiencia; y a los oficiales de la Real Hacienda y al factor Juan de Lerma, por el licenciado Alonso López de Cerrato, juez nombrado para este efecto" (1548–50).

Justicia 301
"Residencia tomada a los licenciados Alonso López de Cerrato, Tomás López, Diego de Herrera y Juan Rogel, presidente y oidores de esta Audiencia de Guatemala, por el doctor Antonio Rodríguez de Quesada, oidor de la Audiencia de México, juez nombrado para este efecto" (1555).

Justicia 332
"Tasaciones hechas por el licenciado Briceño en la Provincia de Guatemala en los pueblos de su Majestad" (1566)

Justicia 1031
"Juan de Espinar con Pedro de Alvarado sobre el pueblo de Huehuetenango" (1537–40).

Patronato Real

Patronato 54-5-2
"Probanza de Diego de Rojas" (1528).

Patronato 58-1-4
"Información de los méritos y servicios de Pedro González Nájera" (1565).

Patronato 59-1-1
"Probanza de los méritos y servicios de Cristóbal Lobo" (1549).

Patronato 59-1-3
"Sobre los méritos y servicios de Pedro González Nájera" (1549).

Patronato 60-5-3
"Información de los méritos y servicios del adelantado Pedro de Alvarado" (11/9/1556).

Patronato 60-5-6
Probanza de los méritos y servicios de Francisco de Utiel (1556).

Patronato 66-1-3
"Probanza de Pedro González Nájera" (1564).

Patronato 68-2-3
"Información de los méritos y servicios de Juan Páez" (1568).

Patronato 70-1-7
"Información de los méritos y servicios de Juan Pérez Dardón, Lorenzo de Godoy y Bartolomé de Medina."

Patronato 70-1-8
"Probanza de méritos y servicios de Cristóbal de la Cueva" (1570).

Patronato 75-2-5
"Información de los méritos y servicios de Juan Pérez Dardón, Francisco de Monterroso y Gonzalo de Ovalle, en la conquista y pacificación de las provincias de Guatemala" (1578).

Patronato 180-1-64
"Autos hechos sobre la tasación de los indios" (8/30/1535).

Patronato 183-1-1
"Relación formada por la Audiencia de Guatemala de todos los pueblos de su jurisdicción y modo de administrar en ellos justicia" (3/20/1583)

Patronato 275-1-19
"Copia de la Real Provisión por la que se manda al licenciado Alonso de Maldonado, oidor de la Audiencia de Nueva España, tomar la residencia al adelantado don Pedro de Alvarado, gobernador de la provincia de Guatemala" (10/27/1535).

Mapas y Planos de Guatemala

Guatemala 74 (Petapa) to Guatemala 186 (Nejapa)
A collection of maps that constitute a cartographic appendix to the "visita general" undertaken by Archbishop Pedro Cortés y Larraz (see Guatemala 948 above) between 1768 and 1770.

Archivo General de Centro América

A1, legajo 4119, expediente 32636
"Autos que siguen diferentes indios del valle de esta ciudad, salineros en la costa de Esquintepeque" (1675).

A1, legajo 5942, expediente 51995
Documents related to land rights and local governance in Sacapulas (1572).

A1, legajo 6021, expediente 53084
Documents related to a land dispute in the late eighteenth century between San Francisco and Santo Tomás, two *parcialidades* in Sacapulas, over land rights and boundaries. Other documents pertaining to the case may also be found in legajo 6042, expediente 53327; and legajo 6060, expediente 53305.

A1, legajo 6025, expediente 53126
Documents related to land rights and access to resources in Sacapulas in the late eighteenth century, involving in particular the *parcialidades* Santiago, San Sebastián, and San Pedro.

A1, legajo 6037, expediente 53257
Documents related to land rights and boundaries in Sacapulas in the late eighteenth century.

A1, legajo 6037, expediente 53258
Testimony of Andrés Henríquez, parish priest of Sacapulas, concerning the land rights and boundaries of the six different *parcialidades* that make up the town (1786).

A1, legajo 6064, expediente 53974
"Autos de los indios de Comalapa, sobre que don Miguel Casique les impide la labranza
    de sus sales" (1601).

A1.29, legajo 4678, expediente 40244
"Probanza de Juan de Espinar (1539).

A3.16, legajo 249, expediente 5036
Marcos Castañeda, *comisionado*, to the Alcalde Mayor of Totonicapán and Huehue-
    tenango (5/5/1806).

A3.16, legajo 1600, expediente 26371
"Cuenta de los naturales de todos los pueblos de la Verapaz, hecha por el alcalde mayor
    Pedro de Casa de Avante y Gamboa" (1570–71).

A3.16, legajo 1601, expediente 26391
Documents related to tribute payment, by *parcialidad*, at Sacapulas in the seventeenth
    century.

A3.16, legajo 2327, expediente 34374
"Número de tributarios" (1806).

A3.16, legajo 2797, expediente 40466
A register of forty-three "tasaciones de tributos" undertaken during the presidency of
    Alonso López de Cerrato (1553–54).

A3.2, legajo 825, expediente 15207
"Padrón de los indios tributarios" (1681).

Other Repositories

Archivo General de Simancas

Simancas, legajo 6, número 53
"Sumario general de lo que valen todas las Indias a Su Majestad" (1558).

Biblioteca del Palacio Real

Manuscript 175
"Relación de Fray Rafael de Luján" and "Memoria de los frailes menores que hay en la
    provincia de Guatemala" (1604).

Biblioteca Provincial de Córdoba

Manuscript 128
Francisco de Ximénez, "Historia de la Provincia de San Vicente de Chiapa y Guatemala"
    (1715–20).

Hispanic Society of America

"Libro segundo de cabildo," Hiersemann 418/239 (5/27/1530–9/9/1541).

"Libro tercero de cabildo," Hiersemann 418/239 (9/14/1541–9/4/1553).

"Mapas de varias provincias de la República de Guatemala," Hiersemann 418/242 (ca. 1768–70).

John Carter Brown Library

"Vocabulario copioso de las lenguas cakchikel y jiche" (n.d.).

Nettie Lee Benson Library

J. García Icazbalceta Collection, vol. 20, no. 1
"Relación de los caciques y número de yndios que hay en Guatemala, hecha por el deán y cabildo, de orden de Su Majestad" (4/21/1572).

Real Academia de la Historia

Colección Muñoz, A 106
"Probanza de Luis de Soto" (1533).

Colección Muñoz, A 107
Concerning the *tasación de tributos* proposed by Alonso de Maldonado, tribute assessments that Pedro de Alvarado opposed being carried out (ca. 1535).

Colección Muñoz, A 108
Concerning a letter written by Bishop Francisco Marroquín to the King, dated 1/20/1539, related to the tribute assessments undertaken by himself and Alonso de Maldonado.

Collección Muñoz, A 109
Concerning a letter written by Bishop Francisco Marroquín to the King, dated 8/10/1541, related to tribute assessments and notifying the monarch of the death of Pedro de Alvarado.

Colección Muñoz, A 111
Concerning a letter written by Bishop Marroquín to the King, dated 3/15/1545, related to the difficulties involved in undertaking comprehensive tribute assessments.

Papeles del Consejo de Indias, D-95
Copy of Mendiola Artiaga's "Memoria de partidos" (see AGI, Guatemala 394, above).

Papeles del Consejo de Indias, 9-4663
Copy of Francisco de Valverde's "Relación geográfica" (8/28/1590).

Papeles del Consejo de Indias, 9-29-2
"Memoria de los curatos, pueblos, curas, doctrineros, coadjutores y feligreses e idiomas de que se compone el Obispado de Goathemala" (1750).

University of Glasgow Special Collections

Hunter 242 U.3.15
Manuscript copy of Diego Muñoz Camargo's "Historia de Tlaxcala" (1582).

PUBLISHED SOURCES

The items below, forming part of the holdings either of a university library or our own personal collections, were consulted in conventional print format. Two research libraries of inestimable assistance were those of the Centro de Investigaciones Regionales de Mesoamérica (CIRMA) in Antigua, Guatemala, and the Escuela de Estudios Hispano-Americanos in Seville, Spain. We thank the staff of these two research libraries in particular for their assistance and advice. Some of the book titles we reference, and a good many of the journals too, are now available for consultation online.

Akkeren, Ruud van. 2007. *La visión indígena de la conquista*. Guatemala: Serviprensa.

Altman, Ida. 1989. *Emigrants and Society: Extremadura and America in the Sixteenth Century*. Berkeley and Los Angeles: University of California Press.

———. 2010. *The War for Mexico's West: Indians and Spaniards in New Galicia, 1524–1550*. Albuquerque: University of New Mexico Press.

Amaroli, Paul. 1991. "Linderos y geografía económica de Cuscatlán, provincia pipil del territorio de El Salvador." *Mesoamérica* 21:41–70.

Anghiera, Pietro Martire d'. [1530] 1912. *De Orbe Novo: The Eight Decades of Peter Martyr d'Anghera*. Translated and edited by Francis Augustus MacNutt. 2 vols. New York: G. P. Putnam's Sons.

Anglería, Pedro Mártir de. [1530] 1944. *De Orbe Novo*. Buenos Aires: Editorial Bajel. See also Anghiera, Pietro Martire d'.

Annis, Sheldon. 1987. *God and Production in a Guatemalan Town*. Austin: University of Texas Press.

Arévalo, Rafael de, ed. 1932. *Libro de actas del ayuntamiento de la ciudad de Santiago de Guatemala, desde la fundación de la misma ciudad en 1524 hasta 1530*. Guatemala: Tipografía Nacional.

Asselbergs, Florine. 2004. *Conquered Conquistadors: The* Lienzo de Quauhquechollan—*A Nahua Vision of the Conquest of Guatemala*. Leiden: CNWS.

———. 2008. *Conquered Conquistadors: The* Lienzo de Quauhquechollan—*A Nahua Vision of the Conquest of Guatemala*. Boulder: University Press of Colorado.

———. 2010. *Los conquistadores conquistados: El* Lienzo de Quauhquechollan—*Una visión nahua de la conquista de Guatemala*. Translated by Eddy H. Gaytán. South Woodstock, Vt.: Plumsock Mesoamerican Studies.

Barón Castro, Rodolfo. 1942. *La población de El Salvador*. Madrid: Consejo Superior de Investigaciones Científicas, Instituto Gonzalo Fernández de Oviedo.

———. 1943. *Pedro de Alvarado*. Colección Vidas, 9. Madrid: Ediciones Atlas.

Bergmann, John F. 1958. "The Cultural Geography of Cacao in Aboriginal Middle America and its Commercialization in Early Guatemala." PhD diss.,University of California, Los Angeles.

———. 1969. "The Distribution of Cacao Cultivation in Pre-Columbian America." *Annals of the Association of American Geographers* 59 (1): 85–96.

Bermúdez Plata, Cristóbal. 1940–46. *Catálogo de pasajeros a Indias durante los siglos XVI, XVII y XVIII*. 3 vols. Seville: Imprenta Editorial de la Gavidia.

Bertrand, Michel. 1982. "Demographic Study of the Rabinal and El Chixoy Regions of Guatemala." In *The Historical Demography of Highland Guatemala,* edited by Robert M. Carmack, John D. Early, and Christopher H. Lutz, 65–75. Albany: Institute for Mesoamerican Studies, State University of New York.

———. 1987. *Terre et Société Coloniale: Les Communautés Maya-Quiché de la Région de Rabinal du XVIe au XIXe Siècle.* Études Mesoamericaines 14. Mexico: Centre d'Études Mexicaines et Centraméricaines.

Blasco, Julio Martín, and Jesús María García Añoveros, eds. 2001. *Descripción geográfico-moral de la diócesis de Goathemala, 1768–1770, hecha por su arzobispo, Pedro Cortés y Larraz.* Madrid: Consejo Superior de Investigaciones Científicas.

Borah, Woodrow. 1954. *Early Colonial Trade and Navigation between Mexico and Peru.* Ibero-Americana 38. Berkeley and Los Angeles: University of California Press.

———. 1983. *Justice by Insurance: The General Indian Court of Colonial Mexico and the Legal Aides of the Half-Real.* Berkeley and Los Angeles: University of California Press.

Borah, Woodrow, and Sherburne F. Cook. 1960. *The Population of Central Mexico in 1548: An Analysis of the Suma de Visitas de Pueblos.* Ibero-Americana 43. Berkeley and Los Angeles: University of California Press.

———. 1963. *The Aboriginal Population of Central Mexico on the Eve of the Spanish Conquest.* Ibero-Americana 45. Berkeley and Los Angeles: University of California Press.

———. 1967. "New Demographic Research on the Sixteenth Century in Mexico." In *Latin American History: Essays on Its Study and Teaching, 1898–1965,* vol. 2, edited by Howard F. Cline, 717–22. Austin: University of Texas Press.

———. 1969. "Conquest and Population: A Demographic Approach to Mexican History." *Proceedings of the American Philosophical Society* 113 (2): 177–83.

Borg, Barbara E. 1986. "Ethnohistory of the Sacatepéquez Cakchiquel Maya, ca. 1450–1600 A.D." PhD diss., University of Missouri.

———. 1999. "Los Cakchiqueles." In *Historia general de Guatemala,* vol.1, *Época precolombina,* edited by Marion Popenoe de Hatch, 663–72. Guatemala: Fundación para la Cultura y el Desarrollo.

———. 2003. "Iximché and the Cakchiquels, ca. 1450–1540." In *Archaelogy and Ethnohistory of Iximché,* edited by C. Roger Nance, Stephen L. Whittington, and Barbara E. Borg, 17–38. Gainesville: University Press of Florida.

Borhegyi, S. F. 1965. "Archaeological Synthesis of the Guatemalan Highlands." In *Handbook of Middle American Indians,* vol. 2, 3–58. Austin: University of Texas Press.

Brinton, Daniel G., ed. and trans. 1885. *The Annals of the Cakchiquels.* Philadelphia: Library of Aboriginal American Literature.

Cambranes, J. C. [1985] 1996. *Café y campesinos: Los orígenes de la economía de plantación moderna en Guatemala, 1853–1897.* Madrid: Editorial Catriel.

Carmack, Robert M. 1968. *Toltec Influence on the Postclassic Culture History of Highland Guatemala.* Middle American Research Institute Publication 26. New Orleans: Middle American Research Institute.

———. 1973. *Quichean Civilization: The Ethnohistoric, Ethnographic, and Archaeological Sources.* Berkeley and Los Angeles: University of California Press.

————. 1977. "Ethnohistory of the Central Quiché: The Community of Utatlán." In *Archaeology and Ethnohistory of the Central Quiché,* edited by Robert M. Carmack and D. T. Wallace, 1–19. Institute for Mesoamerican Studies Publication 1. Albany: Institute for Mesoamerican Studies, State University of New York.

————. 1981. *The Quiché Mayas of Utatlán: The Evolution of a Highland Guatemala Kingdom.* Norman: University of Oklahoma Press.

————. 1982. "Social and Demographic Patterns in an Eighteenth-Century Census from Tecpanaco, Guatemala." In *The Historical Demography of Highland Guatemala,* edited by Robert M. Carmack, John D. Early, and Christopher H. Lutz, 139–50. Albany: Institute for Mesoamerican Studies, State University of New York.

————. 1995. *Rebels of Highland Guatemala: The Quiché-Mayas of Momostenango.* Norman: University of Oklahoma Press.

Carmack, Robert M., John D. Early, and Christopher H. Lutz, eds. 1982. *The Historical Demography of Highland Guatemala.* Albany: Institute for Mesoamerican Studies, State University of New York.

Carmack, Robert M., and Alfonso Efraín Tzaquitzal Zapeta. 1993. *Título de los señores Coyoy.* Guatemala: Comisión Interuniversitaria Guatemalteca de Conmemoración del Quinto Centenario del Descubrimiento de América.

Carrasco, Davíd, ed. 2001. *The Oxford Encyclopedia of Mesoamerican Cultures: The Civilizations of Mexico and Central America.* 3 vols. New York: Oxford University Press.

Censo Nacional de Población. 1880. Guatemala.

Cieza de León, Pedro de. [1553] 1998. *The Discovery and Conquest of Peru.* Edited and translated by Alexandra Parma Cook and Noble David Cook. Durham: Duke University Press.

Clendinnen, Inga. 1987. *Ambivalent Conquests: Maya and Spaniard in Yucatan, 1517–1570.* New York: Cambridge University Press.

Cline, Howard F. 1956. "Civil Congregation of the Western Chinantec, New Spain, 1599–1603." *The Americas* 12:115–37.

Coetzee, J. M. 2003. *Elizabeth Costello.* New York: Viking.

Collier, George Allen. 1975. *Fields of the Tzotzil: The Ecological Bases of Tradition in Highland Chiapas.* Austin: University of Texas Press.

Collins, Anne Cox. 1980. "Colonial Jacaltenango, Guatemala: The Formation of a Corporate Community." PhD diss., Tulane University.

Contreras, J. Daniel. 1965. "El último cacique de la Casa de Cavec."*Cuadernos de Antropología* 5:37–48.

————. 1971. "Notas para la historia de la conquista." *Estudios* 4:19–27.

————. 2004a. "Dos guerreros indígenas." In Contreras and Luján Muñoz, 65–76.

————. 2004b. "Sobre la fundación de Santiago de Guatemala y la rebelión de los kaqchikeles." In Contreras and Luján Muñoz, 45–64.

————. 2004c. "El Tinamit kaqchikel." In Contreras and Luján Muñoz, 35–44.

Contreras, J. Daniel, and Jorge Luján Muñoz. 2004. *El Memorial de Sololá y los inicios de la colonización en Guatemala.* Guatemala: Academia de Geografía e Historia de Guatemala.

Cook, Noble David. 1982. *The People of the Colca Valley: A Population Study.* Dellplain Latin American Studies, 9. Boulder, Colo.: Westview Press.

Cook, Noble David, and W. George Lovell, eds. [1992] 2001. *"Secret Judgments of God": Old World Disease in Colonial Spanish America.* Norman: University of Oklahoma Press.

Cook, Sherburne F., and Woodrow Borah. 1960. *The Indian Population of Central Mexico, 1531–1610.* Ibero-Americana 44. Berkeley and Los Angeles: University of California Press.

———. 1968. *The Population of the Mixteca Alta, 1520–1960.* Ibero-Americana 50. Berkeley and Los Angeles: University of California Press.

———. 1971. *Essays in Population History: Mexico and the Caribbean.* Vol. 1. Berkeley and Los Angeles: University of California Press.

———. 1974a. *Essays in Population History: Mexico and the Caribbean.* Vol. 2. Berkeley and Los Angeles: University of California Press.

———. 1974b. "The Population of Yucatan, 1517–1960." In *Essays in Population History: Mexico and the Caribbean,* vol. 2, edited by Sherburne F. Cook and Woodrow Borah, 1–179. Berkeley and Los Angeles: University of California Press.

———. 1979. *Essays in Population History: Mexico and California.* Vol. 3. Berkeley and Los Angeles: University of California Press.

Cook, Sherburne F., and Lesley Byrd Simpson. 1948. *The Population of Central Mexico in the Sixteenth Century.* Ibero-Americana 31. Berkeley and Los Angeles: University of California Press.

Cortés, Hernán. [1519–26] 1963. *Cartas y documentos.* Edited by Mario Hernández Sánchez-Barba. Mexico: Editorial Porrúa.

———. [1519–26] 1971. *Letters from Mexico.* Translated and edited by Anthony R. Pagden. New York: Grossman.

Cortés y Larraz, Pedro. [1768–70] 1958. *Descripción geográfico-moral de la diócesis de Goathemala.* Edited by Adrián Recinos. 2 vols. Guatemala: Sociedad de Geografía e Historia de Guatemala.

Cumberland, Charles C. 1968. *Mexico: The Struggle for Modernity.* New York: Oxford University Press.

Dakin, Karen, and Christopher H. Lutz. 1996. *Nuestro Pesar, Nuestra Aflicción—Tunetuliniliz, Tucucuca: Memorias en lengua náhuatl enviadas a Felipe II por indígenas del Valle de Guatemala hacia 1572.* Facsímiles de lingüística y filología nahuas 7. Mexico City and Antigua, Guatemala: Universidad Nacional Autónoma de México and Centro de Investigaciones Regionales de Mesoamérica.

Denevan, William M., ed. [1976] 1992. *The Native Population of the Americas in 1492.* 2nd ed rev. Madison: University of Wisconsin Press.

Díaz del Castillo, Bernal. [1632] 1853. *Conquista de Nueva España.* Madrid: Imprenta M. Rivadeneyra.

———. [1632] 1968. *Historia verdadera de la conquista de la Nueva España.* Mexico: Editorial Porrúa.

Editorial del Ejército. 1963. *La muerte de Tecún Umán: Estudio crítico del altiplano occidental de la República de Guatemala.* Guatemala City: Editorial del Ejército.

Enríquez Macías, Genoveva. 1989. "Nuevos documentos para la demografía histórica de la Audiencia de Guatemala a finales del siglo XVII." *Mesoamérica* 17:121–83.

Farriss, Nancy M. 1983. "Indians in Colonial Yucatan: Three Perspectives." In *Spaniards and Indians in Southeastern Mesoamerica: Essays on the History of Ethnic Relations,* edited by Murdo J. MacLeod and Robert Wasserstrom, 1–39. Lincoln: University of Nebraska Press.

Feldman, Lawrence H. 1982. "Verapaz Statistics." *Estudios de Cultura Maya* 14:299–310.

———. 1985. *A Tumpline Economy: Production and Distribution Systems in Sixteenth-Century Eastern Guatemala.* Culver City, Calif.: Labyrinthos.

———. 1992. *Indian Payment in Kind: The Sixteenth-Century Encomiendas of Guatemala.* Culver City, Calif.: Labyrinthos.

———, ed. and trans. 2000. *Lost Shores, Forgotten Peoples: Spanish Explorations of the South East Maya Lowlands.* Durham: Duke University Press.

Feldman, Lawrence H., and Gary Rex Walters. 1980. *The Anthropology Museum's Excavations in Southeastern Guatemala: Preliminary Reports.* Miscellaneous Publications in Anthropology 9. Columbia, Mo.: Museum of Anthropology, University of Missouri.

Fischer, Edward F., and R. McKenna Brown, eds. 1996. *Maya Cultural Activism in Guatemala.* Austin: University of Texas Press.

Foster, George M. 1960. *Culture and Conquest: America's Spanish Heritage.* Viking Fund Publications in Anthropology 27. New York: Wenner-Gren Foundation for Anthropological Research.

Fowler, William R. 1987. "Cacao, Indigo, and Coffee: Cash Crops in the History of El Salvador." *Research in Economic Anthropology* 8:139–67.

———. 1989. *The Cultural Evolution of Ancient Nahua Civilizations: The Pipil-Nicarao of Central America.* Norman: University of Oklahoma Press.

———. 1991. "The Political Economy of Indian Survival in Sixteenth-Century Izalco, El Salvador." In *Columbian Consequences: The Spanish Borderlands in Pan American Perspective,* vol. 3, edited by David Hurst Thomas, 187–204. Washington, D.C.: Smithsonian Institution Press.

Fry, Michael Forrest. 1988. "Agrarian Society in the Guatemalan Montaña, 1700–1840." PhD diss., Tulane University.

Fuentes, Carlos. [1985] 2001. *Latin America: At War with the Past.* Toronto: House of Anansi Press.

Fuentes y Guzmán, Francisco Antonio de. [1690–99] 1882–83. *Historia de Guatemala, ó Recordación florida.* Edited by Justo Zaragoza. Madrid: Luis Navarro.

———. [1690–99] 1932–33. *Recordación florida.* Edited by J. Antonio Villacorta. 3 vols. Guatemala: Sociedad de Geografía e Historia de Guatemala.

———. [1690–99] 1969–72. "Recordación florida." In *Obras históricas de don Francisco Antonio de Fuentes y Guzmán,* edited by Carmelo Sáenz de Santa María. 3 vols. Madrid: Ediciones Atlas.

Gall, Francis. 1961–62. *Diccionario geográfico de Guatemala.* 1st ed. 2 vols. Guatemala: Tipografía Nacional.

———. 1963. *"Título del Ajpop Huitzitzil Tzunún: Probanza de méritos de los de León y Cardona.* Guatemala: Editorial José de Pineda Ibarra.

———. 1967. "Probanzas del capitán Gonzalo de Alvarado, conquistador que fue de las provincias de Guatemala." *Anales de la Sociedad de Geografía e Historia de Guatemala* 1–2:192–228.

———. 1968. "La primera relación conocida de Pedro de Alvarado." *Anales de la Sociedad de Geografía e Historia de Guatemala* 41:62–97.

———. 1976–83. *Diccionario geográfico de Guatemala*. 2nd ed. 4 vols. Guatemala: Instituto Geográfico Nacional.

Gálvez Borrell, Víctor, and Alberto Esquit Choy. 1997. *The Mayan Movement Today: Issues of Indigenous Culture and Development in Guatemala*. Guatemala: Facultad Latinoamericana de Ciencias Sociales.

García Añoveros, Jesús María. 1987a. "Don Pedro de Alvarado: Las fuentes históricas, documentación, crónicas y bibliografía existente." *Mesoamérica* 15:243–82.

———. 1987b. *Pedro de Alvarado*. Madrid: Historia 16, Ediciones Quorum.

———. 1987c. *Población y estado sociorreligioso de la diócesis de Guatemala en el último tercio del siglo XVIII*. Guatemala: Editorial Universitaria, Universidad de San Carlos de Guatemala.

García de Palacios, Diego. [1576, 1860] 1985. *Letter to the King of Spain: Being a Description of the Ancient Provinces of Guazacapan, Izalco, Cuscatlan, and Chiquimula, in the Audiencia of Guatemala*. Translated and with notes by Ephraim G. Squier, with additional notes by Alexander von Frantzius and Frank E. Comparato, editor. Culver City, Calif.: Labyrinthos.

Gasco, Janine. 1987. "Cacao and the Economic Integration of Native Society in Colonial Soconusco, New Spain." PhD diss., University of California, Santa Barbara.

———. 1991. "Indian Survival and Ladinoization in Colonial Soconusco." In *Columbian Consequences: The Spanish Borderlands in Pan-American Perspective*, vol. 3, edited by David Hurst Thomas, 301–18. Washington, D.C.: Smithsonian Institution Press.

Gerhard, Peter. 1972. *A Guide to the Historical Geography of New Spain*. Cambridge: Cambridge University Press.

———. 1979. *The Southeast Frontier of New Spain*. Princeton, N.J.: Princeton University Press.

Gibson, Charles. 1952. *Tlaxcala in the Sixteenth Century*. New Haven, Conn.: Yale University Press.

———. 1964. *The Aztecs Under Spanish Rule: A History of the Indians of the Valley of Mexico, 1519–1810*. Stanford, Calif.: Stanford University Press.

———. 1966. *Spain in America*. New York: Harper and Row.

———. 1974. Review of *Spanish Central America: A Socioeconomic History, 1520–1720*, by Murdo J. MacLeod. *Hispanic American Historical Review* 54 (3): 505–507.

Henige, David. 1998. *Numbers from Nowhere: The American Indian Contact Population Debate*. Norman: University of Oklahoma Press.

Herrera, Robinson A. 2003. *Natives, Europeans, and Africans in Sixteenth-Century Santiago de Guatemala*. Austin: University of Texas Press.

———. 2007. "Concubines and Wives: Reinterpreting Native-Spanish Intimate Unions in Sixteenth-Century Guatemala." In *Indian Conquistadors: Indigenous Allies in the Conquest of Mesoamerica*, edited by Laura Matthew and Michel R. Oudijk, 127–44. Norman: University of Oklahoma Press.

Hill, Robert M. 1992. *Colonial Cakchiquels: Highland Maya Adaptation to Spanish Rule, 1600–1700*. Forth Worth, Tx.: Harcourt Brace Jovanovich.

———. 1996. "Eastern Chajoma (Cakchiquel) Political Geography: Ethnohistorical and Archaeological Contributions to the Study of a Late Postclassic Highland Maya Polity." *Ancient Mesoamerica* 7:63–87.

Hill, Robert M., and John Monaghan. 1987. *Continuities in Highland Maya Social Organization: Ethnohistory in Sacapulas, Guatemala*. Philadelphia: University of Pennsylvania Press.

Isagoge histórica apologética de las Indias Occidentales. [1711] 1935. Guatemala: Sociedad de Geografía e Historia de Guatemala.

Johannessen, Carl L. 1963. *Savannas of Interior Honduras*. Ibero-Americana 46. Berkeley and Los Angeles: University of California Press.

Jones, Grant D. 1983. "The Last Maya Frontiers of Colonial Yucatan." In *Spaniards and Indians in Southeastern Mesoamerica: Essays on the History of Ethnic Relations*, edited by Murdo J. MacLeod and Robert Wasserstrom, 64–91. Lincoln: University of Nebraska Press.

———. 1989. *Maya Resistance to Spanish Rule: Time and History on a Colonial Frontier*. Albuquerque: University of New Mexico Press.

———. 1998. *The Conquest of the Last Maya Kingdom*. Stanford, Calif.: Stanford University Press.

Juarros, Domingo. [1808] 1981. *Compendio de la historia de la ciudad de Guatemala*. Guatemala City: Editorial Piedra Santa.

Kelley, Jane, Marsha P. Hanen, and William R. Fowler. 1988. *Cihuatán, El Salvador: A Study in Intrasite Variability*. Vanderbilt University Publications in Anthropology 35. Nashville, Tenn.: Vanderbilt University.

Kelly, John E. 1932. *Pedro de Alvarado, Conquistador*. Princeton, N.J.: Princeton University Press.

Kramer, Wendy. 1994. *Encomienda Politics in Early Colonial Guatemala, 1524–1544: Dividing the Spoils*. Dellplain Latin American Studies 31. Boulder, Colo.: Westview Press.

Kramer, Wendy, W. George Lovell, and Christopher H. Lutz. 1986. "Las tasaciones de tributos de Francisco Marroquín y Alonso de Maldonado, 1536–1541." *Mesoamérica* 12:357–94.

———. 1990. "Encomienda and Settlement: Towards a Historical Geography of Early Colonial Guatemala." *Yearbook of the Conference of Latin Americanist Geographers* 16:67–72.

———. 1991. "Fire in the Mountains: Juan de Espinar and the Indians of Huehuetenango, 1525–1560." In *Columbian Consequences*, vol. 3, edited by David Hurst Thomas, 263–82. Washington, D.C.: Smithsonian Institution.

———. 2011. "Hemorragia en los archivos: Reflexiones sobre la pérdida de documentos coloniales guatemaltecos, tesoros de un país despojado." *Mesoamérica* 53:236–45.

Kubler, George. 1942. "Population Movements in Mexico, 1520–1600." *Hispanic American Historical Review* 22 (4): 606–43.

La Farge, Oliver. 1940. "Maya Ethnology: The Sequence of Cultures." In *The Maya and Their Neighbors*, edited by Clarence L. Hay, Ralph L. Linton, Samuel K. Lothrop, et al., 282–91. New York: D. Appleton-Century.

Langenberg, Inge. 1979. "Urbanización y cambio social: El translado de la Ciudad de Guatemala, 1773–1824." *Anuario de Estudios Americanos* 36:351–74.

———. 1981. *Urbanisation und Bevölkerungsstruktur der Stadt Guatemala in der ausgehenden Kolonialzeit: Eine sozialhistorische Analyse der Stadtverlegung und ihrer Auswirkungen auf die demographische, berufliche und soziale Gliederung der Bevölkerung (1773–1824)*. Vol. 9. Lateinamerikanische Forschungen. Vienna, Cologne, and Weimar: Böhlau Verlag.

Las Casas, Bartolomé de. [1552] 1982. *Brevísima relación de la destrucción de las Indias*. Madrid: Cátedra.

Leighly, John L., ed. 1963. *Land and Life: A Selection from the Writings of Carl Ortwin Sauer*. Berkeley and Los Angeles: University of California Press.

Lockhart, James. 1969. "Encomienda and Hacienda: The Evolution of the Great Estate in the Spanish Indies." *Hispanic American Historical Review* 49 (3): 411–29.

Lokken, Paul. 2000. "From Black to Ladino: People of African Descent, *Mestizaje*, and Racial Hierarchy in Rural Colonial Guatemala." PhD diss., University of Florida.

———. 2008. "Génesis de una comunidad afro-indígena en Guatemala: La Villa de San Diego de la Gomera en el siglo XVII." *Mesoamérica* 50:37–65.

———. 2013. "From the 'Kingdom of Angola' to Santiago de Guatemala: The Portuguese Asientos and Spanish Central America, 1595–1640." *Hispanic American Historical Review* 93 (2): 171–203.

López de Gómara, Francisco. [1554] 1932. *Cortés: The Life of the Conqueror by His Secretary*. Translated and edited by Lesley Byrd Simpson. Berkeley and Los Angeles: University of California Press.

———. [1552] 1922. *Historia general de las Indias*. 2 vols. Biblioteca de Autores Españoles 22. Madrid: Ediciones Calpe.

López de Velasco, Juan. [1571–74] 1971. *Geografía y descripción universal de las Indias*. Edited by Marcos Jiménez de la Espada and María del Carmen González Muñoz. Biblioteca de Autores Españoles 248. Madrid: Ediciones Atlas.

Lovell, W. George. [1985] 2005. *Conquest and Survival in Colonial Guatemala: A Historical Geography of the Cuchumatán Highlands, 1500–1821*. 3rd ed. rev. Montreal and Kingston: McGill-Queen's University Press.

———. 1988. "Surviving Conquest: The Maya of Guatemala in Historical Perspective." *Latin American Research Review* 23 (2): 25–57.

———. 1990. *Conquista y cambio cultural: La sierra de los Cuchumatanes de Guatemala, 1500–1821*. Antigua, Guatemala, and South Woodstock, Vt.: Centro de Investigaciones Regionales de Mesoamérica and Plumsock Mesoamerican Studies.

———. [1992] 2001. "Disease and Depopulation in Early Colonial Guatemala." In *"Secret Judgments of God": Old World Disease in Colonial Spanish America*, edited by Noble David Cook and W. George Lovell, 49–83. Norman: University of Oklahoma Press.

———. [1995] 2010. *A Beauty That Hurts: Life and Death in Guatemala.* 2nd ed. rev. Austin: University of Texas Press.

———. 2000. "The Highland Maya." In *The Cambridge History of the Native Peoples of the Americas,* edited by Richard E. W. Adams and Murdo J. MacLeod, vol. 2, pt. 2, *Mesoamerica,* 392–442. Cambridge: Cambridge University Press.

———. 2002. Review of *Numbers from Nowhere* by David Henige. *Ethnohistory* 49 (2): 468–70.

———. 2004. "A Measure of Maturity: Advances and Achievements in Mesoamerican Studies." *Journal of Historical Geography* 30:173–78.

———. 2009. Review of *Indian Conquistadors* by Laura E. Matthew and Michel R. Oudijk, eds., *Ethnohistory* 56 (4): 749–53.

Lovell, W. George, and Christopher H. Lutz. 1994. "Conquest and Population: Maya Demography in Historical Perspective." *Latin American Research Review* 29 (2): 133–40.

———. 1995. *Demography and Empire: A Guide to the Population History of Spanish Central America, 1500–1821.* Dellplain Latin American Studies 33. Boulder, Colo.: Westview Press.

———. 2000. *Demografía e imperio: Guía para la historia de la población de la América Central Española, 1500–1821.* Guatemala: Editorial Universitaria, Universidad de San Carlos de Guatemala.

———. 2001. "Pedro de Alvarado and the Conquest of Guatemala, 1522–1524." In *The Past and Present Maya: Essays in Honor of Robert M. Carmack,* edited by John M. Weeks, 47–62. Lancaster, Calif.: Labyrinthos.

———. 2003. "Perfil etnodemográfico de la Audiencia de Guatemala." *Revista de Indias* 63 (227): 157–74 and 63 (229): 759–64.

Lovell, W. George, Christopher H. Lutz, and William R. Swezey. 1984. "The Indian Population of Southern Guatemala, 1549–1551: An Analysis of López de Cerrato's *Tasaciones de tributos.*" *The Americas* 40 (4): 459–78.

Lovell, W. George, and William R. Swezey. 1981. "La población del sur de Guatemala al momento de la conquista española." *Antropología e Historia de Guatemala* (2nd series) 3: 43–54.

———. 1982. "The Population of Southern Guatemala at Spanish Contact." *Canadian Journal of Anthropology* 3 (1): 71–84.

———. 1984. "La población del sur de Guatemala en vísperas de la conquista española." In *Investigaciones Recientes en el Área Maya: Proceedings of the XVII Mesa Redonda of the Sociedad Mexicana de Antropología.* Vol. 2, 329–40. Mexico City: Sociedad Mexicana de Antropología.

———. 1990. "Indian Migration and Community Formation: An Analysis of *Congregación* in Colonial Guatemala." In *Migration in Colonial Latin America,* edited by David J. Robinson, 18–40. Cambridge: Cambridge University Press.

Luján Muñoz, Jorge. 1976. "Fundación de villas de ladinos en Guatemala en el último tercio del siglo XVIII." *Revista de Indias* 36 (145–46): 51–81.

———. 1985. "Cambios en la estructura familiar de los indígenas pokomanes de Petapa (Guatemala) en la primera mitad del siglo XVI." *Mesoamérica* 10:355–69.

————. 1988. *Agricultura, mercado y sociedad en el Corregimiento del Valle de Guatemala, 1670–1680.* Guatemala: Dirección General de Investigaciones, Universidad de San Carlos de Guatemala.

————. 1993. "Balance." In *Historia de Guatemala*, vol. 2, *Dominación española: Desde la conquista hasta 1700*, edited by Ernesto Chinchilla Aguilar, 803–12. Guatemala: Fundación para la Cultura y el Desarrollo.

————. 1995. "Centro y periferia en el Reino de Guatemala durante la dominación española." *Anales de la Academia de Geografía e Historia de Guatemala* 70:7–20.

————. 2003. "El sentido urbano de la colonización española: El proceso fundacional en el Reino de Guatemala." *Anales de la Academia de Geografía e Historia de Guatemala* 78:49–57.

————. 2004. "Historia del Memorial de Sololá." In Contreras and Luján Muñoz, 4–18.

————. 2005. "Un documento demográfico de la Arquidiócesis de Guatemala de 1812." *Anales de la Academia de Geografía e Historia de Guatemala* 80:121–40.

————. 2006. *Relaciones geográficas e históricas del siglo XVIII del Reino de Guatemala.* Guatemala: Universidad del Valle de Guatemala.

————. 2011, ed. *Atlas histórico de Guatemala.* Guatemala: Academia de Geografía e Historia de Guatemala.

Luján Muñoz, Jorge, and Horacio Cabezas Carcache. 1993. "La conquista." In *Historia general de Guatemala*, vol. 2, *Dominación española: Desde la conquista hasta 1700*, edited by Ernesto Chinchilla Aguilar, 47–74. Guatemala: Fundación para la Cultura y el Desarrollo.

Lutz, Christopher H. 1981. "Population Change in the Quinizilapa Valley, Guatemala, 1530–1770." In *Studies in Spanish American Population History*, edited by David J. Robinson, 175–94. Boulder, Colo.: Westview Press.

————. [1982] 1984. *Historia sociodemográfica de Santiago de Guatemala, 1541–1773.* Antigua, Guatemala: Centro de Investigaciones Regionales de Mesoamérica.

————. 1993. "Evolución demográfica de la población no indígena." In *Historia general de Guatemala*, vol. 2, *Dominación española: Desde la conquista hasta 1700*, edited by Ernesto Chinchilla Aguilar, 249–58. Guatemala: Fundación para la Cultura y el Desarrollo.

————. 1994a. "La evolución demográfica de la población ladina." In *Historia general de Guatemala*, vol. 3, *Siglo XVIII hasta la Independencia*, edited by Cristina Zilbermann de Luján, 111–26. Guatemala: Fundación para la Cultura y el Desarrollo.

————. 1994b. *Santiago de Guatemala, 1541–1773: City, Caste, and the Colonial Experience.* Norman: University of Oklahoma Press.

————. 1996. "Introducción y notas históricas." In *Nuestro Pesar, Nuestra Aflicción—Tunetuliniliz, Tucucuca: Memorias en lengua náhuatl enviadas a Felipe II por indígenas del Valle de Guatemala hacia 1572,* by Karen Dakin and Christopher H. Lutz, xi–xlvii.

————. 2005. *Santiago de Guatemala: Historia social y económica, 1541–1773.* Guatemala: Editorial Universitaria, Universidad de San Carlos de Guatemala.

Lutz, Christopher H., and W. George Lovell. 1990. "Core and Periphery in Colonial Guatemala." In *Guatemalan Indians and the State*, edited by Carol A. Smith, 35–51. Austin: University of Texas Press.

————. 1991. "Centro y periferia en la Guatemala colonial." In *Territorio y sociedad en Guatemala: Tres ensayos históricos*, edited by Julio Pinto Soria, 9–36. Guatemala: Editorial Universitaria, Universidad de San Carlos de Guatemala.

Mackie, Sedley J., ed. and trans. 1924. *An Account of the Conquest of Guatemala in 1524 by Pedro de Alvarado*. New York: Cortés Society.

MacLeod, Murdo J. [1973] 2008. *Spanish Central America: A Socioeconomic History, 1520–1720, with a new introduction*. Austin: University of Texas Press.

————. 1980. *Historia socio-económica de la América Central española: 1520–1720*. Guatemala: Piedra Santa.

————. 1982. "An Outline of Central American Colonial Demographics: Sources, Yields, and Possibilities." In *The Historical Demography of Highland Guatemala*, edited by Robert M. Carmack, John D. Early, and Christopher H. Lutz, 3–18. Albany: Institute for Mesoamerican Studies, State University of New York.

————. 1983. "Ethnic Relations and Indian Society in the Province of Guatemala, ca. 1620–ca. 1800." In *Spaniards and Indians in Southeastern Mesoamerica: Essays on the History of Ethnic Relations*, edited by Murdo J. MacLeod and Robert Wasserstrom, 189–214. Lincoln: University of Nebraska Press.

————. 1985. "Los indígenas de Guatemala en los siglos XVI y XVII: Tamaño de la población, recursos y organización de la mano de obra." In *Población y mano de obra en América Latina*, edited by Nicolás Sánchez-Albornoz, 53–67. Madrid: Alianza Editorial.

————. 1998. "Self-Promotion: The *Relaciones de Méritos y Servicio*s and Their Historical and Political Interpretation." *Colonial Latin American Historical Review* 7 (1): 25–42.

Madigan, Douglas G. 1976. "Santiago Atitlán, Guatemala: A Socioeconomic and Demographic History." PhD diss., University of Pittsburgh.

Martínez Peláez, Severo. [1970] 1998. *La patria del criollo: Ensayo de interpretación de la realidad colonial guatemalteca*. Mexico: Fondo de Cultura Económica.

————. [1970] 2009. *La Patria del Criollo: An Interpretation of Colonial Guatemala*. Translated by Susan M. Neve and W. George Lovell. Edited by W. George Lovell and Christopher H. Lutz. Durham: Duke University Press.

Mártir de Anglería, Pedro. See Anglería, Pedro Mártir de.

Matthew, Laura E. 2004. "Neither and Both: The Mexican Indian Conquistadors of Colonial Guatemala." PhD diss., University of Pennsylvania.

————. 2007. "Whose Conquest?: Nahua, Zapoteca, and Mixteca Allies in the Conquest of Central America." In *Indian Conquistadors*, edited by Laura E. Matthew and Michel R. Oudijk, 102–26. Norman: University of Oklahoma Press.

————. 2012. *Memories of Conquest: Becoming Mexicano in Colonial Guatemala*. Chapel Hill: University of North Carolina Press.

Matthew, Laura E., and Michel R. Oudijk, eds. 2007. *Indian Conquistadors: Indigenous Allies in the Conquest of Mesoamerica*. Norman: University of Oklahoma Press.

Maxwell, Judith M., and Robert M. Hill. 2006. *Kaqchikel Chronicles: The Definitive Edition*. Austin: University of Texas Press.

McCreery, David. 1990. "State Power, Indigenous Communities, and Land in Nineteenth-Century Guatemala." In *Guatemalan Indians and the State, 1540–1988,* edited by Carol A. Smith, 96–115. Austin: University of Texas Press.

———. 1994. *Rural Guatemala, 1760–1940.* Stanford, Calif.: Stanford University Press.

Miles, Suzanne W. 1957. "The Sixteenth-Century Pokom-Maya: A Documentary Analysis of Social Structure and Archaeological Setting." In *Transactions of the American Philosophical Society,* 731–81. Philadelphia: American Philosophical Society.

Miranda, José. 1952. *El tributo indígena en la Nueva España durante el siglo 16.* Mexico: Colegio de México.

Mondloch, James. 2002. "Una perspectiva lingüística." Review of Simón Otzoy, translator, *Memorial de Sololá, Mesoamérica* 44:161–73.

Montejo, Victor. 2005. *Maya Intellectual Renaissance: Identity, Representation, and Leadership.* Austin: University of Texas Press.

Mörner, Magnus. 1964. "La política de segregación y el mestizaje en la Audiencia de Guatemala." *Revista de Indias* 95–96:137–51.

Nance, C. Roger, Stephen L. Whittington, and Barbara E. Borg. 2003. *Archaeology and Ethnohistory of Iximché.* Gainesville: University of Florida Press.

Newson, Linda A. 1981. "Demographic Catastrophe in Sixteenth-Century Honduras." In *Studies in Spanish American Population History,* edited by David J. Robinson, 217–41. Dellplain Latin American Studies 8. Boulder, Colo.: Westview Press.

———. 1982. "The Depopulation of Nicaragua in the Sixteenth Century." *Journal of Latin American Studies* 14 (2): 253–86.

———. 1985. "Indian Population Patterns in Colonial Spanish America." *Latin American Research Review* 20 (3): 41–74.

———. 1986. *The Cost of Conquest: Indian Decline in Honduras under Spanish Rule.* Dellplain Latin American Studies 20. Boulder, Colo.: Westview Press.

———. 1987. *Indian Survival in Colonial Nicaragua.* Norman: University of Oklahoma Press.

———. 1992. *El costo de la conquista.* Tegucigalpa, Honduras: Editorial Guaymuras.

Orellana, Sandra L. 1984. *The Tzutujil Mayas: Continuity and Change, 1250–1630.* Norman: University of Oklahoma Press.

———. 1995. *Ethnohistory of the Pacific Coast.* Lancaster, Calif.: Labyrinthos.

Oss, Adriaan C. van. 1981. "La población de América Central hacia 1800." *Anales de la Academia de Geografía e Historia de Guatemala* 60:291–311.

———. 1986. *Catholic Colonialism: A Parish History of Guatemala, 1524–1821.* Cambridge: Cambridge University Press.

Othón de Mendizábal, Miguel. 1952. *El tributo indígena en la Nueva España.* Mexico.

Otzoy, Simón. 1999, ed. and trans. *Memorial de Sololá.* Guatemala: Comisión Interuniversitaria de Conmemoración del Quinto Centenario del Descubrimiento de América.

Oudijk, Michel R., and Matthew Restall. 2007. "Mesoamerican Conquistadors in the Sixteenth Century." In Laura E. Matthew and Michel R. Oudijk, eds., *Indian Conquistadors,* 28–64. Norman: University of Oklahoma Press.

Padden, R. C. 1967. *The Hummingbird and the Hawk: Conquest and Sovereignty in the Valley of Mexico, 1503–1541*. Columbus: Ohio State University Press.

Palma Murga, Gustavo. 1986. "Núcleos de poder local y relaciones familiares en la ciudad de Guatemala a finales del siglo XVIII." *Mesoamérica* 12:241–308.

Paso y Troncoso, Francisco del. 1939. *Epistolario de Nueva España, 1505–1818*. Edited by Silvio Arturo Zavala. 16 vols. Mexico: Robredo.

Peña y Cámara, José María de la. 1955. *A List of Spanish Residencias in the Archives of the Indies, 1516–1775*. Washington, D.C.: Library of Congress.

Pinto Soria, Julio César. 1980. *Raíces históricas del estado en Centro América*. Guatemala: Editorial Universitaria, Universidad de San Carlos de Guatemala.

———. 1987. *Estructura agraria y asentamiento en la Capitanía General de Guatemala*. 2nd ed. Guatemala: Universidad de San Carlos de Guatemala.

———, ed. 1991. *Territorio y sociedad en Guatemala: Tres ensayos históricas*. Guatemala: Editorial Universitaria, Universidad de San Carlos de Guatemala.

Polo Sifontes, Francis. [1977] 2005. *Los cakchiqueles en la conquista de Guatemala*. Guatemala: Editorial Cultura.

Prem, Hanns J. [1992] 2001. "Disease Outbreaks in Central Mexico during the Sixteenth Century." In *"Secret Judgments of God": Old World Disease in Colonial Spanish America,* edited by Noble David Cook and W. George Lovell, 20–48. Norman: University of Oklahoma Press.

Quiñones Keber, Eloise. 1995. *Codex Telleriano-Remensis: Ritual, Divination, and History in a Pictorial Aztec Manuscript*. Austin: University of Texas Press.

Radell, David R. 1969. "Historical Geography of Western Nicaragua: The Spheres of Influence of León, Granada, and Managua, 1519–1965." PhD diss., University of California, Berkeley.

Ramírez, José Fernando, ed. 1847. *Proceso de residencia contra Pedro de Alvarado*. Mexico: Valdés y Redondas.

———, ed. [1847] 1930–33. "Proceso de residencia contra Pedro de Alvarado." *Anales de la Sociedad de Geografía e Historia de Guatemala* 7:1–4, 95–122, 210–39, 360–87, and 513–28; 8:2–4 and 254–67; 9:1–2, 121–29, and 256–64.

Recinos, Adrián, ed. and trans. 1947. *Popol Vuh: Las antiguas historias del Quiché*. Mexico: Fondo de Cultura Económica.

———, ed. and trans. 1950a. *Memorial de Sololá: Anales de los Cakchiqueles*. Mexico: Fondo de Cultura Económica.

———, ed. and trans. 1950b. *Popol Vuh: The Sacred Book of the Ancient Quiché Maya*. English version by Delia Goetz and Sylvanus G. Morley. Norman: University of Oklahoma Press.

———. 1952. *Pedro de Alvarado, conquistador de México y Guatemala*. Mexico: Fondo de Cultura Económica.

———. 1953. Introduction to *The Annals of the Cakchiquels*, edited by Adrián Recinos and Delia Goetz, 3–42.

———, ed. 1957. *Crónicas indígenas de Guatemala*. Guatemala: Editorial Universitaria, Universidad de San Carlos de Guatemala.

———. 1958. *Doña Leonor de Alvarado y otros estudios*. Guatemala: Editorial Universitaria, Universidad de San Carlos de Guatemala.

Recinos, Adrián, and Delia Goetz, eds. and trans. 1953. *The Annals of the Cakchiquels*. Norman: University of Oklahoma Press.

Recopilación de las leyes de los reynos de las Indias. [1681] 1973. 4 vols. Madrid: Ediciones Cultura Hispánica.

"Relación de los caciques y principales del pueblo de Atitlán." [1571] 1952. *Anales de la Sociedad de Geografía e Historia de Guatemala* 26:435–38.

Remesal, Antonio de. [1619] 1964–66. *Historia general de las Indias occidentales, y particular de la gobernación de Chiapa y Guatemala*. Edited by Carmelo Sáenz de Santa María. 2 vols. Madrid: Ediciones Atlas.

Restall, Matthew. 2010. "Perspectivas indígenas de la conquista de Guatemala: Descifrando relatos escritos por los nahuas y mayas." *Mesoamérica* 52:190–97.

Restall, Matthew, and Florine Asselbergs. 2007. *Invading Guatemala: Spanish, Nahua, and Maya Accounts of the Conquest Wars*. University Park: Penn State University Press.

Robinson, David J., ed. 1990. *Migration in Colonial Latin America*. Cambridge: Cambridge University Press.

Rodríguez Becerra, Salvador. 1975. "Metodología y fuentes para el estudio de la población de Guatemala en el siglo XVI." In *Atti del XL Congresso Internazionale degli Americanisti*, vol. 3, edited by Ernesta Cerulli and Gilda Della Ragione, 243–53. Genoa, Italy: Tilgher.

———. 1977. *Encomienda y conquista: Los inicios de la colonización en Guatemala*. Seville: Universidad de Sevilla.

Rosenblat, Angel. 1967. *La población de América en 1492: Viejos y nuevos cálculos*. Mexico: Colegio de México.

Rubio Sánchez, Manuel. 1982. *Los jueces reformadores de milpas en Centroamérica*. Guatemala: Academia de Geografía e Historia de Guatemala.

Sáenz de Santa María, Carmelo. 1964. *El licenciado don Francisco Marroquín, primer obispo de Guatemala (1499–1563)*. Madrid: Ediciones Cultura Hispánica.

———. 1969. "Estudio preliminar." In *Obras históricas de D. Francisco Antonio de Fuentes y Guzmán*, vol. 1, v–lxxxii. Biblioteca de Autores Españoles 230. Madrid: Ediciones Atlas.

———. 1972. "La reducción a poblados en el siglo XVI en Guatemala." *Anuario de Estudios Americanos* 29:187–228.

Saint-Lu, André. 1968. *La Vera Paz: Esprit évangélique et colonisation*. Paris: Centre de Recherches Hispaniques, Institut d'Études Hispaniques.

Sanchíz Ochoa, Pilar. 1976. *Los hidalgos de Guatemala: Realidad y apariencia en un sistema de valores*. Seville: Universidad de Sevilla.

Sanders, William T. 1976. "The Population of the Central Mexican Symbiotic Region, the Basin of Mexico, and the Teotihuacán Valley in the Sixteenth Century." In *The Native Population of the Americas in 1492*, edited by William M. Denevan, 85–150. Madison: University of Wisconsin Press.

Sanders, William T., and Carson Murdy. 1982. "Population and Agricultural Adaptation in the Humid Highlands of Guatemala." In *The Historical Demography of Highland*

Guatemala, edited by Robert M. Carmack, John D. Early, and Christopher H. Lutz, 23–34. Albany: Institute for Mesoamerican Studies, State University of New York.

Santos Pérez, J. Manuel. 1999. *Élites, poder local y régimen colonial: El Cabildo y los regidores de Santiago de Guatemala, 1700–1787.* Antigua, Guatemala, and Cádiz, Spain: Centro de Investigaciones Regionales de Mesoamérica and the Universidad de Cádiz.

Sapper, Karl. [1936] 1985. *The Verapaz in the 16th and 17th Centuries: A Contribution to the Historical Geography and Ethnography of Northeastern Guatemala.* Translated by Theodore E. Gutman. Occasional Paper 13. Los Angeles: University of California, Institute of Archaeology.

Sauer, Carl O. [1956] 1963. "The Education of a Geographer." In *Land and Life: A Selection from the Writings of Carl Ortwin Sauer,* edited by John Leighley, 389–404. Berkeley and Los Angeles: University of California Press.

Schäfer, Ernst. 1935–1947. *El consejo real y supremo de las Indias.* 2 vols. Seville: Centro de Historia de América.

Schirmer, Jennifer. 1998. *The Guatemalan Military Project: A Violence Called Democracy.* Philadelphia: University of Pennsylvania Press.

Sherman, William L. 1969. "A Conqueror's Wealth: Notes on the Estate of Don Pedro de Alvarado." *The Americas* 26 (2): 199–213.

———. 1971. "Indian Slavery and the Cerrato Reforms. *Hispanic American Historical Review* 51 (1): 25–50.

———. 1972. Personal letter to Christopher H. Lutz, January 7, 1972.

———. 1979. *Forced Native Labor in Sixteenth-Century Central America.* Lincoln: University of Nebraska Press.

———. 1983. "Some Aspects of Change in Guatemalan Society, 1470–1620." In *Spaniards and Indians in Southeastern Mesoamerica: Essays on the History of Ethnic Relations,* edited by Murdo J. MacLeod and Robert Wasserstrom, 169–88. Lincoln: University of Nebraska Press.

———. 1987. *Aspectos del cambio social en Guatemala, 1470–1620.* Guatemala: Seminario de Integración Social Guatemalteca.

Simpson, Lesley Byrd. 1934. *Studies in the Administration of the Indians in New Spain.* Ibero-Americana 7. Berkeley and Los Angeles: University of California Press.

———. [1950] 1966. *The Encomienda in New Spain: The Beginning of Spanish Mexico.* Berkeley and Los Angeles: University of California Press.

Slicher van Bath, B. H. 1978. "The Calculation of the Population of New Spain, Especially for the Period before 1570." *Boletín de Estudios Latinoamericanos y del Caribe* 24:67–95.

Smith, A. Ledyard. 1955. *Archaeological Reconnaissance in Central Guatemala.* Washington, D.C.: Carnegie Institution.

Smith, Carol A. 1978. "Beyond Dependency Theory: National and Regional Patterns of Underdevelopment in Guatemala." *American Ethnologist* 5 (3): 574–617.

———. 1984. "Local History in Global Context: Social and Economic Transitions in Western Guatemala." *Comparative Studies in Society and History* 26 (2): 193–228.

———. 1987. "Regional Analysis in World-System Perspective: A Critique of Three Structural Theories of Uneven Development." *Review* 10 (4): 597–648.

Smith, Carol A., ed. With the assistance of Marilyn M. Moors. 1990. *Guatemalan Indians and the State.* Austin: University of Texas Press.

Solano, Francisco de. 1969. "La población indígena de Guatemala, 1492–1800." *Anuario de Estudios Americanos* 26:279–355.

———. 1974. *Los mayas del siglo XVIII: Pervivencia y transformación de la sociedad indígena guatemalteca durante la administración borbónica.* Madrid: Ediciones Cultura Hispánica.

Solombrino Orozco, Vincenzo. 1982. *Legislación municipal de la República de Guatemala: Antecedentes legislativos históricos, legislación fundamental vigente, acuerdos y reglamentos municipales.* Guatemala: Tipografía Nacional.

Solórzano Fonseca, Juan Carlos. 1985. "Las comunidades indígenas en Guatemala, El Salvador y Chiapas durante el siglo XVIII: Los mecanismos de la explotación económica." *Anuario de Estudios Centroamericanos* 11 (2): 93 130.

Spores, Ronald. 1967. *The Mixtec Kings and Their People.* Norman: University of Oklahoma Press.

Stanislawski, Dan. 1983. *The Transformation of Nicaragua, 1519–1548.* Ibero-Americana 54. Berkeley and Los Angeles: University of California Press.

Suñe Blanco, Beatriz. 1984. *La documentación del cabildo secular de Guatemala (siglo XVI): Estudio diplomático y valor etnográfico.* Seville: Universidad de Sevilla.

Swezey, William R. 1985. "Cakhay: La ubicación original de Tecpán-Atitlán." *Mesoamérica* 9:154–69.

Tax, Sol. 1937. "The Municipios of the Midwestern Highlands of Guatemala." *American Anthropologist* 39 (3): 423–44.

Tedlock, Dennis, ed. and trans. 1985. *Popol Vuh: The Definitive Edition of the Mayan Book of the Dawn of Life and the Glories of Gods and Kings.* New York: Simon and Schuster.

Thomas, David Hurst, ed. 1991. *Columbian Consequences.* 3 vols. Washington, D.C.: Smithsonian Institution.

Thompson, J. Eric S. 1966. *The Rise and Fall of Maya Civilization.* Norman: University of Oklahoma Press.

———. 1970. "The Maya Central Area at the Spanish Conquest and Later: A Problem in Demography." In *Maya History and Religion*, 48–83. Norman: University of Oklahoma Press.

Tovilla, Martín Alfonso. [ca. 1635] 1960. *Relación histórica descriptiva de las provincias de la Verapaz y de la del Manché.* Guatemala: Editorial Universitaria, Universidad de San Carlos de Guatemala.

Universidad Francisco Marroquín. 2007. *Quauhquechollan: A Chronicle of Conquest.* Guatemala: Universidad Francisco Marroquín.

Vallejo García-Hevia, José María. 2008. *Juicio a un conquistador: Pedro de Alvarado.* 2 vols. Madrid: Marcial Pons.

Vázquez, Francisco. [1688–95] 1937–44. *Crónica de la provincia del santísimo nombre de Jesús de Guatemala de la Orden de N. Seráfico Padre San Francisco en el Reino de la Nueva España.* 2nd ed. 4 vols. Guatemala: Sociedad de Geografía e Historia de Guatemala.

Vázquez de Espinosa, Antonio. [ca. 1629] 1948. *Compendio y descripción de las Indias Occidentales.* Smithsonian Miscellaneous Collections 108. Washington, D.C.: Smithsonian Institution.

Veblen, Thomas T. 1977. "Native Population Decline in Totonicapán, Guatemala." *Annals of the Association of American Geographers* 67 (4): 484–99.

Veblen, Thomas T., and Laura Gutiérrez-Witt. 1983. "Relación de los caciques y número de yndios que hay en Guatemala, 21 de abril de 1572." *Mesoamérica* 5:212–35.

Viana, Francisco, Lucas Gallego, and Guillermo Cadena. [1574] 1955. "Relación de la Provincia de la Verapaz." *Anales de la Sociedad de Geografía e Historia de Guatemala* 28:18–31.

Vos, Jan de. [1980] 1993. *La paz de Dios y del rey: La conquista de la Selva Lacandona, 1525–1821.* Mexico: Fondo de Cultura Económica.

Wagley, Charles. 1969. "The Maya of Northwestern Guatemala." In *Handbook of Middle American Indians,* vol. 7, edited by Robert Wauchope, 46–68. Austin: University of Texas Press.

Warren, Kay. 1998. *Indigenous Movements and Their Critics: Pan-Maya Activism in Guatemala.* Princeton, N.J.: Princeton University Press.

Wasserstrom, Robert. 1983. *Class and Society in Central Chiapas.* Berkeley and Los Angeles: University of California Press.

Webre, Stephen A. 1980. "The Social and Economic Bases of Cabildo Membership in Seventeenth-Century Santiago de Guatemala." PhD diss., Tulane University.

———. 1981. "El Cabildo de Santiago de Guatemala en el siglo XVII ¿Una oligarquía criolla cerrada y hereditaria?" *Mesoamérica* 2:1–19.

Weeks, John M., ed. 2001. *The Past and Present Maya: Essays in Honor of Robert M. Carmack.* Lancaster, Calif.: Labyrinthos.

Wolf, Eric R. 1957. "Closed Corporate Peasant Communities in Mesoamerica and Central Java." *Southwestern Journal of Anthropology* 13 (1): 1–18.

———. 1959. *Sons of the Shaking Earth.* Chicago: University of Chicago Press.

———. 1986. "The Vicissitudes of the Closed Corporate Peasant Community." *American Ethnologist* 13 (2): 325–29.

Woodbury, Richard B., and Aubrey S. Trik, eds. 1953. *The Ruins of Zaculeu, Guatemala.* Richmond, Va.: United Fruit Company.

Wortman, Miles L. 1982. *Government and Society in Central America, 1680–1840.* New York: Columbia University Press.

Ximénez, Francisco. [1715–20] 1929–31. *Historia de la provincia de San Vicente de Chiapa y Guatemala de la Orden de Predicadores.* 3 vols. Guatemala: Sociedad de Geografía e Historia de Guatemala.

Yannakakis, Yanna. 2008. *The Art of Being In-between: Native Intermediaries, Indian Identity, and Local Rule in Colonial Oaxaca.* Durham: Duke University Press.

Zambardino, Rudolph A. 1980. "Mexico's Population in the Sixteenth Century: Demographic Anomaly or Mathematical Illusion?" *Journal of Interdisciplinary History* 11:1–27.

Zamora Acosta, Elías. 1983. "Conquista y crisis demográfica: La población indígena del occidente de Guatemala en el siglo XVI." *Mesoamérica* 6:291–328.

———. 1985. *Los mayas de las tierras altas en el siglo XVI: Tradición y cambio en Guatemala.* Seville: Diputación Provincial.

Zilbermann de Luján, María Cristina. 1987. *Aspectos socioeconómicos del traslado de la Ciudad de Guatemala (1773–1783).* Guatemala: Academia de Geografía e Historia de Guatemala.

INDEX

A letter "t" or "f" in italic type following a page reference indicates a table or figure, respectively.

Acalá territory, 200
Acazaguastlán, 241
African slaves, 80, 83–84, 92, 224, 228–29
Agriculture: colonial cash crops in, 80,
   82–85, 87–88; *encomienda* obligations,
   261*t*, 263–69*t*; exploitation of labor
   for, 86–90; ranching in, 82, 84–85,
   89–90; *tasaciones* of, 160–70, 192, 200,
   201–202, 240; wheat farming in, 80,
   82, 85, 170
Aguilar, García de, 191
Ahau Galel, 13
Ahpoxahil, 34n6. *See also* Belehé Qat
Ahpozotzil. *See* Cahí Ymox
Ahtzic Vinac Ahau, 13
Akkeren, Ruud van, 14n25, 46n40,
   54n63, 54n65
Almagro, Diego de, 68, 69, 161
Almarsa, Bernardo de, 217
Almolonga, 80, 82, 92n31; flight
   of Kaqchikel kings from, 62–65;
   Spanish capital (Santiago) in, 56, 58,
   62–63, 65, 71, 141, 160, 162; Spanish
   settlement in, 80, 82, 92
Altman, Ida, 74n, 212n, 213n3
Alva Ixtlilxóchitl, Fernando de, 9n12
Alvarado, Diego de, 9, 51, 53–54, 65–66
Alvarado, Gómez de, 9, 53–54
Alvarado, Gonzalo de (brother), 9,
   53–54; expedition against the Mam

of Zaculeu of, 131–34; Kaqchikel
   rebellion and, 41–42, 48–49, 52
Alvarado, Gonzalo de (cousin), 10,
   53–54, 56
Alvarado, Hernando de, 9, 53–54
Alvarado, Jorge de, 9, 23; *encomiendas*
   of, 259*t*; governance of Guatemala by,
   58, 68–70; Kaqchikel rebellion and,
   48n46; role in conquest of, 53–56,
   135n9; royal concubine of, 27n52
Alvarado, Leonor de, 161–62
Alvarado, Pedro de, 4, 250–51;
   biographical and historical accounts
   of, 5n3, 10n, 150n3; children of, 16–17;
   death of, 74, 77, 157; *encomiendas* of,
   159–61, 259*t*; Espinar's confrontation
   with, 129–30, 135–41, 147–48;
   expeditions to Honduras of, 49–51,
   70–72; exploitation of Huehuetenango
   by, 142–43; family solidarity of, 9–10,
   53–56; indigenous names for, 14;
   inquiries for misconduct of, 26, 46–47,
   71–72, 150n3; Kaqchikel surrender
   to, 58–74; letters to Charles V of, 5;
   mutiny against, 49–50; official rank
   of, 62, 71–72; opposition to tribute
   assessment regulations by, 149–54;
   Peru expedition of, 68; slaughter in
   Tenochtitlán by, 37–39; Spanish wives
   of, 72, 161, 250; temperament of, 36–38;

Alvarado, Pedro de, *continued*
  unions with indigenous women of,
  16–17, 25–28, 162; wounding in battle
  of, 24; written reports of, xv, 8n, 10n.
  See also Conquest and rebellion
Alvarado Arévalo, Francisco de, 61n3
Alvarado y Chávez, Gonzalo de. *See*
  Alvarado, Gonzalo de (cousin)
Amaq', 106, 109–10
Amatitlán, 82–83
Andrade, Pedro Fernández de, 226
Anghiera, Pietro Martire d', 6–7, 33
Apaneca, 220
Archival sources, xv–xvi; on conquest,
  3; indigenous accounts in, 5, 12;
  lost documents among, 7n, 14;
  translations of, 10n
Arévalo, Francisco de, 141
Arias, Gaspar, 259*t*
Artiaga Mendiola, Pedro, 202–204, 207
Asselbergs, Florine, 9n12, 10n; on
  demands for gold, 29–30nn56–58; on
  Jorge de Alvarado, 54n63, 56n68; on
  the Kaqchikel rebellion, 40, 42–43n30,
  46n40, 48n46; on Kaqchikel response
  to the Spaniards, 18n38, 19n39; on the
  Lienzo de Quauhquechollan, 54n65;
  on Mesoamerican alliance formation
  traditions, 35; on Mexica diplomatic
  mission to Iximché, 33n2
Atitlán. *See* Santiago Atitlán
Atlas histórico de Guatemala (Luján
  Muñoz), 78–79n5, 82nn7–8
Aztecs, 17

Barahona, Sancho de, 159–60
Barrios, Justo Rufino, 248
Beleheb-Tzii, 14
Belehé Qat, 6, 18; death and successor
  of, 63; Kaqchikel rebellion of, 42n28,
  42–43n30, 53, 57; Spanish name for,
  42n28, 43–44, 72–73n31; surrender
  by, 58–62
Bergmann, John, 124

Berkeley School, 174–76, 194
Bertrand, Michel, 200, 202, 206n21
Black population, xvii, 245. *See also*
  African slaves
Blasco, Julio, 244
Bobadilla, Ignacio de, 144
Borah, Woodrow, 174–83, 189,
  192–94, 224–25
Borg, Barbara E., 28n55, 49n51, 55n66,
  64n8, 179n18
Brasseur de Bourbourg, Charles
  Etienne, 6n7
Briceño, Francisco, 199–200
Brinton, Daniel G., 6n7
Briones, Pedro de, 48

Cabezas Carache, Horacio, 5–6; on
  Alvarado's injuries, 24n; on Jorge de
  Alvarado, 54n63; on the Kaqchikel
  rebellion, 39–40, 53; on Tecún
  Umán, 12–14
Cacao, 84–85, 87–88, 89, 160–70
Cadena, Guillermo, 205–206
Cahaboncillo, 226
Cahí Ymox (Sinacán), 6, 18, 26;
  execution of, 72–73; exile of, 63–64;
  Kaqchikel rebellion of, 42–43, 53, 57;
  reports of second uprising of, 64–70;
  Spanish pursuit and capture of, 66–
  68, 70; surrender by, 58–62
Caibal Balam, 131–34
Calpules, 106
Calvo Nájera, Juan, 59, 61n3
Cárcamo, Valdés de, 221
Cárdenas, Tomás de, 111–13, 199
Carmack, Robert M., 7, 105, 154n9;
  on the Kaqchikel rebellion, 42n29,
  43n31; on population assessments,
  179–81, 194, 207, 220–21, 270*t*; on
  Tecún Umán, 13–14
Carrillo, Hernán, 54
Casa de Avante y Gamboa, Pedro de,
  200–201
Castañeda, Marcos, 252

Castas (mixed blood population), xvii, 80, 94; population surveys of, 235, 242, 245, 280*t*; settlement patterns of, 83–85
Castrón, Juan de, 217
Catálogo de pasajeros, 212–13
Catholic Church. *See* Missionaries and clergy
Cédulas de encomienda, 126
Cereceda, Andrés de, 70, 167–68
Cerrato, Alonso López de, 86–87, 94, 154n8, 184–95; colonist resentment of, 184–85, 190–91; *encomiendas* of, 259*t*; on Espinar's *encomienda*, 137; New Laws implemented by, 123, 158, 184–85, 190; tribute assessments by, 101–102, 105, 124–25, 127–28, 146n, 159–67, 177, 185–88, 219–20, 256*t*, 270–74*t*, 277*t*; tribute reforms by, 108–109, 124, 158, 167, 168–70
Chacón y Abarca, Jerónimo, 233–34
Charles V of Spain, 4–6, 50–51, 123
Chaunu, Huguette, 251
Chaunu, Pierre, 251
Chávez, Juan de, 70, 92
Chiantla, 136–37, 142–43, 145, 148, 262*t*
Chiapas, 227–29, 240, 241
Chichicastenango, 127, 259*t*, 271*t*, 272*t*
Chimaltenango, 80, 82–83, 194–95, 255*t*, 262*t*; population surveys of, 243, 260*t*, 274*t*; tribute assessments of, 197–98
Chinamitales, 105–107, 109
Chiquimula, 80, 242–43, 255*t*
Chiquimula de la Sierra, 225, 234–35
Chol Manché Maya, 85
Choluteca (Honduras), 227–29, 240
Cieza de León, Pedro de, 68n19
Cija, Juan de, 217
Ciudad Vieja. *See* Almolonga
Clendinnen, Inga, 250
Clergy. *See* Missionaries and clergy
Cline, Howard, 194
Cloth/clothing, 160–70, 192, 261*t*, 263–69*t*
Coatle, lord of Chiantla, 143–44

Cobán, 201, 208
Cochumatlán, 190–91
Collier, George, 98
Collins, Anne, 119
Comalapa: agriculture of, 82–83; *encomienda* obligations in, 267*t*; tribute assessments of, 158–59, 164–66, 169–70, 192–98, 219, 274*t*
Comayagua, 233–34
Compendio de la historia de la Ciudad de Guatemala (Juarros), 247, 282*t*
Compendio y descripción de las Indias Occidentales (Vázquez de Espinosa), 229–30
Congregación resettlement projects, 86, 96, 101–13, 119, 251; enforcement practices for, 129; fugitivism attributed to, 143, 191, 192; link with epidemics of, 206; *tasaciones* and, 191
Conquest and rebellion, xiv, 3–31; Alvarado family in, 9–10, 53–56; Battle of El Pinar of, 11–15; cartographic rendering of, 30n59, 55; at Cuzcatlán, 21–25, 30; establishment of Santiago and, 56; indigenous accounts of, 9n12, 45–50, 53, 55–56; indigenous population size at, 173–83, 270*t*; Jorge de Alvarado's campaigns in, 53–56; Kaqchikel alliance in, 16–19, 25–27, 32–36; Kaqchikel rebellions and, 3, 44–57, 58n1, 64–70; Kaqchikel surrender in, 58–74; of the K'iche', 10–18, 34; *Lienzo de Quauhquechollan* on, 54n65, 55, 61n3; Spanish accounts of, 39–44, 50–56; Tecún Umán in, 12–14; Tz'utujil defeat in, 20–21; at Utatlán, 14–17
Contreras, Daniel, 5, 6n7; on executions of indigenous rulers, 73n33; on the Kaqchikel rebellion, 42n28, 42–43n30, 44–45; on Kaqchikel rulers, 72–73n31; on the second Kaqchikel uprising, 64–65, 70n25
Contreras, Leonor de, 16

Cook, Noble David, 229
Cook, Sherburne, 174–83, 189, 192–94, 224–25
Corregimiento del Valle, 78–79n5, 80
Cortés, Hernán, 27, 37; on Alvarado's conquest of Guatemala, 8–9; construction of Mexico City by, 50n52; first contact with Maya of, 4–6, 33–34, 34n5; Honduran expedition of, 48–50; on the Kaqchikel rebellion, 50–52
Cortés y Larraz, Pedro, 115–17, 118f, 244–45
Cotoha, lord of Huehuetenango, 145
Cozumaçutla (Santo Domingo Usumacinta), 262t
Criollos (Spanish descendants), 83, 245
Crónica de la provincia del santísimo nombre de Jesús de Guatemala (Vázquez), 40
Cueto, Pedro de, 259t
Cueva, Beatriz de la. See De la Cueva, Beatriz
Cueva, Cristóbal de la. See De la Cueva, Cristóbal
Cueva, Francisca de la. See De la Cueva, Francisca
Cueva, Francisco de la. See De la Cueva, Francisco

Debt peonage, 88–89
De la Cueva, Beatriz, 72, 161, 250
De la Cueva, Cristóbal, 158, 167–68
De la Cueva, Francisca, 72, 250
De la Cueva, Francisco, 72, 73n34, 159, 161–64, 259t
De la Parra, Francisco, 9n12, 185n3
Denevan, William, 174–76, 182
Descripción geográfico-moral (Cortés y Larraz), 244–45
Díaz del Castillo, Bernal, 8n; on Cerrato's tasaciones, 190; on Espinar, 136–37; in Honduras, 50–51; on the Kaqchikel alliance, 16–17; on the Kaqchikel rebellion, 48n46, 51–53; on plots against Alvarado, 14, 15n27; on

Tecún Umán, 12; on Tenochtitlán and La Noche Triste, 37–39
Dominicans, 86, 108; pastoral administration of, 232; population assessments by, 205–206, 226–27, 230, 236–38, 276t; towns founded by, 255t
Don Jorge (Kab'lajuj Tijax), 63

El Pinar, 11–12
El Progreso, 80, 255t
El Quiché, 80, 255t
El Salvador, 227–29, 240, 241, 245
Encomienda system, 86–87, 123–28, 251–52; allocation process in, 126, 259t; burning and resettlement of Indian towns and, 144–48, 262t; Cerrato's reforms of, 101–102, 105, 124–25, 127–28, 146n, 159–70, 185–95, 256t; Crown holdings in, 87, 141, 160, 168, 186, 199–200, 218–19; of Espinar in Huehuetenango, 129–48, 260t, 261t; individual records on, 125–27, 130, 259; Maldonado's and Marroquín's assessments of, 152–70; New Laws regulating, 123, 140–41, 157–58; obligation of indigenous peoples in, 141–44, 169–70, 213–16, 261t, 263–69t; origins of, 123–24; Valverde's reforms of, 212–33; women's burden in, 169
Enríquez Macías, Genoveva, 235–36, 239
Escuintla (Izquintepque), 19, 21–22, 170n52, 234–35, 255t
Espinar, Juan de, 129–30, 134–48, 251–52, 260t; agricultural enterprises of, 139–40; burning and resettlement of Indian towns by, 144–48, 262t; mining interests of, 136–37, 139–41
Estancias, 84
Estrada, Juan de, 196–97, 275t

Farriss, Nancy, 105–106
Feldman, Lawrence, 176–77, 179n19, 186, 199, 205, 270t

Fernández Nájera, Juan, 61n3
Flores, Francisco, 15n27, 45n37
Foster, George, 79
Fowler, William R., 270*t*
Franciscans, 86, 108; pastoral
    administration of, 232; population
    assessments by, 206–207, 226–27, 230,
    236–38, 276*t*; towns founded by, 255*t*
Fraso, Pedro, 230
Fuentes, Carlos, 95, 209
Fuentes Mairena, Manuel, 186
Fuentes y Guzmán, Francisco Antonio
    de, 12–13, 14n25, 37n14; on conquest
    of the Mam of Zaculeu, 131–32, 133*f*;
    on Corregimiento del Valle, 78–79n5;
    on dissolution of *congregación*, 115,
    116*f*; on Espinar, 136–37; on the
    Kaqchikel rebellion, 39–44; on
    Kaqchikel rulers, 72–73n31;
    Recordación florida of, 238–39

Gage, Thomas, 236–38
Galel Ahpop, 13
Gall, Francis, 8n, 107
Gallego, Lucas, 205–206
Garay, Francisco de, 8, 34n5
García, Francisco, 60
García, Mateo, 217
García Añoveros, Jesús María, 244–45
García de Palacios, Diego, 209–11
García Peláez, Francisco de Paula, 6n7
Gavarrete, Juan, 6n7, 238–39
Geopolitical traditions, 34–36, 58–59
Gerhard, Peter, 194
Gibson, Charles, 77–78, 169, 194
Gómez, Juan, 61n3
Gómez, Ortega, 259*t*
González, Francisco, 217
González Nájera, Alonso, 61n3
González Nájera, Pedro, 9n12, 59–62
Guatemala City, 83, 233–34
Guatemalan civil war, xiii–xiv, 119
Guazacapán, 225, 234–35, 274*t*
Guillemin, George, 28n55, 49n51

Gumarcaah. *See* Utatlán
Gutiérrez-Witt, Laura, 204–205
Guzmán, Diego de, 210–11
Guzmán, Juan de, 211

Hassig, Ross, 35
Henequen, 164
Henige, David, 173–76
Henríquez, Andrés, 109
Hernández Arana, Francisco, 16, 18–19, 20
Herrera, Diego de, 157–58
Hidalgos, 38, 135
Hill, Robert M., 18n38, 19n39; on
    Alvarado's demands for gold,
    29–30nn57–58; on Belehé Qat's
    death and succession, 63nn5–6; on
    chinamitales, 106; on executions of
    indigenous rulers, 73n33; on the
    Kaqchikel rebellion, 42–43n30; on
    Kaqchikel tribute, 62n; on Mexica
    diplomatic mission to Iximché, 33n2;
    population estimates of, 179n18; on
    Sacapulas *parcialidades*, 107, 109
*Historia de la Provincia de San Vicente
    de Chiapa y Guatemala* (Ximénez), 44
Holguín, Diego de, 51
Holom Balam, 53
Honduras, 227–29, 240; Alvarado's
    expeditions to, 49–51, 70–72; Cortés
    in, 41, 48–49; Cristóbal de la Cueva
    in, 167–68; demographic recovery in,
    183; mining in, 89; population surveys
    of, 185, 204, 218, 228, 233–34, 238,
    275*t*; taxation in, 225, 227
Huehuetenango, 80, 85, 193, 255*t*;
    burning and resettlement of Indian
    towns in, 144–48, 262*t*; conquest of,
    131–34; Espinar's *encomienda* in,
    129–30, 134–48, 260*t*, 261*t*; native
    leaders of, 143–44; *parcialidades of*,
    106–107; population surveys of, 220,
    235, 241, 260*t*, 274*t*; preconquest
    status of, 130–31; Zurrilla's
    encomienda in, 130, 141–43, 148

Indigenous peoples, xvi–xvii; agency
demonstrated by, 79, 113–19, 123,
143, 191, 192, 215, 250; alliance
traditions of, 34–36, 58–59; ancestral
land of, 111–13; cacao production
by, 84; colonial-era organization of,
96–119; in core-periphery divide,
80–82; enslavement and forced labor
of, 82, 86–90, 92, 140–42, 184, 221,
261*t*; intimate unions with Spanish
of, 16–17, 25–28, 162; land base of
communities of, 86, 91; landlessness
and ladinoization of, 83; obligations
in the *encomienda* system of, 141–44,
169–70, 213–16, 251–52; population
nadir of, 224–30, 240; population
recovery of, 224, 231–48, 252; sacrifice
customs of, 11, 23; skilled labor of,
91, 198; social organization of, 91–93,
105–13; systems of production and
exchange of, 89. *See also* Population
decline; *names of specific groups*,
e.g. Kaqchikel
Indigo, 84–85, 88
Indios (as term), xvi–xvii
Ingenios, 82, 84
Isagoge histórica apologética, 13
Ixil Maya, 85–86
Iximché (Yximché), 77, 134; Alvarado in,
19–21, 25–28; Cahí Ymox in, 63–64;
as Kaqchikel capital, 3, 4, 6, 18, 34n6,
59; Kaqchikel rebellion and, 39,
52–53; Spanish burning of, 49–50; as
Spanish capital, 28–30, 32–34
Izabal, 80, 255*t*

Jalapa, 80, 255*t*
Johannessen, Carl, 183
Jones, Grant, 176–77
Juarros, Domingo, 247, 282*t*
Jueces repartidores, 88
Jumaytepeque, 154n9, 159, 162–64, 265*t*
Jutiapa, 255*t*

Kahi' Imox. *See* Cahí Ymox (Sinacán)
Kaqchikel Maya: accounts by, xv, 44–50,
53, 55–56; alliance with Alvarado
of, 16–19, 26–28, 32–36; Alvarado's
demands of gold from, 28–31;
on Alvarado's seizure of Súchil,
26–27; capital at Iximché of, 6n7, 28;
congregación experiences of, 104–105;
conquest of Peru and, 68; earliest
contact with Spaniards of, 5–8; forced
labor of, 82; indigenous enemies of, 7,
17–19; population estimates of, 178–
81; rebellion against the Spaniards of,
3, 44–57, 58n1, 64–70; rulers of, 34n6,
42–43; secession from the K'iche of,
131, 179–81; surrender to Spaniards
by, 58–74; tribute imposed on, 62–64.
See also *Memorial de Sololá*
Kelly, John E., 10n
K'iche' Maya: earliest Spanish contact
with, 5–6; executions of rulers of,
73n33; indigenous enemies of, 7, 17;
Kaqchikel rebellion and, 42n28, 43–
44, 47; Kaqchikel secession from, 131,
179–81; population estimates of, 179–
81; of Gumarcaah, 131–34, 144–45,
158; social structure of, 105; Spanish
conquest at Utatlán of, 10–18, 34;
Tecún Umán of, 12–14; territory ruled
by, 6n6; Utatlán court of, 11, 158;
Xetulul (town) of, 10

Labor and tribute, xiv, 62–64, 86–88,
101, 251–52; of African slaves,
80, 83–84, 92, 224, 228–29; cacao
and, 84–85; of enslaved indigenous
peoples, 86–90, 140–42, 184, 221,
261*t*; excess payments and, 216;
exemptions from, 198, 199–200,
201; Maldonado and Marroquín
assessments of, 152–70; New Laws
on, 123, 140–41, 157–58, 184–85, 190;

obligations of indigenous peoples and, 141–44, 169–70, 213–16, 251–52, 261*t*; population decline from, 213–15, 219–23; revenues from, 90; *servico del tostón* and, 224–29; *tributarios* and *reservados* in, 189, 193n22, 194–95, 274*t*. See also *Encomienda* system; Population surveys

Labores de pan llevar, 170

Lacandón Maya, 85, 86n16, 115

Ladinos. See *Castas* (mixed blood population)

La Farge, Oliver, 98, 102

Lamadrid, Lázaro, 237

Las Casas, Bartolomé de, 37n14, 149

Las dos repúblicas, 93–95

Las Navas, Andrés de, 115, 236

Laws of the Indies, 103–104, 106

Libro primero de cabildo, 52n57

Libros de cabildo (Santiago de Guatemala), 7n, 65n12, 65nn11–12

Libro segundo de cabildo, 64–67

Libro tercero de cabildo, 64–65, 67–68

Lienzo de Quauhquechollan, 54n65, 55, 61n3

Liévano, Pedro de, 217, 223

Little-Siebold, Todd, 78–79n5, 94n36

López, Alonso, 9n12

López, Francisco, 137

López de Gómara, Francisco, 6–7, 33, 37n15, 50n52

López de Yrrarraga, Nicolás, 60–61

Luján, Rafael de, 226

Luján Muñoz, Jorge, 5–6, 10n, 65n12; on Alvarado's injuries, 24n; on the core-periphery construct, 78–79n5, 82nn7–8; on the *encomienda* system, 128n; on Jorge de Alvarado, 54n63; on the Kaqchikel rebellion, 39–40, 53; on population estimates, 179n18, 198–99, 248; on *pueblos de indios*, 101n24; reproductions of Cortés y Larraz's maps by, 244n28; on Tecún Umán, 12–14

Mackie, Sedley J., 10n, 34n5, 48n44, 50n54

MacLeod, Murdo J., 141; on Cerrato's reforms, 185n3; on colonial settlement patterns, 77–80, 94; on epidemics among indigenous peoples, 19n40; on Maldonado, 154n8; on population assessments, 161, 194, 200, 202n12, 210–11, 219n15, 270*t*; on Valverde, 216

Maldonado, Alonso de, 71–72, 94, 197; enforcement of tribute regulations by, 149–70; as governor of Guatemala, 149, 157–58

Mam Maya, 45, 131–34, 144–45

Maps: of core-periphery divide, 80, 81*f*; in Cortés y Larraz's *Descripción geográfico-moral*, 244; of demographic regions, 180*f*; of *pueblos de indios* in the Cerrato *tasaciones*, 187*f*; of Sacapulas landholding, 112*f*

Marín, Luis de, 50, 51

Mármol, Sebastián de, 163

Marroquín, Francisco, 71, 94, 197; on Cerrato's *tasaciones*, 190; *encomiendas* of, 259*t*; *tasaciones* of, 154–67

Martínez Peláez, Severo, 230; on colonial reality, 249–50; on Cortés y Larraz's *Descripción geográfico-moral*, 244n28; on Fuentes y Guzmán's *Recordación florida*, 238–39; on *pueblos de indios*, 105

Matthew, Laura E., 9n12, 42–43n30, 54n63–64

Maudsley, Alfred P., 52n58

Maxwell, Judith M., 18n38, 19n39; on Alvarado's demands for gold, 29–30nn57–58; on Belehé Qat's death and succession, 63nn5–6; on *chinamitales*, 106; on executions of indigenous rulers, 73n33; on Kaqchikel tribute, 62n; on the Mexica diplomatic mission to Iximché, 33n2

Memorial de Sololá, 5, 6n7; on alliance formation traditions, 35–36; on

Memorial de Solóla, continued
Alvarado in Utatlán, 14–15, 16; on
Alvarado's battle for Cuzcatlán, 21;
on Alvarado's demands for gold, 29–
30; on Alvarado's seizure of Súchil,
27; on *congregación* experiences,
104–105; on executions of indigenous
rulers, 73n34; on Kaqchikel alliance
with Alvarado, 34; on Kaqchikel
rebellion, 40–41, 44–50, 53; on
Kaqchikel response to Alvarado's
arrival, 18n38; on Kaqchikel
secession, 181; on Kaqchikel
surrender, 58–64; on Maldonado,
71–72; on Mexica delegation to
Iximché, 32–33; Recinos's translations
of, 45; safekeeping in Santiago of, 40;
on Spanish conquest, 55–56; Tecún
Umán's omission from, 12
Méndez, Gonzalo, 108
Mendoza, Antonio de, 61n3
Mercedarians, 86, 226, 230; pastoral
administration by, 232; population
assessments by, 236, 276t; towns
founded by, 255t
Miles, Suzanne, 194, 270t
Mining, 88–90, 136–37, 140–44, 261t
Miscegenation, 88–89, 93
Misco (Mixco), 220–21
Missionaries and clergy: *congregación*
resettlement projects of, 86, 96,
101–13, 119, 206, 251; conversion
goals of, 103, 105, 108; population
assessments by, 202–205, 208–209,
226–30, 236–38, 242, 244–45; towns
founded by, 255t
Mixed-blood population. See *Castas*
(mixed blood population)
Moctezuma II, Emperor of Aztecs,
32–33
Momostenango, 158–59, 166–67, 268t
Monaghan, John, 106, 107, 109
Mondloch, James, 29n56
Morales, Antón de, 108

Mörner, Magnus, 93–94
Municipios, 97–102, 119

Nance, C. Roger, 28n55, 49n51
Narváez, Pánfilo de, 37
Native agency, 79, 123, 250; through
fugitivism, 113–19, 143, 191, 192, 215
Nestiquipaque, 220–21
New Laws of the Indies, 123, 140–41,
157–58, 184–85, 190
Newson, Linda, 183; on population
assessments, 192, 194, 228, 233–35; on
the *servicio del tostón*, 225; on survival
variables, 175n10
Niño, Juan, 146
Niquitlán, 260t, 262t
Núñez, Bartolomé, 60
Núñez, Juan, 61n3

Olín, lord of Huehuetenango, 147
Orduña, Francisco de, 60, 138, 145,
147, 259t
Orellana, Sandra L., 170n52, 270t
Ostuncalco, 159, 161–62, 264t
Otzoy, Simón, 18n38; on Alvarado's
demands for gold, 29n56, 30n58;
on executions of indigenous rulers,
73n34; on the Kaqchikel rebellion,
41; on Mexica diplomatic mission to
Iximché, 33n2
Oudijk, Michel, 34–35, 68n19
Oxib-Queh, 14

Padden, R. C., 37n14
Páez, Alonso, 108
Panajachel, 118f
Panchoy, 80, 92n31
Parcialidades, 100, 106–13, 119
Pardo, José Joaquín, 237
Parra, Francisco de la. See De la Parra,
Francisco
Patria del Criollo, La (Martínez Peláez),
238–39, 249–50
Patulul, 220

Paz, Alonso de, 201
Pazón (Patzún), 220
Pérez, Bernaldino, 207n24
Pérez Dardón, Juan, 67n18, 136, 158–59,
    165–67, 169–70
Peru: Alvarado's expedition to, 68–70,
    250; population statistics for, 66, 229
Petapa, 194–95, 197–99, 229, 274t
Petén, 176, 179, 193, 195, 255t
Philip V, King of Spain, 67n18
Pinart, Alphonse Louis, 6n7
Pipil nation: Alvarado's conquest of,
    21–25; indigenous enemies of, 17, 19;
    Kaqchikel rebellion and, 45
Pizarro, Francisco, 68, 69, 161
Pleitos, 125, 126–27
Pochutla, 220
Polo Sifontes, Francis, 5–6; on Kaqchikel
    alliance with the Spaniards, 35–36;
    on Kaqchikel rulers, 72–73n31; on
    second Kaqchikel uprising, 64–65, 70;
    on Xinca flight, 22
Popol Vuh, 5, 13, 14, 44
Population decline, 80–84, 91–93, 140,
    170, 209, 252, 283t; from 1520–1550,
    195; from 1550–1578, 196–211; from
    1578–1587, 212–23; from 1594–1664,
    224–29; counting controversies on,
    173–83; from epidemics, 7, 17, 91,
    160n, 167, 175, 178, 183, 191, 192,
    201–202, 205–206, 223, 224, 252; from
    fugitivism, 143, 191, 192, 215; from
    labor exploitation, 213–15, 219–23;
    nadir of, 224–30, 240; from non-
    biological forces, 175–76; recovery
    from, 224, 231–48, 252; threat to
    colonial economy of, 228–29; of
    women, 206
Population recovery, 224, 231–48, 252
Population surveys, xiv, xvii, 80–83,
    91, 180f, 252; in 1548–51 (Cerrato's
    tasaciones), 184–96, 256t, 270–74t,
    277t; of 1550 (Estrada), 196–97,
    275t; of 1562 (eight communities),

196, 197–99, 274t; of 1566 (Francisco
    Briceño in Verapaz), 199–200; in 1570
    (Artiaga Mendiola's "Memoria de
    partidos"), 202–204; in 1570–71 (Casa
    de Avante in Verapaz), 200–202; of
    1572 ("Relación de los caciques"),
    204–207; of 1575 ("Descripción de los
    Corregimientos"), 207–209; of 1575
    ("Memoria de los Pueblos"), 206–207,
    221n20; of 1575 ("Relación de la
    Provincia de la Verapaz"), 205–206;
    of 1578–82 (Valverde's "Razón de las
    tasaciones"), 212–23, 277t; of 1594–95
    (*Contaduría* 969), 224–26; García de
    Palacios's instructions on, 209–11; of
    1604, 226–27; of 1629 (Vásquez de
    Espinosa's *Compendio*), 229–30; of
    1664, 230; of 1681 ("Padrón de los
    Indios Tributarios"), 231–33; of 1683
    (Contaduría 815), 233–35; of 1683
    ("Razón de las Ciudades"), 233–35;
    of 1684 ("Graduación de salarios"),
    235–36, 278t; of 1690 (Vázquez
    and fellow clerics), 236–38; of 1710
    (*Contaduría* 973), 227–29, 240, 279t;
    of 1712–1812 (Juarros's *Compendio de
    la historia de la Ciudad de Guatemala*),
    247, 282t; of 1719 (*Contaduría* 977),
    240–41, 279t; of 1722–26 (*Contaduría*
    976), 241; of 1750 ("Memoria de
    los Curatos"), 242, 280t; of 1768–69
    ("Testimonio para averiguar el
    aumento de tributarios"), 242–43,
    280t; of 1768–70 (Cortés y Larraz),
    244–45; of 1772 (*Indiferente General*
    1525), 245–46; of 1772 ("Vista
    política de la América española"),
    246, 281t; of 1778 ("Numeración de
    Tributarios"), 246–47, 281t; of 1802
    (*Gaceta de Guatemala*), 246; of 1806
    (*Número de tributarios*), 247, 282t;
    of 1811 (*Numeración y tasación de
    tributos*), 247, 282t; of 1812 (*Relación
    de la población*), 248, 282t; counting

Population surveys, *continued*
controversies on, 173–83; García de
Palacios's instructions on, 209–11; on
preconquest population levels, 173–
83, 270*t*; royal orders on, 243. *See also*
Population decline
Poqomam Maya, 45
Portocarrero, Pedro de, 10, 23, 24;
campaign leadership by, 53–56; on
Espinar's reputation, 138; Kaqchikel
rebellion and, 43; pursuit of Cahí
Ymox by, 66–67
Prem, Hanns, 175–76
Priests. *See* Missionaries and clergy
Probanzas de méritos y servicios, 125–27
Pueblos de indios, 100–101; ancestral
land and, 111–13; in the Cerrato
tasaciones, 187*f*; communal
landholding of, 110–11; *congregación*
settlement project of, 86, 96,
102–13, 119, 206, 251; dispersal
and decongregation from, 113–19;
parcialidades of, 100, 106–13, 119;
strategic acculturation in, 105–107,
111; *tributarios* and *reservados* in, 189,
193n22, 194–95, 274*t*
Pueblos de vista, 206–207

Q'anjob'al Maya, 85–86
Q'eqchi' Maya, 70n24, 86, 200
Quetzal birds, 201–202
Quetzaltenango, 13, 255*t*; agricultural
land in, 85; *encomienda* of, 161–62;
population surveys of, 179, 188, 207,
225, 234–35, 241, 243
Quiyavit Caok, 70, 72–73

Ramírez, Diego, 217
Ramírez de Quiñones, Pedro, 113–14
Real servicio, 224–29, 240. *See also*
Labor and tribute
Rebellion, 240–41; first Kaqchikel
uprising, 3, 44–57, 58n1; second
Kaqchikel uprising, 64–70. *See also*
Conquest and rebellion; Native agency

Recinos, Adrián, 5n3, 6, 244; on
Alvarado's character, 37; on
Alvarado's combat skills, 9; on
Alvarado's conquest of the K'iche',
16; on Alvarado's demands for
gold, 29–30nn56–58; on Alvarado's
expedition to Peru, 68n19, 69n22;
on Alvarado's injuries, 24n; on
Alvarado's seizure of Súchil, 27; on
Belehé Qat's death and succession,
63nn5–6; on Cortés's records on
Alvarado, 8n; on executions of
indigenous rulers, 73nn33–34; on
Jorge de Alvarado, 54n65; on the
Kaqchikel rebellion, 41, 42n28, 45–49;
on Kaqchikel responses to Spanish
arrival, 18n38, 19n40, 32–34; on
Kaqchikel rulers, 34n6; on Kaqchikel
tribute, 62n; on Mexica diplomatic
mission to Iximché, 33n2; on the
second Kaqchikel uprising, 64n7; on
Xinca flight, 22
Recordación florida (Fuentes y Guzmán),
238–39; on conquest of the Mam of
Zacaleu, 131–34; on Corregimiento
del Valle, 78–79n5; on the Kaqchikel
rebellion, 42–43; population
assessment in, 239
Remesal, Antonio de, 108, 236–38
Repartimiento obligations, 88
Reparto de efectos, 90
República de indios, 94
Requerimiento, 10
Reservados, 189, 193n22, 194–95, 201,
274*t*
Restall, Matthew, 10n; on Alvarado's
demands for gold, 29–30nn56–58;
on Alvarado's expedition to Peru,
68n19; on Jorge de Alvarado,
54n63; on Kaqchikel response to
Alvarado's arrival, 18n38, 19n39; on
Mesoamerican alliance formation
traditions, 34–35; on Mexica
diplomatic mission to Iximché, 33n2
Retalhuleu, 255*t*

Rivera, Payo de, 230
Rodríguez Becerra, Salvador, 124,
    154n9, 158n21, 186
Rogel, Juan, 157–58
Rojas, Diego de, 48, 66–67
Ruiz, Marcos, 191

Sacapulas, 107–13, 258*t*
Sacatepéquez, 80, 255*t*; *encomienda* of,
    161–62; tribute assessments of, 159,
    194–95, 197–98, 274*t*
Sachil. *See* Súchil
Sáenz de Santa María, Carmelo, 14n25,
    66n14, 154n8
Saint-Lu, André, 200
Salazar, Antonio de, 134
Salinas, García de, 146
Salt, 106, 110; production of, 192, 207;
    as tribute payments, 108, 123, 160–68,
    198, 215
Salvatierra, Cristobál, 108
San Agustín, 225–26
San Antonio Suchitepéquez, 234–35, 243
Sanchíz, Pilar, 135
Sanders, William, 182, 194
Sandoval, Rodrigo de, 153–54
San Esteban Tamahú, 202
San Juan Amatitlán, 197–98
San Juan Atitán, 260*t*, 262*t*
San Juan Chamelco, 205–206
San Juan Ostuncalco, 234
San Juan Sacatepéquez, 194–95,
    197–98, 274*t*
San Marcos, 255*t*
San Martín Sacatepéquez, 159,
    161–62, 264*t*
San Miguel (El Salvador), 227–29,
    240, 241
San Miguel Tucurú, 202
San Pedro La Laguna, 118*f*
San Pedro Necta, 260*t*, 262*t*
San Pedro Sacatepéquez, 194–95,
    197–98, 274*t*
San Salvador (El Salvador), 227–29,
    240, 241, 245

Santa Inés, 197–98
Santa Rosa, 255*t*
Santa Úrsula, 219
Santiago Atitlán, 114, 118*f*; *encomienda*
    obligations in, 263*t*; population
    assessments of, 241, 260*t*, 262*t*, 274*t*;
    population surveys of, 154n9, 159–62,
    192–93, 226, 234–35, 274*t*
Santiago de Guatemala: as colonial
    core, 78–80; *congregación* in, 114–15;
    establishment of, 82; indigenous
    population of, 91–92, 196–97;
    population surveys of, 199–202,
    204–209, 221–22, 229, 232, 235,
    241, 243
Santiséban, Juan de, 217
Sauer, Carl, 100–101
Schirmer, Jennifer, 14n25
Secular clergy, 86, 101; jurisdiction of,
    203–205, 208; population assessments
    by, 226–27, 230–38, 275*t*
Sequechul, 42n28, 43–44, 72–73n31. *See
    also* Belehé Qat
Servicio del tostón, 224–29, 240. *See also*
    Labor and tribute
Servicio ordinario, 159, 162, 164, 167
Servicio personal, 86–87
Settlement and colonization, xiv, xvi–xvii;
    African slavery of, 80, 83–84, 92;
    agriculture in, 80, 82–85; of cities and
    towns, 82–83; *congregación* policies
    of, 86, 96, 101–107, 109–13, 119,
    206, 251; continuity of indigenous
    communities and, 96–102; core-
    periphery construct of, 78–86, 94;
    dissolution of *congregación* in,
    115–19; economic life of, 78, 86–90;
    encomienda grants and, 86–87, 101–
    102, 123–28; entrepreneurial focus
    of, 79; historiography of, 77–78;
    indigenous enslavement in, 82, 86–90,
    92, 140–42, 184, 221, 261*t*; indigenous
    parcialidades of, 100, 106–13, 119;
    labor exploitation in, 82, 86–87;
    landholding in, 78, 82–86, 110–11;

Settlement and colonization, *continued*
  miscegenation in, 88–89, 93; resource
  exploitation of, xv, 78–82, 249;
  segregation of communities in,
  93–95, 103–104; social life of, 78, 90–93;
  tribute payments of, 87–88, 101
Sherman, William L., 154n8, 168;
  on Alvarado's expedition to Peru,
  68n19, 69n22; on Alvarado's role
  in Guatemala, 250n6; on Cerrato's
  reforms, 184–85; on population
  assessments, 194, 197, 198, 270t
Sierra de Chamá, 80
Sierra de los Cuchumatanes, 78, 80,
  85, 129–48
Sierra de Santa Cruz, 80
Simpson, Lesley Byrd, 194, 218, 222
Slicher van Bath, B. H., 194
Smith, Carol, 78, 99–100, 106
Soconusco (Mexico), 80, 218, 219, 228,
  240, 241
Solano, Francisco de, 124, 182–83, 186,
  188; on clerical assessments, 226–27,
  230, 237–38; on *Contaduría* 973, 228;
  on Cortés y Larraz's *Descripción
  geográfico-moral*, 245; on "Memoria
  de los Curatos," 242; on "Memoria de
  Partidos," 202–203n13; on "Padrón
  de los Indios Tributarios," 232–33; on
  "Razón de las ciudades," 233–34; on
  "Relación de los Caciques," 204n
Solís, Gonzalo de, 134
Sololá, 118f, 193, 255t, 274t
Sonsonate (El Salvador), 80, 245
Soto, Luis de, 66n14
*Spanish Central America: A
  Socioeconomic History, 1520–1720*
  (MacLeod), 77–78
Súchil, 26–28, 72–73n31
Suchitepéquez (Department), 255t
Suchitepéquez (Partido), 225, 234–35,
  243, 280t
Suma de visitas, 189, 193
Sumpango, 82–83, 193, 194–95, 197–98, 274t

Tacuba (El Salvador), 154n9, 159,
  162–64, 266t
Tasaciones de tributos, 101, 105, 154–67;
  Cerrato's assessments of, 101–102,
  105, 124–25, 127–28, 146n, 159–67,
  177, 185–95, 219–20, 256t, 270–74t,
  277t; population estimates from,
  188–95; vital statistics of, 177–79.
  See also Population surveys
Tax, Sol, 96–98, 117
Tecoçistlán (Rabinal), 225, 274t
Tecpán Atitlán (Sololá), 235, 241, 274t
Tecún Umán, 12–14, 42–43n30
Tepepul, 42n28, 73n33
Terrazgo system, 87
Thompson, J. Eric S., 176–77, 270t
Título del Ahpop Quecham, 12
Título del Ajpop Huitzitizil Tzunún, 12–13
Título de los Señores Coyoy, 12–14
Título de Santa Clara, 131
Títulos de la Casa Izquín Nehaib, 12–13
Tlaxcalans (Tlaxcala), 17
Torres, Juan de, 111–13
Totonicapán, 85, 115–16, 255t;
  parcialidades of, 106–107; population
  surveys of, 188, 207, 219, 225, 235,
  241, 243, 257t
Tovilla, Martín Alfonso, 109, 111
Tresino, Juan, 217
Tributarios, 189, 194–95, 274t
Tz'utujil Maya: Alvarado's defeat of,
  20–21; indigenous enemies of, 7, 17,
  19; Kaqchikel rebellion and, 45, 47

Utatlán, 77, 167–68, 269t; conquest of,
  10–18; tribute assessment of, 158–59

Valle de Guatemala, 225, 241
Valverde, Baltasar de, 212
Valverde, Diego García de, 94, 191,
  196; *encomienda* reforms of,
  212–23; "Razón de las tasaciones"
  of, 217–22, 277t
Valverde, Francisco de (brother), 212

Valverde, Francisco de (son), 212–13
Van Oss, Adriaan, 91, 101, 247
Vásquez de Espinosa, Antonio, 229–30
Vázquez, Francisco, 37n14; on Alvarado's
    absences from Guatemala, 72–73;
    on the Kaqchikel rebellion, 39–44;
    on population surveys, 236–38; on
    possible second Kaqchikel uprising,
    64–70; on Sacapulas, 108
Veblen, Thomas T., 179–81, 194,
    204–205, 270t
Vecinos (Spanish residents), 82, 202–204,
    207, 221n20, 226–27
Verapaz, 80, 255t; congregación in, 114–15;
    population surveys in, 199–202,
    204–209, 225–26, 229, 234–35, 241;
    Spanish conquest of, 47, 55, 65–66
Viana, Francisco, 205–206
Vides, Alonso de, 225–26
Villalobos, Pedro, 207–209
Villanueva, Dr., 215–16, 219
Vivar, Luis de, 143–44
Vos, Jan de, 176–77

Wagley, Charles, 98
Warren, Kay, 14n25
Wasserstrom, Robert, 98, 102

Webre, Stephen, 83
Whittington, Stephen L., 28n55, 49n51
Winäq, 106n40
Wolf, Eric, 93, 98–99, 100n21, 106–107,
    111, 119
Women: death rates of from epidemics,
    206; encomienda system burden on,
    169; intimate unions with Spanish of,
    16–17, 25–28, 162
Wortman, Miles, 90

Xicoténcatl, 16–17, 27, 27n52
Ximénez, Francisco, 44, 52n57, 72–
    73n31, 108, 236–38
Xinca nation, 22–23, 163
Xiquilite. See Indigo

Yaquis (Aztecs or Mexica), 33

Zacapa, 80, 242–43, 255t
Zambo and Mosquito nation, 241
Zamora, Elías, 111, 182, 204n, 206–207,
    218n14
Zumpango. See Sumpango
Zurrilla, Francisco de, 69, 130,
    141–43, 148